Introduction to Comput.

Introduction to Computing

Percy Mett

Department of Computing
The Open University

MACMILLAN

First published 1990

Published by
MACMILLAN EDUCATION LTD
Houndmills, Basingstoke, Hampshire RG21 2XS
and London
Companies and representatives
throughout the world

Printed in Hong Kong

British Library Cataloguing in Publication Data
Mett, Percy
  Introduction to computing.
  1. Computer systems
  I. Title
  004

ISBN 0–333–39336–8

Lotus 1–2–3 is a trademark of Lotus Development Corporation.
UNIX is a trademark of AT&T Bell Laboratories.
MicroSoft Word is a trademark of MicroSoft Corporation.
VAX is a trademark of Digital Equipment Corporation.
CP/M is a trademark of Digital Research Inc.

Contents

Preface

This is a book, not about computers, but about computing—the science of using the computer. The study of computing as a science in schools and colleges has grown dramatically in recent years. From a position as a Cinderella subject on the periphery of the curriculum, it has developed into a mainstream area of study examined by all the public examining bodies both in the GCSE and in the Advanced Level GCE examinations. The increase in the number of candidates taking the subject has not been matched by up-to-date textbooks to provide adequate instruction in the subject. It is the aim of this book to fill this void by providing a main text which gives a broad coverage of the new Advanced level syllabuses.

Despite a massive increase in popularity among candidates, A-levels in Computing fail to command a positive image. Universities and Polytechnics continue to prefer candidates with traditional A-levels for admission to degree courses in Computer Science, rather than those with A-levels in Computing. The reason is not hard to find. The emphasis in A-level courses has been on the wrong topics and the wrong methods. The Alvey Report stated (page 62): "Universities in fact are having to give remedial education to entrants with A-level computer science. Uncorrected, the explosion in home computing with its 1950s and 60s programming style will make this problem even worse."

The new syllabuses which the GCE Boards introduced in the mid-1980s have gone some way towards redressing the balance. However, the main improvement will come from the use of proper design methods in the development of software. This important message is put across in the first four chapters of this book. Software development—including design—is still a much neglected topic in the teaching of the subject, and early exposure is required to ensure that students appreciate its importance. Left to their own devices, students are quick to acquire bad programming habits; it is preferable to inculcate in them the correct techniques at the earliest possible stage.

Hardware topics are not introduced until later on. Those used to earlier textbooks on Computing may find this approach unusual. However, the subject is Computing rather than Computers—our interest in computers stems only from their role in Computing.

The A-level syllabuses do not presuppose any previous knowledge of the subject. This book aims to be intelligible as a first course in Computing. It does not, however, teach any programming language as such. This has to be covered by a parallel course, using a language that is locally available.

The first three chapters introduce the use of program control structures as design tools. The method of top-down stepwise refinement is taught with the aid of structure diagrams, followed by a more general look at software design and program development in chapter 4. These topics include program correctness, maintainability and efficiency. The operation of the hardware, including peripheral devices, is discussed in chapter 5. The function of the hardware is specified in terms of its machine instruction set; this is most easily taught by way of assembly language, in chapter 6. Binary arithmetic is left until this point, as its main relevance is at this level of the computer hierarchy.

The organisation of data is an important topic which spans chapters 7 to 9. The methods used to access data have been influenced by the choice of storage media available. A continuous thread is woven through the hardware and software aspects so as to present a coherent picture. Operating systems and other systems software which, together with the hardware, make up the complex machine described indiscriminately as a computer, form the subject matter for chapter 10.

In chapter 11 we discuss communication, at both the human–computer and the computer–computer levels. This discussion includes a brief introduction to networks. The final chapter looks at some of the ways in which the computer is currently put to use and the social issues raised thereby.

Readers familiar with traditional texts will notice a complete absence of that so-called programming tool, the flowchart. I make no apology for its omission. Far from aiding program design, flowcharts hamper it, forcing the programmer to think in terms of the computing device and not the problem. A more useful design tool, the structure tree, is introduced early on to aid high-level programming. Flowcharts have their uses in the documentation of complex programs, but these are beyond the scope of this book.

No single text can hope to cover fully the whole of a two-year course, especially in such a wide-ranging subject as Computing. The contents of this text do, however, address most of the major topics common to the several syllabuses of the various examining boards. In addition, a number of subsidiary topics are included; the selection and the depth of coverage of each reflects the author's view of how the subject should be taught. This book is not intended, though, to constrain the teacher, who will undoubtedly wish to amplify certain topics and introduce further examples from his or her own experience. A Bibliography of other source material is included to provide additional background reading for instructors.

The defining occurrence of each important technical term is indicated by the use of **bold** typeface; as well as highlighting the defining context, this will enable rapid identification of key terms for revision purposes. Less significant technical words are indicated in *italics*, which are also used for occurrences of technical terms before they have been defined.

Within each chapter there is to be found a number of exercises, to be worked as they are encountered. These exercises are mostly designed to give practice in newly taught techniques; consequently, the frequency of their appearance is not uniform throughout the book. Solutions to these exercises are given at the end of the chapter. It must be emphasised that the solutions offered are usually not unique. Particularly in the case of programming exercises, there may be many equally valid alternatives. In certain chapters there are *activities* for the reader. These are either exercises of an extended nature, or practical activities to gather information in a particular context. Instructors may wish to select such activities as are suitable for their pupils. Further exercises are included at the end of each chapter; many of these have been taken from recent A-level papers.

The teaching material is in no way tied to a specific computer, and is usable in conjunction with any hardware. In those cases where it is necessary to illustrate a point with a program fragment, this is usually done in BBC BASIC, which is accessible to most educational institutions. An appendix provides the conversion to RM BASIC for other schools and colleges. Where necessary, programming features are illustrated in Pascal. Any serious student of programming will have to learn a language like Pascal, in the long term, in order to implement the design philosophy which this book sets out to teach.

Acknowledgements

A number of people have been most helpful to me in the writing and production of this book. I should particularly like to place on record my thanks to Professor Manny Lehman of Imperial College, London, and Professor Frank Sumner of the University of Manchester for advice on the content of the book and for their comments on the drafts. I hope that no errors remain, but if any do the responsibility for them remains my own. I should also like to thank Doreen Tucker of the Faculty of Mathematics Word Processing Unit at the Open University for assistance in typing various drafts of the manuscript, and Malcolm Stewart of Macmillan Education for constant encouragement in seeing this book through.

My most special thanks go to my wife Judith, and to my children who are waiting eagerly to see this text in print, having so frequently heard that 'Daddy is busy on his book'.

Acknowledgement for the use of copyright material is hereby made to the Civil Aviation Authority (figures 5.7 and 10.9), AGFA-Gevaert Ltd (figure 5.17), Southdown Bus Company (figure 7.1), ICL (figures 11.5 and 11.7), Halifax Building Society (figure 11.6) and Sun Microsystems UK Ltd (figure 12.1). Questions from past examination papers are acknowledged individually to source. They are reproduced by permission of the Associated Examining Board, Joint Matriculation Board, University of Cambridge Local Examinations Syndicate and University of London Schools Examination Board.

1989   Percy Mett

1 Information Processing—Why and How?

> **Computer:** A calculating-machine; *esp*. an automatic electronic device for performing mathematical or other operations.
>
> *Shorter Oxford English Dictionary*
>
> **Computer:** A machine which, under the control of a stored program, automatically accepts and processes data, and supplies the results of that processing.
>
> *BCS: A glossary of computing terms*

The first entry above implies that the purpose of a computer is to perform operations, with a strong hint that these operations are likely to be mathematical in nature. Indeed, *compute* is a synonym for 'calculate', and the initial development of the modern computer in the 1940s and 1950s was as a device for speeding up lengthy and complex calculations. The second definition indicates, however, that nowadays this definition must be considered as out of date.

During the past quarter of a century, progress in the use and applications of computers has been dramatic on all fronts. The computer is now used to solve problems of all kinds; it is, *par excellence*, a general-purpose problem-solving tool.

This book is about the science that has grown up around the computer, its design and use, and the art of instructing or *programming* the computer. The designation *information processing* might be a more accurate description, but the term 'computing' has stuck, with an enhanced meaning.

This chapter commences with two examples which illustrate the scope of information processing. These are intended to answer, at a superficial level at least, the 'why' of the title. The rest of the chapter begins to tackle the 'how'. The development of good computer programs is not a haphazard process. In recent years it has become apparent that the *ad hoc* methods favoured in the earlier years lead to the production of programs which require excessive maintenance, both as a result of the discovery of errors late in the day, and in any attempt to modify programs in the light of changed circumstances.

The stages through which computer programs or *software* develop have much in common with the design stages of the actual machinery or *hardware*. Modern techniques of software development are based on the tried and tested methods of engineering design. For this reason these techniques are known as *software engineering*. We shall be studying how an information processing problem can be analysed, from a complete specification of the problem through to a design for a working program, using a *top-down* design technique known as *stepwise refinement*.

1

The terms *stored program* and *data* in the second definition are then elaborated in the context of a program design. We shall take a look at the way data may be represented using named variables and the use of arrays for identifying data aggregates.

1.1 Two Examples

All human endeavour requires information. The housewife who undertakes the weekly shopping chore requires information about the cost of likely purchases, and needs to relate the prices of goods to the amount of money she has available to spend. On completion of the process of selecting the purchases, the total price must be calculated, as must the amount of change due—both straightforward pieces of information processing. Notice, though, that the first calculation uses information which must be provided—by ringing up the price of each item on a cash register, for example, or by obtaining the price from a catalogue held in a computer. In the second case, however, the change is calculated using a previously computed piece of information—the total cost.

The need to process information did not begin with the invention of the computer. Far from it. Man has processed information throughout history. But the computer has, by virtue of its capability to process rapidly large quantities of information, focused attention on the nature of information processing.

To set the scene, we shall describe just two examples of everyday problems involving the handling of information. In both of these examples computers are now used to process and handle the information requirements.

An airline booking system

Have you ever considered what is involved in booking a passenger ticket on an airline flight? In order to obtain a ticket you must not only decide between which airports you wish to fly, but also on which airline. And to make these decisions information is needed. Suppose you decide to fly from London to New York—you can then get your ticket. Or so you may think. More than twenty scheduled flights leave London for New York each day, run by some fifteen different airlines. Maybe you have a preference for a particular airline, or wish to arrive in New York at a particular time. Before you can choose, you need the information. You might consult a travel brochure or a timetable.

Once you have chosen, the rest is plain sailing (or maybe plain flying). But is it? An aircraft is limited in seating capacity, and your chosen flight may be fully booked. The airline must maintain a central record of tickets issued for each flight. This will very likely involve you, or your travel agent, in a telephone call to the central office of your chosen airline, to establish the availability of a seat. If you then book a seat, your booking will be added to the central record.

What information requirements have we identified so far? Provision must be made for details of flights between various destinations, times of departure and arrival, and intermediate stops if any. The fare charged for a ticket is also of considerable interest to the traveller. All this information must be circulated to potential customers, possibly in the form of timetables held by travel agents. The information may be dependent on the day of the week, but generally speaking this information is static and predictable over long periods of time. Details of seat bookings for individual flights must be available to be consulted on a central basis, so all bookings must be *communicated* to a controller.

We have by no means discussed the full extent of travel information, or even explored in depth the details of an airline booking system, yet we begin to perceive the enormity of the underlying systems. A vast store of information is required, together with the ability to maintain an up-to-date view of the booking situation. Users of the system may be at widespread geographical locations, so communication links are required between providers and users of the information and service. A typical booking system may link more than 10 000 user terminals, each requiring a response to messages within three seconds. The hardware at the hub of the system will typically consist of something like six mainframe processors.

You should bear in mind that there is nothing in a booking system that *requires* the use of a computer. All the processing can be done manually, as indeed was the case until computers developed to the stage which made them suitable and beneficial for this application. The introduction of computers has, however, enabled developments in air travel booking which were not possible hitherto. It has also allowed the implementation of solutions in problem areas, such as overbooking, which were previously deemed insoluble. The truly enormous amount of information, held at numerous locations around the world, makes it difficult for manual systems to cope. The speed with which responses are required to requests for information is, in fact, not achievable without the assistance afforded by computers. The computerised booking systems currently used by airlines incorporate a bewildering array of computers of all sizes, connected by telecommunications links. Many of the features of these systems find their realisation in the topics which form the subject matter of this book.

Banking systems

Banks and building societies provide a range of banking services to the community. Funds belonging to individuals or companies do not need to be held by them as cash; instead they can be deposited with a bank or building society for use when required.

A bank may have hundreds, or even thousands, of clients at each branch. Each client may maintain one or more separate accounts. In a deposit account, a depositor's funds earn interest which may be added to the balance, or sent to the depositor, at regular intervals. Other transactions which change the balance in an account include further deposits and the withdrawal of sums of money. A bank may offer several different types of account. These may provide alternative methods of withdrawing funds—by cheque or by giving advance notice—and may offer various rates of interest. The banking service gives clients a safe and secure means of holding funds, opportunities for investment and, by way of current accounts operated with chequebooks, a method of making cashless payments to third parties.

To back up these financial services, it is necessary to maintain records. A journal holds a daily list of individual transactions, while a ledger is used to summarise the effect of each transaction on the appropriate account. At regular intervals, or on request by a client, the bank issues a statement of the account. This statement lists transactions and updated balances since the previous statement was issued for that account; typically it is a copy of recent ledger entries for the account. Within any one branch of the bank this work entails a great deal of record keeping. As an additional service a bank may wish to allow clients to deposit money in an account, and withdraw from it, at a different branch from the one holding the account. To support these activities it is necessary to transmit information about transactions between branches. In the United Kingdom there is a highly developed inter-bank clearing house arrangement which allows account holders to undertake transactions at branches of other banks, too.

The sheer volume of transactions performed daily in each branch has encouraged even the smallest banks and building societies to use computers to handle the processing of this information. Indeed, banks were among the earliest commercial users of computers in the late 1950s. Since then, they have developed their services, making use of the facilities provided by computerisation.

As an example of the way that banking services are used, consider the payment of salaries. A firm of modest size, with about one hundred staff, each earning a salary in the range of £10 000 to £20 000 *per annum*, has a monthly salary bill of about £100 000. If the staff were paid in cash, this would require a vast sum of money to be delivered safely to the firm's premises on the pay day each month. Payment by cheque is a safer method. Each employee can deposit a salary cheque to the credit of a bank account, avoiding the need for handling a large sum in cash. This procedure can be simplified further still. Many firms use computers to calculate each employee's monthly salary entitlement. Instead of printing the amount on a cheque, the salary can be credited directly to the employee's bank account. To achieve this the employer's computer communicates the payment details to the bank's computer. The actual process is more complicated than this, but we are trying to illustrate the way in which funds may be transferred—in this case from the employer to the employee—without using cash or a cheque. Of course, the employee will need to receive a statement from the employer indicating how the 'pay packet' has been determined. This statement, too, will have been printed under computer control.

More recently, further advances in technology have made it easier to draw cash on an account. Previously a client could draw cash at a distant branch of the bank either by advance arrangement or by telephone authorisation. Today a bank terminal anywhere in the country enables you to withdraw money from your account, at any time of the day or night, or to ascertain your bank balance. These facilities barely resemble the old manual procedures, and were not even thought of when computerisation of banks began.

Banks pioneered the commercial use of computers a quarter of a century ago. Indeed much of the terminology of data processing betrays the banking origins of the terms used. The uses of computers in banking and for payrolls will serve to provide us with the background for many of the examples in this book.

1.2 Computerisation

The widest benefits of computerisation should be seen in terms of the expansion of activity. Organisations which introduce computers rapidly come to realise that they have acquired a tool which not only rationalises their previous work procedures but also enables the introduction of new activities which were hitherto not engaged in.

In principle, any kind of information processing can be done with the aid of a computer. However, the computer is not always the best tool for the job. It should not be assumed that every task which involves the processing of information can benefit from being automated. Indeed, some types of processing are much better candidates for computerisation than others, and some are best performed by manual methods.

There are some tasks for which computers offer clear advantages. Long and complex calculations which require great precision, such as may be required in scientific research, weather forecasting and control of space modules, may be quite infeasible without the aid of a computer. Repetitive tasks in commerce and industry may be boring for humans, leading to fatigue-induced errors; a computer can take on such tasks with a consistent level of reliability. Manual methods of storing data may require a large amount of storage space, making access difficult and creating opportunities for internal contradictions where the same data is required for different purposes. Here the computer can help by miniaturising the spatial dimensions of the store, by providing remote access using communications links, and by enabling the data to be organised in a manner satisfying to all users.

These are some of the factors which may weigh in favour of computerisation—carrying out long and precise calculations within a reasonable timescale, performing repetitive tasks reliably, and accommodating large volumes of information.

The adoption of a computer-based approach does, however, involve expense in the purchase of equipment. In addition, it is necessary to invest staff time in order to match up the task in question to possible computerised solutions and also to train staff in the use of a new technology. The decision to computerise an activity will require consideration of the benefits as against the costs of so doing. A full appreciation of the advantages, and limitations, of computerisation can come only with an adequate understanding of the relevant areas of computer science.

1.3 Problem Analysis

Any activity for which a computer is required must produce some output. Unless the activity is identical on each occasion, there will also be some input each time the activity takes place. The activity produces the output when given the input. In its broadest terms we consider the problem of obtaining the output, given the input. It is the task of the programmer to compose and write down a suitable sequence of instructions which will, when the correct information is input, produce the required output. However, before the instruction sequence can be written down, or **coded**, there are a number of prior stages.

The programmer's starting point is a real-world problem. The first stage is to establish the *requirements* of the user. This can be quite a tricky job. Frequently the user has not formulated the requirements precisely. Moreover, in the process of clarifying those requirements—and, sometimes, even long after the programmer has begun developing the software—the user's perception of the requirements may change. It should, therefore, not be thought that establishing the requirements is an insignificant activity. Analysis of these requirements enables the programmer to specify precisely the function of the software, that is, the relationship of the output from the software to given sets of input. The *specification* is an important document which states precisely what the program, or suite of programs, will achieve. For all but the most trivial problems this stage will entail a breakdown of the problem into a number of smaller sub-problems. Working from the specification, the programmer can design an *algorithm* for the program. Only when a program has been fully designed can the coding stage begin. In this stage the programmer reformulates the design terminology used in the algorithm as a formal document, the **program**, which can be executed on a computer. Figure 1.1 shows the process of analysis schematically.

The various stages in this process do not have to be carried out by one person. Indeed many programmers may work simultaneously on a large project. It is therefore vitally important that each stage is watertight. For example, the specification must be produced in sufficient detail so that another programmer can use it to design the program. If, as is usual, the design phase yields a set of related algorithms, these must be expressed sufficiently clearly so that different programmers can code them separately and obtain a successful match when the suite of software is run.

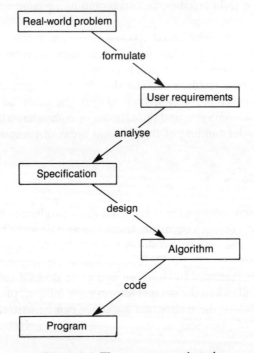

Figure 1.1 The programmer's task

By way of example, let us consider an aspect of the airline booking system. In particular, we shall tackle the problem of providing a facility for the travel agent, which will enable him to obtain answers to queries about the availability of places on flights and make bookings for available seats.

The first stage is to formulate a clear statement of the problem. The user in this situation is the travel agent; it will be necessary to ask him some questions in order to establish clearly what is required. The following are examples of questions which might be asked in this situation to obtain further particulars.

- Does the system have to keep accounts and charge travel agents for the booking that they make, or is the accounting function part of a separate system?
- Should it be possible to enquire about all the flights on the same day between two given airports?
- Are details about fares required?

It should not be assumed that all possible questions can be anticipated at this stage; some questions may only become apparent at a later stage of the analysis. We might now arrive at the following formulation of requirements.

A system is to be devised to handle information on all scheduled flights by carriers who are members of the International Air Transport Association. The information already held for each flight consists of: the names and codes of the airports of departure and arrival and intermediate stopping points, the times of departure and arrival, the aircraft used and its seating capacity for each class of passenger, and the fares available on the flight. The new software will augment this information with details of seat bookings.

The system is to answer queries about seat availability, times of departure and arrival and fares, given the towns of departure and arrival and the date or dates. The system is further to accept bookings by travel agents for specific seats on a named flight on a given date.

It is not suggested that this is a complete formulation for a realistic booking system, but it will be sufficient for our purpose in this chapter. We wish to show how to proceed through the various steps from a real-world problem to an algorithm, or program design. The techniques for deriving program code from a given design will be left until chapter 3.

Specification

The statement of the problem given above spells out the travel agent's requirements as a user of the system. It does not, however, spell out a number of things which the programmer needs to know in order to design the program. For example, the statement of requirements refers to queries input by the travel agent but says nothing about their format. Indeed, the travel agent may not care too much about the specific format so long as it is easy to understand and use. The specification must therefore lay down these matters. It may specify that the name of the airport must be input but that the software should handle possible misspellings (in case the travel agent makes a minor typing error). For convenience, it is wise to give users the choice of using the international three-letter airport codes (such as LHR for London Heathrow). Unless such details are specified, they cannot be incorporated into the design. The manner in which information must be input by the user, the sources of stored data available and the nature of the data to be output must be fully specified. The job of the designer is then to determine a suitable sequence of steps which will generate the output corresponding to the given input.

Top-down design

The aim of the algorithm design stage is to express unambiguously the steps which fulfil a precise specification. It is clearly desirable that this design process should use the words and language appropriate to the problem whose specification has been given. In designing the algorithm, the programmer may take into consideration similar problems which have been previously encountered. In a complex situation it is always advisable to break the problem into a few such manageable pieces. If the analysis is too large a task for one programmer, each piece can be handled separately by a different programmer. By progressively dividing a problem in this manner the pieces become more tractable. This technique of divide and conquer is known as **top-down design**.

Using a broad brush approach we might make the following initial analysis of the seat-booking problem. The first step is

   1 begin processing queries and bookings
to get things started. Before any computer activity can take place there is some setting up to get things ready for the actual activity. This should not surprise you. When you settle down to some activity you too must begin, by assembling pen, paper and dictionary, and possibly borrowing a calculator. It may also be necessary to clear from your desk the debris of a previous activity. The next step (very broadly) is
   2 process each transaction
where a transaction is a query or a booking; the final step is
   3 stop processing.

We have included very little detail here at the top level, although you may note that step 2 lends itself to immediate further analysis.

Stepwise refinement

The virtue of the top-down process is that at each level the individual steps can be treated as separate problems which can themselves be analysed in a top-down fashion. Thus, for example, step 2 of our top level can be fleshed out further as follows. We note first that a succession of transactions is to be catered for. Eventually, the travel agent will decide to send no further queries or bookings. So we can rewrite step 2 as

   2 while there are more transactions process the next one.

The processing of a transaction depends very much on whether it is a query or a booking. We may therefore refine step 2 as follows.

2 while there are more transactions
  2.1 select
  2.2   if transaction is a query: answer query
  2.3   if transaction is a booking: make booking
  2.4   endselect
  2.5 endwhile

There are two things to note here. Firstly, we have introduced a second level of numbering to indicate where a single step of the top-level design has been refined into a number of steps at the next level. Secondly, we have indented certain lines to indicate that they are subordinate to previous lines. Thus all steps 2.1 to 2.5 are governed by the overriding step 2. Likewise, steps 2.2 to 2.4 are subordinate to step 2.1. The final step in each subordinate sequence, 2.4 endselect and 2.5 endwhile, are included to clarify the interpretation of the design.

We can now proceed further to refine yet again steps 2.2 and 2.3. This process of **stepwise refinement** continues until each step represents an atomic activity—a single action which does not merit further subdivision. Step 2.2 might be replaced by

  2.2.1 input flight data
  2.2.2 search information bank for matching flights
  2.2.3 output list of flights with vacant seats

We have used the word *input* here to mean obtain data from the outside world (that is, the travel agent) and *output* to mean transfer data to the outside world. You should note carefully the construction of this last refinement—input, process, output—as it occurs repeatedly in the design of programs.

Exercise 1.1

Refine step 2.3 in the design above.

Exercise 1.2

A sum of money is deposited in an existing account with a building society. Produce a top-level design for the problem of computing the new balance in the account after this deposit. Assume that the current balance is known to the system, and allow for any interest earned but not yet included in the balance.

Following the refinement in exercise 1.1, the design of our airline booking system looks like this:

  1 begin processing transactions
  2 while there are more transactions

2.1 select
2.2   if transaction is a query:
          2.2.1 input flight data
          2.2.2 search information bank for matching flights
          2.2.3 output list of flights with vacant seats
2.3   if transaction is a booking:
          2.3.1 input booking data
          2.3.2 update information bank with booking details
          2.3.3 confirm booking
          2.3.4 output seat numbers
2.4   endselect
2.5 endwhile
3 stop processing

It is evident that we can continue to refine any step within this design as far as necessary. The exact words used are not important, but the more detailed the design becomes, the more specific must be the activities. We have used a numbering system to indicate the level of refinement and also an indentation scheme to indicate the pattern of processing.

There are a few design structures, like while . . . endwhile and select . . . endselect, which occur naturally in program designs. These structures help you to think about problems in words which you can use. We shall develop these structures in chapter 2.

First, though, we shall introduce a system of diagrams which help to make clear the design process.

Structure trees

There is no harm in continuing to produce the complete design of the booking system as a stylised list of steps in the manner described above. We shall, however, use a diagrammatic convention to display graphically the relationship of the steps in an algorithm. Each step representing an *activity* is enclosed in a box, and the *refinement* of a step is indicated by a sequence of steps drawn at a lower level. Thus figure 1.2 illustrates the current version of our algorithm for the airline booking system.

Figure 1.2 reflects the structure of our design for an airline booking system. Each box describes an action and the diagram as a whole represents a hierarchy of levels. The top box, which labels the problem as a whole, is called the *root*. Several branches are seen to radiate from the root and from the intermediate boxes. Action boxes from which no further branches radiate are called *leaves*, and the diagram as a whole is a **structure tree**. (Computer scientists grow their trees upside down.)

The structure tree of figure 1.2 is interpreted as follows. The three branches coming from the root are to be executed in left to right sequence. Branches 1 and 3 require no further elaboration. In branch 2, corresponding to step 2 of the top-level design, the *while* repetition is indicated by an oval and the *select* construction is indicated by a hexagon. Do not concern yourself with these at present as they will be discussed fully in the next chapter. For the time being it is sufficient to

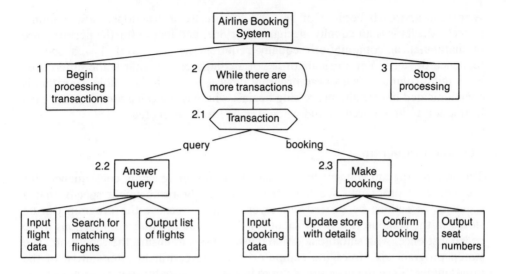

Figure 1.2 Structure tree for an airline booking system

appreciate that the whole of the *subtree* coming from branch 2 may be repeated several times, and that only one of the branches 2.2 and 2.3 is selected for execution on each repetition.

The structure tree is not the only method of representing an algorithm—many programmers are quite happy to use numbered steps as in our earlier discussion, or different diagrammatic conventions. During the development stages it is generally simpler to perform stepwise refinement on numbered steps; the numbering system helps to keep the design intact without rewriting it completely at every stage. However, the human mind can more easily encompass a complex situation using two-dimensional diagrams. The structure tree provides this graphic view of an algorithm, and any part of it can be scanned downwards to reflect its top-down design.

Exercise 1.3

The Telecom company sends out quarterly bills to each of its subscribers. Each subscriber pays rental charges for the line and for telephone equipment and a call charge which is calculated using meter readings at the telephone exchange. Illustrate an algorithm for producing the bill for one subscriber by means of a structure diagram.

1.4 Algorithms and Data

The construction of an algorithm which specifies a solution to a problem is a valid method of approach whether the solution is to be implemented by manual or mechanical means. The computer does give an additional impetus to the use of a systematic approach because of its need for precise instructions. Now a simple pocket calculator is an equally mechanical device, and its use for the performance of mathematical computations equally requires the user to follow a specific sequence of steps. Yet a calculator is not a computer. So what is the difference? The digital computer is a **stored program** device, to which the whole algorithm is communicated before any processing begins, whereas the calculator requires each instruction to be entered as and when it is due to be executed.

The stored program

The stored program concept has fundamental and far reaching consequences for the nature of programs. We have seen how an algorithm might specify that a sequence of actions be carried out several times. Because the program can be stored in the computer, it is sufficient for this repeated sequence of actions to be coded just once, with suitable additional instructions to ensure the repetition. The stored program also frees the computer from the continual intervention of the programmer. Since the program is stored inside the computer, the computer can be given autonomous control over program execution. This autonomy allows the high potential speed of the computer to be exploited. Any external intervention is slow by the standards of achievable computing speeds. The full benefit of high-speed computing is available whenever there is no need for external communication. Between inputs and outputs, the computer can operate at full speed, accessing its instructions internally.

When we talk about about a computer we mean an *electronic, general-purpose, stored-program* computer. So, although a pocket calculator is an electronic device for performing calculations, it is not a computer because it needs to have each instruction keyed in prior to execution, and cannot store a program of instructions. A digital watch incorporates a stored program to change the display each second, minute, hour and day—but it is limited to its pre-programmed function and so is not a general-purpose device. A computer, on the other hand, can be programmed to function as a calculator or a digital watch (or even to control a washing machine), or to implement an algorithm within a wide range of capability.

Data

One of the aims of algorithm design is to abstract from a real-world problem—that is to say, to strip away details not relevant to the problem while concentrating on the process. Consider the following simple problems, which differ in underlying detail but all describe a common process:

(a) total the number of pints of milk taken during a week;
(b) total the number of gallons of petrol purchased in a month;
(c) determine the total daily takings by a department store.

In each case the algorithm includes the same sequence of instructions. In (a), starting with a zero total, the daily number of pints is added to the current total for each day of the week. In (b), starting with a zero total, the number of gallons purchased on each occasion during the month is added to the current total. And finally in (c), starting with a zero total, the daily takings for each department is added to the current total. Each algorithm contains the following skeleton:

    1 initialise total to zero
    2 while there are more numbers to add
    2.1 input next number
    2.2 add next number to total
    2.3 endwhile
    3 output total

The algorithm expresses the instructions for the computation, in their proper sequence, without reference to the details of the application. It applies equally to any of our examples and does not have to be varied to suit the changing context. (The actual program code derived from it might, however, include parts which are sensitive to the particular context of application.) The noteworthy feature of the algorithm is that it specifies unambiguously what should be done, and how, for a class of similar problems.

However, the interpretation of the algorithm depends on the application. In case (a), the input and output numbers refer to pints of milk, whereas in case (b) they refer to gallons of petrol, and in case (c) they refer to takings in some unit of currency. The context may or may not be included in the statement of the algorithm, but it must surely be stated somewhere.

The numbers which are fed into the algorithm as input are referred to as **data**. As such they convey no meaning beyond that required to add them and obtain a total. However, in context each data item *represents* specific information. In general, the term 'data' is used to describe a number or word, or a collection of numbers or words, without necessarily referring to a particular context. Information, on the other hand, requires a context within which to interpret the data. One of the functions of problem analysis is to abstract the data (or rather the types of data) from the nature of the information upon which the algorithm is to act.

Atomic data types

Just as programs can be analysed into individual instructions, so too complex data items may be analysed into *atomic* data, capable of direct representation in the computer. Numbers, or **numeric data**, form an important class of atomic data. The arithmetic operations on numbers are understood well and are clearly defined. Numbers themselves may be further subdivided into **integers** (whole numbers) and **real** numbers, which in the context of computers means numbers expressed using a decimal point. In practice additional subdivisions may be desirable. Thus, although integers may be positive or negative, stock levels can generally be measured by positive numbers only. Likewise the date in a month is not just an integer, but an integer in the range 1 to 31.

Non-numeric processing is every bit as important as numeric processing, and to cater for it we require a type of data which can handle characters, words and symbols. We call this data type a string of symbols, or just **string** for short. A string is usually presented as a sequence of symbols enclosed between quotes, like "Fred" or 'Fred'.

integer	27	-100
real	47.72	3.0
string	"computer"	"27"

The preceding table gives some examples of atomic data. Note that there is a difference between the string "computer" and a computer. The former is an English word with eight characters which may be printed in a book, whereas the latter is the name of a device for processing information. The same distinction applies to the quoted string "27" and the number 27. The former is the character "2" followed by the character "7", whereas the latter is the name of an abstract idea. Whether you write 27 (conventional decimal notation) or XXVII (Roman numerals) or even 1B (hexadecimal notation—we shall be discussing this in later chapters), the underlying idea is the same. For most purposes it suits us to write 27, especially when we perform arithmetic. On the other hand "27" cannot be added, subtracted or multiplied. The use of quotes makes clear the distinction between strings (which stand for themselves) and character sequences which are names of concepts.

Variables

An algorithm is a template for execution—it describes the method, but does not include actual data. In this way the same algorithm can be used repeatedly for computations with different data.

It is necessary though for the algorithm to refer to the different data items. This is achieved by giving each data item a name or **identifier**. The named data item is referred to as a **variable**; its value (numerical or other) may *vary* during program execution or on different occasions when the program is executed. Thus the statement

price = cost + profit

can be implemented on different occasions with different values of *cost* and *profit*; on each occasion the value of *price* will bear the correct relationship to the values of *cost* and *profit*.

The ability to name variables has had a profound effect on the development of programming tools. The use of names to stand for the unknown values of numbers, strings and even collections of data enables the programmer to work at a level of abstraction and generality. This improves the effectiveness of the programmer in producing a correct, working program which meets the user's requirements.

The computer provides the hardware for advances in information processing. The stored program enables the computer to operate autonomously. The notion of a variable enables the programmer to express a processing algorithm in general terms.

Arrays

We have introduced the named variable as a means of referring to individual data items. When a process is applied to one or more items from a collection of related data, it is convenient to have a method of representing the aggregated data. We shall describe here one form of data aggregate, the **array.** Other data structures will be introduced in chapters 7 and 9.

The array provides the means for grouping a collection of variables of the same type which may require similar processing. In the skeleton program design earlier in this section, each number in the sequence to be totalled was required to be input separately, on each successive occasion that step 2.1 is encountered. It might be considered more appropriate to think of the whole collection of data to be totalled as a single aggregate. For the sake of being specific, we shall use terminology appropriate to case (a), the milkman's problem, but the principle applies equally to any totalling problem.

There will be seven numbers in the aggregate, each representing the number of pints taken on a particular day of the week. We therefore use an array of seven integer variables, described collectively by the name *pints()*, say. We use the parentheses here as a reminder that the name is not a simple variable but an array. When it is desired to access the value of *pints()* for a particular day, say Tuesday, we use the notation *pints(Tuesday)*. The individual variables which make up the array are called the **elements** of the array. In our example, the array *pints()* has seven elements, each taking an integer value. The value which selects a particular day is called the **index** or **subscript** of the element. Thus *pints(Tuesday)* is called the element of *pints()* with index *Tuesday*.

The following data table summarises the variables which will be used in our revised program design.

Name	Description	Type
pints()	number of pints of milk taken each day	integer array
day	current day of the week	
total	total number of pints so far	integer

Note that the table does not specify a type for *day*. Since the values which *day* takes are not numbers or strings, we really want a special day type which allows the values Sunday, Monday, Tuesday and so on.

We shall now modify the program design so that the input step initialises the whole array *pints()*. Indeed we shall refine step 1 to initialise all the variables. The resulting design will look something like this:

1 initialise
1.1 input values for *pints()*
1.2 set *total* to pints(Sunday)
1.3 set *day* to *Sunday*

2 while there are more *days* in the week
2.1 set *day* to next day
2.2 add *pints(day)* to *total*
2.3 endwhile
3 output *total*

In step 2.2 the value of *pints(day)* is the number of pints taken on the current day. On each traversal of the while . . . endwhile section the same actions are performed in steps 2.1 and 2.2, namely adding the number of pints for the current day to the total. However the current day is different on each traversal, because the index variable *day* is updated.

Of course our new design fragment does not in itself achieve any more than the original design. What has been achieved, though, by the use of an array is that the elements of *pints()* remain available to be accessed in any subsequent step. In the original design the values were totalled and discarded.

The array is a flexible data structure because each array element is independently accessible through its index.

1.5 Library Routines

Each step of an algorithm is capable of successive refinement until at some stage an *atomic* step is reached, requiring no further refinement. An atomic step is an action for which a defined mechanism exists. So if your target programming language can express simple arithmetic operations—add, subtract, multiply—these actions can appear in the final version of an algorithm without further refinement. However, the action or process of drawing a square, for example, may require several program actions (depending on the language) and so may require further refinement. But, if many algorithms are likely to be written, all incorporating square drawing, it is preferable that drawing a square should be available to program designers as an atomic action.

Algorithms for problems which arise in many contexts are collected to form a library of *routines*. These routines may have been supplied with the computer system, bought off the shelf or designed in-house. The source of a library routine is irrelevant to the programmer who needs to know only at which stage of the design he can stop refining the algorithm. The library routine is plugged into the algorithm as a self-contained module. The essence of successful program design is thus to reduce a problem to a combination of previously solved problems.

Parameters

It is conceivable that a library routine is required to perform exactly the same function on every occasion that it is used. For example, a library routine could be used to draw the layout of a chart or table which is then completed with detail by other program steps. However, a routine is likely to be more useful if an element of flexibility can be built in. Thus a routine which draws squares can allow the user the freedom to specify the size of the square. We say that size is a **parameter** of the square-drawing routine.

Input and output

Every program design must make provision for some sort of output, so as to communicate the results, either to the outside world or to some other computer program. In many cases the design will also include specific instructions for the input of data from an appropriate source. Few of the details of how the input and output are actually performed are likely to be relevant to the algorithm. The details depend critically on the mode of processing, and even on the assumption that a computer is used for the processing. Indeed, there are as many different implementations of input and output as there are different models of computers.

The actions which input and output data are left as atomic steps within an algorithm. It is assumed that they are available as library routines, to be incorporated into program designs as required.

Summary of Chapter 1

The world abounds with problems which require information to be processed. Some are fairly simple while others are highly complex. In all cases careful analysis can help in the design of a solution to the problem. The advent of the digital electronic computer has brought hitherto intractable problems within the realm of feasibility, and has encouraged the development of new procedures which make use of high-speed processing and error-free repetition. If the solution to a problem is to be implemented automatically, using a computer, careful analysis and design are indispensable, so that a precise set of instructions for the solution can be drawn up. A complete specification of the processing required for a given task, expressed in terms of the set of operations available on a computer, is called a program.

The first stages in programming the solution to a problem entail determining what the problem is, and specifying precisely the relationship of the results which are to be output to the initial data fed in.

An algorithm for solving a problem may then be designed in top-down fashion. First the method of solution is described in terms of a limited number of component steps. Each step may be further analysed in a continual process of stepwise refinement, until each step is manageable in its own right. The resulting design is a formal description in words of the solution to the problem. The sequence of steps may be numbered to display the hierarchy of the algorithm. The design may also be displayed as a structure tree. The structured algorithm is used by the programmer as the basis for writing the program code which can be executed by the computer.

A program designed in top-down fashion develops a clear structure. This has advantages for both the users of the program and the programmers who have to maintain it.

The program, when written, is stored in the computer for autonomous execution. Interaction with the outside world takes place only as directed by the program. A program consists of a sequence of instructions which manipulate data. The fundamental data types include integers, real numbers and strings. A collection of data of a given type may be packaged in an array. The array is regarded as a single compound object.

Within the program code, the program statements do not necessarily manipulate specific numbers and strings. Instead, names are used to stand for variables which take on particular values on each occasion when the program is executed.

Answers to Exercises

1.1 An appropriate refinement might be
    2.3.1 input booking data
    2.3.2 update information bank with booking details
    2.3.3 confirm booking
    2.3.4 output seat numbers.

1.2 1 input amount of deposit
    2 add deposit to current balance to produce new balance
    3 add any outstanding interest due
    4 output balance.

1.3

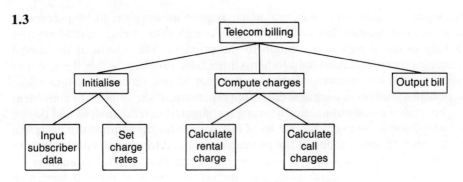

Figure A1.3 Telecom subscriber billing

Further Exercises

1. Give two reasons why it might be desirable to provide the Directory Enquiries operators of a telephone company with a computer-based directory to replace printed telephone directories.
   Discuss whether your reasons apply to telephone subscribers.

2. What advantages are to be gained by designing an algorithm using a top-down approach?

3. A building society has decided to use a computer to maintain members' accounts. Using structured English or a suitable diagrammatic convention, devise an algorithm to update the balance in an account following a withdrawal.

Consider how you would set about designing a program which could handle both deposits and withdrawals.

4. Explain briefly the method of designing programs by stepwise refinement.

5. Illustrate, using an example, the difference between data and information.

2 Program Control

Programming, in the broadest sense of the word, is the total task of stating (to the necessary degree of precision) a problem, the domain in which it applies and a method for its solution. The statement must be complete, that is precise, unambiguous and sufficiently detailed so that a computer may be used to implement the method and obtain the solution. We saw in the previous chapter that such a complete statement may be developed by the method of top-down successive refinement: an action is first described in a single word or phrase and is then refined in successive steps until the description is sufficiently detailed and precise to be presented to the computer for execution.

The statement will include an *algorithm*, a detailed description of the computational (and other) steps which must be carried out. It is also necessary to set out the dependencies between individual steps. Sometimes the steps form a logical sequence, in which a given step cannot be performed until certain data is available from one or more other steps; these other steps need to be executed prior to the given step. The order of execution of certain other steps may be immaterial and, if resources permit, it may be possible to allow execution of these steps to overlap, or to be performed in parallel.

The computers now available commercially are all essentially sequential machines, that is, in general they are able to perform one action at a time. Thus a program for such a machine specifies effectively a linear sequence of instructions. Current research work is in progress towards the building of highly parallel computers which, for example, can execute concurrently several computational sequences. The structure of such machines, and how to program them, are topics which cannot be studied in an introductory course. Throughout what follows we shall assume execution on a sequential computer.

We saw, in some of the program designs in chapter 1, that the sequence in which the program steps are to be executed is not necessarily the linear sequence in which they are written. Very often a sequence of steps may have to be executed several times; this requirement can be specified (by the word *while*, for example) without actually writing out the sequence of steps numerous times. On the other hand, it may be necessary at some point in the sequence to choose between alternative sets of steps, depending on some external condition or on a previously computed result. We saw an example of such a choice construction in the analysis of the airline booking system in section 1.3. These three logical constructions—sequences, repetitions and choices—are sufficient for controlling the execution of a program design by a sequential computer.

It may also be desirable, in the top-down design process, to defer further refinement of a particular step. The set of execution steps into which the step is refined may be recorded elsewhere, packaged and made available as a single entity, called a *module*, for execution as and when required.

The complete statement of the solution—that is, the *program*—may include such groupings of steps as required by the specification of the solution.

2.1 Control Structures

The principal aim at the higher levels of refinement is to allow the programmer (and his client) to express his understanding of the problem and its proposed solution. That is, he must write down, using some appropriate language, a sequence of successively more detailed descriptions of the problem and its solution which can be read and understood by a human being (another programmer, perhaps), and so checked for correctness.

As we have seen, the design of a program entails the use of two types of control structure, allowing for repetition and choice. Imagine a sequence of steps in a program design being written on a piece of paper which has been stuck back upon itself to form a loop. Then, after the last step of the process, the first step is met again. A repetitive program construct is therefore called a **loop**. On the other hand, recall the way a selection is incorporated into a structure tree. There may be several branches coming from the hexagonal choice box, but only one branch has to be executed. A selective program construct is called a **branch**.

A loop construct provides a mechanism whereby an action, or group of actions, can be repeated. A branch construct allows a choice, controlled by a stated condition, to be made between alternative sequences of actions.

We had a brief glimpse at these control features in the airline booking system in chapter 1. We now examine them in greater detail.

Loop constructs

In exercise 1.3 we posed the problem faced by the Telecom company in billing its subscribers. We also presented a design to compute the amount owing and produce a bill for a single customer. The task is, however, to bill *all* customers of Telecom. The actual process for producing each bill is the same but, naturally, the data varies among subscribers. A description of this task will therefore require the use of a loop. A loop causes execution of a computational process repeatedly until some condition is satisfied. In our example, the process must be repeated until the list of customers is exhausted.

The top-level design for the overall billing system might be:

    1 initialise
    2 produce bills for all subscribers
    3 close files

Step 1 in this program design sets up the data to control the loop which will process the bill for each customer. It may achieve this by setting the number of subscribers who have to be billed. Let us call this number *no_of_subscribers*. The individual subscriber data which has to be processed may be held in a file, so the initialisation step will open the file prior to commencement of the loop. At this stage it does not matter whether this file is a conventional paper file or a modern computerised file. Step 2 is refined into a loop describing the action required for each subscriber. In the refinement below an additional dummy step 2.3 is included to show clearly the extent of the loop.

    1.1 open subscriber file
    1.2 input *no_of_subscribers*
    2.1 loop *no_of_subscribers* times
    2.2   produce subscriber's bill
    2.3   endloop
    3   close subscriber file

The computations included in step 2.2 may be broken down further into three steps—initialisation of the data specific to the current subscriber, computation of the balance owing and printing of the bill—as shown below.

    1.1 open subscriber file
    1.2 input *no_of_subscribers*
    2.1 loop *no_of_subscribers* times
    2.2.1   input subscriber data
    2.2.2   compute charges
    2.2.3   output bill
    2.3   endloop
    3   close subscriber file

We may also represent the program design by a structure tree; we then use an elongated oval to depict a loop, as shown in figure 2.1. The number inside the loop oval specifies the number of repetitions.

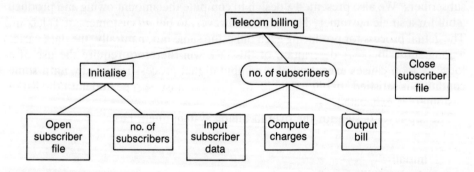

Figure 2.1 Example of a loop construct

The structure tree is interpreted by working from the root. At the next level there are three *subtrees*: initialisation (corresponding to step 1 in the top-level design), followed by the loop (step 2) and finally closure of the file. The interpretation of the loop oval is that the actions in the subtree coming from the oval are to be performed (in the usual left-to-right sequence) *repeatedly* for the required number of times, as specified in the oval.

A common mistake made by novice programmers is to use a numeric constant in step 2 instead of an identifier. For example, if there are currently 275 812 Telecom subscribers, there might be a temptation to write

2 loop 275 812 times

Such a program design would not be very useful. After all, new subscribers are likely to be taken on, and old ones may discontinue their telephone service. The program design would be obsolete before the program code is written. It is important to realise that, although the number of subscribers remains constant throughout a particular execution of the billing program, it may change before the next occassion on which the program is executed. The essential program steps, however, do not change. Thus the number of subscribers is a *parameter* of the billing program. The use of an identifier for the number of subscribers allows for the value of the parameter to be set on each execution rather than be enshrined in the program design.

We call a loop in which the number of repetitions in the loop is fixed at the outset a **fixed loop**.

Conditional loops

The use of a fixed loop in our program design is satisfactory only when the number of subscribers is already known. In practice, since the subscriber data is held in a file, it is not necessary to know the number of subscribers before processing the file—processing of subscriber data can continue as long as unprocessed data remains in the file. To accommodate this form of repetition, step 2.1 of the billing algorithm must be replaced by

2.1 loop while there is more data in the file

Note carefully that this loop will work satisfactorily for an empty file, containing no subscriber data. A loop which is repeated *while* a given condition holds is called a **while loop**. A while loop is described in a structure tree by inserting a suitable condition into the loop oval.

The following exercise requires the use of an appropriate loop construct.

Exercise 2.1

A sequence of names is to be read and the corresponding telephone numbers are to be printed out. The sequence of names is terminated by the hash symbol #. Draw a structure diagram for this process, without refining the step required to obtain the telephone number corresponding to a given name.

It is instructive to note that the loop in the answer to exercise 2.1 has to be primed by reading the first name in the sequence before entering the loop; otherwise there would be no condition to test. This feature is known as *look-ahead*. Whenever further processing depends on the nature of the next item, it is necessary to look ahead and inspect the next item before processing. In this case the first item must be inspected before the whole process is started.

By way of contrast, some repetitive processes are required to continue *until* a predetermined situation arises.

Consider a process which poses a question and seeks the answer "yes" or "no"; any other answer is rejected and the question is asked again until one of these answers is given. A suitable design for this process is:

```
1 loop
2      pose question
3      input answer
4      until answer = "yes" or answer = "no"
5 process answer
```

This type of loop construct is called an **until loop**. The extent of the loop is clearly indicated by the until condition (step 4). It is not necessary, therefore, to add the word endloop. Note that, in this example, it is possible for the loop to be repeated endlessly, if neither of the preferred responses, "yes" and "no", is input.

There are two fundamental differences between the until loop and the while loop. The first difference is that the until condition is tested *after* the steps in the loop; in other words an until loop is always traversed at least once, whereas a while loop is skipped altogether if the condition fails on the first entry to the loop. The other point is that the steps in a while loop are repeated *as long as* the condition holds; in an until loop, execution of the steps in the loop *ceases* as soon as the condition holds.

An algorithm should normally be expressed in terms of whichever type of loop matches the problem most closely.

Exercise 2.2

Give a top-level design for the process of reading a paragraph of text and copying it out with each sentence starting on a new line. Refine the step which handles a single sentence, assuming that a full stop occurs only at the end of a sentence.

It is worth noting at this stage that our program designs have evolved a definite style, using a limited repertoire of control words such as *loop*, *endloop*, *while* and *until*. The structure of the program is delineated by appropriate indentation to indicate which steps comprise the loop. This form of expressing program designs is called **structured English** or **pseudocode**.

Branch constructs

A number of candidates sit an examination. They are to be graded into several categories of pass and fail according to their marks. Assuming that the names and marks of candidates are held on file, a top-level design for this process might be:

```
1 open candidate file
2 loop
3    obtain candidate data
4    allocate grade
5    until end of candidate file
6 close file
```

In allocating the grade a suitable action must be selected. Suppose the possible grades for candidates are *fail*, *pass* and *distinction*. The pass mark is 40 and distinctions are awarded to those candidates who score above 85. Step 4 can be refined as follows:

```
4.1 select
4.2    if mark < 40 : award fail grade
4.3    if mark between 40 and 85 : award pass grade
4.4    if mark > 85 : award distinction grade
4.5    endselect
```

The control structure which allows selection from a set of possible actions is called a **branch construct**. To incorporate a branch construct in a structure diagram, we use a hexagon. The condition or expression which is tested to determine which choice of action to take is written inside the hexagon. Each branch coming from the hexagon is *labelled* with a value (or set of values) which can arise on testing the condition. Only one branch is selected for execution—the one corresponding to the value of the condition.

Our grade allocation procedure can be illustrated diagrammatically as in figure 2.2.

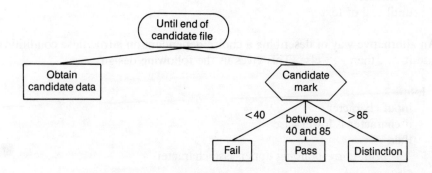

Figure 2.2 Example of a branch construct

Where a branching condition has only two possible values, it is usually phrased in terms of a *true/false condition*. Consider, for example, a text processor which prepares output for a printer which has no lower-case alphabet. It is therefore necessary to convert all lower-case characters to upper case before printing, but to copy without alteration digits and other symbols. A corresponding structure tree is given in figure 2.3.

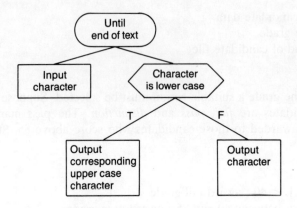

Figure 2.3 Text conversion algorithm

A program design in structured English for this process could use the select format introduced above, as follows:

```
loop
    input character
    select
        if character is lower case:
            print corresponding upper-case character
        if character is not lower case:
            print character
    endselect
until end of text
```

An alternative way of describing a choice dependent on a true/false condition is to use if . . . then . . . else. This gives us the following design:

```
loop
    input character
    if character is lower case
    then
        print corresponding upper-case character
    else
        print character
    endif
until end of text
```

Note as in previous constructs, the dummy step *endif* which delineates the extent of the steps subordinate to the else condition.

Exercise 2.3

A program is required to handle client transactions for the National Midlays Bank. The transactions to be catered for are deposits, withdrawals, notification of current balance and requests for statements (which are sent subsequently through the post). A client must identify the name and number of his or her account, and may perform several transactions on one visit.

The following is a top-level design.

   1 initialise client details
   2 process transactions for client

Refine this design in the form of a structure tree.

Exercise 2.4

An output selector module has the following specification. The output is to be sent to one of these devices: screen, printer, lineprinter, indicator board. The device is selected by typing its initial letter at the keyboard.

Devise a suitable program design.

2.2 Assignment

In the course of developing our program designs we have incorporated expressions such as

  mark < 40

and

  answer = "yes"

Such expressions use the current value of a variable. This implies that a value was *assigned* to the variable at some previous step. Variables serve as a useful means of holding values until they are used. In the initialisation process, values are established for certain variables which may be required at various points in the algorithm. Thus, in the bank transaction handler (figure A2.3) the balance was obtained during the initialisation phase so that it could be used subsequently in the processing of individual transactions. This amount can henceforth be referred to by the name *balance*. This enables the name *balance* to be used anywhere in the design, rather than having to issue a request to obtain the current balance (from a file) each time it is needed.

During initialisation, variables which have not yet been used are introduced and given values. Variables may also be introduced at intermediate steps in a computation to hold temporary values. Thus the value

balance + deposit

may be assigned to the variable *new_balance* after a deposit transaction.

In many situations it is appropriate to update the value of a variable, changing its current value for a new one. Thus, for example, the effect of a deposit transaction may be succinctly described by assigning the new value

balance + deposit

to the variable *balance*. Similarly a withdrawal may be described by giving *balance* the value

balance − withdrawal

In this way a variable may take on a succession of values during the execution of an algorithm; however, at any point in the execution it has just one value. The action of assigning a value (which may be an integer, real, string or of some other type) to a named variable is called an **assignment**. Assignment to a variable is useful in the course of processing to hold temporary results.

We shall use the = sign to indicate the assignment to a named variable of the result of a computation. The = sign in this context is called the **assignment symbol** and should be read as 'takes the value of'. (Other authors use alternative symbols, such as := or ←, to denote assignment.) The variable name to which the value is being assigned appears on the left of the assignment symbol, while the method of computation of that value appears on the right.

Input and output

Besides processing the data, an algorithm must provide for communication with the outside world. There is little point in performing the processing if the results are never *output*. Likewise an algorithm may be very limited in scope if there is no opportunity for alternative data values to be *input*.

The fundamental input action assigns a name to an item of data fed into the computation. This is just a special form of assignment, in which the value assigned is obtained from an external medium rather than a computational process. We use a notation like

input *price*

for the step which obtains a data value from an external medium and assigns it to the variable *price*. The actual method of data input—keyboard, document reader, bar code scanner, to name just some—is immaterial at this level of program design.

The fundamental output action communicates a value, or the result of a computation, to the outside world. We may write

output *salary*

for the step which outputs the current value of salary. The actual method of outputting the value—numerical, graphical or by diagram—does not matter; nor does the device, which could be, for example, a screen or a printer.

The structure diagram of figure 2.4 describes a simple payroll.

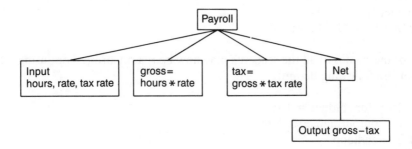

Figure 2.4 Simple payroll

The input box is used to input values to the three variables *hours*, *rate* and *tax_rate*. The next two action boxes compute values and assign them to *gross* and *tax*. The values are calculated as simple multiplications (we use the * for multiplication). The final action—output box—specifies the value to be output, namely the result of the computation *gross-tax*.

Exercise 2.5

A payroll program is required to calculate an employee's pay as follows: the gross pay for the hours worked is calculated taking into account basic pay and overtime; deductions are made for tax and superannuation; and the consequent net pay is determined. Draw a structure diagram which incorporates a top-down design for the corresponding algorithm.

Exercise 2.6

Textual analysis, a boring and repetitive task, is an ideal candidate for computerisation. One of the tasks of textual analysis is to count the average number of occassions that a given word appears in a piece of text. Draw the structure tree for an algorithm to find the average number of occurrences of the word 'has' in a piece of text.

Controlled loops

A variable which is updated on each traversal of a loop may be used as a parameter within the body of the loop. Here is an example which uses a loop with a fixed number of repetitions.

There are twenty students in a class, and it is required to print a list of their names. An array *name()* is used to hold the names of the students. The **elements** of the array are string variables called *name(1)*, *name(2)*, *name(3)* and so on. Each of these elements can be assigned a distinct value; for example

        name(1) = "F. Jones"
        name(2) = "S. White"
        name(3) = "D. Edwards"

A list of the names of all the students may now be readily printed out using a fixed loop of the following design:

        1 loop for student = 1 to 20
        1.1   output name(student)
        1.2   endloop

On each traversal of the loop the same action is performed, namely, the printing of an array element. But the array element printed is different each time round. The **control variable** *student*, which appears as the index of *name()*, is updated each time round the loop. Step 1 incorporates the instruction that the loop be traversed twenty times, with *student* taking the value 1 on the first traversal, 2 on the next, and so on until the final traversal when it has assumed the value 20. The net effect is identical with the sequence of steps

        output name(1)
        output name(2)
        output name(3)
        .
        .
        .
        output name(20)

Suppose now that each student in the class sits an examination and is awarded a mark, which is an integer in the range 0 to 100. These marks can be held in a parallel array *mark()*. If J. Finegold achieves a mark of 91, this information might be recorded by the following assignments:

        name(17) = "J Finegold"
        mark(17) = 91

Both arrays *name()* and *mark()* have an index variable in the same range (a number from 1 to 20) but the former is an array of string variables whereas the latter is an array of integer variables. The arrays may be visualised as shown in figure 2.5.

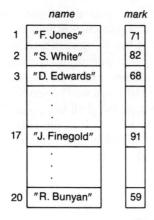

Figure 2.5 The arrays *name()* and *mark()*

Having recorded the marks for all the students it is instructive to classify them into categories of fail, pass and distinction, using the algorithm of figure 2.2. The performance of the class can be appraised by accumulating the total in each category. For this purpose an array *total()* may be used. The index range for *total()* is *fail*, *pass* and *distinction*, and the values of the array elements are positive integers, namely, the number of students in the corresponding categories. Let us now develop a program design. A top-level design might be:

```
1 initialise
2 loop for student = 1 to 20
3    increment appropriate element of total()
4    endloop
```

Since the grades are accumulated by incrementing the elements of *total()*, they must first be set equal to zero. This is achieved in the initialisation step, using a fixed loop whose control variable (called *grade*, perhaps) runs through the values *fail*, *pass* and *distinction*.

Exercise 2.7

Refine the program design to accumulate the total number of students in each category by inspecting the array *mark()*. Present your design as a structure tree.

Searching an array

It is evident that the array is a useful data structure when the desired index is known. Suppose, however, that you know the name of a student and wish to find out his mark. It will be necessary to determine his index number first. This may be achieved by searching the array for the required name. Beginning with the first array element, each element is inspected and compared with the name sought. When the desired name is found, the current index can be used to determine the student's mark. This method of marching sequentially through an array is called a **linear search**. A loop is clearly the appropriate construct here, and the array index can be controlled by incrementation. However, we do not use a fixed loop as that would inspect the whole array, whereas we can terminate our search as soon as the desired element is found. Instead, we shall use an until loop.

As an example, suppose we wish to find the mark of T. Brown, whose index number is unknown to us. The following algorithm performs a linear search of the array *name()* and determines the mark.

```
1 initialise: student = 0
2 loop
    2.1    increment student
    2.2    until name(student) = "T. Brown"
3 output mark(student)
```

Search algorithms have wide application and are discussed at greater length in chapter 3.

2.3 Modular Design

The design of a program entails breaking down a problem into a sequence of subordinate steps. Each of these steps is in turn analysed into further subordinate steps and this process can continue until each step is a simple action. It is often desirable to consider a certain step as a self-contained module. We have already made reference to library routines which can be incorporated into an algorithm as a single step. We now develop the use of routines, to allow the programmer to specify and design customised modules for a particular application. The technique of designing a program using modules to break up the task is known as **modular design**. The following are some of the advantages of developing an algorithm in modular fashion:

- the structure of the algorithm is easier to follow;
- each module can be developed separately (by a different programmer, if desired) and tested independently;
- where appropriate, the internal details of a module can be altered without requiring any changes in the main program module;
- a frequently needed module can be kept in a library for use by other programmers;
- the text of the main program can be kept short, reflecting the reduced size of the main algorithm;
- where the same module is required at several points in the algorithm, the corresponding program code need be written just once.

As an example, let us consider further the Telecom billing algorithm of section 2.1. For each subscriber the following actions are required:

2.2.1 input subscriber data
2.2.2 compute charges
2.2.3 output bill

Step 2.2.1 can be refined as follows:

2.2.1.1 input telephone number, name, address
2.2.1.2 obtain number of telephones rented, initial and final meter readings

Steps 2.2.2 and 2.2.3 involve a fair amount of complexity and might need to be changed as a result of new charging policies or a new design of bill. It is therefore best to leave the detail to named modules, so that the main program design contains just a reference to the module. Such a reference is not refined any further within the main design. Analysis of the module is treated as a separate problem. A convention is required to indicate a module reference. We shall use the word **call** when we wish to refer to a module. So we have:

2.2.2 call compute charges module
2.2.3 call output bill module

Figure 2.6 illustrates part of a structure tree which corresponds to the refinement of step 2.2 of the Telecom billing algorithm.

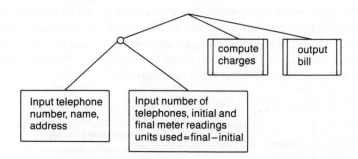

Figure 2.6 Modular Telecom billing algorithm (part)

In the structure tree for a modular design, a module call is shown as a *leaf* of the tree with no further branches. It is delineated with double lines, as shown in figure 2.6. The name in the action box is the name by which the module is known.

Step 2.2.1 of the design has been replaced here by a small circle. When it is not necessary or useful to retain any detail from an earlier level, the corresponding box is replaced by a circle to preserve the structure of the levels.

Modules

We look now at the modules in more detail. The *compute charges* module needs to begin with its own initialisation step. This will set up, for example, the charge for a telephone line, the rental per telephone receiver, and the charge per call unit. Likewise, the *output bill* module must begin by setting up the rate of VAT (value added tax). Here are top-level designs for the two modules:

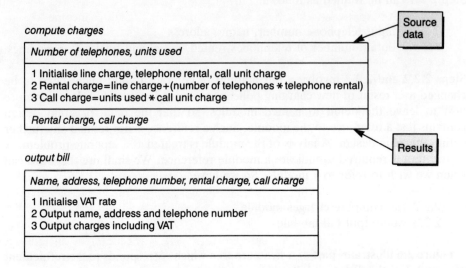

compute charges

Number of telephones, units used
1 Initialise line charge, telephone rental, call unit charge 2 Rental charge=line charge+(number of telephones ∗ telephone rental) 3 Call charge=units used ∗ call unit charge
Rental charge, call charge

Source data

Results

output bill

Name, address, telephone number, rental charge, call charge
1 Initialise VAT rate 2 Output name, address and telephone number 3 Output charges including VAT

Notice how the format for a module design includes two additional lines. The top line describes the *source data* which are provided for the module by the main program. The bottom line describes the *results* which are returned to the main program. The *output bill* module produces the output; its results line is blank as it does not return any values to the main program. Figure 2.7 illustrates the flow of data between the modules and the main program.

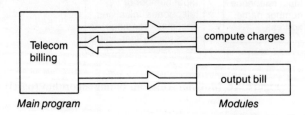

Telecom billing

compute charges

output bill

Main program   *Modules*

Figure 2.7 Flow of data in a modular design

The module calls in the main program design can be treated as black boxes describing specific visible actions. Thus *compute charges* calculates the values of variables called *rental_charge* and *call_charge*, and *output bill* prints the bill. These module calls are not refined further within the main program design—instead, they are designed separately as programs in their own right, with named source data and results.

Exercise 2.8

An annual tax assessment is raised on a person's taxable income.
(a) Draw a structure tree of an algorithm which produces the assessment based on the person's income and tax allowance.
(b) If tax is applied at a standard rate of 30 per cent on taxable income, design a module to compute the tax due.

2.4 Nested Control Structures

The steps which are repeated in a loop construct, or chosen in a branch construct, may themselves be refined into subordinate steps. These subordinate steps may, in turn, be loop or branch constructs, or modules. Likewise, the algorithm for a module may include steps which are control structures or module calls. The inclusion of a control structure within a superior structure may be described as *embedding* one structure within another. Examples of embedded structures may be seen in figures 2.2, 2.3, A2.6 and A2.7.

When designing a program using structured English we indent subordinate steps. Embedded structures should be indented further to show the hierarchy of steps. (It is good policy to maintain this form of indentation when writing program code, as this makes the program more readable.)

Where a control structure includes an embedded structure of the same form as itself, this is described as a **nested** structure. Thus a **nested loop** is a loop construct within a loop, and similarly for the other structures. If the nested (inner) loop requires six traversals, and the outer loop requires four traversals, then the inner loop is actually executed $4 \times 6 = 24$ times. With *while* and *until* loops the number of times that the inner loop is actually executed may vary between traversals of the outer loop.

Two-dimensional arrays

Let us return to the class of 20 students, which we discussed in section 2.2. If each student sat three papers in the examination, there will be a separate mark in each paper. Suppose we wish to find the total mark achieved by each student. We shall need to add up the marks (using a loop over the three papers) for each student (requiring a loop over the students). Thus we need a nested loop.

We record the marks for each student in each paper by allowing each array element to have *two* indices. If the array is called *marks()*, the marks for student 19 are held in the three array elements *marks(19,1)*, *marks(19,2)* and *marks(19,3)*. The whole array can be thought of as a grid with twenty rows and three columns, as shown in figure 2.8. This is called a **two-dimensional array**.

The interpretation of the grid is that *marks(1,1)* = 71, *marks(1,2)* = 43, *marks(1,3)* = 52, *marks(2,1)* = 82, and so on. A two-dimensional array can be

Paper	1	2	3
Student			
1	71	43	52
2	82	67	61
3	68	71	54
.			
.			
.			
19	92	81	84
20	59	61	43

Figure 2.8 The array *marks()*

processed in either dimension. So, for example, the total marks for student 19 are found as follows.

```
1 tot19 = 0
2 loop for paper = 1 to 3
2.1    add marks(19,paper) to tot19
2.2    endloop
```

The average mark for paper 2 in the examination is found by processing downwards.

```
1 total = 0
2 loop for student = 1 to 20
2.1    add marks(student,2) to total
2.2    endloop
3 average = total/20
```

To find the total for each student a nested loop is used. The total may be held in an integer array *score()*, with index range from 1 to 20.

```
1 loop for student = 1 to 20
2    score(student) = 0
3    loop for paper = 1 to 3
3.1    add marks(student,paper) to score(student)
3.2    endloop {paper}
4    endloop {student}
```

Exercise 2.9

(a) The crossword in figure 2.9 is to be implemented as a two-dimensional array. How should it be initialised?

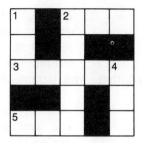

Figure 2.9 Crossword

(b) Upon consideration of the clues, it is decided that the answer to 5 across is "RAM". How can this be inserted into the array?

(c) Describe the additional steps required to ensure that entering a new word into the crossword does not overwrite an existing letter or cover a shaded square.

Summary of Chapter 2

This chapter could have been entitled 'The Anatomy of an Algorithm'. The design process for an algorithm by stepwise refinement aims at analysing a large problem into simple steps. These simple steps are grouped by various control features—loops for repetition, branches for the selection of alternatives and modules for deferred refinement. The use of these control features simplifies the program design.

An algorithm designed in top-down fashion benefits from several advantages. Firstly, its structure is clear to both the programmers who have to implement it as a program and the end users. Secondly, it can be implemented in several modules reflecting its structure. Furthermore, program code has a notorious propensity for attacting errors; in a modular program each module can be checked out separately and the code for the main program can be tested (albeit on a skeleton basis) before all the lower-level modules are completed.

In the belief that the human designer can assimilate a pictorial pattern more readily than a written sequence, we introduced diagrammatic conventions for structure trees. These are summarised below for convenience.

This box encloses an *action*. Branches coming from the box are interpreted as a refinement of this action. The sequence of actions is determined by taking the branches from left to right. This box may be replaced by a small circle if there is no action or if there is no need to name a composite action.

This box names a *module*. It appears either as a leaf of an algorithm, or as the root of the module algorithm. Its interpretation as a leaf is the complete execution of the module algorithm, with parameters as supplied by the main program.

 The oval has a sequence of branches coming from it which are repeated until the *termination condition* in the oval is satisfied. The repetition may be zero, one or many times. The oval with its branches forms a fixed-, until- or while-loop.

 The branches coming from the hexagon are alternatives. Only one is actually executed during a particular execution of the algorithm, as determined by the value of the expression in the hexagon. Two-branched constructs may represent an if . . . then . . . else . . . logic.

Answers to Exercises

2.1

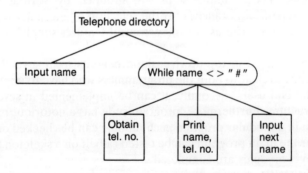

Figure A2.1 Telephone directory

The symbol <> used here means 'not equal to'.

2.2 The following is *one* possible solution.

Top-level design:
    1 loop
    2   start new line
    3   read and print sentence
    4   until end of paragraph
Refinement of Step 3:
    3 loop
    3.1   read a character
    3.2   print character
    3.3   until character is full stop.

2.3

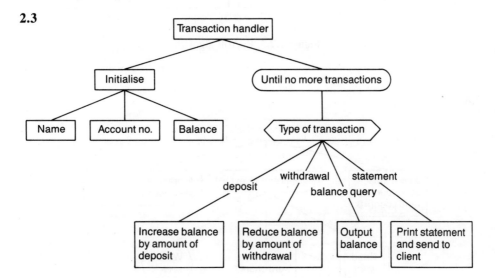

Figure A2.3 Bank transaction handler

2.4 The following is a possible solution.

    1 input character
    2 select
    3   if character is 'i': send output to indicator board
    4   if character is 'l': send output to lineprinter
    5   if character is 'p': send output to printer
    6   if character is 's': send output to screen
    7   endselect

2.5

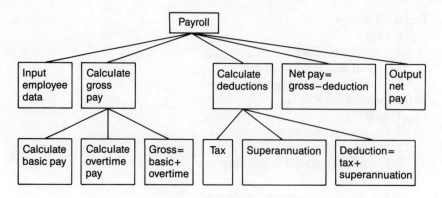

Figure A2.5 Payroll algorithm

2.6

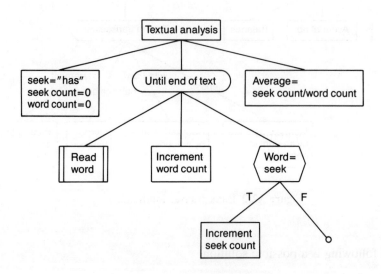

Figure A2.6 Text analyser

Note the use of a dummy branch to indicate no action.

2.7

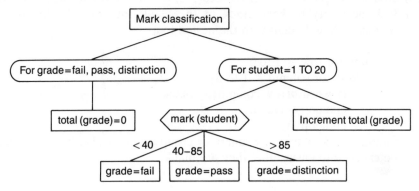

Figure A2.7 Classification counting algorithm

2.8 (a)

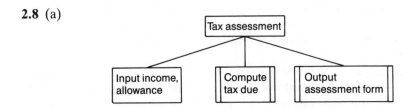

Figure A2.8 Tax algorithm

As the tax computation and the assessment form are separate activities in their own right, these are best left as module calls.

(b) compute tax due

income, allowance
1 taxable = income − allowance 2 tax due = 0.3 ⋆ taxable
tax due

2.9 (a) A two-dimensional array *crossword()* in which each index takes a value between 1 to 5 is appropriate. Initialisation is needed to shade the appropriate squares.

crossword(1,2) = shaded : crossword(2,2) = shaded
crossword(2,4) = shaded : crossword(2,5) = shaded
crossword(4,1) = shaded : crossword(4,2) = shaded
crossword(4,4) = shaded : crossword(5,4) = shaded

(b) crossword(5,1) = "R" : crossword(5,2) = "A" : crossword(5,3) = "M"

(c) It is necessary to keep track of the blank squares. The initialisation
     sequence should begin with the nested loop:

```
loop for row = 1 to 5
  loop for column = 1 to 5
    crossword(row,column) = blank
    endloop {column}
  endloop {row}
```

Subsequently, before any square or group of squares is filled, they should
be checked to ensure that they are blank.

Further Exercises

1. The National Midlays Bank operates an automated bank facility by which
    account holders may withdraw money up to a fixed weekly limit. Each Monday
    morning the limit is reviewed, and the automatic bank will dispense withdrawals
    up to the fixed limit. Write a top-level design for the operation of the facility.

2. An employee has to pay National Insurance contributions on earnings which are
    at least £34 a week. If the employee is not contracted out of part of the state
    pension scheme, the contributions are 9 per cent of all earnings up to £250 a
    week. If the employee is contracted out, the contributions are 9 per cent of
    earnings up to £34 a week plus 6.85 per cent of earnings between £34 and £250 a
    week.

    A married woman or widow who has the right to pay reduced rate contribu-
    tions pays 3.85 per cent of all earnings up to £250 a week; it makes no difference
    whether she is contracted out or not. These rates and figures applied to the tax
    year 1984/1985; they are changed annually on 6 April.

    Design a program for calculating an employee's National Insurance contribu-
    tions. Your design should make due allowance for the annual changes.

3. A college timetable is constructed round a five-day week (Monday to Friday)
    with six lecture periods a day. Choose a suitable data structure to hold the
    timetable.

    In the Physics department the subjects taught are Mechanics, Heat, Elec-
    tricity and Optics. Give program designs, using a suitable notation, for programs
    (a) to set up the timetable, and (b) to list the times of all the lectures on
    Electricity. State clearly any assumptions you have to build into the specifica-
    tion.

3 High-level Programming

The aim of computer programming is to transform a description of a user's problem and an approach to its solution into a form whereby it may be executed by a computer. We saw in the first two chapters how a problem may be analysed to derive a clear statement of the program design. In order to achieve the computational objective, the program must be expressed in a precise language, so that it is capable of being transformed—or *translated*—into a form in which it can be used to control the execution of the target computer. Better still, the program should be suitable for use on many different computers. On the other hand, the program statement should be intelligible to the human reader. This is necessary for two reasons. Firstly, it must be possible to check that the program meets the user's requirements. In addition, in any practical application, the problem will evolve over a period of time as conditions change. Thus programs inevitably have to be modified to meet the needs of a changing environment. This can be done only if the human programmer who implements the change understands the form and content of the program. High-level programming languages provide facilities for meeting these twin aims. They allow programs to be expressed in a form which is both intelligible to humans and capable of automatic transformation to internal code which may be executed on a computer to achieve the desired end result.

In principle, high-level programming languages are *machine independent*, so that programs can be written without prior knowledge of the machine on which they are to run. Also, having run on one machine they can be transported (or *ported*) to run on other machines. In practice, this machine independence is usually not complete, and some account may have to be taken of local peculiarities before the program will be acceptable to a particular computer.

The general aim of high-level languages is to enable a programmer to state the computational solution to a specified problem in a notation which is both formal and human-intelligible. If this aim is met it becomes simpler to create programs that can be shown to solve the stated problem correctly. Our method of program construction is to create a sequence of representations by successive refinements. The aim of the design process is to produce a program in the chosen programming language. It is clear, therefore, that our design process is ultimately influenced by our choice of programming language. The use of a well-chosen language with an adequate 'vocabulary' and a good 'sentence' structure will result in programs that describe real problems well.

There are numerous high-level languages available for writing programs. They differ in style, corresponding to the various types of problem for which computers are used. They fall broadly into two classes—*imperative* and *declarative*.

Declarative languages are associated with *fifth-generation* computers. These languages are intended to be closer to problem descriptions than conventional high-level languages and indeed have inspired the design of new computer architectures to support them. A declarative program may consist of a collection of function definitions or logical relationships; the program is *run* by issuing an appropriate query. This mode of programming is beyond the scope of this book.

We shall concern ourselves in this chapter with the imperative style of programming, using *procedural languages* (as they are more commonly known). In these languages the fundamental structure of a program follows a sequential pattern. Each program statement represents an action (simple or compound) which is completed before the action of the following statement begins. Different procedural languages cater for different types of applications. COBOL is widely used in business and commercial applications where there is a high volume of processing activities, each activity being fairly simple. The COBOL language has developed considerably since it was first pioneered by Commander Grace Hopper of the United States Navy in the mid 1950s. At about the same time the scientific and engineering community developed FORTRAN as a language for expressing mathematical computations, especially those involving considerable numerical processing. With the availability of multiple on-line access via terminals to larger computers in the early 1960s, the BASIC language was developed at Dartmouth College for the purpose of teaching programming to students. Some attempts at bringing to BASIC the philosophy of a structured problem-oriented approach may be seen in languages derived from BASIC—COMAL, BBC BASIC and RM BASIC.

The languages mentioned so far, designed with different aims, all sought to provide the programmer with only a limited degree of high-level language capability. The first serious attempt at a language which incorporated control structuring facilities into its initial design was Algol 60 (developed in the late 1950s). Subsequent improved languages include Pascal, which attempts to serve as a general-purpose language with *data-structuring* facilities as well as control structures. The data structures available in Pascal include not only arrays, which aggregate data items of the same type, but also records, which allow programmers infinite variation in constructing mixed data types to suit the current application.

A more recent development has been inspired by the United States Department of Defense in an attempt to standardise the programming of complex systems (including embedded systems such as satellite control). This has resulted in the highly sophisticated Ada language, whose development began in the late 1970s and which is now beginning to be used for operational programs.

In this chapter we shall be looking at the essential features of programming in a high-level language. An important function of high-level languages is the provision of a means whereby programs may be written in a form that is intelligible to the programmer and other human readers. To this end it is insufficient for a program to contain merely a list of the computational steps which make up the algorithm. It is also necessary for the program—or supporting documentation—to set out clearly how the program functions in relation to the problem which it solves. Programming languages make a number of provisions to enable programmers to write clear programs. These include *data types* which can be defined by the user to match his problem, a free choice of *identifier* names which can be chosen to reflect the data items being modelled in the program, and a *comment* feature to allow the insertion of free text in programs to provide signposting.

The principal building blocks of our program designs are loops, branches and modules. Facilities for coding these constructs are also available in a high-level language. In the programming of loops and branches we frequently have to test conditions. These are expressed in programs as *logical expressions*. We shall see that arithmetic expressions may be written into programs to perform simple calculations. Other computations may use string expressions. For more complex calculations (which might be designed as a module) the appropriate programming construct is a *function*. On the other hand, modules which encapsulate a sequence of actions in a single, higher-level action are coded as *procedures*. Data values are passed into and out of functions or procedures as *parameters*.

As a particular example of the use of functions and procedures, the chapter concludes by considering how to program modules which search and sort collections of data. Both these operations are frequently required, particularly in commercial applications, which may spend an appreciable amount of time engaged in these activities.

3.1 Writing Readable Programs

A program is not just written once and then deposited in the computer. Frequently a program may be constructed in several phases, possibly by more than one programmer. On other occasions a program which has worked well for several years may need to be partially rewritten to take into account new circumstances. For example, a payroll program must compute tax deductions in order to determine net pay. Each year minor alterations to the program will be needed as new interpretations of tax rules are promulgated. Once every five or ten years, a major overhaul of the tax system may be announced by the Government, requiring a major rewrite of the payroll program.

What is all this leading to? Programs are not only written, they must also be read. In order that programs can be read, they must be written in a comprehensible style.

The first consideration in this direction is that the program should have a clear structure, which mirrors the structure of the program design. Another contribution towards greater readability of programs is the choice of meaningful names both for data and for executable actions. A further requirement is proper documentation. This means an adequate description of the nature of the objects (such as variables) in the program and how the algorithm is constructed. High-level programming languages feature a facility for internal documentation, that is, the inclusion of sufficient information with the program text to make it self-documenting. This ideal is achieved to differing extents in different programming languages.

The way in which the global structure of a high-level program is represented is covered in the remaining sections of this chapter. In this section we look at the facilities available for enhancing the expressive power of a piece of code.

Choosing identifiers

The predominant form of data description within programs is in terms of variables. Numeric (real and integer) and character variables are examples of *simple* (unstructured) data. In Pascal the user may also define additional forms of simple data by enumerating the allowable data values. For example

> **type** *colour* = (*red, amber, green*)

can be used to define a new simple data type *colour* with three possible values— *red, amber* and *green*.

One of the features of a high-level language is a facility for the programmer to choose his own mnemonic names for program objects (such as variables and data types), ignoring how and where the data is actually represented within the computer. The name of a program object is called an **identifier**.

Each language implementation imposes specific rules for the formation of identifiers. The following rules are typical:

1. An identifier consists of a sequence of **alphanumeric** characters; that is, each character is either a letter (alphabetic) or a digit (numeric).
2. Often some additional characters are allowed, such as _(the underline character), £ and $.
3. Spaces are not allowed within identifiers (as the space character is used to mark the end of the identifier).
4. The first character must not be a digit (to help distinguish an identifier from a number).
5. Some reserved words have specific meanings in the language and are not available as identifiers. (A **reserved word** is a word whose meaning is fixed as though it were a symbol. Typical reserved words are PRINT, READ and FOR in BASIC; **if, while** and **do** in Pascal.)

Identifiers should be chosen by the programmer for clarity, for example

> month
> name_of_pupil   {underlines used to simulate spaces}
> Text
> number7
> SizeOfFamily   {upper case used to mark beginning of a new word}

Most input devices nowadays allow both upper- and lower-case alphabets, and a judicious mixture can be used to good advantage. The programmer should have some convention for identifiers composed from multiple words—for example, *nameofpupil* is unsatisfactory because it is difficult to read.

It is also important to discover the way in which the local implementation handles upper- and lower-case characters. Some implementations treat, for example, *DIRECTION, Direction* and *direction* as three distinct identifiers whereas others consider all three to be the same identifier. An added complication is introduced by many BASIC implementations which do not accept an identifier such as *PRINTER*; they treat this sequence of symbols as the reserved word PRINT followed by the identifier *ER*.

Exercise 3.1

Using rules 1–5 above, determine which of the following are valid identifiers.

> double
> date-of-birth
> Clok
> item$price
> FRED
> third
> 3rd
> item_no3
> item 7

Determine also which are valid identifiers in the version of BASIC or Pascal which is available on your computer.

Data tabulation

Consider the problem of adding a sequence of *n* numbers and printing the sum. A refined program design for this problem may be given by the structure diagram of figure 3.1.

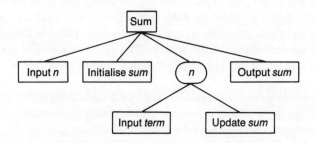

Figure 3.1 Design for summation program

The data objects which will be needed to code this as a program are summarised in the following **data table**.

Name	Description	Type
count	control variable for summation loop	positive integer
n	number of terms to be summed	positive integer
sum	sum of terms so far	real
term	current term	real

The data table lists the identifiers to be used in the program, with a description of the purpose of each variable and its type. By maintaining a data table, the programmer has a clear identification of the role and the allowable values for each identifier. Conversely there is a clear record of the identifier to be used for each data object. This can be invaluable as the number of identifiers used in a program grows, and where more than one programmer is working on a project. It is indispensable when a program needs to be modified some time after it was originally written.

The type of a variable determines the range of allowable values for the variable and also the allowable operations on the variable. Thus, *sum* can take any real value—or, more correctly, any real value which can be represented in the computer which is to execute the program. In addition it can participate in the arithmetic operations of addition, subtraction, multiplication and division. Likewise, *n* can take any positive integer value within the available range and can participate in addition, subtraction, multiplication and integer division. (Integer division is the operation taught in primary schools which yields an integer quotient and an integer remainder.) It is sometimes necessary to combine integer and real numbers in one calculation; this is a complication which we shall consider later in the context of arithmetic expressions.

A **boolean** type is frequently available in high-level languages. Unlike real or integer or string variables which can assume any of a vast range of values, a boolean variable is restricted to the two values *true* and *false*; no other value is possible. The conditions which have to be tested in loop and branch constructs yield a value at each test—they are either *true* or *false*. Since a condition can yield no other value, it is convenient to have a boolean data type. Boolean variables can represent conditions. For example, in a search program a boolean variable *found* can be used to describe the current status of the search. The variable *found* is given the value *false* initially; if and when the item being sought is found, the value of *found* is reset to true.

The set of possible values that may be taken by a variable is called its **domain**. By specifying the type of a variable you are determining its domain. Typically, the domain of an integer variable may be the set of all integers in the approximate range -10^9 to 10^9. The domain of a string variable is, in principle, the set of all possible sequences of characters. In fact, since a real computer is a finite machine, there is an upper limit (frequently 256 characters) on the length of a string. The domain of a boolean variable is the set of values (*false, true*).

BASIC provides three simple data types: integer, real and string. The rules for forming identifiers in BASIC require that every integer identifier terminates with a

% symbol, and that every string identifier terminates with a $ symbol. Other than in these instances, the symbols % and $ are not used within identifiers. Thus, *item* names a real variable, *item%* an integer variable and *item$* a string variable; all three are distinct and may appear in the same program.

Besides clarifying the intention of a program, the classification of variables into types has other advantages. For a start, in any program there is a danger of logical errors creeping in. Since it is often difficult to detect the source (or even the existence) of an error, the program may fail to execute or, worse still, may execute and yield unintended results. The use of types may help to reduce the incidence of certain errors, by means of automatic checking for type incompatibility. This provides a measure of protection against inadvertent corruption by the programmer.

As a side-effect, storage of values and efficiency of computation may sometimes be improved, since the type of a variable is known from its identifier. (The BBC computer allocates four bytes of storage to an integer variable and five to a real variable; and integer arithmetic is faster than real arithmetic.)

If we wish to program our summation program in BBC BASIC, we must modify our data table as shown.

Name	Description	Type
count%	control variable for summation loop	integer
n%	number of terms to be summed	integer
sum	sum of terms so far	real
term	current term	real

Enumerated types

It is possible to write programs using just the simple types real, integer and string, with the corresponding array types. But programming is not the art of devising tricks which exploit a limited set of capabilities. (If that were the case, the autocodes of the 1950s—precursors of high-level languages which resembled a rudimentary form of BASIC—would never have given way to the powerful facilities now available.) A good language must be sufficiently expressive to enable the programmer to use the natural data format of the problem under consideration. To this end, additional types of data are needed. A good high-level programming language provides the programmer with the flexibility to define additional types to enhance program development.

One way of defining a new data type is by giving its domain explicitly, as a list of values. Such a data type is called an **enumerated** type. For example, an algorithm which references the months of the year is best programmed in terms of an enumerated type

(Jan, Feb, Mar, Apr, May, Jun, July, Aug, Sept, Oct, Nov, Dec)

A variable *month* should have this data type.

Enumerated types arise naturally in multi-way conditional constructs. In the mark classification algorithm (figure A2.7) we used the grades *fail*, *pass* and *distinction*. Thus a *gradetype* domain (*fail*, *pass*, *distinction*) would be helpful to facilitate writing a clear program for this algorithm. The expressiveness of a program written in Pascal, ALGOL-68, or Ada can be enhanced considerably by the introduction of new enumerated types.

Data declaration

When an array variable is used, there is no way of knowing how large the array might be. Before it may be used, an array variable must be *declared* to reserve the necessary storage space. In BASIC this is achieved using a DIM statement. In this case the function of declaring the identifier for an array includes the allocation of storage for the array.

In many languages (such as Pascal) it is a requirement that all identifiers in the program be declared before use. Each program contains a declaration section which incorporates (the relevant part of) the data table for the program. This serves as a considerable aid in avoiding unintentional errors. Firstly, since the type of the identifier is known in advance, an automatic syntax check can detect illegal uses of the identifier. In addition, this requirement can trap spelling mistakes, whose effect on a program can be disastrous. For example, if the assignment

    current = 7.5

is miscoded as

    currant = 7.5

then subsequent uses of the variable *current* will have the previous, wrong value. Provided *currant* has not been declared as a *real* variable, this error will be caught, before the program can run, as an *undeclared variable*.

Self-documentation

The program described by figure 3.1 may be coded into BBC BASIC by taking the branches from left to right, using the appropriate keywords in the loop. (The corresponding program in another high-level language can be coded from the diagram in a similar manner.)

```
10    REM {PROGRAM SUM}
20    REM *** Program to read in and sum a sequence of numbers ***
30    INPUT n% : REM n% is the number of terms to be summed
40    sum = 0 : REM sum gives the sum so far
50    FOR count% = 1 TO n%
60        INPUT term : REM term is the current term
70        sum = sum + term : REM update sum
80    NEXT count%
```

```
 90    REM Final value of sum is sum of terms read in
100    PRINT sum
110    END
```

The use of well-chosen identifiers is just one method by which programs can be made more comprehensible. Two further techniques are available which help to clarify the intention and purpose of the program.

Firstly, the program text itself gives a clear description of its purpose, by the insertion of **comments** at strategic positions. Comments do not affect the way in which a program runs, but they perform a vital function in turning a program into a meaningful text. Thus they serve to *document* the program. Comments in programs are distinguished by the use of a reserved word or a special symbol. (In BASIC this is REM; any statement commencing with the REM keyword is ignored during execution. In Pascal the braces { and } are used; any text between a pair of braces is ignored.)

Likewise, the layout of the program text, although of no consequence to the computer, can make an enormous difference in comprehensibility to the human reader. Just as a long sentence is more easily understood if broken into shorter clauses, and a page of text can be grasped more readily if divided into paragraphs, so too proper spacing and indentation of a program can work wonders. The judicious insertion of blank lines, which have no effect on processing, can be used to good effect to improve the layout of a program listing, by breaking up the text into sections which are more easily assimilated.[*]

Now consider the following program, also written in BASIC, to implement the design of figure 3.1.

```
10    INPUT n
20    S = 0
30    FOR J = 1 TO n : INPUT t : S = S + t : NEXT
40    PRINT S
50    END
```

Both versions of the program take the same input format and output the sum of the terms input; both will run under BBC BASIC. Nevertheless, there is a clear difference between the two versions. The first version provides a much clearer presentation.

The use of meaningful identifiers and comments thus allows a self-documenting programming style.

Constants

It is frequently desirable to name a quantity in a program, where the name refers not to a variable but to the same fixed value throughout the program. In a mathematical program, for example, the constant 3.141 592 65 may be required on

---

[*] Line-oriented editors, including most versions of BASIC, do not allow the insertion of blank lines; however, a line containing only a space character will appear as a blank line.

many occasions, and it is convenient to call this constant *pi*. In a word-processing program the number of characters per line may be fixed for each application; say 80 on some occasions and 96 on others, but never varying during an individual run of the program. In this case *linesize* might be an appropriate name; the definition

    linesize = 80

may be given at the beginning of the program and all references within the program to this number can then use the name *linesize*. If this constant definition is replaced by

    linesize = 96

the program then works, without further amendment, for the new line length.

Similarly, an invoicing program will require the rate of VAT. Suppose this rate is 15 per cent when the program is written. At a later date the Government might change the rate of VAT to 18 per cent. If the symbolic constant 0.15 is used on each occasion in the program, each occurrence must now be amended. Not only is this a laborious job, but it is also error-prone, because it is only too easy to miss one occurrence. Worse still, there might be an occurrence of the constant 0.15 in the program which does not refer to VAT, and this constant could easily get changed to 0.18 inadvertently during the changeover. However, if a constant identifier *vat* is defined at the beginning of the program, all subsequent references to the rate of VAT can use the same identifier. A rate change can be implemented painlessly by amending the constant definition from

    vat = 0.15

to

    vat = 0.18

A number of languages (such as Pascal, Ada and ALGOL-68) allow constant identifiers to be used for this purpose. Any attempt to reassign the value of a constant would immediately be detected as a programming error. BBC BASIC, though, does not allow constants to be defined. The next best thing is to use a variable name for a constant. A section at the beginning of each program, accompanied by a suitable comment, can set up the identifiers which represent constants within the program. However the onus is on the programmer to ensure that the values of these variables do not change during execution of the program. BBC BASIC does, however, provide three fixed constants which may be used in programs:

    TRUE   − 1
    FALSE   0
    PI   3.141 592 65

3.2 Statements

The basic building block in conventional programming language is the **statement**. A statement corresponds to a step in a program design. The main body of a program consists of a sequence of statements reflecting the sequence of steps which comprise the program design.

A **simple statement** contains a single description of an action. Such an action may be an assignment, an input or output action, or a procedure call. Loops and branches are coded as **compound statements**, composed of one or several simple statements.

Simple statements

A program statement which assigns (or reassigns) a value to a variable is called an **assignment statement**. The form of an assignment statement is

<variable identifier> <assignment symbol> <expression>

We have discussed identifiers in section 3.1. The assignment symbol actually used in a program depends on the programming language, as the following table shows.

Languages	*Assignment symbol*
BASIC, C, FORTRAN	=
Ada, ALGOL, Pascal	:=
APL	←

(The method of assigning a value to a variable is somewhat different in COBOL; details may be found in an appropriate manual.)

The expression whose value is to be assigned may be a constant, as in

    salary = 18500

or the value of another named variable, as in

    salary = clerk_salary;

or it may specify a computation, as in

    salary = base_salary + increment ∗ number.

The value yielded by the expression must be **compatible** with the type of the variable on the left-hand side. Thus the following are inadmissible as assignment statements.

item% = 2.7   {integer variable, real value}
item% = "Fred"   {integer variable, string value}
person$ = 3.0 + age   {string variable, real value}
distance = "two miles"   {real variable, string value}

It is however, permissible to assign an integer value to a real variable; for example:

distance = 71
speed = 5 + 10 ★ time%

A variable may also receive a value from an external medium (such as the keyboard or a file or a sensor) via an input action. This is coded as an *input statement*. Examples in BASIC are

INPUT price

or

INPUT name$, works_number, tax_code, date.

The corresponding Pascal statements would be

read(price)

and

read(name, works_number, tax_code, date).

The specific word (or symbol) used to denote an input action varies between languages, but is frequently something like *input* or *read* or *get*. Note that INPUT accepts one or more variables as parameters; these parameters may be real, integer or string variables, and may be mixed within one input statement. (Similar rules apply to *read* in Pascal.)

When a new variable is introduced it has no value. A variable may be *initialised*, or given a starting value, in one of two ways. This can be either using an input statement or by an assignment statement in which the variable appears on the left of the assignment symbol. No variable can appear on the right-hand side of an assignment unless it has previously been initialised. A program which breaks this rule cannot be correct. Consequently, every program should be scanned to check that no variable is used before it has been initialised. Since it is possible to specify this task unambiguously, the computer can be used itself to check this aspect of correctness in a program presented to it for execution. All good programming systems make provision for such checks.

Once a variable has been initialised, its value may be used on the right-hand side of an assignment or in any other context where an expression is computed. So, for example, we might have

```
old_total  = 70.0
this_week = 21.9
new_total = old_total + this_week
```

In particular, a variable which has been initialised may participate in an *output statement* which transfers a value to an external medium. Assuming that values have previously been assigned to *forename$*, *surname$*, *rate* and *hours*, a typical output statement in BASIC is

PRINT forename$, surname$, rate ⋆ hours.

The Pascal equivalent is

write(forename, surname, rate⋆hours).

The specific words PRINT and *write* used in BASIC and Pascal, respectively, have their origins in the early days of computing, when all output was to a printer. These words are still in use although the external medium may be a screen, a disc file or the setting of a machine valve.

There is an interesting dual aspect to initialisation. Just as it is incorrect to attempt to use a variable which has not yet been initialised, so too it is foolish to assign a value to a variable which is never used subsequently. It would seem a matter of sheer prudence to make a corresponding check on a program to ensure that every assigned variable is subsequently used, either in the right-hand side of a subsequent assignment or in an output action. Yet it is rare indeed to find a language implementation which reports such blind-alley assignments.

We have not yet discussed an important form of simple statement, the *procedure call*. Source data supplied to a procedure may be constants, or variables which have already been initialised. Results are retrieved from a procedure using variables whose values are assigned within the procedure. We shall consider procedures at length in sections 3.4 and 3.5.

A sequence of steps in a program design is coded as a sequence of statements. In Pascal, statements are separated by a semi-colon. BASIC has two methods of separating statements. The principal method is by giving each statement a different line number. However it is possible to put several statements on a single line, separated by colons.

Updating a variable

A fairly common program step is that of updating a variable. A variable may hold a current value which needs to be changed during execution of the algorithm. This may require a variable whose value already exists to appear again as the destination of an assignment (that is, on the left-hand side). If the new value of the variable is computed from the old value, the same variable will appear on both sides of the assignment, for example

balance = balance + deposit

A common form of updating arises from incrementing a counter. In BASIC, Pascal and many other languages this is achieved by a statement like

number = number + 1

The right-hand side calculates a new value, *number* + 1, from the current value of *number*. The result of this calculation is assigned to the variable whose name appears on the left-hand side; in this case it is also *number*. The net effect of the assignment is to update the variable *number*, incrementing it by 1.

The corresponding statement in COBOL,

ADD 1 TO NUMBER

avoids duplicate reference to the variable NUMBER, and is clearly seen to be an updating assignment. A similar approach is available in the C language, in which the corresponding statement

number += 1

has the same effect. In addition to the advantage this form of statement has in expressing clearly an updating action, it also has the beneficial by-product that the machine code produced is more efficient.

Similar remarks apply to *decrementation*, that is, reducing the value of a variable by 1.

Repetitive statements

We have encountered two important types of control structure in the construction of program designs—repetitive constructs (loops) and alternative constructs (branches). In high-level languages these constructs are typically expressed as compound statements.

Repetitive control structures (loops) occur either as fixed loops or as conditional loops (*while* loops and *until* loops). They are implemented in programs as follows.

Basic	*Pascal*
	while <condition> **do**
	begin
	<statements>
	end
REPEAT	**repeat**
<statements>	<statements>
UNTIL <condition>	**until** <condition>
FOR j = 1 TO 20 DO	**for** *j:*= 1 **to** 20 **do**
<statements>	**begin**
NEXT	<statements>
	end

In BASIC all reserved words must appear in upper case. It is sensible to adopt a similar rule when you key in a Pascal program. For convenience, we print the reserved words in Pascal programs in bold face.

Similar formats for loops are used in other high-level languages. (Note that BBC BASIC fails to provide a *while* loop. When a program design which requires a *while* loop has to be coded in BBC BASIC, it it necessary to rewrite the algorithm using an extra conditional test.)

In Pascal, the body of a *while* loop and a *for* loop must be sandwiched between **begin** and **end**. However, if the body of the loop is a simple statement, the **begin** and **end** are not required.

Exercise 3.2

What are the values output by each of the following fragments?

(a)
```
p:= 5;
for count:= 1 to 3 do
begin
  q:= count;
  p:= p+1
end;
write(p,q)
```

(b)
```
p:= 5
for count:= 1 to 3 do
q:= count;
p:= p+1;
write(p,q)
```

We shall now look at the form of the conditions which may appear in a conditional loop. The simplest form of condition tests whether two items of data are equal or not. Thus, the condition

mark = 85

would be used to test whether the value of the variable *mark* is currently equal to 85. Likewise a test to see whether the variable *day* is equal to "friday" would be achieved using the condition

day = "friday"

Tests for equality or inequality can be applied to data items of any type, including arrays or records. It is necessary to be more careful with values of type real. Real values are converted for computer storage (as will be explained in chapter 6). It is therefore possible for two values which are supposed to be the same, say 5.58, to be represented slightly differently within the computer. Thus there can be no guarantee that the test $x = y$ will succeed even if the values are supposed to be equal. The recommended way of overcoming this problem is to allow a small *tolerance* for equality, say 10^{-6}. The absolute difference between x and y can then be tested to see if it lies within this tolerance:

IF ABS(x − y) < 10^{-6} THEN . . .

Some data types (such as numeric and string) impose an ordering on values of that type. For such data types the relative order of two values can be tested. In the case of numeric data the appropriate conditions are *less than* and *greater than*. For example, the condition *total > 38* tests whether the value of the variable *total* is currently greater than 38. High-level languages provide a set of these **relational operators** similar to that shown below.

=	equal to
<>	not equal to
<	less than (precedes)
>	greater than (follows)
<=	less than or equal
>=	greater than or equal

Relational operators

The relational operators are defined for strings by dictionary order; so

"green" < "red"   {read as: green precedes red}

and

"red" >= "blue"   {read as: red follows or equals blue}

are true, whereas

"Smith" < "Jones"   {read as: Smith precedes Jones}

is false. Conditions may therefore contain string relationships as well as numeric relationships.

The actual ordering of strings depends on the internal code sequence used in the computer, and may vary between machines. It is safe to assume that the alphabet is correctly ordered, with all upper-case letters preceding all lower-case letters. The digits are ordered, but may appear either before or after the alphabet. For other characters the precise sequence has to be known. The space character usually precedes all printable characters (although this cannot be guaranteed). Thus

"West End" < "WestEnd"

is true.

Several conditions may be combined to form a compound condition using the **logical connectives** AND and OR, and a condition may be negated using the *unary* logical operator NOT. A compound condition is necessary to define a range of values. For example, the condition that *price* lies in the range 25 000 to 40 000 is expressed in the form

price > 25000 AND price < 40000.

Exercise 3.3

Assume the following assignments:

salary = 12550
name$ = "Rowley"
cost = 21.00
price = cost + 3.50
colour$ = "yellow"
shade$ = "orange"

Are the following conditions true or false?

(a) salary > 10000
(b) price = 25.50 OR colour$ = "yellow"
(c) name$ <= "Scott"
(d) name$ > "Rowley"
(e) shade$<> "Orange"

Exercise 3.4

A program is being written to process objects having a colour attribute. A statement has to be written to process all objects whose colour attribute is *red* and costing more than £30, and also all objects having the colour attribute *green* and costing more than £90.

Formulate an appropriate condition so that the statement can be written as

loop while *condition*
   process object
   endloop

In contrast to conditional loops, the number of repetitions of a fixed loop is determined by a control variable. Where the type of the control variable is integer or an enumerated type the constructions

for id := 100 **to** 176 **do**

and

for day := Monday **to** Friday **do**

repeat the body of the loop for each value of the control variable in turn from the
starting value to the final value. If the final value is less than (or precedes) the
starting value, the loop will not be executed at all.

When the control variable is an integer, it is possible to execute the loop body for
a regular sequence of values. Thus a loop controlled by

for id := 100 **step** 5 **to** 170 **do**

will be executed for *id* having the values 100, 105, 110 and so on until 170. In fact, it
does not matter if the final value is one of the stepped values of the control
variable—the loop will be repeated as long as the current value of the control
variable is less than the final value. So

for id := 100 **step** 5 **to** 176 **do**

controls a loop which is repeated with the values 100, 105, 110 until 175 for *id*.

You need to be careful, however, when a program design calls for a fixed loop
controlled by a real variable, for example

```
loop for x = 1.0 to 2.0 in steps of 0.1
    {some computation}
    endloop
```

The intention here is to perform eleven repetitions for values of *x* equal to 1.0, 1.1,
1.2 until 2.0 inclusive. Since real numbers are not stored accurately in a computer,
it is impossible to determine whether this intention will be carried out. It is possible
that when the control variable *x* reaches the value 2.0, the final value against which
this is tested, may have been overshot. This may result in losing the final iteration
of the loop.

Therefore, when coding a fixed loop controlled by a real variable, it is necessary
to introduce a suitable integer variable. In the example given above, a possible
solution would be to introduce the integer variable *xcount*, as follows:

```
for xcount := 10 to 20 do
begin
    x := 0.1 * xcount;
    {code for computations}
end
```

If statements

Alternative control structures arise as either a two-way or a multi-way branch. We
consider first the two-way branch. This is typified by the following example:

```
select
    if mark < pass mark: grade = fail
    if mark >= pass mark: grade = pass
endselect
```

The two-way branch is frequently expressed in terms of a true/false condition, as follows:

```
if mark < pass mark
then
     grade = fail
else
     grade = pass
endif
```

This form of **if statement** can be coded, with only minor changes, in many languages. (In BBC BASIC the whole *if* statement must appear as a single line.)

Many languages also provide a simplified version of the two-way branch which omits the else part. This is convenient where no action ensues on failure of the condition, for example

```
310 hourly_rate = 4.62
320 total = 0
330 FOR day = Monday TO Friday DO
340    INPUT hours_worked
350    total = total + hours_worked
360 NEXT
370 IF total > 38 THEN
        overtime = total − 38 : total = 38 + 1.5 * overtime
380 wage = total * hourly_rate
```

By padding out the line with spaces you can achieve the tabulation shown in line 370. Most systems allow lines up to 256 characters long—with a 40 column screen this gives six screen lines for each program line.

Exercise 3.5

A particular programming language does not have the *while* construct. Use a branch structure and a *repeat* construct to code the following design fragment:

```
loop while count > 0
    process(count)
    count = count − 1
endloop
```

Case statements

We now look at the multi-way branch, in which one statement (or sequence of statements) is selected from several. The following structure diagram displays the rule for evaluating the number of days in a month when it is not a leap year. Recall that in a multi-way structure a choice is determined by the value of the control variable.

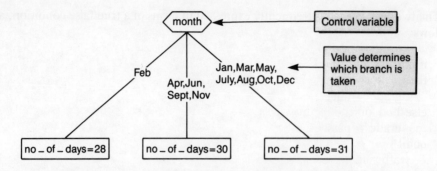

A multi-way branch structure can be coded in some high-level languages (such as Pascal) as a **case statement**. The structure tree shown would appear in Pascal as:

```
case month of
                    Feb: no_of_days :=28;
            Apr,Jun,Sept,Nov: no_of_days :=30;
    Jan,Mar,May,July,Aug,Oct,Dec: no_of_days :=31
end
```

(It is assumed that the variables *month* and *no_of_days* are of appropriate types.)
   Of course any two-way branch could be coded as a case statement, for example

```
case age > 18 of
true: person := adult;
false: person := minor
end
```

However this statement is clearer when coded as an *if* statement:

```
if age > 18 then
person := adult
else
person := minor
```

Conversely, a multi-way branch can be coded using *if* statements. Some languages (BBC BASIC is one) do not provide a construct for the multi-way selection. This deficiency can be overcome by breaking a multi-way branch into several two-way branches. Consider, for example, the following design fragment:

```
select
    if traffic light = red : stop
    if traffic light = amber : slow down
    if traffic light = green : go
    endselect
```

This is coded most easily using a case statement:

case *traffic_light* **of**
red: stop;
amber: slow_down;
green: go
end

One method of coding this design in BASIC is as the following (single-line) statement:

IF traffic_light=red THEN PROCstop
         ELSE IF traffic_light=amber THEN PROCslow_down
         ELSE IF traffic_light=green THEN PROCgo

Alternatively, the following three-line construction can be used.

IF traffic_light = red THEN PROCstop
IF traffic_light = amber THEN PROCslow_down
IF traffic_light = green THEN PROCgo

The second of these two alternatives reflects the intention of the multi-way branch more clearly than the first; nesting IFs tends to obscure the meaning. Besides the loss of clarity in using *if* statements for a multi-way branch, there is a further consideration—efficiency. The case construction is more efficient than the multiple *if* construction. In the case construction, the control variable *traffic_light* is tested just once; its value determines which branch statement should be executed. In the nested *if* construction, each condition is tested individually, so that in the example given below, if the value of *traffic_light* is green on entry, three conditions will be tested before the appropriate statement is executed. The second *if* construction is less cumbersome, but beware—it is even less efficient, as all three conditions are tested, even if the first is found to be true.

3.3 Expressions

Much computational effort is devoted towards obtaining a final or intermediate value from values previously stored or computed. These values are frequently numeric (real or integer), but could also be strings or boolean values (truth values of conditions). Wherever values are used in a program an *expression* may be used which effectively instructs the computer to compute a new value. In an assignment statement the right-hand side must produce a value (of the right type) to be assigned. This value may be computed in an expression. Likewise the condition in a conditional control structure may be a (boolean) expression.

In a similar manner, procedure statements, which call routines, may depend on parameters, as in

process(count).

A parameter which is used in a procedure statement to represent source data may be a constant, or a variable name (such as *count*), but more generally will be an expression which yields a value, for example

   print_balance(capital ★ (1 + interest_rate ★ no_of_days)).

When we meet *functions* in the next section we shall see that these too have parameters, which may be in the form of expressions.

In whichever context it may be used, an expression can incorporate several computations which yield a value. This is one of the principal advantages of high-level programming, enabling the text of a program to resemble the form in which an algorithm is actually written. In a low-level language each expression would have to be broken down into a sequence of simple operations.

Part of the price paid for the conceptual elegance of high-level programming is the translation phase which a high-level program must go through before it is executed. This will be discussed in greater detail in chapter 10, where we shall see that the analysis of expressions into machine operations is an important function of the *compilers* and *interpreters* which perform the translation.

Algebraic expressions

The first type of expression that springs to mind is one that computes an arithmetic value. The expressions of algebra occur frequently in programs to provide new values for variables. Typically they are formulas like $2\pi r$ for the circumference of a circle. In a program this might appear as

   circumference = 2 ★ pi ★ radius.

A programmer is not limited to testing standard algebraic formulas; he can invent any expression he requires to perform the desired computation, using the fundamental binary operations of algebra $+, -, ★$ and $/$. (Note the conventional use of a ★ for multiplication on computer installations.)

+	plus
−	minus
★	times
/	divided by
DIV	integer division
MOD	remainder after division
ˆ or ↑	to the power of

Algebraic binary operations

The operators $+$, $-$ and $★$ may be used for reals or integers. If both operands are integers the result is again an integer; otherwise the result is real. The result of a division using $/$ is always real. In contexts where integers are used, DIV is available for whole number division (as in primary school arithmetic) to provide an integer answer. The corresponding remainder is obtained using MOD. Thus

> 7 DIV 3   has the value 2
> 7 MOD 3 has the value 1

Some languages allow the use of a power operator, ^ or ↑. The result of a power operation is always real. Thus

> 2 ↑ 3 stands for 2^3 and has the value 8.0

Parentheses may be used within an expression to clarify the meaning and also to determine the sequence of computation, for example

> 2 ⋆ (4 − 3)   has the value 2

whereas

> 2 ⋆ 4 − 3   has the value 5

The rules of precedence in algebraic expressions provide that brackets have the highest priority, followed by the power operation; multiplication and division come next, while addition and subtraction are performed last.

Exercise 3.6

Use values to show the difference between

> size − (this + that) and size − this + that

String expressions

Numeric values are not the only ones to be manipulated, although this might be our most familiar experience. Two or more strings may be joined together—this operation on strings is known as **concatenation**. Programming languages frequently allow the use of the symbol + for concatenation of strings. So

> "Good" + "morning" has the value "Goodmorning"

If a space is required, it must be included explicitly. Suppose the string variables *title$*, *first_name$* and *surname$* have been given suitable values. The following program fragment might be used to print the complete name.

```
sp$ = " "
IF title$ = "Mr"
THEN PRINT first_name$ + sp$ + surname$ +", Esq"
ELSE PRINT title$ + sp$ + first_name$ + sp$ + surname$
```

BBC BASIC also provides facilities for extracting part of a string. These may be used, as required, in building up a string expression.

Function	Value
LEFT\$(string\$, n)	The string consisting of the *n* leftmost characters of *string\$*
RIGHT\$(string\$, n)	The string consisting of the *n* rightmost characters of *string\$*
MID\$(string\$, m)	The string obtained from *string\$* by deleting from the left up to, but not including, the *m*th character
MID\$(string\$, m, l)	The string, of length *l* characters, obtained from *string\$* starting with the *m*th character

As an example of how these string functions are used, if we have

    king\$ = "All the king's"

then

LEFT\$(king\$, 3)	has the value	"All"
MID\$(king\$, 5, 3)	has the value	"the"
MID\$(king\$, 5) + "head"	has the value	"the king's head"

Exercise 3.7

What is unusual about the following expression?

    king\$ + "horses and " + king\$ + "men"

Boolean expressions

In section 3.2 we saw that conditions can be simple relations (for example, price < 40000) or could be built up from simple relations using the boolean operators AND, OR and NOT. Such a compound condition is a **boolean expression**. In Pascal and some other languages (but not in BBC BASIC) it is possible to declare variables of type boolean. Such a variable can take one of two values—true or false; it can then participate in a boolean expression and be used wherever a condition is appropriate (for example, after *if*, *while* and *until*). Thus, assuming the following declarations:

    var *cheap, expensive, foreign, worthwhile: boolean;*
         price: real;
         origin: (English, French, Italian, Swiss);

these program statements might appear:

cheap:= (price < 100);
expensive:= (price > 500);
foreign:= (origin <> English);
worthwhile:= cheap **or** *(***not** *expensive* **and not** *foreign);*
if *worthwhile*
then *write('buy')*
else if *expensive* **then** *write('too expensive');*

The parentheses in these statements are not essential, but they serve as a considerable aid to clarity. In the first three statements no other meaning could be intended; in the fourth the meaning would in fact remain the same because of the order of priority of the operators. The unary operator **not** always takes precedence over anything else, while **and** takes priority over **or**. Nevertheless a few, carefully chosen, extra parentheses can make an enormous improvement in the readability of a program.

NOT, ( )   ↑ highest
=, <>, <, >, <=, >=
AND
OR, EOR   ↓ lowest

Table of operator priority in boolean expressions (BBC BASIC)

Within expressions, operations with higher priority are understood to be performed before operations with lower priority. The boolean operator EOR (in BBC BASIC) gives an **exclusive-or**; so

p EOR q

takes the value true if either p or q (but not both) is true. Thus

x > 4 EOR x < 5

has the value TRUE if x <= 4 or x >= 5 but FALSE if x is between 4 and 5. We shall study the algebra of boolean expressions in chapter 5.

Exercise 3.8

Write boolean expressions which take the value true if

(a) x is positive but less than 100
(b) the sum of $p\%$ and $q\%$ is greater than 20 but their product is less than 90
(c) *next_name$* appears before "Smith" in a telephone directory or is "Taylor"

Exercise 3.9

A program addresses the screen using the variables *line%* and *col%*. The lines on the screen are numbered from 0 to *maxline%* and the columns are numbered from 0 to *maxcol%*. Write a section of program which tests that the current values of *line%* and *col%* are legitimate, and then updates these values so that they refer to the next position on the screen.

3.4 Subprograms

The stepwise refinement approach to problem analysis allows one to defer detailed decisions. When the structure so far is sufficiently detailed it may be advisable not merely to defer a decision to the next stage of refinement, but to treat the deferred decision as a separate problem. In this way the detailed design may be constructed as a series of *modules*. Each module interfaces with one or more of the remaining modules and, in a large programming project, may be designed independently by a different programmer.

A module may be designed as a program in its own right, with the complete software solution for a problem being a suite of modules which communicate in an appropriate fashion. For example, the common task of sorting data into some predefined order (which may be numeric or alphabetic) may be implemented as a pair of modules, *sort* and *merge*. The sort module takes as input a file of data and outputs the same data in correct sequence. The merge module takes as input two or more sorted files and outputs the data as a single file in correct sequence.

In other cases a module may be implemented as part of a main program. It is desirable for programs to be coded as closely to their design as possible; the program unit corresponding to a module (in a design) is called a **subprogram**. The ability to write subprograms as separate program units is a major feature of *block-structured* languages. Subprograms also have an advantage where the name (or similar) group of actions is required in more than one part of a program. In this case it may be possible for the main program to reference several occurrences of the same subprogram.

The full scope of subprograms is beyond the level of this book. We shall restrict our discussion to two types—*procedures* and *functions*. These types of subprograms correspond with the simple module designs we encountered in chapter 2. They may perform actions and deliver values to the main program.

Procedures

The first type of subprogram which we consider is the **procedure**. Input to and output from programs are well-defined actions; they are achieved using input and output statements, which are in fact procedures although they are not always recognised as such. Other procedures may be built into a programming language to open and close files and to control the layout of output (by starting a new page, say).

A module design may be coded as a (user-defined) procedure. Names for procedures usually follow the same rules as for variables. Thus a procedure to draw a square could be named

square

in Pascal. In BBC BASIC every procedure name must commence with the four upper-case characters PROC. A procedure to draw a square might therefore be named

PROCsquare

This name appears on its own in a program as a *procedure statement*, with PROC playing the role of a keyword. Execution of this statement results in a square being drawn. If we want to allow the possibility of drawing squares of different sizes, the procedure must be defined with a **source parameter**, enclosed in parentheses. We could then write procedure statements such as

PROCsquare(100),

or

PROCsquare(size),

where the variable *size* has previously been assigned. We could even use an expression as the parameter, for example

PROCsquare(2 $\star$ t $-$ 1)

Indeed wherever a number is required in a program we might reasonably hope that a numeric variable, or an algebraic expression which produces a numeric value, be equally acceptable. Similarly, a procedure might call for a string parameter. In this case the parameter actually used in the corresponding procedure statement could be a string constant, a string variable or a string expression. Thus a procedure to display a text in a particular format might appear in a program as

PROCdisplay("The quick brown fox jumps over the lazy dog.")

or

PROCdisplay(sentence$)

or

PROCdisplay(STRING$(3, "$\star$") + title$ + ".")

The variable or expression which appears in parentheses in the procedure statement to particularise the action of the procedure is called an **actual parameter**.

To illustrate how procedures are coded we shall develop further part of the Telecom billing system which you studied in chapter 2. Coding directly from the structure tree (figure 2.6), we may get the following:

```
REM***Telecom billing***
INPUT telephone_no$, name$, address$
INPUT number_of_telephones, initial, final
used = final − initial
PROCcompute_charges(number_of_telephones, used)
REM The results data of compute_charges are rental_charge and call_charge
PROCoutput_bill(name$, address$, telephone_no$, rental_charge, call_
charge)
END
```

Comparing this with the structure diagram, you will see that each statement in the program corresponds to an action in the diagram. The input statements initialise the variables used in the program, and the assignment statement is straightforward. The next two lines are procedure statements, in which each procedure is referred to by name. The actual parameters of these procedures correspond with the source data variables in the module designs given in section 2.3.

Let us now see how to code the *output_bill* procedure. For convenience, the design developed in section 2.3 is repeated here.

output bill

---

name, address, telephone number, rental charge, call charge

---

1 initialise VAT rate
2 output name, address and telephone number
3 output charges including VAT

When coding a procedure design, it is necessary to set up a *procedure head*. This begins with a reserved word (DEF in BBC BASIC, **procedure** in Pascal), followed by the procedure name and a set of **formal parameters**. The formal parameters are identifiers (of appropriate types) which act as placeholders for the source data and results data which are communicated between the procedure call (in the main program) and the procedure definition. The *output_bill* procedure may be coded thus in BBC BASIC:

```
500
510 DEF PROCoutput_bill(name$, address$, tel_no$, rental_charge, call_
    charge)
520 LOCAL vat, vat_charge
530 vat = 0.15 : REM constant value
```

```
540 PRINT name$ ' address$ ' tel_no$
550 REM ★★★output charges★★★
560 PRINT "apparatus:", rental_charge
570 PRINT "calls: ", call_charge
580 vat_charge = vat★(rental_charge + call_charge)
590 PRINT "vat:      ", vat_charge
600 PRINT "total:    ", rental_charge + call_charge + vat_charge
610 ENDPROC
```

Note that we have refined step 3 of the design.

The procedure pre-supposes values for the parameters, which represent source data. These values are represented by the corresponding identifiers which appear in the procedure head, namely, the formal parameters. These formal parameters may be used freely in program statements within the procedure definition. Additionally, we have introduced two identifiers, *vat* and *vat_charge* to stand for quantities which are required during the execution of the procedure but then have no further use. In BBC BASIC, these identifiers are declared using a LOCAL statement. In Pascal, *local* identifiers are declared within a procedure in the same way as they are declared within a main program—using **const**, **type** and **var** declarations.

Note that the line numbers used in subprogram definitions are at the programmer's discretion, but they may not overlap with each other or with the line numbers of the main program. We have adopted the useful convention that each subprogram definition should begin with a blank line numbered on a round hundred. (A REM statement with a row of asterisks would do as well.) As a result the final program listing acquires a clear layout.

The *compute charges* procedure is coded in a similar manner. For convenience, the top-level design of section 2.3 is repeated here.

compute charges

---

number of telephones, units used

---

1 initialise line charge, telephone rental, call unit charge
2 rental charge = line charge + (number of telephones ★ telephone rental)
3 call charge = units used ★ call unit charge

---

rental charge, call charge

Here is how it might be coded in Pascal:

procedure *compute_charges(no_of_telephones, used: integer;*
                                    var *rental_charge, call_charge: real);*
const
        line_charge = 13.60;
        receiver_rental = 2.45;
        unit = 4.4 {pence};

begin
　　rental_charge := line_charge + (no_of_telephones ⋆ receiver_rental):
　　call_charge := used ⋆ unit/100
end

Note that in Pascal the type of each formal parameter must be *specified* within the procedure head. Formal parameters which correspond to results, that is, values which are communicated from the procedure to the calling program, must also be prefixed by the reserved word **var**. Step 1 of the design is performed by the **const** section. The other steps are coded in the two assignment statements.

In BBC BASIC it is not possible to export values from procedures. The reason for this will be explained in the next section, when we discuss how parameters are passed. Instead, results from procedures are assigned to **global** variables, which are visible both within the procedure definition and within the main program. This is a deficiency of BBC BASIC compared with most other high-level languages.

The flow of control through the main program is sequential from beginning to end. This gives us a simple view of the program design, ignoring the details of the procedures. In fact, as each procedure call is encountered, the sequential flow of control is interrupted while the *procedure body* (that is, the sequence of actions specified by the procedure design) is executed. This is illustrated in figure 3.2. At each procedure call, control passes to the first line of the corresponding procedure body; when all the statements in the procedure body have been executed, control reverts to the next action in the original sequence.

Functions

A procedure is incorporated into a program by writing a procedure statement, as described above. An alternative type of subprogram delivers a value which can be used in an expression or on the right-hand side of an assignment. Such subprograms are called **functions**.

For example, in a payroll program it is necessary to compute an employee's gross wage, and also the tax and National Insurance deductions. The employee's gross wage depends on the employee's hourly rate of pay and the number of hours worked in a given week. The calculation of the gross wage may be designed as a subprogram module whose result consists of a single value. Although such a module can be coded as a procedure with a single output parameter, it is frequently convenient to code it as a function. In BBC BASIC, function identifiers begin with the upper-case characters FN; for example, we might write

　　gross_pay = FNwage(rate, hours)

The function named FNwage calculates the gross wage, given the rate of pay and the number of hours. The details of the calculation do not appear in this statement—they are deferred to another part of the program. FNwage delivers a value, which is a number; this value is assigned to the variable *gross_pay*.

In a similar manner, a function may be used for the calculation of the tax and National Insurance deductions, given the gross wage. It too delivers a value which

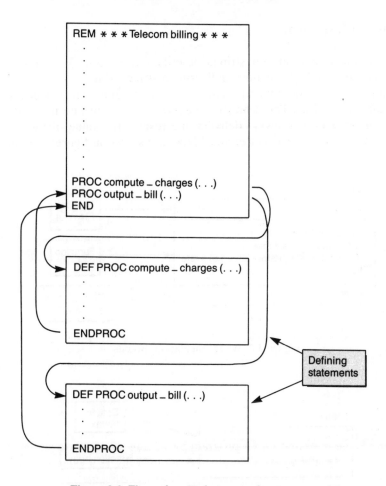

Figure 3.2 Flow of control at procedure statements

may participate in an algebraic expression on the right-hand side of an assignment, such as

net_pay = gross_pay − FNtax(gross_pay)

Note that by leaving FNtax as a function and not spelling out the calculation in the main body of the program, a change in tax law can be implemented merely by rewriting the definition of FNtax, leaving the main body of the program unaltered.

Our two examples of functions so far both deliver numeric values, and are controlled by numeric parameters. However, depending on the language used, functions can deliver values of any data type and there may be a wide range of allowable types for parameters.

Thus, the length of a string may be computed using the standard BASIC function *LEN*, which delivers an integer value, but takes a string parameter, as in length = LEN(word$)

Likewise all the operations on strings described in section 3.3 (under String Expressions) are standard functions delivering a string value.

For a function whose definition is provided by the programmer, it is necessary to design a function module. This is much like a procedure module design, except that a function module design always delivers one result—the value of the function. Simple module designs for FNwage and FNtax are shown in figures 3.3 and 3.4.

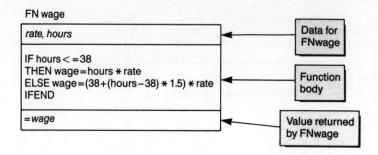

Figure 3.3 Wage calculation module

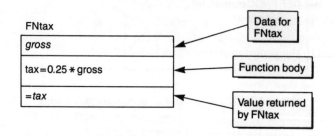

Figure 3.4 Simple tax module

These designs may be coded in BBC BASIC as function definitions, as follows.

```
1200
1210 DEF FNwage(rate,hours)
1220 LOCAL wage
1230 IF hours <= 38 THEN wage = hours * rate
        ELSE wage = (38 + (hours−38) * 1.5) * rate
1240 = wage
1300
1310 DEF FNtax(gross)
1320 = 0.25 * gross
```

or

```
1300
1310 DEF FNtax(gross) = 0.25 * gross
```

There are several points to note in these *function definitions*. Each function definition commences with a *function head*; like a procedure head, this consists of a reserved word (DEF in BBC BASIC, **function** in Pascal) followed by the name of the function and, in parentheses, a list of formal parameters. The *values* of the parameters are determined outside the function definition; it is when a function is called (for example, in the main program) that these values are computed from the actual parameters.

The *function body* is coded like a procedure body, making use of the formal parameters and the local variables. It is also possible for the function body to use the values of variables in existence in the main program; such variables are called *global variables* (or sometimes *global parameters*) as their values are visible not only in the main program but also within all function and procedure definitions. Global variables must be used with great care, as their current values in a given context may not be immediately apparent. It is even possible to reassign a global variable with a new value inside a function body. This dangerous practice is called a *side-effect* as it happens by the way when evaluating the function. Some languages nowadays (such as Ada) expressly forbid the programmer from including such side-effects in a function definition.

The final statement of the function definition—corresponding to the ENDPROC statement of a procedure definition—commences with the = sign. It looks like an assignment with no left-hand side—the value is not, in fact, assigned to a variable but is returned to the program statement which *called* the function; it is the *value of the function*. Note that the right-hand side of this final statement can be an expression and so may subsume part (or even all) of the function body. (When the whole function body is subsumed in the right-hand side of the = statement, it is permissible to collapse the function definition into one line.) The form of the statement which returns the function value varies between languages. In Pascal, for example, it is a special form of assignment statement which uses the function name on the left-hand side; in Ada it commences with the reserved word **return** instead of =.

The functions defined in a program are available for use throughout that program in any appropriate context. Since *FNwage* returns a numerical value it may be used wherever a numeric value is legal. Thus

    PRINT "Your wage this week is £"; FNwage(7,25)

would output the line

    Your wage this week is £175

Note how the actual parameters 7 and 25 in the function call are interpreted as *rate* and *hours* respectively—they must appear in the correct order. The statement gross_total = gross_total + FNwage(7.5, 40)

updates the variable *gross_total* by the week's wage of 307.5. In printing the wage
slip the tax deduction could be printed by the program statement

    PRINT "Tax: " FNtax(FNwage(rate, hours))

where the value returned by *FNwage* is used as the single actual parameter of
FNtax.

Block structure

The rules about where subprogram definitions should be placed within the program
code depend on the particular language used. In BBC BASIC, the appropriate
place for procedure and function definitions is after the END statement of the
program.

   A complete program consists of a *main program*, which must be terminated by an
END statement, followed (at higher line numbers) by subprograms (function and
procedure definitions) which may appear in any order. BBC BASIC is fully
democratic—all subprograms have the same status and may be called anywhere,
either in the main program or by other subprograms. A subprogram may even call
itself, as we shall see in section 3.6. Most imperative languages (for example,
Pascal) require the main program to be written *after* the subprogram declarations;
this has the unfortunate result of making programs difficult to unravel. BBC
BASIC is more civilised in this respect, having the main program first; this
corresponds to the first stage in a top-down design.

   In typical block-structured languages, such as Pascal, subprograms are defined
among the declarations for the main program; these subprograms are then visible
throughout the program. But each subprogram has the structure of a complete
program; it may define local types, local variables and even its own local
subprograms. These local subprograms are visible only within the defining
subprogram but not in the main program. In this way further subprograms may be
nested providing a *hierarchy* of subprograms.

3.5 Execution of Subprograms

When a subprogram is called by the main program (either in a procedure statement
or by the use of a function value) the normal execution sequence of the main
program is suspended while the subprogram body is executed. It is pertinent to
pause here to consider the *dynamic* structure of program execution. Unlike the
static program text, which lists the main program and the subprogram definitions,
the dynamic structure of a program provides a snapshot of the actual execution
sequence. This is worthy of consideration because subprograms exert a powerful
influence on the control sequence of a program.

Flow of control

A payroll program may be written along the following lines.

```
       ⎛ REM [payroll]
       ⎜ .
       ⎜ .
       ⎜ .
Main   ⎜ REPEAT
program⎜ INPUT #employees, EMPno, EMPrate
       ⎨ PROCESS(EMPno, EMPrate)
       ⎜ UNTIL EOF
       ⎜ .
       ⎜ .
       ⎜ .
       ⎝ END

         DEF PROCESS(emp%, rate)
         LOCAL hours, gross _ pay, tax
         INPUT #time _ cards, hours
           .
           .
           .
         gross _ pay=FNwage(rate, hours)
         tax=FNtax(gross _ pay)
           .
           .
           .
         PROCpayslip(emp%, gross _ pay, tax)
           .
           .
           .
         ENDPROC

         DEF FNwage(rate, hours)
         LOCAL wage
            IF hours < =38 THEN wage=hours * rate
            ELSE wage=(38+(hours-38) * 1.5) * rate
         =wage

         DEF FNtax (gross)=0.25 * gross

         DEF PROCpayslip(id _ no%, gross, tax)
           .
           .
         ENDPROC
```

> Transaction files are dealt with in Chapter 8

When this program is executed, on reaching the statement

PROCESS(EMPno, EMPrate)

the procedure body of *PROCESS* is activated. Suppose *EMPno* is 479123 and *EMPrate* is 3.15 at this stage; then the parameter *emp%* is initialised to the value 479123, and *rate* is initialised to 3.15. Throughout this activation of *PROCESS*, *emp%* and *rate* exist as local variables in addition to the variables specified in the LOCAL statement. On encountering the statement

    gross_pay = FNwage(rate, hours)

execution of *PROCESS* is suspended while the value of *FNwage* is calculated by activating its function body. Suppose that, at this stage, *hours* = 41.5; and the initial values of the formal parameters of *FNwage* are taken as 3.15 (for *rate*) and 41.5 respectively. When the activation of *FNwage* is complete, its parameters and the local variable *wage* cease to exist. Control passes back to the calling statement and the value returned by *FNwage* is assigned to *gross_pay*. When the activation of *PROCESS* is complete, the local variables *hours, gross_pay* and *tax* and the parameters *emp%* and *rate* cease to exist; control then reverts to the main program at the statement following the procedure call.

Whenever a subprogram call is encountered, the formal parameters of the subprogram are initialised to the values of the actual parameters in the calling statement. Execution of the calling statement is then suspended while the subprogram body is executed. When execution of the subprogram is complete the local variables and the parameters cease to exist and control passes back to the calling statement. In the case of a function call a value (which may be integer, numeric or string) is returned to the expression and the computation of the calling statement is resumed; in the case of a procedure call the current values of the result parameters (if any) are assigned to the *actual* result parameters and the next statement (following the procedure call) is executed.

Dynamic structure

Transfer of control into and out of subprograms can occur to any level of nesting, as each subprogram can call further subprograms, thus implementing the modular structure of the algorithm. Of course, the process cannot continue indefinitely—eventually control must return to the main program, allowing a graceful conclusion. This dynamic structure of a program is illustrated in figure 3.5 for the payroll program, in which each subprogram is called only once during a single traversal of the repeat loop.

In practice, one of the reasons for using subprogram is to contain a segment of code which is executed more than once during a program run. In this case the (static) program text will contain the subprogram definition only once. However, there will be several calls of this subprogram (possibly with differing choices of parameters); this will be reflected in the dynamic structure by a corresponding number of activations of the subprogram.

Parameter-passing mechanisms

The dynamic structure diagram shows clearly how each activation of a subprogram implicitly defines additional local variables corresponding to the formal parameters, which are initialised to the values of the actual parameters. It is apparent that these formal parameters can be used as extra local variables within the

```
REM [payroll]
.
.
.
REPEAT
  INPUT #employees, EMPno, EMPrate
  PROCESS(EMPno, EMPrate)              [EMPno=479123, EMPrate=3.15]
  +----------------------------------------------------------------+
  | emp%=479123, rate=3.15                                         |
  +----------------------------------------------------------------+
  | LOCAL hours, gross_pay, tax                                    |
  | .                                                              |
  | .                                                              |
  | FNwage(rate, hours)            [hours=41.5]                    |
  | +--------------------------+                                   |
  | | rate=3.15: hours=41.5    |                                   |
  | +--------------------------+                                   |
  | | LOCAL wage               |                                   |
  | | .                        |                                   |
  | | .                        |                                   |
  | | .                        |                                   |
  | +--------------------------+                                   |
  | | 136.2375                 |                                   |
  | +--------------------------+                                   |
  | gross_pay=136.2375                                             |
  | FNtax(gross_pay)                                               |
  | +-----------------------+                                      |
  | | gross=136.2375        |                                      |
  | +-----------------------+                                      |
  | | =0.25 * 136.2375      |    [=34.059375]                      |
  | +-----------------------+                                      |
  | | 34.059375             |                                      |
  | +-----------------------+                                      |
  | tax=34.059375                                                  |
  | .                                                              |
  | .                                                              |
  | PROCpayslip (emp%, gross_pay, tax)    [emp%=479123]            |
  | +---------------------------------------------------------+    |
  | | id_no%=479123: gross=136.2375: tax=34.05935             |    |
  | +---------------------------------------------------------+    |
  | | .                                                       |    |
  | | .                                                       |    |
  | | .                                                       |    |
  | +---------------------------------------------------------+    |
  | | ENDPROC                                                 |    |
  | +---------------------------------------------------------+    |
  | .                                                              |
  | .                                                              |
  +----------------------------------------------------------------+
  | ENDPROC                                                        |
  +----------------------------------------------------------------+
UNTIL EOF
.
.
.
END
```

Figure 3.5 Dynamic structure diagram of payroll program, indicating subprogram activation. Values of actual parameters are shown in brackets to aid clarity

subprogram body. Most languages provide for *call-by-value* parameters of this nature, which cater for source data. The Ada language, however, does not allow parameters of this sort. Instead, it provides *call-as-constant* parameters for source data. This means that the corresponding formal parameters must not be used as local variables, but only as local *constants*, within the subprogram body.

In order that a procedure may return results data to the calling program, a *call-by-reference* parameter is used. This does not define a new local variable; it defines an alias (a new local name) for an existing variable of the calling program. This means that the actual parameter in the subprogram call must be a variable name (it must not be an expression). Within the subprogram body the formal parameter can be assigned new values; when the subprogram body is concluded, the final value of the formal parameter is in fact the new value of the actual parameter, its alias. A function always delivers a single result, so it is not desirable for a function to alter the values of its parameters. Such a change in value during a function evaluation would be an undesirable side-effect. It should be noted, though, that some languages fail to prohibit the use of call-by-reference parameters in function declarations.

Note that in BBC BASIC, since only call-by-value parameters are permitted, a function can return one value to its calling program, and a procedure can return none. This restriction can be overcome by passing values through *global variables*, but this represents a side-effect which may have undesirable or unnoticed consequences. In Pascal, the programmer can designate parameters as call-by-reference by using the reserved word **var**. Undesignated parameters are treated as call-by-value.

The pioneering programming language, ALGOL-60, did not provide for call-by-reference parameters. Instead it allowed parameters to be called *by name*. This means that *wherever* a formal parameter appears in a subprogram body, the actual parameter is effectively substituted on activation. In simpler cases this yields results identical with those obtained using call-by-reference; however, by skilfully relating the actual parameters to each other, more sophisticated effects can be achieved. The programming of these special effects belongs more properly to a study of ALGOL-60.

The stack model

The identifiers which are used to name the formal parameters and local variables do not have to be distinct from the identifiers used outside the subprogram. Identifiers from outside a subprogram are visible within the subprogram—as global identifiers—provided that their names are not reused. If the identifier of a local variable or a formal parameter is identical with a global identifier, the latter is temporarily invisible for the duration of the subprogram. On conclusion of the subprogram execution, the local variables and formal parameters are discarded, and any hidden global identifiers reappear.

The method by which this reuse of names is achieved is by using a special area of memory called the **run-time stack**. Whenever a new identifier is encountered it is placed on the stack. Each time an identifier is used, the stack is inspected to ensure that the identifier has already been declared. New items are always added at the top of the stack; likewise the stack is always searched downwards from the top. On activation of a subprogram, a marker is placed on the stack. The formal parameters and local variables are then entered into the stack above the marker. This is illustrated in figure 3.6. When an identifier is used inside the subprogram body, the stack is searched downwards from the top until the corresponding name is found. If a local identifier has the same name as a global identifier, the local one will be found first. Thus the global identifier of the same name is effectively invisible during the execution of the subprogram. On termination of the subprogram, all the identifiers down to the marker are erased. Thus, those global identifiers which were hidden previously become visible again.

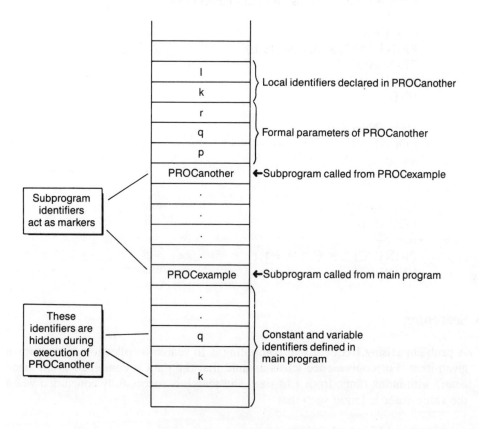

Figure 3.6 The run-time stack

This stack model is a considerable improvement over the subroutine jumps which are available in lower-level languages (including many versions of BASIC). Subroutines are invoked by jumping to the first statement of the subroutine and preserving a *return address* to which control can be redirected on conclusion of the subroutine. Thus a subroutine call identifies a line number, rather than an identifier which can describe its aim. In addition, subroutines do not allow the use of formal parameters and local parameters which are available for subprograms. With the stack model, moreover, it is perfectly in order for a statement in one subprogram to generate a call to another subprogram. What happens is that a new marker is placed on the stack to indicate the subprogram entry, and new local identifiers can be introduced as before. In fact, as we shall see in the next section, it is even possible for a subprogram to issue a call to itself.

Exercise 3.10

What output is produced by the following program?

```
REM ★★★★Procedures and Parameters★★★★
a = 4
b = 3 ★ a
PRINT "A) ", a, b, FNex(a,b)
PROCex(a)
PRINT "B)", a, b
END

DEF FNex(p,q)
LOCAL a
a = p+q
=a ★ p

DEF PROCex(z)
LOCAL b
b = z−3
PRINT "C) ", a, b, FNex(1,1)
ENDPROC
```

3.6 Searching

A problem arising frequently in computing is to search a collection of data for a given item. For convenience let us assume that the data is contained in an array *data()* with index range from 1 to *size*. The search is successfully concluded when the value *index* is found such that

> *data(index)* is equal to *item*

Since we need to discover the value of *index*, a suitable programming structure for the search routine is a function which returns the value of *index*. We shall develop two types of search routine—*linear search* and *binary search*.

Linear search

A straightforward search algorithm would inspect *data(1)*, *data(2)*, *data(3)* and so on in sequence until the value *item* is found, as we saw in section 2.2. This is fine if *item* is one of the values in the array—it will be found sooner or later. It is a fundamental principle of programming, though, to allow for all eventualities. In this case we must be prepared to allow for the possibility that *item* is not in the array. A suitable convention is for the search function to return the value 0 in this case (in BBC BASIC this has the desirable feature that FALSE = 0). This is illustrated by the algorithm of figure 3.7.

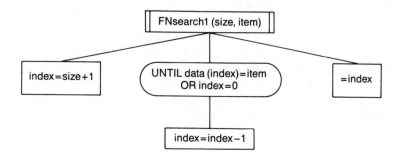

Figure 3.7 Linear search—version 1

There is a neat device to force this result. The index range is extended to include 0. An extra step is added to the function body initialisation to augment the array by assigning the value of *item* to the array element *data(0)*. This is called a **sentinel**. The search then proceeds backwards from *data(size)*; if *item* has not been found until *data(0)* is examined, it will certainly be found at this stage (since we put it there!), returning the appropriate value. The corresponding algorithm, given in figure 3.8, implements the linear search algorithm of section 2.2 on the augmented array.

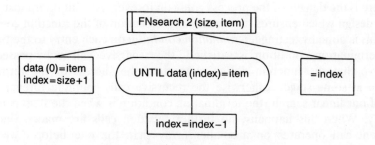

Figure 3.8 Linear search—version 2

Note that the array *data()* should be a parameter of the function. (This is possible in Pascal, but in BBC BASIC this is not allowed and the array *data* must be inspected by the search function as a global array.)

Exercise 3.11

Code the program of figures 3.7 and 3.8 as function definitions. (If you are coding in BASIC, you should assume that the data to be searched exists as strings.)

Exercise 3.12

Write a suitable test program to see that your search functions work.

There is an alternative method of describing a linear search, as in the following analysis. Inspect the last element of the array, *data(size)*. There are two possibilities: if *item* has been found, we have finished, otherwise we can discard *data(size)* and search the remainder of the array. The beauty of this approach is that the remainder of the array is just the original array *data()* from index 1 to index *size−1*. The remainder of the array can therefore be searched using the same search function. This approach is illustrated by the structure tree in figure 3.9.

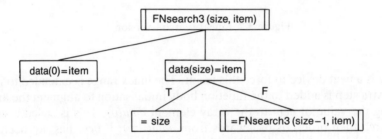

Figure 3.9 Linear search—version 3

An arrangement of this sort whereby a function calls itself is a very neat idea: we call it a **recursive** function. You have to be careful, though; since the function calls itself there is the danger of the process going on forever. An exit door must be built into the design which ensures that eventually execution of the function comes to a close. This is done by testing a *termination condition* on each entry to the function. If the termination condition is satisfied, the recursive call is by-passed. It is imperative that the function design guarantees the success of the termination condition at some stage—otherwise the recursive calls continue forever. In the design of our linear search, the terminating condition is when the item is found in the array. When this happens, no further function calls are made. Since each subsequent call operates on a smaller array than the one before, we ensure termination by putting the item into *data(0)* in the initialisation phase.

Exercise 3.13

This exercise requires you to write a recursive subprogram.
    Design and code a recursive function to determine the position of the largest element of a given sequence of numbers. You should assume that the numbers are held in a suitable array.

Binary search

For small arrays, linear search is an adequate method. For example, with eight elements stored in the array, nine comparisons are needed for an item which is not in the array, and fewer for an item which is in. For larger arrays, linear search is totally inefficient.

Suppose you want to look up 'concatenation' in a dictionary. You would certainly not proceed to work in sequence through aardvark, abacus, abandon, abate and so on until you found 'concatenation'. This method of searching would require hundreds of items to be checked before the desired word is found. Instead you would open the dictionary somewhere in the middle. Suppose you hit upon the word 'messenger'. Using the fact that the dictionary is arranged in lexicographic order you would concentrate on the section of the dictionary preceding 'messenger' in which to continue your search. Opening the dictionary somewhere in the first half, you hit upon 'explain'. Since the word sought precedes 'explain', the search is now narrowed down to the first quarter of the dictionary. Proceeding in this fashion, you eventually hit upon your chosen word 'concatenation', or discover its omission from the dictionary. With this method of searching, far fewer items are actually checked, because the field of search is cut in half at each step. The chosen word can thus be found in a dozen steps maybe.

This technique can be applied to any sequence of data items, provided the sequence is arranged in a definite order so that you can decide which of two items precedes the other (such as words, numbers). Any ordered sequence can be searched by splitting it into two portions, and then searching only the portion which can contain the required item; this method is known as **binary search**. For all but the smallest arrays this is, in general, a much faster method, as the size of the array is reduced by half following each unsuccessful comparison. Figure 3.10 shows a

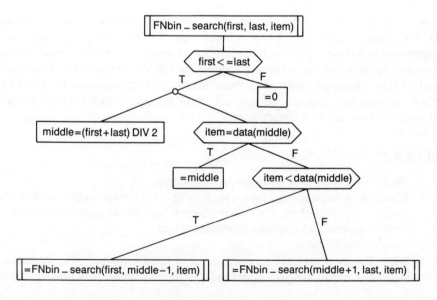

Figure 3.10 Binary search

structure diagram for binary search; as before, it returns either the position of the required element or 0 if the item is not found. When using this method it is not appropriate to insert the desired item at the beginning of the array, as the point where an unsuccessful search ends is actually in the array near where the item should be!

Figure 3.11 shows a formalised view of the array *data()* which is being searched, and the interpretation of the (local) variables *first*, *middle* and *last*. If the item is not equal to *data(middle)* a new value of *first* or *last* is chosen, and the search is continued on the restricted array portion.

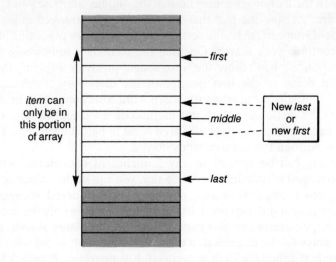

Figure 3.11 Diagrammatic representation of array during binary search

For an array of about 1000 elements, the maximum number of comparisons is 1000 for a linear search and 10 for a binary search. On average, the number of comparisons is 500 for a linear search and 9 for a binary search; using binary search, about half the items in the array will require the full 10 comparisons. Thus binary search is generally much faster than linear search. In fact, doubling the size of the array to be searched doubles the time taken for a linear search routine, but adds only one function call to a binary search.

Activity 3.1

1. Write a function definition for binary search.
2. Construct a large enough array, such as an array containing the names of all students in your class. Use binary search and linear search to search for various names and compare the times taken.

   Note: Binary search works only on an *ordered* sequence. The ordering of strings in BBC BASIC and Pascal is lexicographic (dictionary order), provided that they are all in upper or all in lower case. For mixed case strings, all upper-case letters are assumed to precede all lower-case letters.

3.7 Sorting and Merging

In the previous section we saw how, using binary search, an ordered sequence could be searched much faster than an unordered sequence. It stands to reason that if data is already arranged in some suitable order, access to it will be more rapid. When data is generated or collected, be it by interview or questionnaire, by people or by computers, it may well not be in a useful order. It may be necessary to sort the data to bring it into order. Even more so than with search routines, there are numerous sorting algorithms with differing degrees of complexity. While a simple algorithm is frequently adequate for a small collection of data, a more sophisticated and efficient algorithm may be needed to handle a large volume of data. For a given volume of data, two factors measure the efficiency of a sorting algorithm—the number of comparisons required and the number of occasions in which data elements are moved. In this section we study sort algorithms for data held in an array; other data structures may also be suitable for this purpose and in section 9.4 we shall meet the concept of a *sort tree*.

Selection sort

The **selection sort** selects, in correct sequence, the elements of an array. At any stage of the process, the array will consist of two parts—an unsorted portion and a sorted portion. We shall find it convenient to sort the array so that 'later' elements are sorted first, as shown in figure 3.12.

Figure 3.12 Partially sorted array

The top-level design for the procedure is as follows, yielding the structure tree of figure 3.13.

Selection sort

data(), size

1 If *size* of array *data()* is >1
2 then
    2.1 Select the element of the (unsorted) array that is last in order.
    2.2 Exchange the selected element with the final element of the (unsorted) array.
    2.3 Disregard the final element (which is now in the correct position) and sort the remaining unsorted array.
    2.4 endif

data()

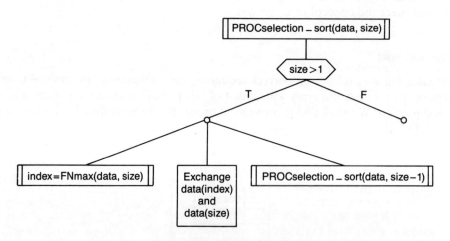

Figure 3.13 Selection sort module

Exercise 3.14

Refine the program design of figure 3.13, and write a program using your design.

The method of performing the selection sort is highly reminiscent of the linear search, and indeed this method is sometimes called **linear selection**. The number of comparisons required at step 2.1 is *size−1*; so the total number of comparisons in all the recursive calls of *selection_sort* is

$$(N - 1) + (N - 2) + (N - 3) + \ldots + 1$$

which may be shown mathematically to equal $\frac{1}{2}(N^2 - N)$. Additionally, up to N exchange moves are required, depending on the degree of order displayed by the unsorted array. Thus for large N the time taken to sort the array will be roughly proportional to N^2; so we may expect an array of 50 elements to take one hundred times as long to sort as an array of 5 elements.

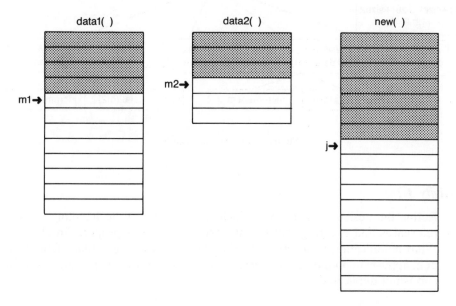

Figure 3.14 Merging two arrays

Merging

Before considering a more efficient sorting algorithm, we shall take a look at the allied problem of merging two ordered sequences. One circumstance in which we may wish to merge two sequences is when adding a number of data items to an established sequence. If each item is added individually, the main sequence will have to be scanned on each occasion. To speed things up, it is desirable to first sort the new data items—this is a relatively fast operation. Only now do we merge the two sequences, requiring just one scan of the main sequence.

Another practical need for merging arises when sorting very large collections of data which cannot be held in main memory. In this case the data may need to be sorted in sections, and the sorted sections then merged externally.

Suppose the two streams of data to be merged are held in a pair of arrays *data1( )* and *data2( ),* and the merged data will be stored in *new( ),* as shown in figure 3.14. We shall need pointers *m1* and *m2* to delineate the unprocessed data, and a marker to indicate when to switch from copying *data1( )* to copying *data2( ),* and vice versa. The pointer *j* indicates the position in *new( )* where the next element will be added. Figure 3.15 gives a partial design for the merge algorithm based on an iterative solution.

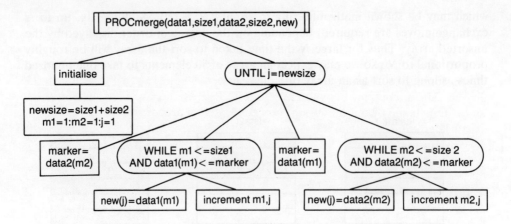

Figure 3.15 Merge module

Activity 3.2

Refine the design of figure 3.15, including tidying up the handling of array references and ensuring that the algorithm terminates properly in all cases. What modification is necessary to the algorithm to ensure that, if the same item appears in both data sequences, it is inserted only once into the new array and is not duplicated?

Merge sort

Now that we have a procedure for merging two arrays, we can devise an accelerated method for sorting an array. Without going into great detail, the general idea is to split the array into two halves, sort each half, and then merge the two halves. The half arrays are themselves sorted using the same method. Continual halving of the size of the array eventually results in an array containing just one element, which requires no sorting. To see how much time is taken to perform this procedure, assume that the initial array has 16 elements. So two arrays of 8 elements must be merged, requiring 15 comparisons. This argument can be extended as follows.

merge 1 pair of arrays of 8 elements: $1 \times 15 = 15$ comparisons
2 pairs of arrays of 4 elements: $2 \times 7 = 14$ comparisons
4 pairs of arrays of 2 elements: $4 \times 3 = 12$ comparisons
8 pairs of arrays of 1 element : $8 \times 1 = 8$ comparisons
Total $= 49$ comparisons

In general, the number of comparisons for an array of size N is somewhat less than N times the number of merge levels required. The following table shows how many merge levels are required for certain values of N; the number of levels is equal to the number of times the array size can be halved.

N	2	4	8	16	32	1024
levels	1	2	3	4	5	10

For an array of size 30, say, there are almost five complete levels. The number of levels for a given N is known mathematically as $\log_2 N$. (It is not equal to the mathematical functions LN and LOG, but is closely related to them.) An estimate of the time taken by our merge sort procedure is then proportional to $N \log_2 N$. This is considerably faster than the N^2 associated with the selection sort, especially for large values of N.

Summary of Chapter 3

The problem analysis and program design of the previous chapters lead to a specific program when coded in a suitable high-level language. The features of the language naturally have a bearing on the direction of problem analysis, without tying the analysis to the peculiarities of any one computer.

Program comprehensibility is improved by the following high-level features:

- clear program structure;
- meaningful identifiers;
- data typing (for example, numeric, string and enumerated types);
- comments in programs.

Some high-level languages allow constant identifiers to be defined and require variables to be declared before use. These programming facilities allow better organisation of programs and provide some protection against programming errors.

A high-level language may provide all or some of these control features:

- *while* loops;
- *repeat* loops;
- fixed loops, with a choice of step size for an integer control variable;
- *if* statements;
- case statements

If some of these features are unavailable, at least sufficient must be provided to enable all the types of program control features introduced in chapter 2 to be programmed.

Numeric and boolean data can be built into expressions which encapsulate much of the processing achieved by a program. Subprograms are used to execute a self-contained piece of processing; their execution may be parameterised using parameters for source data. A function delivers a unique value which may participate in an expression; a procedure need not deliver any result, but may do so through result parameters. The most common characteristics of parameters available in programming languages are call-by-value (for source data) and call-by-reference (for result data). Functions and procedures may be designed to call themselves recursively.

Searching and sorting aggregates of data comprise an important area of information processing; we have used these topics as case studies to illustrate some features of high-level programming. The methods we discussed are

> linear search and selection sort   for small arrays
> binary search and merge sort   for large arrays

Answers to Exercises

3.1
double	valid
date-of-birth	invalid—hyphens not allowed
Clok	valid—misspelt English words can be valid identifiers
item$price	valid
FRED	valid
third	valid
3rd	invalid—begins with a digit
item_no3	valid
item 7	invalid—spaces not allowed

3.2 (a) 8, 3.   (b) 6, 3.

3.3 (a) False. (b) True. (c) True. (d) False. (e) True—upper- and lower-case letters are always distinct within strings.

3.4 condition = (colour=red AND price > 30) OR (colour=green AND price > 90).

3.5 IF count > 0 THEN
REPEAT
   process (count)
   count = count − 1
UNTIL count = 0

> This test is necessary to avoid processing when the initial value of count is not positive.

Notice that count is decremented within the loop, so the end condition used in the *until* loop differs from the start condition in the original *while* loop. This alteration is needed to ensure that the two versions have the same meaning.

3.6 Let size = 50, this = 10, that = 5. Then

> size − (this + that) = 50 − 15 = 35
> size − this + that = 50 − 10 + 5 = 45

3.7 The second "All" begins with a capital letter.

3.8 (a) x > 0 AND < 100   (0 < x < 100 is unacceptable)
(b) (p% + q%) > 20 AND (p% ⋆ q%) < 90
(c) next_name$ < "Smith" OR next_name$ = "Taylor"

3.9 100 IF (line% < 0) OR (line% > maxline%) OR (col% < 0) OR (col% > maxcol%)
        THEN PRINT "⋆⋆⋆ screen error ⋆⋆⋆"
        ELSE col% = (col% + 1) MOD (maxcol% + 1)
110 IF col% = 0 THEN line% = (line% + 1) MOD (maxline% + 1)

[There are many equally valid solutions to this problem. In our version we have used the MOD operation to reset a value to 0 to prevent it overshooting. Line 110 advances the line number after the end of the previous screen line; it is assumed that the next position after the last position on the last line is the beginning of the screen again.]

3.10 A) 4, 12, 64.
    C) 4, 1, 2.
    B) 4, 12.

3.11 The following are possible solutions.

```
DEF FNsearch1(size, item$)
REM GLOBAL data$(size)
LOCAL index
index = size + 1
REPEAT
    index = index − 1
UNTIL data$(index) = item$ OR index = 0
= index

DEF FNsearch2(size, item$)
REM GLOBAL data$(size)
LOCAL data$(0), index
data$(0) = item$
index = size + 1
REPEAT
    index = index − 1
UNTIL data$(index) = item$
= index
```

3.12

```
REM {search test}
size = 8
DIM data$(size)
FOR i = 1 TO size: READ data$(i): NEXT i
DATA cornflakes, rice krispies, weetabix, shredded wheat
```

```
DATA porridge, all bran, coco pops, muesli
FOR test = 1 TO 3
    READ cereal$
    found = FNsearch(size, cereal$)
    IF found THEN PRINT cereal$ "is item" found "in list"
        ELSE PRINT cereal$ "not found"
NEXT test
END
DATA weetabix, toasties, muesli
```

In BBC BASIC (and other interpreted languages) you can avoid writing a complete test program for a function by using statements at command level, such as

```
PRINT FNsearch(size, "cornflakes").
```

Do not forget to initialise any global variables (such as the *data$()* array).

3.13 We adopt the following design

max

data(), size		
1 if size=1		
2 then		
3 posmax=1		
4 else		
4.1 CALL max(data(), size − 1) to obtain interim position		
4.2 if data(size) > data(interim position)		
4.2.1 then		
4.2.2 posmax = size		
4.2.3 else		
4.2.4 posmax = interim position		
4.2.5 endif		
posmax		

The following BASIC program is a possible implementation. It assumes that the numbers are held in the global array *data*.

```
DEF FNmax(size)
REM GLOBAL ARRAY data(size)
LOCAL pos%
IF size=1 THEN pos%=1 ELSE
    pos%=FNmax(size − 1)
    : IF data(size) > data(pos%) THEN pos%=size
= pos%
```

3.14 The refinement of *FNmax*, which finds the index of the array element that comes last in order, is essentially identical to the solution of exercise 3.13.

The exchange of two elements requires the introduction of a temporary variable:

> 2.2.1 temp = data(size)
> 2.2.2 data(size) = data(index)
> 2.2.3 data(index) = temp

The final step, 2.3, is implemented as a call back to *selection_sort* with the array *size* parameter reduced by 1, and requires no refinement.

In BBC BASIC, the array *data()* cannot be passed as a parameter but has to be a global variable. Since *data()* is altered by the procedure (that is its purpose!), and assuming that the data items are strings, we shall use *_data$()* as the name of the global variable which holds the data array. The initial underline is a useful convention for a global variable which suffers side-effects. (In Pascal, you would have a parameter *data* of a suitable array type.)

Two local parameters are used: *index* (integer type) and *temp* (data type).

```
1000
1010 DEF PROCselection_sort(size%)
1020 IF size% = 1 THEN ENDPROC
1030 REM GLOBAL ARRAY _data$(size%)
1040 LOCAL index%, temp$
1050 index% = FNmax(size%)
1060 temp$ = _data$(size%)
1070 _data$(size%) = _data$(index%)
1080 _data$(index%) = temp$
1090 PROCselection_sort(size% - 1)
1095 ENDPROC
1100
1110 DEF FNmax(size%)
1120 REM GLOBAL ARRAY _data$(size%)
1130 LOCAL pos%
1140 IF size%=1 THEN pos%=1 ELSE
         pos% = FNmax(size% - 1)
         : IF _data$(size%) > _data$(pos%) THEN pos%=size%
1150 = pos%
```

Further Exercises

1. Give one major feature which distinguishes an *until* loop from a *while* loop. Show how an *until* statement can be recoded as a *while* statement, illustrating your answer with an example. What implication does this have for a language designer?

Under what circumstances would it be undesirable to use a *while* loop instead of an *until* loop?

2. Name one programming language which requires identifiers to be declared before use. Give two advantages for such a rule. What disadvantages might there be in having this rule?

3. Where in a program would you use local variables, and why?

4. Identify two features of high-level languages which aid writing a program for the solution of a set of linear equations.

5. Explain three features of a particular high-level language which contribute to the readability of programs, with illustrative examples.

6. Discuss the relative merits of a linear search and a binary search.

7.

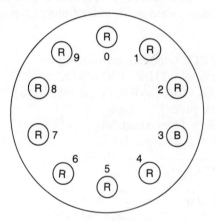

Figure 3.16 Puzzle board

Figure 3.16 shows one possible starting position for a simple puzzle. There is a board with ten positions, numbered 0 to 9, arranged in a circle. At the start, any one position is occupied by a black piece (B), and the other nine positions are occupied by red pieces (R). A number n, between 2 and 9, is chosen and then, starting from position 0, every nth piece around the circle clockwise is removed. So, for example, if $n = 7$, the pieces removed are on positions 7, 4, 2, 1 and so on. If the black piece is the last one to be removed, a solution to the puzzle has been found. The solution is represented by two values, the position of the black piece and the number chosen.

Analyse the problem of finding a list of all possible solutions to the puzzle. Describe an algorithm for a program to generate the list, or write a clearly annotated program.

(Camb.—1983)

8. A program is to process a stream of data items. Discuss the relative merits of

   (a) specifying the number of items as part of the data;
   (b) terminating the data with a bogus value.

   Explain which high-level programming constructs are required in each case.

9. Write a recursive procedure which takes as input parameter a string containing commas, and prints each part of the string (between the commas) on a separate line. Thus the input string

   "Macmillan Education Ltd, Houndmills, Basingstoke, Hampshire, RG21 2XS"

   would be printed as

   Macmillan Education Ltd
   Houndmills
   Basingstoke
   Hampshire
   RG21 2XS

   Make sure that your solution works for a string containing no commas.

10. Name one programming language which allows the programmer to define constants. Describe briefly two advantages of using named constants in programs.
    Can a constant identifier be used as

    (a) an input parameter,
    (b) an output parameter

    in a procedure call?

11. (i) Using a high level programming language of your choice show without using an unconditional jump instruction how a loop can be executed as follows:
    (a) a certain number of times using a variable as a counter (counted loop)
    (b) until some condition is true (until loop)
    (c) while some condition is true (while loop)
    (ii) Show how a counted loop can be expressed:
    (a) by a while loop
    (b) by an until loop (assume that the loop is executed at least once).
    (iii) One of the three loop constructs can be used to perform the same functions as the other two (without using an unconditional jump). Which one is it? Explain.

    (ULSEB—1986)

12. The following pseudo-code algorithm describes one method of finding an arbitrary name in an alphabetically ordered array of N unique names.

```
set first to 1
set last to N
repeat
    set mid to the integer part of (first + last)/2
    if the midth name precedes the wanted name then
        set first to mid + 1
    else
        set last to mid − 1
    endif
until first > last or midth name is the wanted name
```

(a) If 142 names are stored in the array, and HAMMOND is the 44th name, which elements of the array are examined when searching for HAMMOND?

(b) If a search is made for a name that is not in the array, what is the largest number of elements that might need to be examined before one could say that the name is not present? Explain how you arrive at your answer.

(c) What are the advantages of describing an algorithm in pseudo-code before it is written in a programming language?

(Camb.—1987)

4 Program Development Issues

We have, in the first three chapters, taken you through the various stages encountered in translating a real-world problem into a functioning computer program which delivers the solution. In this chapter we shall take a brief look at some issues which were skated over in our original discussion.

In the real world, errors are liable to find their way into software. This can generate problems of massive proportions, as programs in daily use contain typically hundreds of thousands of lines of program code. The scope for error, and the difficulty of tracking down errors even when they are known to exist, provide solid reasons for developing software in a manner which minimises errors in the first place.

In describing how to analyse a problem and design a corresponding computer program, we have presented a particular development method—top-down stepwise refinement. In practice, it is not always easy to apply this method to complex systems. We shall begin this chapter by reviewing the development cycle for a software system, and take a brief look at some of the tools in use for studying complex systems.

At the other extreme, computer programs—even when developed using structured design methods—do not always (or even often) work entirely to the users' satisfaction. It is one thing to describe in a book what ought to happen when developing a program, but what actually happens may be quite different from the theory. Section 4.2 takes a look at the repair of errors in programs and the use of test data to help discover errors.

It is advantageous if exceptional situations are dealt with explicitly by the program, rather than letting the program crash in these circumstances. In section 4.3 we take a brief look at mechanisms for handling exceptions.

4.1 The Software Life-cycle

A program (or suite of programs) begins a life as a real-world problem, or a system with particular requirements. From system to working program there are several stages of development; subsequently the working program may be subject to continual maintenance as the real-world system, which is modelled by the program, itself changes in the course of time.

Systems development

The first stage of development is a **systems analysis**. The requirements of the user must be clearly specified in terms of the information content of the system. Analysis will reveal the components of the system and the flow of information between those components. The whole, or maybe some parts, of a system may entail procedures which can and should be performed using a computer; one function of systems analysis is a *feasibility study* to identify such procedures. A decision to automate a given procedure must be based on estimates of cost and effort in implementing a computerised version of the procedure, on the cost (in terms of money, goodwill and staff time) in training staff in the new operational methods, and on the ability of a computerised system to fulfil adequately the user's needs. A feasibility study may also be applied to an existing computer-based system to consider how best to implement improvements to the system. As a result of the study, appropriate management information will be provided. Sometimes it will be appropriate to make amendments to the existing software; on other occasions it will prove to be beneficial on grounds of cost or obsolete hardware, say, to replace the system by developing a new system.

When an operational procedure is selected for computerisation, particular care must be taken to formulate precisely the *functional requirements* for the software and the *data interface*. The data interface specifies the format in which the data is presented to the procedure and the format of the output; the functional requirements specify the relationship which the output must have to the input. In other words, there will be a clear definition of the nature of the input data, the processing function of the software and the nature of the output data.

The user's requirements are typically determined in a series of interviews between the user and the **systems analyst**. Analysis of these requirements leads to the production of a specification document, the *statement of requirements*, which serves as the basis of the contract between the supplier of the computer system and the user.

The statement of requirements, which can run to hundreds of pages for a complex application, may include a large element of preliminary design. The systems analyst is concerned with the efficiency of the application and the speed with which each transaction is completed when the system is running. The statement of requirements will therefore also include proposals for hardware—what performance is expected from the processor, and how much backing storage is required. It may also include some elements of *system design*, such as how the software should be partitioned into a suite of separate programs, and the interface between each program and the files which are to be maintained.

When the system is finally implemented, it will be necessary for appropriate documentation to be available, both for users on a day-to-day basis, and for programmers who will subsequently maintain the software. The statement of requirements should lay down what documents need to be produced in conjunction with the software.

Formal methods

In order to provide the most rigorous standards in the development of software, it is desirable to use formalised methods as early as possible in the life-cycle. These methods typically seek to apply a structured approach to both the analysis and design phases of software development. Detailed discussion of such methods is out of place here, but we shall give a brief indication of some of the techniques currently being used.

SSADM (Structured Systems Analysis and Design Methodology) is the approved development method whose use is required on all projects for UK Government departments. An important part of the method is the use of diagrams which show the processes which make up the system and the various *data flows* between these processes. The resulting diagram is a network which describes the flow of data through the system. SSADM also lays down detailed procedures to be followed in the analysis and design phases. The Yourdon method is a commercially marketed development method which follows similar principles. With these methods the individual processes can be designed in detail using top-down stepwise refinement as described in chapter 2.

Another method which uses diagrams as a design tool is the Jackson Development Method. This method differs, though, from SSADM and Yourdon by identifying real-world entities as the fundamental building blocks. These entities are analysed in terms of the sequence of activities in which they engage. The whole system is then described by piecing together the entities in a system implementation diagram. This approach is quite different from the stepwise refinement of processes which has been used so far. The Jackson method is quite sophisticated, and considerable training is required before it can be used. It has been used successfully in developing business systems as well as computer operating systems and missile guidance systems.

The most formal methods do not use diagrams. Instead they use mathematical specifications as a basis for software development. VDM and Z are the names of two popular specification techniques for developing sequential programs. The use of a strict formalism allows the resulting programs to be checked mathematically for correctness.

Software design

Following systems analysis and design, the next stage for a system which is to be computerised is the design of the software. A large part of the effort expended in this direction will be devoted to the design of the algorithm and its development into a computer program, topics discussed in the first three chapters of this book.

In designing the software, especially for a large project, it is necessary to build a **data dictionary**. We have mentioned previously the need to choose suitable identifiers for data items. Each data item has an entry in the dictionary. The entry relates the identifer used in the software to the corresponding real-world entity and describes the range of permissible values and links with other entities in the system. The data dictionary serves as a valuable source of *documentation*, both while writing the software and for subsequent use during maintenance. It should include a description of data items held in files (on backing storage) as well as input and output data. The compilation of a data dictionary is an established practice for database management systems, but it is an equally useful tool for all kinds of software. The dictionary may be held as a manual file or as a machine-readable file—after all, the computer is available for this purpose, so why not use it.

When the software design is implemented, the documented program which is produced may no longer be faithful to the original user specification. The user's requirements have been interpreted by a systems analyst, whose software design has been interpreted in turn by a programmer. On a large project, a section may be developed by one programmer, who then delegates the task of refining certain elements in the design to other programmers. It is in the nature of the top-down design method that the highest levels of the design may be coded as a sequence of subprogram calls before the subprograms themselves have been refined. All that is necessary is that each subprogram is fully specified as to its data interface and its functional requirements. At each phase of this development process, there can be no guarantee against misinterpretation.

With the best will in the world, the software may not perform its specified task. The choice of programming language can be a crucial factor here. Although the software can be designed quite independently of the programming language used to implement it, each language has its own modes of expression and modes of thought associated with it. There is therefore a tendency to design software in the way in which it can be most readily implemented. In practice, this may mean compromising the specification. On the other hand, if the software design fulfils the specification faithfully, but is out of step with the language style, there is an increased risk of writing a program which does not truly reflect the design. This may happen as a result of transforming the program design into code.

Choice of language

We have referred to the choice of programming language as a factor influencing program correctness. The language chosen is likely to be dictated by the nature of the application. This will depend, of course, on the availability of compilers for the chosen language if the hardware has already been installed. When a new computer system is going to be supplied, then the choice of language may restrict the choice of hardware. The familiarity of programming staff with the language must also be considered. Training the staff to learn a new language may be expensive, and may meet with staff resistance. Furthermore, programmers may not deliver code of the best quality if they are coding in a newly learned language.

We shall now give a brief description of the area of application of some of the more common languages.

COBOL was designed to meet the needs of commerce. It has a fairly plain English style and is suited well to file manipulation activities. Simple arithmetic is catered for, but more complicated mathematics would require a slow and cumbersome program. The standard definition of COBOL has been revised about once every ten years to bring the language in line with current good programming practice. Extensions to COBOL are available which provide for database operation.

RPG is another language designed for use in the commercial environment. It is used to write programs which analyse data files to generate statistical reports and tables of data.

BASIC was initially introduced as a teaching language for interactive use. Its line-by-line structure hails back to an era when the prime input medium was punched cards and low-level assembly coding was widespread. Very limited facilities were available and BASIC represented a considerable improvement over assembly language. The BASIC system also introduced interactive programming using a teletype. Various enhancements over the years have produced a hotch-potch of versions, all masquerading under the name BASIC. BBC BASIC, with long identifiers, control structures, procedures and functions, provides most of the features of a clean programming language and has been used successfully for writing games programs (requiring a modicum of calculation) and business programs. The file-handling facilities are adequate for many applications. BBC BASIC Version 5 includes a number of valuable improvements over the original BBC BASIC—in particular the provision of output parameters for procedures.

Pascal also made its debut as a teaching language but has proved immensely popular for a range of scientific and descriptive calculation. Pascal has a full range of both control structures and data structures, and also the ability for user types to be defined. As such, it is a self-expanding language. Weak file-handling facilities make it a poor choice for large commercial applications, and standard Pascal has rather primitive string-handling facilities. Since its definition is the subject of an international standard, programs are portable between validated compilers. Extended versions of Pascal have been implemented to allow concurrent processing and hidden data types. These are widely used for systems programming, such as writing compilers.

C grew out of earlier languages designed specifically for writing compilers, and was initially devised as a systems programming language. In particular, it was developed to write the UNIX operating system for the PDP-11 minicomputer. In recent years, UNIX has become very popular and UNIX systems have been written for a large variety of minis and micros. In C there is no strong data typing as in Pascal, and programmers have to keep their wits about them to avoid writing code which performs operations on inappropriate data. It is sometimes described as a structured, machine-independent, low-level language.

Ada is a Pascal-like language commissioned by the United States Department of Defense. It has numerous powerful program structures to handle complex situations, and is intended for use in embedded systems which control aeroplanes, rocket paths and industrial processes. The data-structuring facilities of Ada allow programmers to define data types (such as queues) in which only the operations on the data type (for example, add item to queue, inspect head of queue) are visible within the main program, but the representation details are hidden.

Prolog has been developed by computer scientists interested in artificial intelligence. In imperative block-structured languages, programs describe the flow of control through an algorithm. In Prolog, on the other hand, the programmer is not unduly concerned with the control aspect of the algorithm. A program consists of a description of the relationship of the output to the input, and it is the task of the language processor (not the programmer) to discover the chain of command from input to output. The thrust of Japanese research into computing during this decade is to build suitable hardware which will execute Prolog programs; the hardware has been dubbed the **fifth generation**. For the time being, Prolog programs can be run on a conventional computer architecture using an interpreter. Prolog is seen as the appropriate language in which to construct **expert systems** (programs which simulate an experienced professional) and natural language processors (programs which allow communication using ordinary language instead of special programming languages).

Exercise 4.1

(a) For a given program specification, what feature should dictate the choice of programming language?

(b) Name two important features which are desirable in *any* programming language.

(c) Suggest two reasons why the actual language chosen for a software project may differ from the ideal choice.

Verifying the program

Throughout the process of program design and coding, steps have to be taken to ensure program correctness. Even so, there can be no guarantee that the program is correct. A useful tool in the hands of the programmer which aids matching up the algorithm implemented by the program with the specification of the software is **program verification**. As an example, consider a sorting algorithm (it does not matter which). We assume that the data is initially contained in an array

item(1), . . . ,item(N)

The specification has two requirements. Firstly, the final data must be a permutation of the original data, that is, the same data initially contained in the array *item()* but (possibly) in a different sequence. Additionally the final data must be sorted, that is,

item(1) < item(2) < . . . < item(N)

This latter requirement can be checked easily, and this should indeed be done, within the program, to verify the validity of the algorithm. The former requirement may be difficult to perform if the data has been sorted *in situ*, for the original data is now lost. An approach to this requirement is to verify *on each occasion* when elements of *item()* are reassigned that the new values are indeed a rearrangement of the old. By extension, if integrity of the data is preserved at each stage, it has been preserved through the program. This approach is best illustrated with an example.

The following procedure performs a linear selection sort.

```
1000
1010 DEF PROCselection_sort(size)
1020 IF size = 1 THEN ENDPROC
1030 REM GLOBAL ARRAY item(size)
1040 LOCAL index, temp
1050 index = FNmax(size)
1060 temp = item(size)
1070 item(size) = item(index)
1080 item(index)= temp
1090 PROCselection_sort(size − 1)
1095 ENDPROC
1100
1110 DEF FNmax(size)
1120 REM GLOBAL ARRAY item(size)
1130 LOCAL pos
1140 IF size=1 THEN pos=1 ELSE
        pos = FNmax(size − 1)
        : IF item(size) > item(pos) THEN pos = size
1150  = pos
```

The two conditions which require verification can be treated as follows. As explained above, we shall show that each change to an element of the array *item()* permutes the data. In fact, the only assignments to *item()* are contained in the sequence of statements which swap *item(index)* with *item(size)*. Before the swap let the values be as shown.

variable	value
item(index)	A
item(size)	B

After the statement *temp = item(size):*

item(index)	A
item(size)	B
temp	B

After the statement *item(size) = item(index):*

item(index)	A
item(size)	A
temp	B

After the statement *item(index) = temp:*

item(index)	B
item(size)	A
temp	B

Since no other elements of *item()* have been reassigned, it is clear from the table that, after a single swap, the new values of *item()* are a permutation of the old. Since each swap preserves the set of values in the array, it follows that the final set of values of *item()* is a permutation of the original set.

To establish the order of the final set of values, the procedure PROCverify may be called immediately following the call of PROCsort.

```
DEF PROCverify(size)
REM To verify that item(i) <= item(i + 1)
REM GLOBAL item()
LOCAL i
FOR i = 2 TO size
IF item(i - 1) > item(i) THEN STOP
NEXT i
PRINT "Verification complete"
ENDPROC
```

This example has illustrated two methods of verification. The first method is that of proving that a section of program maintains or creates a certain condition—the set of values in *item()*; this is a formal verification which asserts the validity of a piece of code. The second method is by inserting code which confirms that a certain condition obtains—that *item()* is sorted; this method does not verify the code in general, but asserts the success of the current execution of the program. A completely verified program should fully meet its specification and contain no logical or semantic errors. In practice, it is often not feasible for a program to be completely verified while writing it. Thus errors may remain in programs. Some techniques for detecting and handling these errors are discussed in sections 4.2 and 4.3

Some languages (such as Euclid) have been specifically designed to aid program verification.

Efficiency

Even when a program has been coded correctly, it will not be the unique software solution. Many different programs can be written which achieve the same task. In some cases one program may perform twice as fast as another. Some thought must be given to maximising speed. Where time has to be paid for on the computer, the gain in speed will be reflected in a direct cost saving. Even with an in-house machine there are indirect savings in using less computer time. Furthermore, quick results may be more useful than those which take longer to produce.

To some extent the speed of a program is in the hands of the designer, who must take speed of execution into account when choosing between different strategies which meet the same specification. But the coding phase may also allow some flexibility. Ultimately the time taken to run a program reflects the number of instructions in the program. It is incumbent upon the programmer to minimise the number of slow instructions contained in his program. For example, each function call takes time. If repeated function calls are required with the same arguments in a section of code, the code will run faster if the values are computed once and saved in an array.

Here is an example. A program to draw a clock makes frequent use of sin 6°, sin 12°, . . . , sin 360°. Rather than recalculate these values each time they are required, an array *sin()* can be set up and initialised with the code:

```
DIM sin(60)
FOR i = 1 TO 60
   sin(i) = SIN(RAD(i * 6))
NEXT i
```

The execution of this piece of code introduces a time penalty. But subsequently every call to *sin(i)* will save time, because an array access is much faster than a function evaluation.

Exercise 4.2

The following code makes repeated identical calculations. Suggest an improvement which will run faster.

```
FOR i = 1 TO m
   x = i/2 + LN(i/4) − i/8
   y = i/3 + LN(i/4) − i/8
NEXT i
```

Since the body of a loop is executed many times, care must be taken to maximise the efficiency of loop bodies. Often it is possible to identify a critical portion of the program which occupies a high proportion of the program's execution time. This may be the inner body of a nested loop, or a function which is called recursively. It is this portion whose efficiency is vital to the program. As far as possible, computations should be taken out of loops, where the result of a given computation is the same on each traversal of the loop body.

Improving the speed of a program may require the use of additional variables, which may occupy extra space. In a single-user system this does not matter. Unless all the available memory is used up, there is no point in 'saving' memory, and the programmer might as well use up more space in order to achieve an improvement in speed or elegance. In a multi-user system, however, memory is shared between users and a significant increase in memory usage may result in more swapping in and out of memory pages with a concomitant loss in overall speed (although the processing may be faster). In writing the most efficient program, the programmer must exercise judgement over the trade-off between space and time. There will also be circumstances in which a less efficient program is justified because the corresponding program text is more readable and elegant. Efficiency must be seen in the total environment, and the efficiency of the programmer is no less important than the efficiency of the program.

Exercise 4.3

Give three circumstances in which program efficiency is not of paramount importance.

Maintenance

The minimal requirement for a program is that it should be able to process successfully any valid data with which it is supplied. A good program should do better than that. Ideally a program should be robust, that is, capable of functioning adequately in all circumstances. It should be able to discriminate valid and invalid input and handle exceptional cases. These cases may only come to light after the program has been working successfully for a while, so that subsequent program modification may even be necessary. This is one form of program maintenance.

More generally, a major piece of software may remain in use for many years. During this time the fundamental system may evolve. Changes in the system will require corresponding changes in the software. A major maintenance function is to keep the software up-to-date with developments in the system. The ease and success with which software can be maintained reflects the care taken in the original written. Well-structured, clearly written and fully documented programs allow for simple maintenance. Poorly structured and poorly documented programs, on the other hand, may be difficult or impossible to maintain. No programmer should rely on keeping things in his head. Once a software package is delivered it should be complete. All the details should be provided with such clarity that another maintenance programmer, new on the scene, can understand how the program works. Even if the original programmer does the maintenance, he will not be sorry to have a clean, well-documented program to maintain. Between the time of original writing and the time of carrying out maintenance tasks on a piece of software, the programmer may have undertaken many other tasks which could easily cloud the memory.

The purchaser of a motor car is provided with clear user and maintenance manuals, and prefers a simple-to-maintain model; the purchaser of a piece of software is not likely to want anything less.

4.2 Program Testing

Even after a program has been developed as carefully as possible, it may yet contain a variety of errors. To understand this, you should realise that the program code is frequently divorced several stages from the original application; at each stage there is an element of modelling which may not provide a faithful replica of the situation being modelled. Firstly, the program design may not truly reflect the user's actual requirements. Even if it does, the transformation from design to code creates a further opening for errors, or *bugs*, to creep in, so that the program does not actually perform what it is designed to do.

Program errors may usefully be considered according to the type of error. *Syntax errors*, representing a failure of the program code to meet the exacting constraints of the programming language, can be discovered automatically by the *compiler*. The compiler is a specific piece of software which will be discussed at length in chapter 10. Its function is to translate the program code so that it can be executed by the machine. As part of its function, the compiler can discover all errors caused by code which breaks the syntax rules of the language.

Semantic errors, in which a syntactically correct program attempts to perform activities devoid of meaning or beyond the allowed meaning, may be caught in a variety of ways—by hardware, software (the compiler again) or specifically programmed actions. It should be part of the designer's job to incorporate suitable tests into the program design to prevent semantic errors occurring, and to flag their existence when they do occur.

Logical errors arise when a computer program does not match its specification. The method of trapping such errors is by running the program with suitable test data.

To the extent that a program cannot be proved to be error free, tests must be devised to show up as many errors as possible. Program errors are known as bugs; once their existence has been established, the process of locating and eliminating them is **debugging**. By devising careful tests we may hope to show up bugs in the program, but we shall never be sure whether any more remain. In the words of E. W. Dijkstra: "Program testing can be used to show the presence of bugs, but never to show their absence!" For this reason, there are many software systems in existence and regular use which are not completely reliable.

Error diagnosis

Some bugs may interfere with the normal running of the program. These are semantic errors, which may be trapped by the run-time system. Some errors, like division by zero, are trapped by the hardware and propagated through to the running program. Others, like array subscript out of range are trapped by the interpreter or by code inserted by the compiler. What happens next depends on the language implementation. Normally the program is aborted and an error message is displayed indicating the nature of the error which arose. With luck you may also be told on what line of code, or in which procedure, the error arose. The amount of information supplied varies a great deal between languages and between different implementations of the same language. A **store dump** may be invoked, indicating the current values of all variables visible when the program crashed. The information provided may be sufficient to diagnose the bug. However, that is only half the job done. It remains necessary to modify the program to prevent the situation arising again.

Exercise 4.4

A division by zero error is found when using the procedure PROCexample
defined below. Suggest an improvement which will trap this error.

```
1010 DEF PROCexample(n)
1050    FOR i = 1 TO n
1060       this = i/n
1070    NEXT
1099 ENDPROC
```

Test data

When all syntax and semantic errors have been debugged the program will be able
to run to its conclusion. But is the conclusion successful? Do the results produced
meet the user specification? In a few cases it will be obvious that they do. In many it
will be obvious that they do not (for example, alignment of output). In most, it will
be impossible to tell merely by looking at the output whether it is correct or not.

How is the programmer to increase his confidence in the accuracy of this
program? The answer must be to provide some input data which is in some sense
typical and for which the output can be predicted. The actual output can be
compared with the predicted output and, if the two disagree, there must be a bug in
the program. Discovering the actual bug may require exhaustive **tracing** of the
values of particular variables through the program execution and of the flow of
control through the program. Where the language processor does not provide an
adequate tracing facility, it will be necessary for the programmer to insert suitable
(temporary) output statements for this purpose.

The form of testing can be enhanced when the program conforms to a clean
modular structure. In this event each subprogram can be separately tested to
ensure that it performs satisfactorily. Such **modular testing** should eliminate many
problems at a stage when they can be identified easily. When a program is
developed by the top-down method, testing can follow the same pattern. The top
levels of the program design can be coded early on in the process. In order to test
them, the subprograms called from the top level, which have not yet been
developed, are replaced by simple subprograms with the correct interface (parameter set) and a simple body with minimal processing. Such testing can help to
identify design flaws early on before the whole project is almost complete.

When the lowest-level subprogram or module is developed it should not be
inserted into the main program before it is tested independently; if it is, it will be
difficult to track down the errors which are found. Instead, it is desirable to test the
subprograms in a *bottom-up* fashion. Each subprogram is tested on its own by
inserting it into a special piece of main program whose sole purpose is to drive and
test the subprogram. This is called a **driver program**. Only when individual
subprograms are considered to be error free are they combined into the higher-
level structures of the program design. These are then tested to ensure that
modules which work successfully on their own also perform correctly when linked
together. This linked test is called **integration testing**.

The choice and design of sets of test data need careful consideration. In addition to typically correct data, it is wise to include unlikely and marginally incorrect data and also to cover marginal cases. For example, a search procedure should work when the array being searched contains no data, when the item being searched is the first or last in the array, and when the item is not present in the array. A file-handling program should not break down on encountering an empty file.

One technique for measuring the quality of test data is *mutation testing*. In this technique a suite of test data is constructed and used to test the program. When the program performs satisfactorily on the test data, mutant versions of the program are concocted, containing deliberate bugs.

Now here comes the crunch. The test data is input to the mutant programs. If any of the mutant programs is able to reproduce the same output as the (notionally) correct program, the test data is inadequate. It cannot discriminate between a good and a bad program. The test data must then be improved so that it rejects the mutant programs. The performance of the correct program on the improved suite of test data gives us a measure of confidence in the program.

Exercise 4.5

Devise a set of test data for a routine which takes as input two dates and outputs the number of days between them.

4.3 Exception Handling

We have made reference to situations where program execution may be aborted on encountering an error. This is not always the best way of coping with the error situation. Semantic errors are predictable in nature. For example, every array access must be viewed as a potential hazard of subscript out of range. If a programmer introduces a new structure into his program, such as a vector, queue or tree, he should be aware of possible error situations which could arise. Programming in anticipation of errors, rather than hoping they will not happen, is known as **defensive programming**. A program which not only handles expected situations—that is, valid data—well, but also includes procedures for handling unusual situations, is said to be **robust**. The extent to which a programmer can protect a program from execution errors, expected or otherwise, depends on the facilities provided in the language. In other words, some languages provide better facilities for writing clear, robust programs than others.

In some situations the exception does not cause an irretrievable breakdown, and the correct action may be to ignore the input and call for new data. In others, the system will be unable to continue functioning, but certain housekeeping operations can usefully be performed. This has the beneficial effect that, when the system is restarted, it can begin operation with the minimum of disruption. Consider, for example, the system operated by a building society for its automatic teller machines. If a user keys in the wrong personal identification number (PIN), the system may give him another try. However, to prevent breaches of security, the number of tries may be limited, to three. Thus the program which controls the system must not only accept the correct PIN, but must also handle incorrect PINs in a satisfactory manner. After three incorrect tries, the program must specify a suitable action. In this case, the exception may be handled by invoking a procedure which retains the plastic card, on the assumption that it is being used by an unauthorised person. After retaining the card, the program returns to normal operation, awaiting a new card user. On the other hand, if the exception is a breakdown in power supply, the action to be taken is quite different. The program must arrange for a rapid closing of the files currently being accessed. Otherwise the files will not have the proper markers, and when the program attempts to open them on restart, it will find that they have been corrupted. Thus a fundamental aim of exception handling is to help maintain the integrity of the system in unusual circumstances. A program should not just abort on encountering an error—it should close down gracefully. A software system which 'lands softly' in case of a malfunction is said to be **fail soft**.

The proper handling of exceptions is particularly important for **embedded systems**, that is, programs which are part of the operational machinery of a piece of equipment. A simple example is the controller in a washing machine or a compact-disc player. More critical examples are programs which control aeroplanes, space capsules and nuclear reactors. Failure of the computer system in these cases would spell disaster. It is imperative that the software is capable of reacting properly to any fault which may arise. A system which is designed to react in this way is said to be **fault tolerant**.

Many languages make no explicit provision for handling error situations or exceptions. BBC BASIC has a useful procedure, invoked by the use of ON ERROR. This procedure allows defensive action to be specified when an exceptional situation arises. The ON ERROR facility is a catch all, but it can be refined in practice by using the code numbers of the different errors. (In fact it can even be used, quixotically, for handling syntax errors.) Standard Pascal makes no provision for exception handling. The best a programmer can do is to define specific procedures to handle exceptions, and use the normal decision constructs of the language to transfer control to the exception procedure as appropriate. Ada, on the other hand, has developed exception handling to a fine art, and provides the facility for named *exception handlers* to be invoked at any convenient point in a program.

Proper handling of exceptions has a highly beneficial effect in terms of program readability. When an exceptional situation has to be handled within a program, a condition must be tested and acted upon. The appropriate actions have nothing to do with the normal flow of the program—on the contrary, they are there precisely to handle an exceptional situation. Their presence in the body of the program code tends to clutter the program and obscure its intention. The availability of proper exception-handling facilities enables exceptions to be dealt with cleanly without cluttering the main program.

Activity 4.1

If your computer system runs UCSD Pascal, study the *exit* procedure which provides a method of aborting a currently active procedure invocation. Can you see its utility for handling exception conditions?

Summary of Chapter 4

Writing the program code is just one stage in a development process which encompasses many phases. The first phase begins with a feasibility study and an analysis of requirements. This is followed by a system specification, which is ideally a formal document. This specification is then subject to a design phase before being developed into program code. The development process must also produce adequate documentation, both for users and for subsequent maintenance.

It is in the nature of the normal operation of the digital computer that it is utterly precise and utterly predictable—a correctly instructed computer does not make occasional errors. But the program which controls the execution of the computer is written by human beings, and so is prone to human error. Only the most exacting procedures applied to program development can deliver reliable software.

Those who design and operate computer systems, whether on the hardware side or in the writing of program instructions, must keep uppermost in their minds the absolute precision with which the computer interprets what it is told. The digital computer operates with a rigid logic, and does not make allowance for error or inaccuracy unless it is specifically instructed to do so.

The style of program design may be influenced by the choice of language in which the program will be coded. Each language is better suited to some problems than to others. A poor choice of language allows greater scope for errors to creep in and remain unnoticed. A tool available to match the program code to its specification is program verification. Program components should also be tried out with a variety of suitably chosen test data to increase confidence in their validity.

Writing a program is a creative art, in the course of which several issues may need to be balanced. Efficiency of execution is an important issue, for both the systems developer and the programmer. The amount of time taken in executing a program, or the amount of memory occupied either by the program code or by the data structures created during execution, may possibly be excessive. Where cost considerations preclude the purchase of a faster processor or more memory, the efficiency of the program is a candidate for improvement. Readability of the program code is another important issue, and some trade-off between efficiency and readability may sometimes be called for.

If you ever have to design a program which sends out bills to customers, do not forget that a customer will not be impressed at receiving an invoice for £0.00. Yet a computerised billing system will regularly churn out such invoices unless instructed otherwise. The computer is accurate. The computer is fast. But the computer is completely devoid of common sense. Defensive programming is the art of anticipating possible error situations. Exception handling is the name given to special procedures which are activated when special situations (including error situations) arise. Ada makes provision for handling exceptions within programs without interrupting the normal program flow.

Answers to Exercises

4.1 (a) The language should be capable of describing the data structures and problem-solving methods relevant to the specification, using the vocabulary of the real-world problem.

(b) The language should produce readable programs (using appropriate control structures and meaningful names). The language should include facilities (such as data typing) which minimise the occurrence of errors and help locate any which do exist.

(c) The programming staff may not be familiar with the ideal language. Compilers for the ideal language may not be available for the hardware.

In addition, if the programmers are already maintaining one or more software systems in some language, it may not be wise to install a new system written in a different language, as this may cause confusion during maintenance.

4.2 There is no need to calculate $LN(i/4) - i/8$ twice during each traversal of the loop. The following is faster (and clearer).

```
FOR i = 1 TO m
  term = LN(i/4) − i/8
  x = i/2 + term
  y = i/3 + term
NEXT i
```

4.3 Program efficiency is highly desirable, but is not as important as *program correctness*, which is paramount. There is no point in executing an incorrect program efficiently. Additionally, program efficiency may justifiably be downgraded in the interests of *readability* (so that the program can be maintained more easily) and *programmer efficiency* (it may not be worth the programmer's effort to achieve the saving in execution time).

4.4 The error is caused by calling PROCexample with parameter 0. The programmer must decide between two methods of handling the error. One possibility is to trap the error inside the procedure (covering all calls to the procedure). The other alternative is to ensure that the parameter is non-zero in the calling program each time the procedure is called. This decision may well depend on the nature of the program. If the first alternative is chosen, the condition may be trapped within the procedure by inserting the following code at the beginning of the procedure.

```
1015 REM *** error condition
1020 IF n = 0 THEN PRINT "Illegal input parameter to PROCexample"
     : ENDPROC
```

4.5 The following pairs of dates are suggested:

> 1 Jan 1990, 20 Jan 1990 : 19 days   {two dates in same month}
> 1 Feb 1990, 15 Apr 1990 : 73 days   {different months}
> 31 Mar 1990, 5 Apr 1991 : 370 days {whole year}
> 1 Jan 1992, 5 Apr 1992 : 95 days   {leap year}

Further Exercises

1. (a) Define the terms *low-level language* and *high-level language*.
   (b) Working with an engineering research company, a programmer will be using scientific language as the main high-level programming language. Describe five features of a scientific language which make it appropriate in this application area.
   (c) Both FORTRAN and COBOL were devised in the 1950s. Despite the emergence of superior programming languages they are still the most common high-level languages used in industry and commerce today.
       Suggest reasons why a significant proportion of the computing industry has been reluctant to change to more effective programming languages.
       (JMB—1986)

2. Suggest a suitable choice of programming language for weather forecasting software. Identify features of your chosen language which help (a) the programmer (b) the user of the software.

3. Programs written in assembly language can be made more efficient than those written in a high-level language. Why do we need the latter?

4. You have written a program which reads in three positive numbers, which represent the lengths of three lines. The program prints out YES or NO depending on whether the three lines can form a triangle. Give three sets of test data which you would use on this program. State the expected result for each set and say why you chose that set.
   (JMB—1981)

5. You have been given a routine which will

   (a) read and store a list of names
   (b) read a name and reply YES or NO depending on whether the name is in the list or not.

   Give, with reasons, the test data you would use to check this routine.
   (JMB—1984)

6. Consider the testing of a newly developed program that has a modular structure.

    (a) Explain what is meant by a program module.
    (b) Give the reasons why modules are usually tested separately.
    (c) Describe how the modules may be tested separately.
    (d) Even though the testing of all individual modules has been successful, the complete program may fail. Explain how this may occur.
    (e) This program is part of the applications package for a computer system to replace a manual system. A stage in the testing of the package is to run two systems together, in parallel, using the same, live data. What, in your opinion, are the aims of this stage of testing?

(ULSEB—1986)

7. When a manual system is being replaced by a computerised system, the Systems Analyst designs the computer based system and is then responsible for the changeover.

    (a) The Systems Analyst will describe the computerised system using system flow charts. What information will be presented in these flow charts?
    (b) Describe the essential features of three methods of changeover which the Systems Analyst might employ.
    (c) Documentation will have to be provided for the programmers, the users who have no programming skills, and the operations staff. Describe the different documentation which will have to be provided for each of these three groups of people.
    (d) After the changeover has been effected, what further responsibilities does the System Analyst have for the system?

(ULSEB—1987)

8. (a) Three desirable properties of a program are that it should be *well structured*, *readable*, and *maintainable*. By referring to a high level language with which you are familiar describe how a programmer can achieve these aims.
    (b) Different high level languages are designed for scientific commercial and educational applications. For *two* of these application areas, name a language and describe the features which make it particularly suitable for use in that application area.

(ULSEB—1987)

Further Reading

L. Antill and A. T. Wood-Harper, *Systems Analysis*, Heinemann, London, 1985. A very readable introduction to the subject; the most relevant parts are Chapters 4 and 8–11.

5 Hardware

The study of computing is the study of information processing. We have, at some length, investigated the analysis of problems in information processing and the design of solutions. Our investigations have been guided by the techniques available in programming languages on present-day computers. We have mentioned briefly the role of the electronic digital computer in the execution of programs, but it will not have escaped your attention that a program is merely a fully specified design, which could be executed equally by a team of human information processors.

Our aim in this chapter is to give you an understanding of the hardware constituents of the digital computer. There is an enormous range of computer hardware. The small microcomputers often found in homes and schools typically retail at under £500, operate at a speed of about one million instructions per second, and may have a small random-access memory of 32 kilobytes. At the other end of the scale, the CRAY-2 supercomputer used by the United Kingdom Atomic Energy Authority cost about £13 million, executes about 1700 million instructions per second, and has a 2 gigabytes of *random-access memory* (1 gigabyte =1 million kilobytes). Between these two extremes there are minicomputers and mainframes, not to mention the new breed of superminis. While these computers differ in size and in their range of application, many of the principles we discuss are applicable across most of the range.

To set the scene, this chapter begins with an overall view of the hardware components which make up a computer, and the manner in which they interact. This is followed by a discussion of the operation of the *central processing unit*, and how the individual program instructions are executed. We then consider the arrangement of *memory* within a computer. In section 5.4 we discuss the interface with the remaining components of a computer, the *peripheral devices*.

After the broad picture has been given, we look at some of the components in more detail. In section 5.5 we introduce *logic circuits*, which are the fundamental building blocks from which a computer is constructed. We then look, in the final sections, at the main types of input and output devices through which the computer maintains communication with the world at large.

5.1 The Main Processor

The fundamental design of any program contains the sequence

source data → process → results

The design of the hardware follows a similar pattern, namely

input → process → output

The hub of all activity is the *main processor*, which performs the processing and also contains a working store of information. Input and output are handled through *peripheral equipment*.

There are two possible configurations of the hardware, as shown in figure 5.1. The arrows show the direction in which data flows. The input unit converts data from human-understandable to computer-recognisable form, while the output unit performs the reverse role. Much data remains stable over periods of time and may therefore be held in computer-recognisable form on **backing storage** (usually a magnetic medium). The backing storage may, like the working store, hold data of any kind—including programs and procedures held either as text or in internal format.

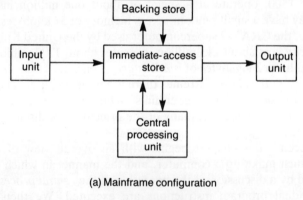

(a) Mainframe configuration

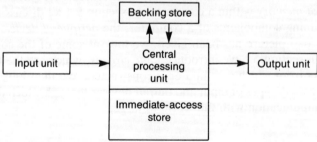

(b) Alternative arrangement for microcomputers and minicomputers

Figure 5.1 Computer hardware configuration

von Neumann Architecture

Our discussions of the inner workings of the computer assume the conventional arrangement, or *architecture*, attributed to the twentieth-century mathematician John von Neumann, who described it in 1945 in the design document for a computer to be called EDVAC. This architecture displays two fundamental features. Firstly, both the stored program and the data on which it operates are held in memory as bit patterns. Secondly, the central processing unit (CPU) executes instructions in sequence, one at a time, unless control is specifically passed elsewhere. These two features have had a fundamental influence on the development of programming during the past three decades. In this design, the CPU is unable to distinguish which bit patterns in storage are program instructions and which are data—the distinction is entirely by context, and it is up to the programmer to ensure that no confusion arises.

In recent years other computer architectures have been developed. The pipeline processor, which can evaluate expressions efficiently, is a minor variant. A number of supercomputers are now available, using two or four processors to share the processing load. The ICL Distributed Array Processor has a matrix of subsidiary processors which carry out identical operations in parallel. But the most revolutionary are the data flow architectures which are driven by data requirements rather than the control sequence underlying the conventional machine. These interesting developments must be left on one side as we study the von Neumann machine.

The main processor of a von Neumann computer consists of a **central processing unit** with associated registers, and a high-speed working store which is often called the **main memory**. A detailed discussion of the main memory is deferred until section 5.3. We shall now take a look at the operation of the central processing unit.

The central processing unit functions by extracting program instructions from the main memory, decoding them and executing them correctly. To achieve this the CPU consists of two parts, the *control unit* and the *arithmetic-logic unit*. These units are complex logic networks. The operation of the processor consists of a continuous sequence of *machine cycles*, each commencing with an action by the control unit. In order to assist the smooth running of the CPU a bank of *registers*, which can hold bit patterns, is used for both housekeeping data and for the program data which participates in the current instruction.

The CPU, registers and memory are linked together by parallel data links. The correct functioning of all the components is ensured by a regular *clock pulse* which initiates transfers of data. A machine cycle may last for two or more clock pulses. This is known as **synchronous** operation. In an asynchronous processor, it is not necessary to wait for the beginning of a clock pulse before commencing another register transfer. However, asynchronous processors require expensive components to detect when the previous transfer is completed, in the absence of a regular clock pulse.

Lines of communication

The various components of the processor require to be linked so that they can communicate with each other. Data transfer between components takes place along bundles of lines called **highways** or **buses**. Data is transferred in *words* and the size of a word is determined by the number of lines in a highway. Highways in some older microcomputers consist of 8 lines; this is a convenient word size because it can be used to transfer a *byte*, which is a common unit for data storage. However, most microcomputers and minicomputers nowadays use a four-byte word (32 lines), whereas in a mainframe the highways may have 64 lines or more. In some CPUs, there is a separate highway between each pair of components. To simplify the wiring, however, there is frequently a main highway or **data bus** along which all data signals pass; individual components are connected via local highways to the data bus. When data is to be transmitted one component is selected as *bus master*, and one or more other components are selected as *bus slaves*; at the next clock pulse the contents of the bus master are transmitted to the bus slaves.

Access to the memory is via a selection mechanism which selects a chosen address. The address is a signal pattern which must be able to distinguish all the memory cells. Those components between which whole addresses need to be transferred are connected by the address highway, or **address bus**. It is not necessary for an address to be the same length as a normal word. In this case the address bus will have a different width from the data bus.

Some components have more than one output. The mechanism which enables a particular output to be selected is controlled by one or more additional signals which are input to that component. These signals are transmitted along individual lines called *control lines*. Another example of the use of control lines is in multiplexers. A **multiplexer** is a logic component which has several input highways and one output. The signal pattern from just one input is placed on the output highway; this input highway is selected by a control signal on a control line. Control lines are also used to select the bus master and bus slaves when data has to be transmitted within the CPU.

In a shared bus system a single highway is used by data, addresses and control signals. This may mean that for some purposes the full width of the bus is not used.

Storage elements

The smallest atom of information in a computer is a **bit**; the lenght of a word is the number of bits in the word. A bit is like a digit except that, since 'digital' computers can distinguish only two states, a bit can take only two possible values—0 and 1. A couple of examples will illustrate how bit patterns can be used to code information. A light switch is a two-state device, being either on or off, so its state can be represented using a single bit. The four states of a traffic signal—red, amber, green, red & amber—cannot be represented by a single bit, but a pair of bits will do, such as 10, 01, 00, 11. The state of a bank of microswitches—often found on computer terminals and printers to control the transmission speed—can be represented by a bit pattern, as shown in figure 5.2. In practice, memory is usually organised in **bytes**, that is, logical groups of eight bits each.

Programs and the data they operate on are held as bit patterns in the *immediate access store*, or memory, of the computer. Unlike the logic networks of the CPU, whose function is to produce an output which responds to the most recent set of inputs, memory has a storage function. Each memory cell stores a value which can

1 0 0 1 1 0 1 1

Figure 5.2 A panel of microswitches and the corresponding bit pattern

be copied, or **read**, by the CPU. The contents of a memory cell change only when a **write** operation takes place.

The smallest storage element is a *flip-flop*. This can hold a single bit, whose value is represented by a voltage level on the output wire. This value does not change immediately when the input value is changed. The output only changes (in response to the input) when a special control signal is given along a third wire, the *strobe*. A storage element which holds a binary word is called a **register**. A byte wide register has eight data inputs, eight data outputs and two control lines. The control lines are used to select reading, writing or storage mode. In the case of a read, the contents of the eight inputs are simultaneously placed in the register. Likewise a write operation activates the eight outputs simultaneously. The register is therefore a **parallel** device.

Registers

The central processing unit requires a small number of special registers for specific tasks. Since there are only a few registers, the address of each is short. If, say, there are 16 registers, four bits are enough to hold a unique address. So, although registers are, in principle, just storage cells, they are faster to access than cells in main memory, because a fast address decoder can be used to choose a register. In addition, they are usually made using a more advanced (and more expensive) technology for maximum speed of access.

The table below indicates some registers and their functions.

Name of register		Bit pattern held in register
MAR	memory address register	address of memory cell to be accessed
MBR	memory buffer register	data (read from/to be written to) memory
IR	instruction register	current instruction code
PC	program counter	address of *next* instruction
AC	accumulator	data used in current instruction
PS	program status register	flags set by previous instructions

The registers in the first group are used by the control unit for housekeeping duties, and are not accessible to the programmer. The second group of registers contain data on which program instructions operate. The accumulator (in which results of instructions are accumulated) is not a unique register—there may be several accumulators in a CPU.

The address held in the **program counter** is automatically advanced during each cycle. This arrangement ensures sequential execution of instructions; it is known as *automatic sequence control*. If instructions have a fixed length (say two bytes), the program counter can be incremented accordingly while the instruction is being fetched. Where instructions have varying lengths, the amount by which the program counter is incremented depends on the current instruction. Incrementation of the program counter is performed by a special hardware unit, which functions in parallel with the arithmetic-logic unit, thus saving time. Jumps to another part of the program are achieved by instructions which reset the contents of the program counter.

The **program status register** holds a collection of bits or *flags* describing the status of the program; some of these bits are used as codes to indicate the presence or absence of some condition. Thus one bit in PS will be the *carry* condition code, which will be set to 1 if the last arithmetic operation executed by the arithmetic-logic unit lost a carry bit 'off the end', and to 0 otherwise. The carry code is frequently the rightmost bit of the PS. Other condition codes indicate whether the last result was negative, zero or overflowed (that is, a number too large to be held in a word). When a flag has the value 1 it is *set*; otherwise it is *not set*. A flag may also be set to indicate whether interrupts are enabled or disabled.

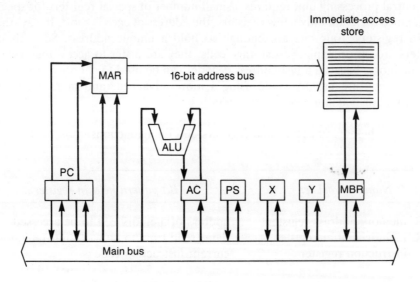

Figure 5.3 Schematic architecture of the 6502 processor

Figure 5.3 illustrates schematically how some of these components are arranged in a small microprocessor, such as the 6502. All highways are eight lines wide except the address highway. Note how the program counter is a double-byte register.

5.2 How the Processor Works

In the first section of this chapter we described the main processor, giving a fairly detailed description of the various components which make up the CPU. The essential feature of the von Neumann processor is the particular way in which it works. The program counter addresses the memory cell which contains the next instruction to be executed. At the beginning of each cycle, the control unit *fetches* the instruction from memory, moves it to the instruction register and decodes it. The arithmetic-logic unit then *executes* the instruction, which may entail fetching data from other memory cells.

The fetch–execute cycle

It has already been stated that the CPU operates in a sequence of cycles. Each cycle commences with the control unit fetching a bit pattern from the memory cell currently addressed by the program counter and copying it to the instruction register. While this is taking place, the program counter is automatically advanced to address the next memory cell. This ensures that, unless overridden by the current instruction, the next cycle will begin by fetching the next instruction in sequence. In the next phase of the cycle the control unit decodes the bit pattern in the instruction register. This then causes the arithmetic-logic unit to perform specific operations which may involve data in the accumulator and in one or more specified memory cells. The control unit then starts another cycle. It is worth noting that the basic control structure of our programming style, the sequential execution of statements, is closely connected with the automatic sequence control of the von Neumann computer.

The fetch and execute phases of the cycle may both require memory accesses. Since memory is not a register, it is worth examining how transfers to and from memory are implemented. For every memory access, the memory address register and the memory buffer register come into play. First, the selected memory address

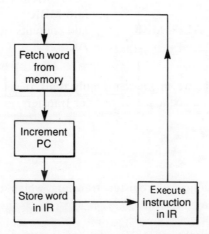

Figure 5.4 The fetch–execute cycle

is placed in MAR. Then the memory cell is accessed (using the built-in address selection mechanism). In the case of a memory read operation the contents of the selected cell are copied into the MBR; for a memory write operation the reverse happens. The memory buffer register is so called because it acts as a buffer between the memory and the CPU. In practice, all memory accesses are treated as transfers to and from MBR. The only difference between MBR and other registers is that MAR must be set in advance of each use of MBR.

This may be illustrated by the following schematic description of the register transfers that take place during the fetch phase. Note carefully line 3: every transfer from memory must include this line.

1. MAR ← PC   :   load the contents of PC into MAR
2. PC   ← PC + 1 :   increment PC
3. MBR ← c(MAR) :   load the contents of the memory cell
                         addressed by MAR into MBR
4. IR   ← MBR   :   load the contents of MBR into IR

A detailed description of what happens next depends on the particular instruction which is to be executed. For example, in the case of an add instruction, the instruction word will contain an indication of what is to be added. (In an 8-bit machine it is necessary to use a two-word instruction for operations such as add—the location of the number to be added is determined by fetching the next word from memory.) Suppose the required operation is to add the contents of memory cell 100 to the contents of the accumulator. The following is a description of the sequence of register transfers.

1. MAR ← 100   :   load the number 100 into MAR
2. MBR ← c(MAR)   :   load the contents of memory cell
                          100 (currently addressed by MAR)
                          into MBR
3. AC   ← AC + MBR :   add contents of MBR to contents of
                          AC

It is evident that what we might reasonably think of as a single instruction is actually implemented as a sequence of register transfers.

Exercise 5.1

Describe the sequence of register transfers which execute the following instruction:

add 24 to the contents of location 60 and store the result in location 60.

Servicing interrupts

After the completion of the execute phase, the cycle recommences with the fetch phase, using the new address now held in the program counter. In the normal course of events, the operation of the CPU consists of an uninterrupted sequence of fetch–execute cycles. However, there are circumstances in which the normal sequence of events must be suspended. This may happen, for example, in connection with the use of peripheral equipment.

When data is transferred to an output device or from an input device, an *interrupt* signal is sent to the main processor to indicate the end of the transfer. This interrupt initiates a break in routine, as a result of which the main processor engages in certain housekeeping duties associated with the data transfer, and checks that the transfer has been performed successfully. After the interrupt has been serviced, execution of the interrupted program continues.

An interrupt is detected by a signal on a special control line, the *interrupt line*. The interrupt is serviced by saving the contents of all the current registers in predetermined locations and loading special values to handle the interrupt. These special values are configured into the hardware. In particular, the program counter is loaded with a special value, which consequently causes the next fetch–execute cycle to commence the *interrupt service routine*. This routine must be written so that its final action is to restore the saved values in the registers. In this way the original computation can continue where it left off.

An interrupt cannot be serviced in the middle of a fetch-execute sequence. When an interrupt is signalled, it must wait for service until the end of the current execute phase. The interrupt service routine can then be entered before the beginning of the next fetch phase.

Microcode

The set of machine instructions which are available on a particular computer is called its *instruction set*. In traditional CPU construction, the execute phase is controlled by the instruction decoder. This component is a hard-wired logic network which interprets the instruction currently held in the instruction register. The larger the instruction set of a machine, the more complex is the instruction decoder required.

Nowadays, most computers have a lower level of **microinstructions**, which carry out specific sequences of register transfers. Each machine instruction is interpreted as a particular sequence of microinstructions, by means of a **microprogram** held in a special high-speed area of memory, the **control store**. The microprogram determines the instruction set of the processor.

Microprogrammed processors are a little slower than hardwired processors, because of the extra level of microinstruction accesses which take place. Against this, they are cheaper and more flexible. The saving in cost arises from the reduced amount of hardwiring necessary and the fact that the same hardwired components can be used in a family of processors, generating economies of scale. Each individual processor design in the family has its instruction set determined by its microprogram.

Machine instructions

A computer is operated using a stored program which is a sequence of instructions; each instruction is an atomic operation of the processor, and is performed in a single fetch–execute cycle. Instructions and data are held in memory cells. In addition to specifying an operation, an instruction must specify the addresses of the cells whose contents participate in the operation. An instruction is therefore divided into several *fields*. The first field contains a binary number called the **operation code**. Each machine instruction (such as addition) has its own operation code. The remaining fields are *address fields*.

Strictly speaking, an instruction may require three addresses. For example, consider the high-level statement.

$$C = B + A$$

This could be achieved by a single machine instruction whose operation code specifies addition. This instruction is performed on the contents of cells numbered A and B, with the result being stored in cell C. It is therefore called a *three-address instruction*. A processor which executes instructions in this format is called a *three-address machine*. On such a machine, an instruction which does not need all three address fields is executed by ignoring one or two address fields.

In practice, the result of the current instruction may overwrite one of the values which participated in the instruction. This immediately enables one of the address fields to be dispensed with. For example, the *two-address* addition instruction, which may be written

ADD A, B

is understood to mean: add the contents of cells A and B and store the result in cell A.

Some processors go further than this. By using registers to hold temporary values, they dispense with the need to access memory cells more often than necessary. The judicious use of registers allows instructions to be specified with less than two addresses. Thus, addition can be performed using the *one-address* instruction.

ADD N

which adds the contents of cell N to the number in the accumulator, and stores the result in the accumulator. Of course, if two forms of the add instruction are available in the same processor, they must be represented by different operation codes, as they correspond to different machine instructions.

Processors are sometimes designed to execute instructions with more than one address format. Thus the 6502 processor, a one-address machine, can also handle *zero-address* instructions. A large family of minicomputers has been designed around the PDP-11 processor, a two-address machine. The PDP-11 does, however, have a number of one-address instructions which it can handle.

Instructions may be classified into three or four types. *Transfer instructions* move data between the accumulator (or an index register) and the main memory. Instructions which read from memory are called *load* instructions; those which write to memory are called *store* instructions. In some processors, the ports for input and output are given addresses as though they were addressable locations in memory. Input is then achieved by loading the contents of an input port, and outport by storing at the address of an output port. This is called **memory-mapped input/output** and avoids the need for a special class of instructions to handle input/output. With **direct input/output**, on the other hand, the instruction set includes a separate class of *input/output instructions*: in this case, memory addresses are not used to identify input/output ports. *Computational instructions* include those which perform arithmetic and logical operations on data (using the arithmetic-logic unit), and those which compare data for equality.

The scheme for machine instructions described so far can implement a sequential program only. There is no means yet for implementing the high-level control structures of programming languages. These are implemented by *control instructions*, which transfer control to another part of the program. A control instruction is implemented by storing a new address in the program counter.

The simplest control instruction is an unconditional jump; as its name implies, it does not depend on any condition or situation. Jumps are often made contingent upon particular conditions. These conditions are usually indicated by the values of flags in the program status register. A conditional jump adjusts the address in the program counter provided a particular flag is set.

Stack processors

Some processors are designed as zero-address machines. With this arrangement, computational instructions act on a special bank of registers, arranged as a *hardware stack*. There are two one-address instructions: *push*, which retrieves the contents of a memory address and loads it on top of the stack, and *pop*, which stores the contents of the top of the stack at a given address in memory. A *stack pointer* keeps track of the current top of the stack to ensure that push and pop instructions access the correct register in the stack. The stack pointer is updated to the new value of the top of the stack after each push and pop is executed.

All the other instructions are zero-address instructions which operate on the contents of an appropriate number of locations at the top of the stack. For example, to add two numbers requires the following instruction sequence:

    push first number onto stack
    push second number onto stack
    add top two numbers on stack, replacing them by the result
    decrement the stack pointer
    store at required address

Exercise 5.2

Which group of instructions can be used to make an explicit change in the value of the program counter? Which other instructions change the value of the program counter?

5.3 Memory

We now turn our attention to the computer's working store, or memory. Computer memories are vast collections of storage elements or *memory locations*. It is convenient to think of each storage element as holding one byte (eight bits), although in practice a single element may hold two, four or more bytes. There are several different technologies for building memories, and each has its uses in particular applications. In general, the greater the speed of data transfer the technology can provide, the more it costs per byte. Thus, when a large memory capacity is required, it is necessary to trade off some speed. Typically, a computer installation will provide two or more levels of memory.

Immediate access store

Transfers of data between the main memory and the CPU must take place at speeds commensurate with the high processing speeds attainable by the CPU. The basic unit of data transfer is the *word*—a single word of data can be transferred between the CPU and a register in main memory at a time. The time taken for this transfer is called the **access time** of the memory. A typical access time is one microsecond (= 10^{-6} second) but on the most powerful computers the access time is less than 10 nanoseconds (1 microsecond = 1000 nanoseconds). These speeds are commensurate with the working speeds of other processor components; a more accurate description of the main memory is therefore the **immediate access store** (IAS). All data transfers to and from the CPU take place via this immediate access store.

The size of the immediate access store may occasionally be 32K words (or even less) in a very small micro, and anything from 512K to 4096K words in a mainframe. The K here (for kilo or thousand) actually stands for 1024.

Direct comparison of the size of two computers by comparing the number of words in the immediate access store is somewhat misleading because of the variety of word lengths used in different computers, as seen in the table below.

Computer	*Word length*
home micro	8 or 16 bits
personal computer	16 or 32 bits
VAX-11 minicomputer	32 bits
mainframe (IBM)	32 bits
mainframe (CDC)	60 bits
transputer (Inmos)	32 bits

The IAS of most present-day computers is made up of a number of silicon chips each consisting of an array of 8K, 16K, 32K or 64K one-bit cells. Some chips are now being manufactured with a capacity of 256K bits, and work is now proceeding on the production of megabyte memory chips (1 megabyte = 2^{20} bytes = 8192K bits). In a mainframe or minicomputer each cell of a memory chip has its own address, and a word is made up of the corresponding cells in an array of memory chips. So 32 chips each of 64K bits would be used to provide 64K words of memory in a 32-bit computer. In microcomputers the cells in memory chips may be grouped physically into bytes, and each byte has its own address. With this arrangement, a 64K bit memory chip in an 8-bit word computer stores 8K addressable words.

The address of a memory location is itself held as a bit pattern within the computer. Within one byte, $2^8 = 256$ different patterns can be formed. So, using one byte to hold an address we could distinguish at most 256 different cells. This is too restrictive—we need to be able to access many more locations than this. The range of addresses which can be stored depends on the number of bits available; that is, on the width of the address bus and the size of the program counter. Many computers allow addresses to occupy four bytes. This provides 32 bits, yielding 2^{32} different addresses. We describe this by saying that using four bytes provides an *address space* of 2^{32} bytes = 4 gigabytes. In general, for a given number of address bits, the available range of addresses will be the corresponding power of two. Computer technology is therefore built round these numbers. (The Acorn BBC uses a 6502 8-bit processor, but addresses are held in 16 bits, allowing 64 Kbytes of memory to be addressed. This means that an address stored in the IAS occupies two bytes.)

$$2^0 = 2 \qquad 2^5 = 32 \qquad 2^9 = 512 \qquad 2^{13} = 8192$$
$$2^1 = 4 \qquad 2^6 = 64 \qquad 2^{10} = 1024 \qquad 2^{14} = 16384$$
$$2^2 = 8 \qquad 2^7 = 128 \qquad 2^{11} = 2048 \qquad 2^{15} = 32768$$
$$2^3 = 16 \qquad 2^8 = 256 \qquad 2^{12} = 4096 \qquad 2^{16} = 65536$$
$$1 \text{ kilo} = 2^{10} \approx 10^3$$
$$1 \text{ mega} = 2^{20} \approx 10^6$$
$$1 \text{ giga} = 2^{30} \approx 10^9$$

The addressing mechanism allows words in the IAS to be identified directly (without the need to step right through the memory, cell by cell, until reaching the desired word). This feature is usually described as **random access**. In practice, the term **random access memory** (RAM) is reserved for that part of the IAS which allows words to be written as well as read. RAM is usually constructed using metal oxide semiconductors. Usually *dynamic* RAM is used, whose contents are electric charges which leak away. Provided that the electric power is connected, their contents can be refreshed every millisecond or so. *Static* RAM does not need refreshing but it is more expensive and uses more power. Both kinds of RAM are *volatile*—when the electric power is disconnected their contents are completely lost. This is one reason why a backing store is needed in addition to the immediate access store—to save data during periods of disconnection.

Permanent data is kept in the **read-only memory** (ROM) section of the IAS; as its name implies, the contents of the ROM can be read, but the ROM cannot be written to. The contents of the ROM are *burnt in* during manufacture, providing a fixed sequence of bytes. A ROM is therefore something of a halfway house between hardware and software. An important use for ROMs, in computers of all sizes, is for the start-up routine, or *bootstrap*, which gets the computer into operation. The control store found in many computers is a ROM which contains the microcoded instructions. In a mainframe, certain commonly used routines may be programmed on a ROM. Historically, the first ROM was pioneered by the Cambridge Mathematical Laboratory where the Edsac 2, built in 1959, included a 1K ROM. (A remarkable achievement at the time, 1 Kbyte of ROM is nowadays a miniscule amount.)

ROMs are much in evidence on the micro scene where they are frequently used for utility programs such as the *operating system* and *language processors*, which will be discussed in detail in chapter 10. For example, the 64K IAS of the Acorn BBC Computer includes a 16K ROM dedicated to the operating system and another 16K ROM for the BASIC interpreter (replaceable by any other language processor or dedicated program); the remaining 32K is available for use as RAM. However, on larger machines the utility programs are held on backing storage, to be loaded into main memory as required.

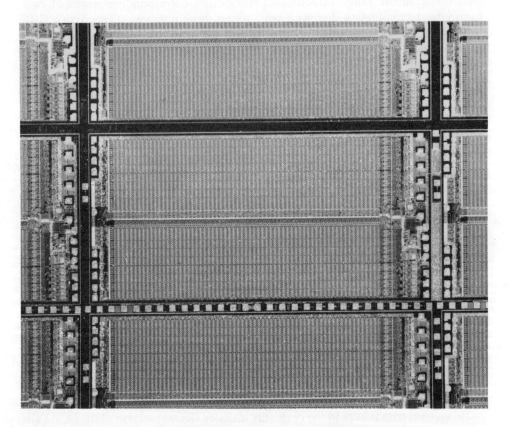

Figure 5.5 Photograph of RAM chips

In situations where the expense justifies it, specially written programs may be coded onto a special type of *programmable read-only memory (PROM)*. A blank PROM consists of cells of fuses, and the PROM programming device blows some of these fuses selectively to inscribe the desired program onto the PROM. With the rapid decrease in the price of ROM chips, is has even been suggested that software be distributed in this way—instead of a shop maintaining a stock of each ROM program it will hold a supply of blank PROM chips, and produce a programmed PROM from a catalogue!

Naturally, the ability to program a chip has led to a demand for PROM chips whose contents can be overwritten. The erasable programmable read-only memory (EPROM) uses ultra-violet light to restore its blank state. (This should be contrasted with RAM whose contents are changed by the CPU under software control).

Machine code

The format in which the instructions are held is strongly influenced by the word length of the processor, that is, the size of the registers. A machine instruction (including the address fields) occupies one word. While this is satisfactory for larger processors, in the case of eight-bit and sixteen-bit processors one word is hardly sufficient to hold one address, let alone the complete instruction. In such cases, the address to be referenced in memory is held in the word or words immediately following the instruction. The number of address fields is determined when the instruction is decoded.

By way of an example, figure 5.6 illustrates a section of memory in an eight-bit processor. The program counter (PC) points to the memory cell containing the instruction 10000101 which is the next instruction to be executed. As explained above, this instruction takes its address from the byte in the next memory cell (01110010). Suppose 10000101 is the machine code instruction 'store the contents of the accumulator in memory', where the location in memory is given by the address field. Then 01110010 is the destination address of the memory location in which the contents of the accumulator are stored.

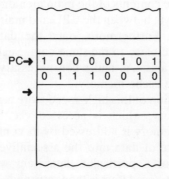

Figure 5.6 Three adjacent memory cells

Note that, in this example, the program counter must actually be advanced by 2 to be correctly positioned for the next instruction (as shown by the arrow). In general, the number by which the program counter must be advanced varies according to the number of bytes (or words) occupied by the instruction and its address fields.

To see an example of a three-byte instruction we shall first examine the method of addressing memory. Each byte can hold $2^8 = 256$ different bit patterns so, using one byte, it is possible to reference 256 different addresses. A memory with only this number of cells would not be of much use. Memory is therefore organised in pages. In an eight-bit machine, a *page* is a block of 256 consecutive memory cells; the IAS may then consist of up to 256 pages. A memory cell is then referenced using two bytes. The first, called the *low byte*, specifies the cell within the page while the second, called the *high byte*, specifies the page. It is clear now that an instruction which includes a full two-byte address occupies three byte-sized memory cells. To cope with this situation the program counter is not advanced until the instruction has been decoded, when the size of the increment in the program counter can be determined.

We note that both the program counter and the memory address registers must be large enough to hold an address; in the 6502 processor they are 16-bit registers.

Cache memory

The transfer of a byte of data between the CPU and the IAS, although very fast, is still slow compared with activities which take place within the CPU. Since access to the IAS forms a large part of the activity of the CPU, it is desirable to speed up such accesses. This may be done by interposing a small high-speed **cache memory** between the main memory and the CPU. The cache memory consists of, say, 16K registers in close proximity to the CPU. Access to cache memory is about ten times as fast as access to the IAS. In a typical mainframe with an IAS access time of 500 nanoseconds, the cache memory may be accessed in 50 nanoseconds. The increase in speed is due partly to the use of more advanced technology, which is too expensive to use for the whole IAS, and partly because the cache is small and close to the CPU. A section of main memory is copied into the cache memory so that high-speed memory accesses can take place. This is faster than accessing the main memory directly because the contents of the main memory are transferred in whole words; transfer of a single byte between the CPU and main memory takes as long as transfer of a whole word. Furthermore, once the data is in cache, repeated high-speed accesses can take place to the same data. Such repeated accesses are a common property of programs. As and when necessary, other sections of main memory are copied into the cache memory.

A particular use for a section of this high-speed store is as an **associative memory**. Unlike conventional memory, which is accessed via the address of a suitable memory cell, associative memory is addressed by its contents. The simplest mode of use is to load a sequence of data into the associative memory and perform a simultaneous comparison of a particular data item with the contents of the memory. The address of the stored item is then returned. This may be subsequently used to retrieve other data associated with the given data item.

cow	black
dog	spotted
cat	striped
elephant	African

By way of illustration, contents addressing enables a line of the array above to be selected by choosing *dog*, say, to yield *spotted*. With conventional addressing, this line would have to be selected by knowing its numerical address in memory. More generally, a long line of data could be held in main memory, with just a *key*, or identifying label, in associative memory. The address of the full data could be retrieved using contents addressing, as in the following table.

cow	14678
dog	45032
cat	35692
elephant	08493

Backing storage

The part of the immediate access store to which data can be written by the CPU, namely the RAM, suffers from a serious defect—it is volatile. Additionally it is also an expensive resource, although prices are continually falling as the technology advances. For these reasons it is both desirable and necessary to have a non-volatile, cheap and plentiful method of generating additional storage. This additional storage is known as **backing storage**. It is usually organised in a filing system much as one would organise information in an office. In an office filing system, related information of a given kind is held together in a file; the files are all kept in a filestore. In sophisticated environments, there may be a hierarchy of filing cabinets and directories for keeping the files well organised. Computerised filing systems are a major topic in their own right; we defer detailed discussion of backing storage and files until chapter 8.

The expense incurred in syphoning off the data overload onto backing storage is the increase in time taken to access this data. The actual access time for data on backing storage must take into account the fact that data held on backing storage is transferred in *blocks* of 64 or more bytes, multiplying the access time almost one hundredfold. In addition there is an overhead, because a sector of data on backing storage must first be written to IAS, and then accessed in IAS by the CPU.

5.4 Peripheral Operation

The term *peripheral equipment* includes all parts of a computer system outside the main processor and its immediate access store. Thus it includes the input and output devices as well as the backing store. These parts of the system are normally put into separate housing and are connected by cables to the main processor. (An exception to this is found with small microcomputers, which may function as an integrated unit, or at least have the keyboard mounted on the main processor housing.) A typical mainframe installation is shown in figure 5.7.

Figure 5.7 A mainframe computer installation (*Courtesy of the Civil Aviation Authority*)

Processor-controlled input/output

There are two main architectures for linking peripherals to the main processor, as was shown in figure 5.1.

The simplest method of transferring data between peripherals and the IAS is under the direct control of the CPU. When date is required by a program, a request signal is sent to the input device. A byte is then sent by the device to an *input register*, and a signal is issued to the CPU to confirm that the input has taken place.

The CPU then copies the data from the input register. Data may be input in this manner, byte by byte. A similar sequence of events governs output. The byte to be output is placed by the CPU in an *output register*. A signal is then sent to the output device to notify it that data is awaiting transfer. On completing the transfer, the output device responds with a signal. This mode of data transfer is called **processor-controlled** input/output.

Since the CPU operates at a much higher speed than the fastest peripheral devices, a scheme of byte-by-byte transfer is very wasteful of processor time. During input, for example, the CPU may have to wait after the receipt of each byte until the peripheral sends the next byte. Similarly, during output the CPU will have to wait before transferring a byte until the previous byte has been processed by the output device. In order to minimise the time wasted by the CPU, various *buffering* arrangements are used.

One possible arrangement is to allocate a reserved set of adjacent memory cells for the temporary storage of data during input and output. This area is called a **buffer**. During input, the buffer can be filled ahead of the CPU's need for data. When the CPU requires data which is already in the buffer, it can be retrieved rapidly at the processor's operating speed. This use of a buffer for keyboard input allows *type-ahead*. Similarly, during output a buffer can be filled by the CPU, with bytes being emptied out of the buffer at the speed of the output device.

Many peripherals are equipped with their own buffering arrangements: a buffer in the device can hold 256 bytes (or more), and is filled (or emptied) by a local microprocessor built into the device. Data to be sent to the main processor is accumulated in the *device buffer* and then sent in one packet or burst; likewise data from the main processor is sent in buffer-sized bursts to the peripheral which then extracts it from its buffer at its own working speed. This eliminates the need for a buffer area in main memory. In addition, since data is sent in packets there is a small saving in the time overhead, as there are fewer occasions when time is lost by the CPU waiting for the peripheral device to become ready.

Even with this arrangement, each time the buffer is emptied by the main processor there is an inevitable delay until it is refilled by the peripheral device. To smooth out the transfer a *double-buffering* arrangement is sometimes employed. When one buffer has been filled, it can be emptied by the processor. While this is taking place, a second buffer is filled. In turn, this buffer is emptied while the first is filled, and so on until the data transfer is complete.

Direct memory access

For mainframes, even the use of buffering is an insufficient answer to match the very high CPU speed. The main processor is completely freed from input/output tasks, which are handled by one or more **channels**. These channels are usually minicomputers which are directly responsible for handling the input/output of data between the IAS and peripheral devices. In this mode of transfer, which is called **direct-memory access**, it is necessary to steal a memory cycle from normal operations.

Backing storage is held on magnetic devices, which operate at higher speeds than input/output devices. It is therefore usual to employ separate channel arrangements for backing storage and for slower peripherals.

Exercise 5.3

What advantage is conferred by the use of

(a) channels
(b) buffers

for peripheral operations? What disadvantages might there be?

Interfacing

It should not be assumed that any peripheral can be linked to any computer. As indicated above, the arrangements by which data is transferred between the processor and the peripherals can vary. Furthermore, although information is communicated between devices in a binary code of electrical pulses, the underlying binary code varies between devices supplied by different manufacturers. Even the interpretation of voltage levels, such as high voltage pulse for 1, low voltage pulse for 0, varies between devices. Thus a computer system configuration can only include peripherals which are compatible with the main processor. It may sometimes be possible to obtain an adaptor or converter to mix different types of equipment.

When signals are sent between the main processors and the peripherals, some convention or protocol is required to establish the meanings of signals, the beginning and end of a message, and the speed of transmission. If extra bits are transmitted to provide a check on transmission errors, the protocol must specify the rule used (for example, parity check bit). For a two-way device it is necessary to distinguish between sending and receiving signals, and the main processor must also decide when to communicate with a peripheral device and which one to communicate with. The hardware which handles the transmission between a pair of devices is known as an **interface**. In practice, most interfaces are manufactured in accordance with one of several international standards. The standards also lay down the type of plug connections (for example 5-pin round connector, 25-pin D-connector) and how the wires should be connected to the pins. The wiring is crucial because there is no point in having standards for transmission if the wires in the plug and the socket do not match up.

The interface between the main processor and a peripheral handles not only the data signals, which carry the data between the processor and the peripheral, but also command signals from the computer, which control operation of the peripheral, and status signals from the peripheral device to the main processor, to indicate whether the device is ready for use.

Interrupt priorities

When data has to be transferred to an output device, say because the output buffer is full, a 'ready to receive' signal must be sent from the device to the CPU. Likewise, when an input device is ready to transfer data, it transmits a 'ready to send' signal. These signals reach the CPU as *interrupts*, and are serviced as soon as the current execute phase is completed.

If several devices need servicing simultaneously, a priority scheme is used to resolve the clash. Slow peripherals (character printers and low-speed terminal links) have the lowest priority, as the waiting time represents a low proportion of their operating time. Fast peripherals (magnetic disc and tape devices) are given a higher priority. The highest priority must be given to real-time devices, where data becomes lost after a certain time has elapsed. In process control, or data logging, the data which needs to be input will change after a while, so if the processor waits unduly before allowing the device to input its data, the information is lost and is overwritten by new data. Likewise if the output from the processor is controlling a fire sprinkler, then undue delay in switching it on may have disastrous consequences. The factor in deciding the relative priorities of real-time devices is the *crisis time*, within which the device must be activated.

Interrupts associated with devices can be disabled—while a high-priority device is being handled, interrupts from all devices with a lower priority are disabled. This ensures that, during an *interrupt service routine*, no interrupts will be accepted from lower priority devices, but interrupts can be accepted if they are sent by a higher priority device. The nesting of interrupts is achieved in much the same way as the nesting of subprograms. For example, the contents of the registers for the current routine can be saved on a stack while the higher priority interrupt is serviced.

Interrupts may also be generated by software. For example, an interrupt will be generated when a program requires some action, such as opening a file, to be carried out by another program. Software interrupts are discussed in chapter 10, in connection with operating systems.

5.5 Logic Circuits

To obtain a detailed understanding of how a computer system works, we shall concern ourselves next with the working of the processor. The CPU is made up of a collection of *logic circuits*, each composed of fundamental parts called *logic gates*. In this section we discuss the rules of logic which underlie the building of networks which perform the machine instructions inside the CPU.

Logic gates

Data flows through the processor as a stream of electronic pulses. These pulses are of two kinds, which may be represented by the symbols 0 and 1. A **logic gate** is a basic electronic component with a number of inputs, through which pulses arrive, and a single output through which pulses leave. The flow is synchronised so that a pulse arrives at each input of a particular component simultaneously. The output from a logic gate at any given instant is a *function* of the input signals at that instant. More generally, the CPU will contain complex components each with a large number of inputs and outputs. Such a component may be thought of as a network of logic gates which are connected so that the signals are carried from one to another.

These gates could be built from mechanical switches, in which case they would operate quite slowly, considering that a reasonable computation may involve millions of logical operations at this level. Since the 1940s three significantly different technologies have been used:

first-generation computers	(1945–1960)	thermionic valves
second-generation computers	(1960–1965)	transistors
third-generation computers	(1965–)	integrated circuits

Integrated circuits include a large number of transistors and all the associated circuitry which are etched, in multiple copies, onto the surface of a silicon wafer. These wafers are then cut up into individual *chips*. In **large-scale integration** (LSI) between 100 and 10 000 logic gates may be put into one chip; in **very large-scale integration** (VLSI) more than 10 000 logic gates are put into the same chip. Apart from the overhead of designing and tooling up for chip manufacture, the marginal cost of producing each extra chip is less than ten pence. It is obvious, therefore, how VLSI contributes to the production of high-powered chips with a price per logic gate of a tiny fraction of a penny.

Besides reducing the cost, VLSI enables higher processing speeds to be attained, as the distances between transistors are reduced to miniscule proportions. This has had an influence on the choice of technology for the manufacture of transistors. Previously, *bipolar* transistors were preferred because they respond faster than metal-oxide silicon (MOS) transistors. However, bipolar transistors suffer from a serious defect—they use more power and so generate more heat. This makes it necessary to take steps to cool devices built with bipolar transistors. With the advent of VLSI, the loss of speed is more than compensated for, so that applications using large numbers of transistors (especially memories) tend to be made using MOS technology.

Truth tables

The use of the terminology logic gates to describe the basic switching elements is no accident. The calculus of logical connectives (such as AND and OR) which we met in chapter 3 is closely analogous to the properties of logic gates. A logical expression consists of a number of conditions (which may be considered as inputs) which together form a compound condition (which may be considered as the output). There is actually an exact parallel between the *propositional calculus* (the algebra of logical expressions) and the functions of logic gates, which can be realised in terms of truth tables. This parallel was first propounded in 1938 by Shannon. Truth tables themselves define operations in a particularly simple mathematical system first formulated by the English mathematician George Boole in 1854. This system is known as *boolean algebra*. We shall study truth tables and the rudiments of boolean algebra to pave the way for an understanding of how logic networks are designed.

The meanings of the logical operators AND, OR and NOT can be fully exemplified by giving tables of values. In these tables a and b stand for statements (that is, they are variables in the terminology of programming languages) which can take one of two possible values—TRUE and FALSE. These values are denoted by T and F respectively.

a	b	a AND b		a	b	a OR b		a	NOT a
F	F	F		F	F	F		F	T
F	T	F		F	T	T		T	F
T	F	F		T	F	T			
T	T	T		T	T	T			

Truth tables for AND, OR and NOT

These truth tables define completely the meanings of the three logical connectives, beyond doubt. Truth tables can also be used to display the value of any logical statement. For example, exclusive OR (XOR), that is, a or b but not both, has the following table:

a	b	a XOR b
F	F	F
F	T	T
T	F	T
T	T	F

Exercise 5.4

Make truth tables for the compound conditions

(i) NOT (a AND b)
(ii) NOT (a OR b).

Exercise 5.5

Suppose a, b and c are statements representing conditions. Use logical connectives to construct an expression which is TRUE only when either a or b is TRUE (but not both) and c is FALSE. Give the corresponding truth table.

Boolean algebra

A **boolean algebra** is a mathematical structure with two elements (usually called 0 and 1), two binary operations (+ and .) and one unary operation ‾ , which are interrelated in a particular way. Before specifying how the operations are related to each other, let us remark that there is already a similarity with the propositional calculus which has two values (F and T), two binary connectives (OR and AND), and a unary operator (NOT).

NOT	$^{-}$
OR	$+$
AND	$.$
F	0
T	1

Correspondence between propositional calculus and boolean algebra

The rules of combination in boolean algebra are precisely those which can be proved to hold for the propositional calculus. What makes them interesting in mathematics is that there are several other examples of boolean algebras (besides the propositional calculus) and a wealth of results can be derived just by studying the basic properties. Here are ten fundamental equations of boolean algebra.

(1a) $a.b = b.a$ (1b) $a + b = b + a$ commutativity
(2a) $(a.b).c = a.(b.c)$ (2b) $(a + b) + c = a + (b + c)$ associativity
(3a) $a.(b + c) = a.b + a.c$ (3b) $a + (b.c) = (a + b).(a + c)$ distributivity

Equations (1), (2) and (3a) are quite familiar from arithmetic, but equation (3b) has a decidedly strange look about it. In fact, in boolean algebra the operators $+$ and $.$ are perfectly symmetrical with respect to each other, and close scrutiny of (3b) will reveal that it mirrors (3a) by interchanging the roles of $+$ and $.$.

(4a) $a.1 = a$ (4b) $a + 0 = a$ identity
(5a) $a.\bar{a} = 0$ (5b) $a + \bar{a} = 1$ complementation

Equations (4) have a familiar look about them, whereas equations (5) establish the unary operation $^{-}$ as complementation. By making the correspondence between boolean algebra and propositional calculus, it may be shown that the ten equations hold in the latter system.

Exercise 5.6

Use truth tables to verify that equations (5) hold in the propositional calculus, that is

a AND NOT a = F
a OR NOT a = T

Other properties of boolean algebras can be proved using truth tables or by applying the fundamental properties (1)–(5).

The following properties are frequently used.

(6a) $a.a = a$ (6b) $a + a = a$

(7a) $a.0 = 0$ (7b) $a + 1 = 1$

Proof

$$
\begin{aligned}
6a:\ a.a &= (a.a) + 0 & \text{using} & \ (4b) \\
&= (a.a) + (a.\bar{a}) & \text{using} & \ (5a) \\
&= a.(a + \bar{a}) & & (3a) \\
&= a.1 & & (5b) \\
&= a & & (4a)
\end{aligned}
$$

$$
\begin{aligned}
7a:\ a.0 &= a.(a.\bar{a}) & (5a) \\
&= (a.a).\bar{a} & (2a) \\
&= a.\bar{a} & (6a) \\
&= 0 & (5a)
\end{aligned}
$$

Properties (6b) and (7b) have similar proofs.

Some other useful properties of boolean algebras, which will not be proved here, are given below.

(8a) $a.(a + b) = a$ (8b) $a + (a.b) = a$ absorption

(9a) $\overline{(a.b)} = \bar{a} + \bar{b}$ (9b) $\overline{(a + b)} = \bar{a}.\bar{b}$ de Morgan's law

Augustus de Morgan, after whom the last two properties are named, was a comtemporary of Boole.

Design and simplification of circuits

The theory of boolean algebra has been introduced to provide a tool for the simplification of logic circuits. How many different types of logic gates do we require in order to enable all possible circuits to be built? On the basis of our experience with logical connectives we would expect to see three types of logic gates. The inverter, AND gate and OR gate are conventionally indicated by the symbols shown in figure 5.8.

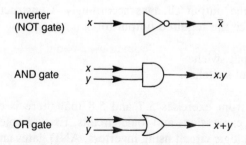

Figure 5.8 The fundamental logic gates

Exercise 5.7

Write down a boolean expression corresponding to the logic network shown in figure 5.9. (A split line sends the same input to more than one gate.)

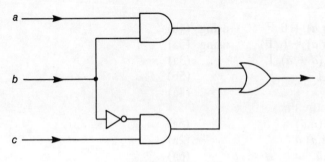

Figure 5.9

Exercise 5.8

A staircase light is controlled by two switches, one upstairs and one downstairs. A logic network is to be designed so that the light may be switched on or off by either switch. If *a* and *b* are boolean variables for the two switches which take values 0 or 1 when the corresponding switch is up or down, respectively, the boolean expression

$$(a.\bar{b}) + (\bar{a}.b)$$

will respond in the required fashion. Draw the required network.

Activity 5.1

If a light is to be switched from two locations, a pair of special light switches (known as two-way switches) is usually installed. This method cannot be extended to enable a light to be switched from several locations. However, using a logic network, as in exercise 5.8, it is possible to arrange for switching to take place at several locations. A separate input senses the position of each switch and the output changes accordingly. Construct boolean expressions which produce the required output for

(i) three input swiches
(ii) four input switches.

It is apparent from exercises 5.7 and 5.8 that there is complete equivalence between boolean expressions and logic circuits. Every boolean expression can be implemented as a logic circuit using inverters, AND gates and OR gates, and vice versa. Likewise it is possible to derive a truth table for any boolean expression.

What about the converse problem: given a truth table, can we write down a corresponding boolean expression (and hence an appropriate logic network)?

Consider the truth table for XOR.

a	b	a XOR b
F	F	F
F	T	T
T	F	T
T	T	F

Picking out the lines whose output is T (that is 1 in boolean algebra), we have

row 2: $\bar{a}.b$
row 3: $a.\bar{b}$

An output of 1 is required for either of these input terms, but in no other, so a XOR b corresponds to the boolean expression

$$(\bar{a}.b) + (a.\bar{b})$$

The corresponding logic network is shown in figure A5.8.

This method will always work for converting truth tables to boolean expressions, but when there are more than two variables, the resulting expressions tend to get clumsy. In these cases, the properties (1)–(9) of boolean algebra may be used to aid simplification.

The NAND gate

Another simplification tool is provided by the NAND gate, shown in figure 5.10. The NAND gate with inputs a and b implements the logic network for NOT $(a$ AND $b)$. In boolean algebra the symbol corresponding to NAND is the vertical stroke, $|$. Thus $a|b$ is equivalent to the boolean expression $\overline{(a.b)}$ which, by de Morgan's laws, equals $\bar{a} + \bar{b}$.

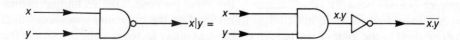

Figure 5.10 The NAND gate with two inputs

The definition of $|$ is summarised in the following two properties

(10a) $a|b = \overline{(a.b)}$ (10b) $a|b = \bar{a} + \bar{b}$

Exercise 5.9

Obtain simplified boolean expressions for the networks of NAND gates shown in figure 5.11.

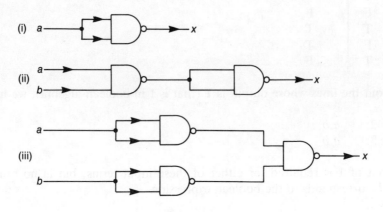

Figure 5.11

Exercise 5.10

Show that

$$(a|b) \mid (c|d) = a.b + c.d$$

The results of exercise 5.9 show that the logical connectives NOT, AND and OR can all be expressed in terms of NAND. This means that the basic logic gates for NOT, AND and OR can all be built using NAND gates. Since all logic networks can be constructed using these basic gates, it follows that any logic network can be built using NAND gates only. In principle it is possible to design a network in the ordinary way, and then replace each logic gate by the appropriate combination of NAND gates. In practice, though, it is almost invariably possible to design a simpler NAND network which achieves the same purpose. One technique, which we shall not describe here in detail, is to manipulate the boolean expression which corresponds to the logic of the network so that as many factors as possible are in the form $\overline{a.b}$ or $\overline{a} + \overline{b}$. These can be represented using NAND gates by virtue of property (10).

The result of exercise 5.10 yields a straightforward algorithm for obtaining a NAND network directly from a truth table. The technique is best illustrated by an example.

Consider the following truth table

a	b	
F	F	F
F	T	T
T	F	F
T	T	T

The corresponding boolean expression is seen to be $\bar{a}.b + a.b$. By virtue of exercise 5.10, this is equivalent to $(\bar{a}|b) \mid (a|b)$. We therefore first set up a NAND gate corresponding to each row with a T output, that is $\bar{a}|b$ and $a|b$; we then combine the outputs from these gates with another NAND gate, as shown in figure 5.12.

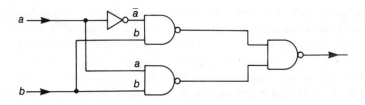

Figure 5.12 A complicated network for obtaining the output b!

Application of this procedure to a truth table may result in a requirement for a NAND gate with more than two inputs; in practice such NAND gates are available. The truth table for such a NAND gate has a T output in all rows *except* when all the inputs are T. A NOT gate can always be realised by splitting the input to a NAND gate but, in fact, a NOT gate is just a NAND gate with one input.

It is also possible to define a NOR gate, according to the rule

a NOR b = NOT (a OR b)

An analysis similar to the one above would reveal that any logic circuit could be built entirely using NOR logic.

Activity 5.2

Design and write a program which will accept as input a boolean expression and output the corresponding truth table. Extend the capabilities of your program

(a) to accept additional operators such as XOR and NAND, and
(b) to handle incorrectly formed expressions.

5.6 Keyboards, screens and printers

Having described at length the internal workings of the main processor, we now turn to look at the most common devices available for input and output. Without the human–computer (or computer–computer) communication achieved in this manner, we cannot obtain any benefit from the workings of the processor.

We shall consider first devices for input and output which allow for communication of character streams. In the next section we look at more sophisticated equipment which may be used for document input and for graphical and voice communication.

Visual display units

Communication with a mainframe computer, or with a minicomputer which supports multiple simultaneous users, is via an input/output unit called a **terminal**. Input is achieved using a keyboard which is very much like the keyboard of an electric typewriter. Instead of the keys activating a hammer, each key sends out a coded binary signal which is interpreted by the processor as a specific character. The part of the terminal which serves as the output device is a cathode-ray tube (just like a television screen) on which the output is displayed. The terminal contains a signal decoder which interprets each binary pattern output to it and displays the corresponding pattern on the screen. Since cathode-ray technology does not preserve the image on the screen, the terminal also includes a component to refresh the image so that it should not fade. A terminal of this description is called a *VDU* (visual display unit) or a *CRT terminal*.

A VDU screen is a versatile output device. Characters and symbols on the screen may be obliterated and overwritten. This allows the image on the screen to be edited and also to provide the illusion of motion. The current position on the screen (that is, the position at which the next output character will be displayed) is usually indicated by a flashing symbol, the *cursor*. The display on the screen is determined by an array of values, one for each character position on the screen. Each displayable character has a unique value associated with it.

Hard-copy terminals are less common nowadays; instead of a screen, these have a printer as the output device. Hard-copy terminals look almost exactly like electric typewriters. With the continual reduction in the price of screen-based terminal equipment, such terminals are now becoming obsolete. Since VDUs do not leave a permanent record, stand-alone printers are often attached for that purpose.

Communication between a computer and a terminal is usually in *echo* mode. This means that each keystroke does not directly produce a character on the screen or printer; instead the computer reflects each input signal as an output signal. On some computer systems the input is not echoed; in order to obtain an image the keyboard must be connected directly to the screen or printer.

Signals between the processor and the terminal travel along a single wire, as the cost of providing a byte-wide channel would be prohibitive. A bit pattern must therefore be transmitted in sequence or **serially**. The speed or serial transmission is measured in baud; with normal methods of transmission, 1 baud = 1 bit per second.

Figure 5.13 A screen terminal [ICL]

Characters are usually encoded as byte patterns, that is, using eight bits. To keep the identity of the separate bytes for a sequence of characters transmitted along a serial line, each byte is packed with one start bit and one or two stop bits. So each character transmitted usually requires ten or eleven bits.

VDUs can operate at speeds up to 19 200 baud, which is something like 1900 characters per second, significantly faster than anyone can read. It goes without saying that no one can type at this speed. VDUs are frequently operated at speed of 1200 or 2400 baud. A skilled keyboard operator may achieve a rate of four key depressions per second, and will not be kept waiting by the lowest transmission speed of 75 baud. A common arrangement is to set up a terminal to transmit (send characters) at 75 baud and receive at 1200 baud. This is described as a 75/1200 setting. Many printing terminals can print at 30 characters per second (equivalent to 300 bits per second), though some have buffers which can accept output transmitted at higher speeds.

Microcomputers for single users do not provide for communication via terminals. Instead, they are commonly built so that the keyboard (the input device) is either a separate unit wired into the processor or indeed the two are housed in the same unit. The normal output is directly to a *monitor* or screen whose display is under the control of a subsidiary processor. Microcomputers for domestic use provide an alternative output signal which can be displayed on a domestic television set.

Printers

Hard copy can be produced on stand-alone printers. *Character printers*, much like the printing unit of a hard-copy terminal, are frequently found on small systems where the volume of print required is not too great. Some small printers now available can print at speeds of up to 200 characters per second—equivalent to about 150 lines per minute. Bidirectional printers can print forwards or backwards along the line, so saving the time lag in returning to the beginning of each line; a small processor in the printer reorganises the character stream so that the characters appear on the page in the intended order. Signal transmission for stand-alone printers is often in **parallel** mode, along a highway which can be made using ribbon cable.

Character printers are mainly of two types—dot matrix and solid face. The dot-matrix printer typically has nine needles arranged vertically. Each character is produced on a notional grid of 9×7 positions—as the print head moves across the seven columns the appropriate needles are fired at the ribbon, producing an image of the character on the paper. This procedure is repeated across the line. In addition to the standard character set, the needles of a matrix printer can be actuated under program control to produce graphic layouts and oversize characters. Some matrix printers use a fine grid of 11×9 positions to produce a higher quality of print.

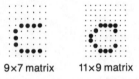

9×7 matrix   11×9 matrix

Figure 5.14 Character produced on a matrix grid

Solid face printers nowadays use a *daisy wheel*. This consists of a circle of plastic spokes with a suitable set of characters embossed on them (see figure 5.15). As the daisy wheel passes each position on the paper, it is rotated to the appropriate character position and a hammer imprints the character onto the paper. In view of the time required to rotate the daisy wheel, the top speed of these printers cannot match the fastest matrix printers. However, the print quality of a daisy-wheel printer exceeds by far what a matrix printer can produce. The character set is fixed, but an alternative character set can be obtained easily by changing the daisy wheel. Different wheels may be used to obtain different typefaces, such as italic. To mix characters from two different daisy wheels it is necessary to run through the whole document twice, with gaps left on the first run to be filled in on the second.

In larger installations where there are many users sharing a single printer, or where long reports are needed, a faster printer is used. **Lineprinters** operate at speeds between 600 and 3600 lines per minute. They do not necessarily print a whole line at a time, but their speed is achieved by having a separate print position

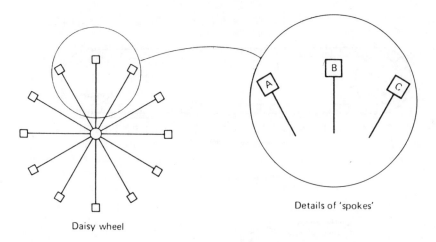

Daisy wheel

Details of 'spokes'

Figure 5.15 Daisy wheel

for each column of the page, avoiding the need for continual movement of the print head across the page.

Lineprinters usually operate at a width of 132 characters, and are equipped with 132 electromagnetic hammers, one for each print position. The characters are embossed on a chain or a barrel. In a chain printer, the character set is repeated several times on the chain which rotates continually across the line. A control mechanism keeps track of the position of the chain and operates the hammers when the required character is in position. When all the characters for a line have been printed, the paper is advanced. In a barrel printer, the whole character set is repeated 132 times. Thus all the 'A's required on a line are printed simultaneously, then all the 'B's, and so on. When the 'A' position on the barrel is once again in line with the hammer, the paper is advanced one line. The time taken to print a line using a lineprinter does not depend on the length of the line or the number of spaces between words.

Many printers are able to embolden text for emphasis. This is achieved by overprinting the relevant characters four times, using a slight offset on each occasion.

Modern reprographic techniques have allowed the development of non-mechanical **laser printers**, which can operate under computer control. The main speed constraint on these printers is the speed with which paper can be fed through, and they can print up to 20 000 lines per minute. They frequently look like photocopiers, with similar feed trays for standard paper sizes. Laser printers operate on the same basic principles as dot-matrix printers. However, unlike dot-matrix printers which are basically character printers, a laser printer is set up to print a whole page at a time. A page of print is made up as a pattern of dots. Even a moderately priced laser printer—about £2000, well within the reach of most offices—has a resolution of 300–600 dots per inch, giving very high quality print. Such laser printers are fitted with ROMs containing many different print fonts and

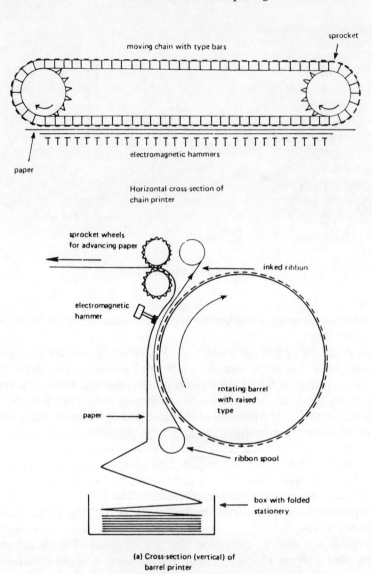

Horizontal cross-section of
chain printer

(a) Cross-section (vertical) of
barrel printer

Figure 5.16 (a) Chain and (b) barrel lineprinters

sizes, and can accommodate bold and italic characters with ease. Typically, these printers have a large buffer memory of, say, 2 megabytes.

The Linotronic laser printer is a professional-quality printing device with an output resolution of 2000 dots per inch. These high-quality printers have reversed the situation of the early 1980s when dot-matrix printers could not match the quality of screen displays. Nowadays, high-resolution screen technology seems to have reached its limit at about 70 dots per inch.

Microfiche and microfilm

The large volumes of output produced by lineprinters and page printers can cause a storage problem if they need to be kept for any length of time. A method of reducing the size of output that needs to be archived is to photograph the screen output. This can be done at high speed and the resulting photographs are stored on a $4 \times 5\frac{3}{4}$ inch (105×150 cm) plastic slide, called a *microfiche*. The usual format is 15×18 frames at 36 times reduction. An individual page or frame can be inspected using a *microfiche viewer*, a stand-alone piece of equipment which projects a single frame onto a screen. The final frame of the microfiche is used for an index, which can be consulted by the user for rapid access to the desired frame. Microfiche is a popular medium for the storage of large volumes of data, such as library catalogues, and the high-street banks use microfiche to give a daily summary of clients' accounts.

Figure 5.17 The AGFA microfiche reader–printer (*courtesy of AGFA-Gevaert Ltd*)

Many firms use *microfilm*—roll film produced by the same process as microfiche—to store details of components stocked. Motor car components stocked by main car distributors and gas cooker parts supplied by British Gas are two examples of the use of microfilm to store catalogues of spare parts.

The technique of photographic reproduction of computer output has also made an impact on the printing industry, where print is typeset by computer on film for the eventual production of books and newspapers. The use of film enables greater flexibility in page layout than is feasible using the older technology of metal type.

5.7 Specialised Input and Output Devices

We now turn our attention to some specialised devices which are used in particular applications.

Document readers

With keyboard input it is necessary to copy information which already exists in a form which cannot be read by machine; this is a prime source of errors. Besides, trained staff are needed for efficient usage of the keyboard. To avoid these problems, many forms of input devices have been designed to handle directly documents which can be completed by unskilled staff on **turnaround** documents, which have been pre-coded by machine. There are several methods of automatic data entry in current use, each with its attendant advantages in specific situations.

Magnetic Ink Character Recognition (MICR) is well-known because of its use on cheques. Each cheque is pre-printed with a serial number, the bank branch number and the client's account number, in a special stylised typeface, using a metallic ink. When a cheque comes into the bank for payment, the amount of the cheque is printed in the same fashion. The characters are printed in a clear zone at the foot of the cheque. The US standard typeface, known as E13B, is used on British and US cheques. This standard uses four special symbols in addition to the ten digits. (British postal orders are also coded for MICR; they are coded in the European standard typeface used by European banks on their cheques.)

The data on the cheques is input to the computer for processing by means of a special reader. The reader has two heads; one magnetises the metallic material in the characters, whereupon the other senses the shape of each character. Because this method of data entry depends on magnetic properties, the data is reasonably secure against defacing. MICR readers can handle over 2000 cheques a minute with a rejection rate of less than two per cent. However, despite these advantages, MICR is little used outside banking applications on account of the high cost of the specialised printers and readers.

Optical devices allow marks or characters written (or printed) on a document to be detected using reflection of light. **Optical Mark Reading** (OMR) requires the uses of standard documents which are pre-printed in pale ink with a set of fixed data or codes. A code is selected by making a pencil mark or blob in the appropriate square. The OMR reader interprets the documents according to the *position* of the marks on the paper. OMR is much beloved of examination boards who use it in objective tests where each question has a limited selection of answers (A to E, perhaps) which can be pre-printed on standard forms. These can then be used for any questions which match this simple answer format. OMR is also used for the recording of examination marks in the same manner, as well as for surveys and order forms. The amount of information that can be captured on a single form is limited, since a separate position is needed for each distinct response. It should be noted, too, that the forms have to be designed and printed for each application, so OMR is only appropriate in high-volume data applications. The users who fill in the forms require minimal training. Moreover, the machines used for reading the documents are relatively unsophisticated, requiring only to recognise the existence of a mark and its position. They are therefore much cheaper than MICR readers. It is usually specified that the marks be made with a soft pencil—inks, especially ballpoint, tend to be reflective and so would not be detected by the reader.

A more sophisticated technique uses **Optical Character Recognition** (OCR), in which human-readable characters are automatically recognised by an optical device. This system allows typed (or, in the case of some highly advanced OCR readers, even carefully handwritten) characters to be read directly, using a machine which senses the shape of the character by measuring its reflective properties. Since the first OCR reader was installed in 1954, the technology has advanced to the stage where present-day readers can recognise 3000 characters a second. The shape detected by the reader is identified by comparing it with the set of character templates held in a ROM.

The most stylised typeface is called OCR-A, and was developed in the USA during the 1960s. It includes the upper-case alphabet as well as digits and special symbols in common use. The digits in OCR-A resemble somewhat the digits used in the E13B MICR typeface. There are three standard sizes, the smallest being used by typewriters and general-purpose printers, while the largest is used to encode embossed plastic cards. In 1970 the European standard typeface, OCR-B, was adopted. It provides 121 characters and is much less stylised than OCR-A, making it more pleasing to the human eye. It is to be widely found nowadays on computer turnaround documents such as bills and paying-in slips issued by public utilities.

OCR is a highly versatile method of automatic data entry using human-readable documents. As the price of OCR readers comes down, this is likely to be the most common general-purpose method in use.

A method of producing machine-readable data which is widely used in the retail trade, as well as by lending libraries, is the **bar code**. This consists of a series of black and white bars of varying thickness which encode an integer (the product code). The bar code requires no additional input by the operator—it is a fully pre-coded input code. If the same bar code is to be read on several occasions, as in library applications, it may be covered with plastic film to increase its durability. The code is read using a *light pen* which focuses a light spot on the target. As the pen is drawn across the bar code, a detector senses the presence or absence of reflected light, and sends an appropriate signal to a **digitiser**, which converts the signal into digital form for input to a digital computer. When the code has been read successfully, the apparatus emits a beep or a light. In case of unsuccessful operation, a further attempt at reading must be made. Light pens are easy to use in awkward positions, being lightweight. The light source is usually a light-emitting diode (LED), which has a low power consumption.

An alternative to the light pen is a **laser scanner** or **laser wand**. In this device the light source is a low-powered laser beam. Although heavier and more expensive than a light pen, the laser scanner has the edge in accuracy and obtaining success on the first try. It also has the advantages of being able to read through protective plastic film and also to read codes on materials which do not present a flat surface. In the *moving-beam* laser scanner, often found at supermarket checkouts, the user does not have to move the wand across the code. Instead, the device is held in a fixed position while the beam moves at high speed several times across the bar code. Since several scans can be compared, this device is even more accurate than the ordinary (fixed-beam) laser scanner.

There are many standard bar codes in use in various applications. To assist in human identification, the integer indicated by a bar code is usually printed, in an OCR typeface, as part of the code.

ISBN 0-333-39336-8

9 780333 393369

Figure 5.18 Bar code

Exercise 5.11

OCR and OMR are two methods of recording data in machine-readable form. Describe these methods briefly, highlighting the major differences.

Digitisation

At this point it is necessary to interrupt the main discussion and interpolate a word in edgeways. Information which is made up of characters is essentially digital in nature; indeed, most of the input and output devices considered until now have made use of this to perform a fairly straightforward conversion between the character images understood by human beings and the binary patterns which are manipulated inside the computer. Thus, both keyboard input and OMR are digital in nature and so directly compatible for use with a digital computer. However, MICR and OCR readers sense the shape of a character, which is decidedly not digital. Shape is an *analogue* property, capable of continuous variation. An **analogue-to-digital** conversion is required so that the signal from the reader can be interpreted by the computer. Likewise the bar-code scanner has to measure the width of the white and black bands and convert these widths to a binary pattern. The device used in these—and other—situations to perform the conversion is called a **digitiser**. Typically, an analogue property—such as position—is realised in the device as a voltage level. The digitiser then converts this voltage into a binary signal sequence. We shall see further uses for digitisers in association with devices for graphical and sound input.

Graphics devices

Human powers of recognition are capable of much more diversity than can be provided by a stream of characters. A picture or diagram can convey information more readily than the printed word, as a rapid flick through the pages of this book will amply verify. In some areas of human endeavour, such as architecture, a limited set of symbols without pictorial representation is totally inadequate to the task. We shall now discuss some devices used for the input and output of pictures and diagrams.

Pictorial or graphic output can be achieved by using an output device which can be considered to be composed of a very large number of small elements. A *graphics terminal* is much like a VDU, but each character position is subdivided into many **pixels** or picture elements, which can be individually addressed. The picture is held in an array whose elements correspond to the pixels; the value stored in each element may represent light intensity and colour. A picture is built up on the screen as a series of dots and lines. The number and size of the pixels on the screen determines the quality of the picture. With low resolution (128×160 pixels), bar charts and approximate pictures can be presented. For accurate engineering drawings, though, high resolution is necessary, such as the 1024×1268 pixels provided on high-quality microcomputers such as the Sun workstation.

For permanent record, *a flat-bed plotter* allows a pen to move over a sheet of paper leaving a graphic trace. These machines can produce dots and lines as fine as 1/10th of the millimetre, but such precision can only be achieved at a slow speed. On *vector graphics* devices, lines do not have to be plotted as a sequence of individual points; instead, the endpoints of the line can be specified and the plotter pen traces out a smooth line between them. Laser printers equipped with appropriate software can produce high-quality printed graphics.

Graphical input to a screen is possible using a **light-detector pen**. (Unfortunately this is frequently called a light pen, although it is a quite different device from the one used to input bar codes.) The VDU screen is illuminated by a continuous electronic scan, which passes each point of the screen once every 1/50th of a second; when the beam is picked up by the light-detector pen, a signal returns the coordinates of the beam. In this way a diagram can be 'drawn' on the screen or a section of a graphics display may be deleted. When the desired picture is displayed on the screen, a permanent record may be obtained by taking a *screen dump*. A light-detector pen is also useful for selecting an item from a menu displayed on the screen. Instead of laboriously directing the cursor to the chosen item, the pen can be used to point to the item.

A *graphics tablet* is a special touch-sensitive pad on which a picture is traced using a pointer. It is particularly useful as a device for inputting to a computer a diagram or map which has already been drawn. The path taken by the pointer is tracked using pulses of sound or by sensing pressure on the board, and the corresponding coordinates are used to produce an image on the screen. The continuous picture is represented by an array of values. Each element of the array corresponds to a pixel; its value may represent intensity (light or dark) and colour.

Speech devices

As well as using pictorial images, human beings communicate with sounds. The mouth and the ears are important sense organs. Adaptation of the computer to incorporate sound communication has, to date, made only slow progress. The problems in this area are akin to those of picture recognition but sound patterns are even more complex. Hopes have been expressed that there will be a spurt in progress using more advanced forms of hardware and software currently under development, but prediction of results remains a hazardous occupation.

Voice synthesisers enable a computer to piece together phrases or parts of phrases, called *allophones*, into mildly recognisable speech output. Typically, a set of 64 allophones is used. Composition of allophones into words can take place under program control; this is an area which requires special skills, though, and usually a pre-packaged dictionary of words is made available.

Music, which is generally more discrete in nature, can be synthesised more readily. However, the quality does not generally match that of musical instruments whose mellow sound is an effect difficult to achieve on a digital device.

Speech input to a computer presents even more difficulties. The patterns of human speech are inherently complex, and the differences between the way in which two people say the same thing aggravates the complexity. However, speech recognition is currently an area of active research and notwithstanding their relatively primitive nature today, speech devices are improving. Speech input is currently available on devices where only a limited vocabulary is required; an example of this is automatic dialling on car telephones.

The essential technique is to digitise the continuous spectrum which comprises human speech. The problem here is that sound varies, in amplitude (loudness) and pitch, in a complex waveform. One method is that of sampling the waveform which describes the speech (or music) at regular intervals, say 1000 times per second. The amplitude is encoded at each sampling point. As the amplitude of the waveform varies between positive and negative values, the sample values automatically incorporate the frequency (that is, the pitch). This system is used in digital telephone networks.

Other forms of input/output

We have spent several pages explaining the workings of peripherals for human–computer communication, but there are other forms of input/output. Input from a remote source such as a temperature or pressure sensor, for example, measures an inherently continuous quality. The interface between such analogue devices and a digital computer must include a digitiser. A remote output may open or close a valve, or set the speed of a stepper motor—these are digital outputs. On the other hand, a conventional motor is an analogue device which can run at a range of speeds. Analogue–digital converters use optical methods for mechanical devices and electronic methods for electrical devices.

Summary of Chapter 5

Programs are the reason for using computers, but without the hardware they are a soul without a body. Conventional digital computer architecture consists of a sequential processor which accesses both its programs and data from the same binary store.

The CPU consists of an arithmetic-logic unit and a control unit which, together with the registers, manipulate the contents of the immediate-access store and control operation of peripheral devices. The whole network of logic circuits is synchronised by a clock pulse and operates in an endless repetition of fetch–execute cycles. A machine instruction, in binary form, is fetched, decoded and executed. Each instruction consists of an operation code and one or more address fields. An instruction may:

- transfer data;
- perform a computation;
- perform input/output;
- redirect control to another instruction.

The operation code of an instruction is a bit pattern. The length of the bit pattern determines the number of distinct operation codes available for a given processor, that is, the number of instructions in its instruction set.

Computer memory is organised on three levels, in decreasing order of speed:

- cache memory;
- main memory;
- backing storage.

The binary computer is built using a large number of logic circuits, whose operation may be understood in terms of boolean algebra. The logic of a boolean expression, or its equivalent, the output of a logic network, may be expressed in terms of a truth table. Conversely, given a truth table, the corresponding logic network (or boolean expression) may be constructed.

Input and output devices enable communication with the world beyond the binary front door. A commonly used device is the visual display unit, but a great variety of special-purpose input and output devices has been described:

Character printers	*Document readers*	*Lineprinters*
Matrix printers	MICR	Barrel printers
Daisy-wheel printers	OCR	Chain printers
	OMR	
Page printers	*Graphical methods*	
Laser printers	Graphics terminal	
	Flat-bed plotter	
Bar-code readers	Drum plotter	
Light pens	Graphics tablet	
Laser scanners	Light-detector pen	

Answers to Exercises

5.1 MAR ← 60
MBR ← c(MAR)
AC ← 24 + MBR
MBR ← AC

5.2 Control instructions (jumps) provide for the transfer of control out of the normal processing sequence; they achieve this by loading a new value into the program counter.

All instructions advance the program counter so that the next instruction is fetched from the correct location.

5.3 The advantage in each case is a saving in time and an increase in CPU utilisation.

A disadvantage of using a channel is the extra expense of a secondary processor. A disadvantage of the use of buffers is the loss of main memory for general use.

5.4

a	*b*	*a* AND *b*	NOT (*a* AND *b*)		*a*	*b*	*a* OR *b*	NOT (*a* OR *b*)
F	F	F	T		F	F	F	T
F	T	F	T		F	T	T	F
T	F	F	T		T	F	T	F
T	T	T	F		T	T	T	F

5.5 A suitable expression is (*a* XOR *b*) AND NOT *c*. The truth table required is shown.

a	*b*	*c*	
F	F	F	F
F	F	T	F
F	T	F	T
F	T	T	F
T	F	F	T
T	F	T	F
T	T	F	F
T	T	T	F

5.6

a	NOT a	a AND (NOT a)	a OR (NOT a)
F	T	F	T
T	F	F	T

5.7 $(a.b) + (\overline{b}.c)$

5.8

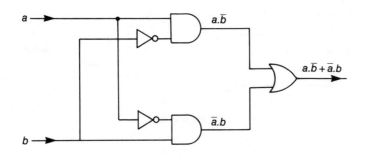

Figure A5.8

5.9 (i) $x = a|a = \overline{(a.a)} = \overline{a}$ {NOT a = a NAND a}

(ii) $x = \overline{(a|b)} \mid \overline{(a|b)}$

$\qquad = (a|b) + (a|b)$ (10b)

$\qquad = \overline{\overline{(a.b)}} + \overline{\overline{(a.b)}}$ (10a)

$\qquad = (a.b) + (a.b)$

$\qquad = a.b$ {a AND b = (a NAND b) NAND (a NAND b)}

(iii) $x = (a|a) \mid (b|b)$

$\qquad = \overline{a} + \overline{b}$ using part (i) and (10b)

$\qquad = a + b$ {a OR b = (a NAND a) NAND (b NAND b)}

5.10 $(a|b) \mid (c|d) = \overline{(a|b)} + \overline{(c|d)}$ (10b)

$\qquad = \overline{\overline{(a.b)}} + \overline{\overline{(c.d)}}$ (10a)

$\qquad = (a.b) + (c.d)$

5.11

OCR	OMR
Can use any document	Special formatted documents needed
Most characters available	Only character is a mark
Special typeface	
Characters must be printed	Marks usually made by hand, in pencil
Recognition by shape	Recognition by position.

Both methods use reflected light to detect the presence of a character/mark.

Further Exercises

1. For the network shown in figure 5.19, draw up a truth table to show the output
   X for all possible input values at P, Q and R.
   Use (a) your truth table, (b) boolean algebra to determine the effect, if any, of
   P on the output X. What gate with two inputs is equivalent to this network?

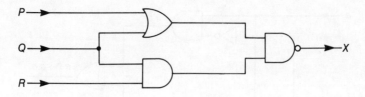

Figure 5.19

2. The prospectus for a University, a 48-page document, is held on disc.
   Discuss the relative merits of making it available to enquirers:

   (a) online,
   (b) as a lineprinter listing,
   (c) on microfiche.

3. Design a logic network which has output 1 if both its inputs are the same, and 0
   otherwise. This corresponds to the boolean algebra binary operation $\equiv$. Write
   down the truth table for NOT $\equiv$. Which logical connective does this correspond to?

4. Show that $\overline{a.(b+c)} = \bar{a} + (\bar{b}.\bar{c})$.

5. How many rows are needed in the truth table for a logic network with four
   inputs?

6. (a) Distinguish between *online* and *offline* methods of data collection.

   (b) Describe how data is encoded when employing
       (i) optical mark sensing,
       (ii) punched cards.

   What are the advantages of each of these input media in relation to each other?
   (AEB—1984)

7. When data is retrieved from the computer's main (immediate access) store, the
   access time depends partly on whether *serial access* or *parallel access* is used. If
   the data is subsequently transferred to a printer under program control, a
   standard *interface* may be employed.

(a) Explain the meaning of each of the **four** terms in italics.

(b) Describe one advantage and one disadvantage of serial access compared with parallel access.

(c) Several items of data are to be transferred in sequence from the processor to the printer under program control. Explain the functions of the interface in ensuring that the data is correctly transferred.

(AEB—1983)

8. Explain why many computers include in their main storage a section of read only memory. What purpose does it serve and how does its use differ from the use of the rest of main storage?

(Camb.—1983)

9. Interrupts are a mechanism that permit various hardware components of a computer configuration to function concurrently.

   (i) Explain what is meant by this statement.

  (ii) Show, with the aid of a flowchart or otherwise, at what stage an interrupt may be detected in the fetch–execute cycle and what happens when one is detected.

 (iii) With the aid of an example, explain why it can be advantageous to have priorities associated with interrupts.

(AEB—1984)

10. Most computer systems have both an immediate access store and a backing store. List two characteristics of each type of store which together show why this is desirable.

(JMB—1984)

11. "A modern home computer exceeds, in terms of speed and immediate-access storage, the specification of a mid-1950s mainframe which occupied a large room, at a fraction of the cost." Why?

12. Some characteristics of the processing unit of a certain computer are as follows.

"The processing unit has an 8-bit data bus and a 16-bit address bus. Registers within the processing unit include an 8-bit accumulator and two 16-bit registers called the program counter and stack pointer. Storage locations 0000_{16} to $1FFF_{16}$ contain the system bootstrap in ROM. The remainder of the computer's addressable storage is provided as RAM."

(a) (i) Explain the purpose of the accumulator, program counter (sometimes called the sequence control register) and stack pointer registers.

    (ii) Name one other register usable by a programmer that you would expect to be present in the processing unit. Explain what purpose it serves.

(b) Using the information given above about the computer's processing unit,

    (i) what is the computer's word length?

(ii) How much RAM storage is available (in Kbytes)?
Give reasons to justify your answers.
(c) What is the system bootstrap? Why is it stored in ROM?

(Camb.—1985)

13. George would like to buy a coffee table and needs to choose from the selection available at his local department store. Tables may be large or small, round or square, and may have their top made from wood or glass. George decides that he will take a table which meets one (at least) of the following criteria:

> round with glass top
> square with wood top
> large with glass top
> small and square
> small with wood top

(a) Express these requirements as
    (i) a truth table,
    (ii) a boolean expression.
(b) Can you simplify George's criteria?

14. Ann, Beatrice and Carol form a panel to decide which attributes should be used in the advertising campaign to launch the new washing powder Sudso. An attribute will be chosen if it gains a majority vote of the panel. Design a logic circuit whose output is 1 if a majority of inputs equal 1. (A vote in favour is treated as an input of 1, a vote against as an input of 0.)

Draw your logic circuit using

(i) AND gates, OR gates and inverters;
(ii) NAND gates only.

Further Reading

Peter Brophy, *Computers Can Read*, Technical Press, Gower, Aldershot, 1986. An interesting account of document-reading techniques and bar codes, with a number of case studies.

M. G. Hartley, M. Healey and P. G. Depledge, *Mini and Microcomputer Systems*, Macmillan, London, 1988.

6 Low-level Programming

It is apparent that there is a gap between the capabilities of the hardware of a computer and the specification of a problem, even when formalised as a program coded in a high-level language. This gap is bridged by a translation process which produces *binary code* (bit patterns) intelligible to the hardware from high-level code. This translation process forms a major topic of chapter 10. In this chapter we study how a program can be written in a form which relates directly to the hardware. In the course of this study we shall see that it is possible to write code in a language that allows easy conversion to binary code. This style of programming is called **low level**, as it is close to the operational level of the hardware.

For most purposes programmers write high-level code, which is closely related to the algorithm under consideration. However, there are specific problems where, for reasons of speed and efficiency, it is desirable to program at a level which is closer to the machine. For a specific given task, a low-level program is able to produce more compact binary code (occupying less memory) and execute faster (using fewer processor cycles). Certain programs might need access to specific memory locations or direct control of peripheral devices. This applies in particular to some *systems programs*; for example, the *compiler* which produces the binary code from a high-level program must itself be written (in part, at least) in low-level code. In addition, the routines which control input and output at the byte level must of necessity be written at the machine level. (The programmers who use these routines, of course, do not want to be bothered with this level of detail—they use the low-level input and output routines by calling them from higher-level programs.)

It is not the purpose of this chapter to turn you into a competent low-level programmer. Rather it is hoped that you will gain an appreciation of low-level programming, so obtaining an additional insight into the processes by which a computer executes a program.

Just as there are high-level languages, so there are low-level languages. The differences between high-level languages reflect the differing aims of high-level programming, that is the differing types of applications for which algorithms are devised. The differences between low-level languages, on the other hand, reflect the different types of hardware available. The allowable binary patterns which form the set of instructions for a processor depend on the architecture of that processor; they define the *machine language* for that processor. Although historically programs *had* to be coded in machine language during the early days of computing, nowadays machine code is produced by automated translation. Low-level programs

163

written by human programmers are expressed in mnemonic form and then translated by an *assembler* into machine code. This mnemonic form is called *assembly language*.

6.1 Binary Representation of Data

At the hardware level, all storage and processing takes place in bit patterns. These patterns are usually organised in bytes of eight bits. The programmer who is working close to the machine has to have an understanding of the way in which data is represented in binary form.

The meaning of a bit pattern depends entirely on its interpretation. Here we shall look at the representation of *data* by bit patterns, where the data can be characters or integers. We shall see in a later section how bit patterns can be interpreted alternatively as negative numbers, floating-point numbers or *instructions*.

Bit patterns for characters

The first data representation we look at is character representation. Documents in Western countries are composed of characters from an alphabet of 26 upper-case letters, 26 lower-case letters, ten digits and a range of punctuation marks and special symbols. The conventional typewriter or computer keyboard can produce approximately 90 distinct characters. In addition there are some control functions such as new line, space and carriage return. A byte of 8 bits can be arranged in 256 different patterns, far more than twice the number required. In fact, even restricting the allowable codes to those whose first, or *most significant*, bit is zero there are still enough patterns to go round. The bits within a byte are conventionally numbered from right to left, with the *least significant* (rightmost) bit being called bit 0.

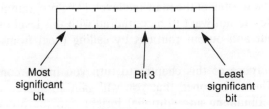

Most
significant
bit   Bit 3   Least
                                                      significant
                                                      bit

Figure 6.1 A byte

The actual allocation of codes to characters, or **collation sequence**, is essentially arbitrary. Nevertheless, in the interest of avoiding a free for all, in which every manufacturer produces hardware utterly incompatible with everyone else's, standards for character representation have been agreed. This helps to ensure, for example, that when you attach a screen or a printer to your computer, the characters are displayed or printed as intended. Unfortunately there are two standard collation sequences in widespread use. The **EBCDIC** (extended binary coded decimal interchange code) representation is used on IBM machines (except personal computers) and equipment made to interface with them. The **ASCII** (American standard code for information interchange) representation is used by almost all other manufacturers as well as on the IBM PC range, and has been adopted (almost entirely) as an international standard. Characters may be classified into *alphabetic*, *numeric*, *special* and *control* characters. The special characters are those printed characters, like % and @, which are not alphanumeric; the space character is also considered to be a special character. Control characters are used for controlling the next printing or cursor position. They include functions such as carriage return, new line and backspace. A special control character, called *delete*, causes the erasure of the previously transmitted character.

Here are some examples of ASCII character codes.

0001000	backspace	0100110	&
0001101	carriage return	1000000	@
1000001	A	1100001	a
1010100	T	1110100	t
0110110	6	1111111	delete

For convenience, a complete table of ASCII character codes is given in Appendix A.

ASCII provides a representation in seven bits. Where characters are stored or transmitted as individual bytes, this leaves a spare bit for each character. The spare bit may be fixed as 1 or 0, but it is often used for some auxiliary purpose, such as error checking. When character codes are transmitted (especially over long distances) there is a danger of corruption through, for example, noise on the line. This may be controlled by a *parity constraint*. This requires that each byte transmitted should have an even number of bits set—*even parity*—or that each byte transmitted should have an odd number of bits set—*odd parity*. One method of achieving even parity, for example, is to set the most significant bit whenever the seven-bit code has an odd number of ones. On arrival, the receiving device can check each byte for compliance.

An alternative use of the most significant bit is to make available additional character sets for special purposes such as graphics, mathematical symbols and the Greek alphabet. This feature is exploited on printers and in screen handlers for microcomputers.

On machines with a word length longer than one byte, several characters may be *packed* into a single word. For example, with a 36-bit word length, five 7-bit ASCII codes may be packed into each word.

Hexadecimal code

Programs and data are held within the computers as bit patterns (binary code). While this format is eminently suited to a machine, it is quite unsuited to human perception. The strings of 1s and 0s are virtually incomprehensible, and trying to count the correct number of each tends to induce dizzy spells. For convenience we shall therefore introduce a representation called **hexadecimal code** (or hex for short). In hex each group of four bits is replaced by a **hex digit** according to the following table.

Bit pattern	Hex digit	Bit pattern	Hex digit
0000	0	1000	8
0001	1	1001	9
0010	2	1010	A
0011	3	1011	B
0100	4	1100	C
0101	5	1101	D
0110	6	1110	E
0111	7	1111	F

There are sixteen different hex digits. A byte can be written as a pair of hex digits. Hex codes are of no interest to a computer, but they do serve as a useful guide to humans trying to understand what is going on inside the processor. Although we use hex code for convenience in representing binary patterns, it must be emphasised that the actual representation within the computer is as sequences of bits.

ASCII character codes may be expressed in hexadecimal notation. Each binary string is padded out with a leading zero so that the bits can be blocked off in groups of four. Thus, the ASCII code for 'T' is 0101 0100, which is written 54 in hex notation. Since some hex codes look like ordinary decimal numbers, a tag is sometimes used to avoid confusion—for example, &54 or 54_{16}.

By and large, a programmer can avoid the use of specific character codes. After all, the computer is far more adept than the human brain in remembering the code for each character. So it is usually best to insert the actual character symbols in programs, and code the conversion. In fact, high-level languages provide built-in functions to perform the conversion between a character symbol and its binary equivalent. However, it is not possible to include control codes in the program text, so a search for a backspace code, say, may have to be explicitly coded by reference to symbol &08.

It should be noted carefully that the ASCII codes &00 to &09 do not correspond to the digits 0 to 9. In fact, all ASCII codes between &00 and &1F are control codes. They serve special functions in controlling print and screen layout and in data transmission; if necessary, they can be input from the keyboard by depressing simultaneously the CTRL key and another key. The ASCII character codes for the digits are &30 to &39. This has no bearing on arithmetic; we are concerned here with the *characters* 0 to 9, whose meanings are quite distinct from the *numerals* 0 to 9.

Older computers used to work with a six-bit byte, which was large enough to represent sufficient characters at a time when the hardware had no lower-case alphabet. A six-bit byte can be blocked off into two groups of three bits, which can each be in one of 8 ($= 2^3$) patterns. The binary patterns from 000 to 111 are labelled 0 to 7 and the resulting representation is called **octal code**.

Exercise 6.1

Complete each line of the following table with alternative representations for the given codes.

Binary	Octal	Hexadecimal
10011010		
	13	
		13

Binary coded decimal

For numeric data there is no point in using the full character representations of the digits. There are only ten different digits, and these can be accommodated comfortably in four bits ($2^4 = 16$). The simplest system is therefore based on the binary scheme up to 9. Here are the binary patterns for the digits, where leading zeros have been introduced to ensure that all patterns have four bits.

0000	0	0101	5
0001	1	0110	6
0010	2	0111	7
0011	3	1000	8
0100	4	1001	9

This code is called **binary coded decimal** (BCD). (There are other BCD schemes; they all have the feature that each digit has a fixed four-bit pattern.) In the BCD scheme, conversion between decimal notation and bit pattern is straightforward. One byte can handle all numbers between 0 and 99, and two bytes can handle numbers from 0 to 9999, which is often sufficient in many commercial applications. (COBOL programmers specify their numeric variables in this way, so that a BCD field of the correct size can be set up.) Signed integers can be handled by an extended version of BCD. The rightmost half byte is coded 1100 to represent + and 1101 to represent −.

The CPU is designed to perform arithmetic in the binary system, as we shall see presently. To perform arithmetic on BCD numbers it is therefore necessary to restore the principles of decimal arithmetic. In particular, a carry must be generated for any number above 9. This may be achieved by suitably modified hardware or by firmware to provide instructions for BCD arithmetic. An alternative approach is to perform arithmetic by looking up a table, rather than by a logical process. Two tables are required, one for the sum digit and the other for the carry.

sum	0 1 2 3 4 5 6 7 8 9	carry	0 1 2 3 4 5 6 7 8 9
0	0 1 2 3 4 5 6 7 8 9	0	0 0 0 0 0 0 0 0 0 0
1	1 2 3 4 5 6 7 8 9 0	1	0 0 0 0 0 0 0 0 0 1
2	2 3 4 5 6 7 8 9 0 1	2	0 0 0 0 0 0 0 0 1 1
3	3 4 5 6 7 8 9 0 1 2	3	0 0 0 0 0 0 0 1 1 1
4	4 5 6 7 8 9 0 1 2 3	4	0 0 0 0 0 0 1 1 1 1
5	5 6 7 8 9 0 1 2 3 4	5	0 0 0 0 0 1 1 1 1 1
6	6 7 8 9 0 1 2 3 4 5	6	0 0 0 0 1 1 1 1 1 1
7	7 8 9 0 1 2 3 4 5 6	7	0 0 0 1 1 1 1 1 1 1
8	8 9 0 1 2 3 4 5 6 7	8	0 0 1 1 1 1 1 1 1 1
9	9 0 1 2 3 4 5 6 7 8	9	0 1 1 1 1 1 1 1 1 1

Look-up tables like these are used for a variety of tasks and are implemented nowadays as firmware in a read-only memory (ROM). Of course, the implementation of these tables is in BCD. Similar tables can be provided for subtraction, multiplication and division.

BCD code, although requiring somewhat contorted arithmetic, uses a simple conversion between internal (binary) and external (decimal) representations. It is therefore an efficient representation for commercial applications which involve minimal arithmetic and a high number of input and output operations.

Binary numbers

We have made frequent reference to binary numbers, but have not as yet explained their format. Our system of numeration takes a great deal for granted. It *assumes* a format of units, tens, hundreds, thousands and so on. This is rarely stated clearly, except in infant schools. When we write 1000, it is assumed that this sequence of digits stands for one thousand, and is one more than 999. The number 256, for example, really means

$$2 \times 100 + 5 \times 10 + 6 \times 1$$

in a *place-value notation*. A digit in the third place (counting from the right—another convention) is interpreted as hundreds. More precisely, our decimal system is based on the number 10, with

$$256 = 2 \times 10^2 + 5 \times 10^1 + 6 \times 10^0$$

(10^0 is a mathematically sound way of writing the number 1.) The word *digit* refers to a finger, and a **base 10** system of counting is ideal when counting on ten fingers. The notational requirements are the existence of the ten symbols, 0, 1, 2, 3, 4, 5, 6, 7, 8 and 9, one for each finger. Yet there is nothing in the place-value system, *per se*, which demands a base of 10. It is equally adaptable to any base.

Present-day computers are short on fingers. At the lowest level of storage or communication they can provide but two distinct states, which we have called 0 and

1. The binary system is adapted to **base 2**. So the meaning of the **binary number** 11010 is

$$1 \times 2^4 + 1 \times 2^3 + 0 \times 2^2 + 1 \times 2^1 + 0 \times 2^0$$

$= 16 + 8 + 2 = 26$ as a decimal number.

Exercise 6.2

Convert the binary numbers 1001 and 100 to decimal form.

Exercise 6.3

Obtain the binary equivalents of the decimal numbers 49 and 21.

Binary addition is performed just like decimal addition, but since

$$1 + 1 = 10 \qquad \text{(binary)}$$

the number two requires a carry. For example, if $a = 10101$ and $b = 1101$, the sum may be set out as follows.

carry	1 1 1 1	
a	1 0 1 0 1	21
b	1 1 0 1	13
	1 0 0 0 1 0 ⟶	34

Subtraction and multiplication in binary can be performed in a similar way, but we shall see that they are usually done quite differently, to take advantage of the properties of binary numbers and the fixed-size store.

Just as it is possible to do arithmetic in base 10 and base 2, there is no reason why someone so minded should not do arithmetic in base 16, using hex codes as numbers. The principles are exactly the same, and the results exactly mirror the corresponding binary arithmetic. Conversion between hex and binary is trivial, blocking off bits in groups of four (from the right).

Conversion between hex and decimal is much trickier; the place values are 1, 16, 256 and so on in powers of 16. Although conversion tables are available to aid the process, in practice this is a task to which the computer is much better suited.

Once again octal arithmetic is much like decimal arithmetic, with a carry for each 8. The conversion from base 8 to decimal works just as for binary to decimal, using powers of 8.

Exercise 6.4

(a) Convert these decimal numbers to hex:

1988, 111, 300

(b) Convert to decimal:

FF, BCD, 111_{16}

6.2 Binary Arithmetic in a Fixed-Length Store

When representing an integer in computer storage, it is necessary to bear in mind the fixed size of a memory cell. The largest integer which can be held in one byte, 1111 1111 equals 255 (decimal). This is uncomfortably small. A few computers work with two-byte integers (maximum positive number is $256 \times 256 = 65\ 536$) and many allow four bytes, which is adequate for almost all work with integers.

A more familiar fixed-length store is the odometer (or mileometer) in a car. When the car has gone 99 999 miles, another mile takes it to 00 000. The carry into the next place is discarded. If the car looks well-maintained, nobody would be any the wiser. Let us consider (for ease of discussion) a computer which handles one-byte integers. The carry into the ninth bit will be lost. So, using decimal notation, the sum $241 + 29$ goes over the top and leaves the result 14 (256 getting lost in the process). The processor does not cheat us, however; it sets the carry bit in the status word as a clear warning. If now we choose to do two-byte arithmetic, this carry can be fed into the high byte.

Negative numbers

Let us consider now the problem of representing negative integers, without which little useful arithmetic can be performed. Since only 256 different numbers can be represented in one byte, it is necessary to compromise and share them out, some positive and some negative. We usually indicate negative numbers with a minus sign; in fixed-length binary representation, the most significant bit will determine the sign. It is conventional to use 0 for positive numbers, 1 for negative numbers. We note that, with this convention, the largest representable number has 0 as its most significant bit and 1s elsewhere. Given these conventions there are three ways of actually representing the negative numbers; the positive numbers have the same representation as hitherto. In order to simplify the calculations, the rest of this section will work with a word length of four bits.

Signed magnitude

The obvious notation for negative numbers is for the most significant bit to act as a minus sign when set. This is called **signed-magnitude** notation, and gives the representation shown in the table.

0000	0	1000	−0
0001	1	1001	−1
0010	2	1010	−2
0011	3	1011	−3
0100	4	1100	−4

0101	5	1101	−5
0110	6	1110	−6
0111	7	1111	−7

We notice immediately one inefficiency—there are two different ways of representing 0, namely 0000 and 1000. A further difficulty is that arithmetic is complicated. The rules for addition of a pair of positive numbers differ from the rules for adding a positive and a negative number; there is a similar difference in subtraction. These difficulties create inefficiencies in computation, and signed-magnitude is therefore not used much for computer representation of integers, although it does have the advantage that it is relatively easy to convert negative numbers between binary and decimal format.

Ones' complement

Another representation of negative numbers is obtained by inverting the bits, that is swapping 1s and 0s. For example, since 6 is 0110 we write 1001 for −6. This method is called **ones' complement**. It is seen that in this system, too, it is not very difficult to convert between binary and decimal negative numbers, although one does have to work via the positive number and, with a long word length, the inversion is inefficient. How about arithmetic? Adding two positive numbers causes no problems, unless the result is out of range. For example, $5 + 3$ becomes

$$
\begin{array}{c}
0\ 1\ 0\ 1 \\
0\ 0\ 1\ 1 \\
\hline
1\ 0\ 0\ 0
\end{array}
$$

yielding the apparent answer −7, which cannot be correct. What has happened is that the answer has overflowed into the negative range. This **overflow** condition can be detected by a suitable algorithm (which checks the sign bits). On detection, the overflow flag in the status register is set, so that the programmer can take appropriate remedial action.

When adding a positive and a negative number, however, a new problem arises; for example, $5 + (-2)$ becomes

$$
\begin{array}{c}
0\ 1\ 0\ 1 \\
1\ 1\ 0\ 1 \\
\hline
(1)\ 0\ 0\ 1\ 0
\end{array}
$$

which equals 2—when the answer should be 3. In ones' complement, whenever a negative number is added to a positive number to yield a positive result, or two negative numbers are added (without overflow), the result will be 1 less than the correct result. These are precisely the cases in which there is a carry out of the most significant bit. This condition can therefore be corrected by adding in the carry bit. Thus $-3 + 4$ becomes

```
  1 1 0 0
  0 1 0 0
─────────
1 0 0 0 0
  └────────▶ 1
─────────
  0 0 0 1
```

which correctly equals 1.

Subtraction is achieved by first negativing the number to be subtracted (by inverting all the bits) and then adding. For example, $6 - 4$ is treated as $6 + (-4)$.

Twos' complement

The rule for adding in the carry in ones' complement addition is awkward, and the majority of processors work with a slightly different format for negative numbers known as **twos' complement**. If you recall the odometer analogy, then running backwards through the positive numbers you eventually get the reading 00 000. Running it further back you get successively 99 999, 99 998 and so on. This suggests that 99 999 is equivalent to -1. The corresponding result in binary notation would give us 11111 as -1. The general rule for twos' complement is that adding a positive number to the corresponding negative number yields zero, ignoring the carry bit. For example

```
    0 1 1 0
    1 0 1 0
  ─────────
(1) 0 0 0 0
```

represents the sum $6 + (-6) = 0$, so 1010 must be -6. A complete table for a four-bit representation appears below

	Ones'	Twos'		
	complement			
1000	-7	-8	0000	0
1001	-6	-7	0001	1
1010	-5	-6	0010	2
1011	-4	-5	0011	3
1100	-3	-4	0100	4
1101	-2	-3	0101	5
1110	-1	-2	0110	6
1111	-0	-1	0111	7

We notice a new feature: in twos' complement there is no longer a double representation of zero. Note also that there is no positive number which can be added to 1000 to give zero. We see, though, that

```
1 0 0 0
0 0 0 1
―――――
1 0 0 1
```

represents the sum $-8 + 1 = -7$, so 1000 represents -8. Thus in twos' complement we have an asymmetry, with an extra negative number being representable. Against that, arithmetic is uncomplicated, following the straightforward rules of binary addition. These can be implemented using logic networks.

It is quite feasible to implement subtraction as addition; for example $7 - 4 = 7 + (-4)$. The fly in the ointment is the conversion from positive to negative numbers, a non-trivial process. The following algorithm is probably the easiest to remember. Treat all bits as usual (for positive numbers), but if the sign bit is set, treat it as *minus its usual value*. For example, $1000 = 8$ as an unsigned number, so we equate it to -8 in twos' complement notation. Here are examples of the conversion method.

$$1011 \longrightarrow -8 + 2 + 1 = -5$$

Conversely

$$-6 = -8 + 2 \longrightarrow 1000 + 0010 = 1010$$

Because this algorithm is somewhat complicated, arithmetic-logic units are frequently provided with hardware subtractors as well as adders.

Overflow is detected in twos' complement arithmetic as follows. If the carry into the most significant bit is 0, and the carry out of the most significant bit is also 0, the correct result is obtained. Likewise, if both carries, into and out of the most significant bit, are 1, the correct result is obtained. If, however, the carries into and out of the most significant bit differ, the true result is out of range. In this case the addition routine sets the overflow flag.

Exercise 6.5

Give the numerically largest negative number representable using twos' complement in a word of six bits.

Exercise 6.6

Add the following and interpret the result in twos' complement:

```
0 1 1 0
1 0 1 1
―――――
```

Multiplication

Computer multiplication of integers is achieved by shifting and addition. The simplest case is multiplication by 2. This is achieved by a machine instruction called **arithmetic shift**, which relies on the fact that in binary arithmetic a number is doubled by inserting a zero at the right-hand end. An arithmetic left shift in twos' complement notation is defined formally as follows:

1. Shift each bit one place to the left.
2. Clear the least significant bit (to 0).

This will yield the correct result of doubling the number if the new sign bit is the same as the old sign bit. The old sign bit is usually put into the carry flag, where it can be tested for overflow.

In general, long multiplication is required. Long multiplication of decimal numbers is well known, even if not always executed correctly. Long multiplication of binary numbers is much easier because the only numbers to multiply by are 0 and 1. For example,

```
        0 1 0 1 ×        5 × 6 =
        0 1 1 0
       _____

        0 0 0 0
  ⋆    0 1 0 1
  ⋆   0 1 0 1
    0 0 0 0
   _____

   0 0 1 1 1 1 0               = 30
```

It is seen that the result of a four-bit multiplication will require eight-bit arithmetic. The important part of the method is to shift left the first factor in the multiplication as many times as necessary, adding in the resulting number. This is seen clearly by inspection of the two lines marked with an asterisk above. In practice, the intermediate terms are added in one at a time, as they are generated. The following is a suitable algorithm for multiplying two numbers, a and b, each n bits long. The result is given by *prod*, which is held in a double byte ($2n$ bits).

1. prod:= 0
2. loop to n
3.   if least significant bit of b is 1
4.   then prod:= prod + a
5.   endif
6.   double a
7.   shift b right
8. endloop

In step 6, *a* is doubled using an arithmetic left shift in a double-byte register, so as not to lose part of the answer. The purpose of the right shift in step 7 is to put the next multiplier bit into the least significant bit of *b*.

The arithmetic left shift is available as a machine instruction on most processors, and can be applied to the contents of either a register or a memory location. In some processors the sign bit is preserved during an arithmetic shift. A corresponding instruction **arithmetic right shift** is achieved as follows:

1. Shift each bit one place to the right.
2. Restore the sign bit.

With this operation the least significant bit is lost. Its arithmetic interpretation is **integer division by two**.

Exercise 6.7

What is the result of applying

(a) an arithmetic right shift
(b) an arithmetic left shift

to the bytes 00111001 and 10111001? Interpret your results in terms of integer arithmetic (twos' complement).

6.3 Floating-point Numbers

The binary representation of integers allows a very limited range of integers to be represented within a reasonable number of bytes. The use of floating-point numbers allows a much larger range of numbers to be represented, as we shall see presently, albeit with some reduction in accuracy. While many commercial applications can manage with the range provided by the integer representation, there are many calculations, especially in the areas of science and engineering, which involve numbers outside this range. Furthermore, fractions are also needed in these calculations. Floating-point numbers can handle these too.

Mantissa and exponent

Working with decimal numbers it is customary to systematise decimal fractions using *scientific notation*; for example

$$234.6 = 2.346 \times 10^2$$
$$0.0713 = 0.713 \times 10^{-1}$$

The number preceding the multiplication sign is called the **mantissa** and the power of ten is the **exponent**. The representation is not unique—we could have written

$234.6 = 23.46 \times 10^1$. It is preferable to **normalise** the representation; in this form the mantissa has a zero before the decimal point and a non-zero digit immediately after. Thus the value of the mantissa is given by

$$0.1 \leqslant \text{mantissa} < 1.0$$

The same principle can be applied to binary numbers. Any number can be converted into binary. The fractional part is handled in much the same way as the integer part. After the units position, a **binary point** is inserted. The value of the first place after the binary point is $\frac{1}{2}$, the value of the next is $\frac{1}{4}$, then $\frac{1}{8}$ and so on. We now have a binary number with a binary point. This number can then be shifted (right or left) so that there is a zero before the binary point and a one after it. The number of shifts required gives the exponent, a positive or negative binary integer. This yields the representation in figure 6.2. In small processors, more than one word is occupied by a floating-point number.

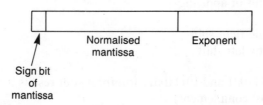

Figure 6.2 Floating-point representation of a binary number

Range and accuracy

Within a given length, we can vary the number of bits allocated to the mantissa and the exponent. The exponent gives the power of two, so a longer exponent increases the *range* of numbers which can be represented. For example, if eight bits are allowed for the exponent, then this part of the number can range from 2^{-128} (close to zero) to 2^{127} (very large). On the other hand, the *accuracy* of the representation is all in the mantissa, and this must be long enough to provide a reasonable number of significant figures. Thus there is a trade-off between accuracy and range for floating-point numbers. For most purposes, a good balance is achieved by having about twice as many bits in the mantissa as there are in the exponent. Note that it is not necessary for either the mantissa or the exponent to occupy a whole number of bytes.

There is a lower limit for the smallest positive number—it must be larger than 0.5×2^{-128} (decimal equivalent) for an eight-bit exponent. Any calculation leading to a positive number less than this generates an **underflow** error. The floating-point number with zeros in all positions represents 0.0. Since the mantissa is normalised, its leading 1 is not usually stored, leaving an extra significant bit. Of course, in all calculations the missing 1 must be restored. (The Acorn BBC represents floating-point numbers in five bytes, four for the mantissa and one for the exponent. This yields a range from 0.5×2^{-128} to 2^{128} (exclusive), that is, 1.5×10^{-39} to 1.7×10^{38}. There is a corresponding range for negative numbers.)

The mantissa is frequently stored in signed-magnitude form. Since the mantissa is normalised, special hardware or software is required for floating-point arithmetic which nullifies most of the advantages of complement notation. It is also common to store an n-bit exponent in **excess** form, in which 2^{n-1} is added to each number. Thus, for example, an 8-bit exponent of 47 is stored in excess 128 form as 10101111 (the binary equivalent of 175). The main advantage of this is where the exponent does not occupy a complete word, so that the sign would have to be inserted in the most significant bit when the exponent is extracted for arithmetic operations.

Exercise 6.8

To what accuracy can a floating-point number be held in 48 bits, if 12 bits are used for the exponent?

Loss of accuracy

Arithmetic using integers is exact; we can add, subtract and multiply integers and obtain an exact answer (provided that the answer is not out of range). Division into a quotient and a remainder is likewise exact. However, fractions cannot always be represented exactly. The decimal fraction for $\frac{1}{3}$ is

0.333 333 333 . . .

continuing for ever. Clearly, using decimal arithmetic this fraction cannot be represented exactly, no matter how much paper and how much time is at our disposal. The situation is retrieved by realising that, beyond a certain accuracy, the finer details do not matter. For example, in monetary calculations, a tenth of a penny is of little consequence.

The simplest approach is to chop off all digits after the position of desired accuracy, and retain just the first so many. This procedure is called **truncation**, and can be performed easily on a digital device. Against this ease of operation must be considered the loss of accuracy. Both 0.339 and 0.331 are truncated to 0.33, which is a much better estimate of the latter than of the former. Surely 0.339 is approximately 0.34; this approach, which increases the last retained digit to give a more accurate estimate, is called **rounding**.

Rounding in binary fractions is quite simple—if the first lost bit is a 0 then rounding is identical with truncation, but if the first lost bit is 1 then 1 must be added to the least significant bit of the retained fraction. Thus 0.101101 rounds to 0.1011 (four places) and 0.101110 rounds to 0.1100.

It follows that the use of fractions can lead to inherent rounding errors. Further rounding errors arise from the use of a fixed-length store, in order to represent numbers with more significant figures than the mantissa provides. When two floating-point numbers are added or multiplied, the result may have a mantissa which does not fit; it will therefore have to be rounded or truncated, introducing a further error. This type of numerical error from the use of a fixed-size mantissa accumulates throughout a long calculation. The study of the propagation of numerical errors is a subject in its own right, and is called *numerical analysis*.

Floating-point arithmetic

We consider multiplication first. The following steps are required

1. multiply the mantissae (taking the leading 1s into account)
2. add the exponents and subtract the *excess*
3. if the product mantissa begins with a zero
4. then
5.   shift the product left—it is now normalised
6.   reduce the new exponent by one
7. endif
8. truncate the new mantissa
9. record the new mantissa and exponent

Addition is more complicated, because the mantissae cannot be added unless the exponents are equal. If they are, then the result of adding two positive (or two negative) numbers will have a mantissa greater than 1. In this case the exponent of the result must be increased. Otherwise, the exponent of the smaller number must be increased to match the larger, shifting the mantissa to the right to compensate. This will always cause a loss of accuracy. The mantissa of the sum will be greater than 0.1_2 and may be less or greater than 1.0. Here is a possible sequence of steps for the addition of a and b.

```
incorporate leading 1s into mantissae
if exponent(a) > exponent(b)
then
      interchange a and b
endif
loop while exponent(a) < exponent(b)
    shift mantissa(a) right
    increment exponent(a)
endloop
expsum := exponent(a)
mantsum := mantissa(a) + mantissa(b)
if carry out of mantsum
then
      expsum := expsum + 1
else
      shift mantsum left (to lose leading 1)
endif
if mantsum too long
```

then

    round mantsum to requisite number of places

endif

store mantsum and expsum in result register

It can be seen that programs for floating-point arithmetic can become quite complicated. They are therefore usually provided as a special package. If floating-point arithmetic is required infrequently, the package can be provided as software to be loaded as needed. However, such software tends to be extensive and can occupy a large area of memory. Where floating-point arithmetic is in regular use, a hardware *floating-point unit* is employed. Although more expensive than software, there is a significant gain in speed of operation. The speed of a floating-point unit is measured in *flops* (floating-point operations per second). Typical speeds are in the range of 100 Mflops (1 megaflop $= 10^6$ flops).

6.4 Assembly Coding

At the machine level, each instruction consists of a binary pattern, which represents both the operation code and the data fields. A machine-code program is thus an enormous string of 1s and 0s. While this is the form in which the computer is able to interpret its input, it is decidedly human unfriendly. If programs had to be written in this form, the margin for error would be so great that few programs could be written correctly, and many would retain undetected errors.

For example, the pattern 10000101 is the operation code for the instruction *store the contents of the accumulator in the cell addressed by one byte* (= eight bits) in the 6502 processor. The address is then given by the byte in the next memory cell. It is clearly awkward to continue our discussion in terms of bit patterns like 10000101.

A first step in the direction of providing a less forbidding programming environment is the use of hex codes to represent binary patterns. This is certainly a considerable improvement. However, a machine-code program, even in hex notation, still provides few useful clues to the human programmer. Instead low-level programs are coded in a format which bears a direct relationship with machine-code, but makes liberal use of notations which can be readily identified by humans. This format is called **assembly language**; programs written in assembly language can be translated automatically and simply into machine code. It is not intended here to teach how to code extensive programs in assembly language. Rather, we shall illustrate assembly code with examples, mostly taken from 6502 assembly language. Since assembly code is essentially a transcription of machine code, assembly languages depend critically on the processor for which they are designed. The details differ between processors, but the broad principles of assembly languages are equally valid for micro and mainframe processors.

Mnemonic operation codes

The first and most far-reaching feature of assembly languages is the use of mnemonics for the operation codes, as shown in figure 6.3. Coupled with the use of

Mnemonic	Meaning
LDA	Load accumulator
STA	Store contents of accumulator (in memory location)
ADC	Add with carry
JMP	Jump (to address)
BEQ	Branch if equal to zero
CLC	Clear carry flag

Figure 6.3 Some 6502 assembler mnemonics

hex codes for binary addresses, this provides the programmer with a reasonable programming language.

A program variable in a high-level language refers to a location in memory to hold data. However, when we write high-level programs we are not interested in the address of the memory cells used. At the machine level, though, we may need to incorporate the address into the program. For example, the effect of the simple high-level assignment

> y = number

is achieved by the following assembly code, using one-address instructions:

>   LDA   &70
>   STA   &0E05

Here the value of *number* is held in cell &70 and the variable *y* references cell &0E05. In this format, each instruction has two fields—an operation code and an **operand**. (We use the ampersand & to signal a hex code. Unfortunately there is no agreement about what symbol to use and when writing hex codes in programs you must establish what convention your software assumes.)

Addressing modes

In the instructions LDA and STA above, the memory cells whose contents are accessed are explicitly stated; this is called **direct** (or **absolute**) **addressing**. If a constant is used in a calculation, it does not have to be taken from a memory cell; it may be given directly in the instruction. To distinguish a constant from a memory address, we prefix the former with the hash symbol #.

>   LDA   &0E05
>   ADD   #3

The sequence above loads the accumulator (using absolute addressing) and adds 3 to its contents. An instruction which uses a constant instead of an address is in **immediate mode**. Note that, in immediate mode, the constant must fit into the operand field. This constraint imposes a limit on the range of numbers which can be used in immediate mode instructions. (For example, the operand field may be limited to eight bits, giving the range from &0 to &FF.)

In many processors the add instruction automatically adds in the contents of the carry flag. To understand why, recall that numbers are held as bit patterns, and addition is performed by the hardware bit by bit. A logic network called a *full adder* adds corresponding bits, taking in the carry from the previous bit. The first adder in the sequence has no carry bit to take in, so it takes the carry flag instead. Any carry generated in the addition is carried into the next adder. The last adder in the sequence sends its carry (if any) back to the carry flag. When the add with carry instruction is used, the carry flag must be cleared to zero first (unless you want to include its contents). This would give the following code sequence for the addition described above.

```
LDA &0E05
CLC
ADC #3
```

Symbolic addressing

When writing assembly code you may need to know where in memory certain instructions will be stored. Just as the programmer is spared the details of the binary instruction codes (or their hex equivalents) by the use of mnemonics, so also provision is made for symbolic representation of addresses.

Assembly languages allow the use of the *symbolic names* to stand for specific addresses. Symbolic names are introduced into programs as **labels** of instructions. The label can then be used in the operand field of another instruction to stand for the address of the operation code where the label is defined. We shall indicate a label definition using a full stop (again there are many different conventions for labels).

```
.start    LDA #0
          CLC
.add      ADC #1
          JMP add
```

This program sets the accumulator initially to zero, then proceeds to add 1 to it time and time again. The label *add* refers to the memory cell in which the operation code for ADC is stored. By using the JMP instruction, the programmer is able to transfer control back to the ADC instruction, blissfully unaware of its actual storage location. Of course, this program is utterly useless as its execution will put the processor into an indefinite loop, with no means of escape (other than an interrupt).

Code assembly

At this juncture it is worthwhile digressing to consider what happens when a program is assembled into machine code. The *assembler* is a special program whose function is to generate machine code from a program written in assembly language. There are essentially four functions to be carried out:

- reservation of storage for the instructions and data;
- replacing mnemonic operation codes by machine codes;
- replacing symbolic addresses by numeric addresses;
- determining the machine representation of constants.

Clearly there is no problem with operation codes, absolute addresses, and immediate constants. These all have bit patterns which are stored sequentially in memory from some start address specified by the programmer. But what happens when a label is encountered? The assembler will have to engage in some book-keeping. A *symbol table* will be set up which matches labels to addresses. In order to do this, the assembler must keep track of the store locations in which the assembled machine code will be held. In practice, these locations are usually held relative to the beginning, or *origin*, of the program, which is called location 0. The assembler calculates how much space is occupied by each program instruction when represented in machine code. As the assembler works through the program code, the *location counter* is updated with the location of the current instruction. When a label is encountered, it is stored in the symbol table together with the current value of the location counter. The label itself can then be removed from the program by the assembler. Thus, for example, in the program above, the ADC operation may correspond to location 5 (*relative* to the origin). The label *add* is inserted into the symbol table with value 5. When the assembler encounters the JMP instruction, the value of *add* is retrieved from the symbol table, and the address field of JMP is replaced by *origin* + 5. If, when the program is run, the origin is set to &0D00 (say), then the JMP instruction above is equivalent to JMP &0D05. This highlights another advantage of symbolic addressing—no matter where in memory the program above is assembled, its execution will produce the same results. The corresponding machine code will, however, always have an absolute address in the jump instruction, and cannot be relocated elsewhere. It is the assembler which takes care to supply the correct addresses when the machine code is produced.

A two-pass assembler

Consider now the following program, which features the use of the X register.

```
          LDX #5              load X register
.loop     DEX                 decrement X register by 1
          BEQ out             branch if zero flag set
                .
                .
                .
          JMP loop
.out
```

The X register is used here just like an accumulator; the DEX instruction decrements its contents by 1, so it serves as a counter. When the loop is traversed for the fifth time, the contents of the X register become zero; this automatically sets the *zero flag* (it would likewise be set if the accumulator of Y register became zero). This provides the loophole taken by the branch instruction so that execution can continue from the instruction labelled out.

But think now—how is this program to be assembled? When the assembler reaches the instruction BEQ *out*, it will search its symbol table for the corresponding address—and find none. The value of the label *out* is not determined until the corresponding instruction is assembled, later on in the program!

To overcome this problem, assembly programs may need to be assembled in two passes. On the first pass, the location of each instruction is calculated and the symbol table is constructed. The operation codes are usually translated to machine instructions during this pass. Any errors discovered during this pass, such as duplicate labels, or inadmissible operation codes, have to be reported. However, symbols in address fields are not processed yet. During the second pass, machine code is generated for the address fields, looking up the symbol table as necessary. Any symbols which remain undefined are reported as errors. In the absence of errors, a listing is produced, which includes the original program text, annotated line by line with the corresponding address and machine-code translation. The machine-code version of the program is then ready to be executed. This process is known as **two-pass assembly**.

Data addresses

Labels enable the programmer to use symbolic names for addresses at which program instructions are stored. We now turn our attention to a corresponding notation which facilitates the use of symbolic names for data addresses. These take the place of variable names in high-level languages. Storage of data in memory cells requires no action at the time of program execution, but a **directive** is required in the program text which directs the assembler to store the data while assembling the program.

EQUB	stores a byte of data
EQUW	stores two bytes (word) of data
EQUD	stores four bytes (double word) of data
EQUS	stores a string

Data directives in the BBC assembly language

Data directives may be inserted into a program as though they are instructions. However no code is generated; the assembler merely stores the binary codes for the number or string specified in the next memory cell or cells. It remains the duty of the programmer to ensure that no attempt is made to execute the contents of these cells. The processor cannot tell the difference. A label attached to a data directive now serves as a symbolic data name. For example, the program fragment

```
.data    EQUB    45
         LDA     data
```

loads into the accumulator the contents of the cell addressed by *data*, namely the number 45. It is therefore equivalent in effect to the instruction LDA #45.

Data directives are typically implemented on the second pass of a two-pass assembler. However, they have to be scanned on the first pass to determine how many memory cells the corresponding data will occupy, so that the location counter can be updated accordingly.

Macros and subroutines

Sections of code which are frequently required can be coded separately and called by the main program as a macro or a subroutine.

A **subroutine** is very much like a subprogram in a high-level language. A JSR (jump to subroutine) instruction is inserted in the main code as required, and assembled into machine code. On execution of the program, when the subroutine call is encountered, control is transferred to the specified address. The subroutine is then executed sequentially until an RTS operation code is encountered. Control is then transferred back to the main program at the next instruction following the JSR which invoked the subroutine.

A **macro** is rather different. The macro definition gives a name to a section of assembly code, possibly including parameters. For example, a section of code to multiply two numbers—not available in the instruction set of most assemblers—might be called MUL. MUL can subsequently be used within the program as though it were a mnemonic code. When the program is being assembled, the macro definition is recorded but not assembled into machine code. When the assembler encounters a *macro call* (a use of the new instruction) within the program, the macro body is assembled into machine code (with appropriate values for the parameters).

The difference between using a macro and a subroutine is illustrated by figure 6.4. The former is assembled into inline code which can be executed sequentially and is often called an **open routine**; the latter requires control to be switched between sections of memory and is called a **closed routine**. Both serve to improve the structure and comprehensibility of assembly programs. However, a subroutine provides a single copy of the code for a particular procedure, providing a saving in memory, whereas a macro is used to produce efficient code which saves processor time while minimising the margin for errors in coding.

Before leaving this topic, it is necessary to say a word about what happens when control is transferred to a subroutine body. The actual transfer of control, a jump, is achieved by modifying the program counter. But there is a subtle difference between a subroutine jump and an unconditional jump. For, at the end of execution of the subroutine body, control must be returned to the calling sequence. To enable this, the address of the next instruction must be preserved, so that, on return from the subroutine, the program counter is reset to the appropriate address.

One method of preserving this data is by the use of an **address vector**. The memory location prior to the first instruction of the subroutine is reserved. On encountering a JSR operation, the contents of the program counter (the next instruction in the main sequence) are saved in the reserved location for future reference. Only then is the program counter updated with the subroutine address.

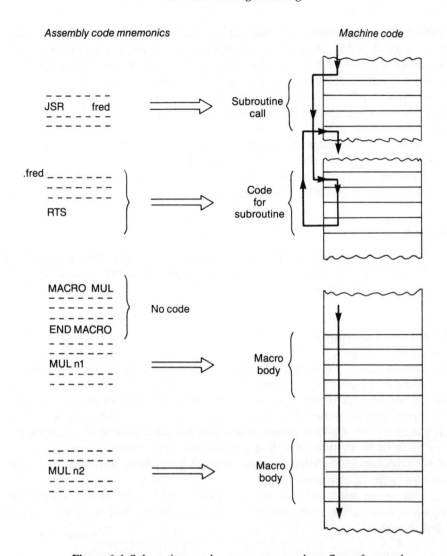

Figure 6.4 Subroutines and macros: arrows show flow of control

When the return operation is reached, the program counter is restored from the address vector. Note that, with this method of storing the return address, one subroutine can be called from another, but it is not safe for a subroutine to call itself recursively. This is because the second call would overwrite the address vector for returning control on conclusion of the subroutine execution.

An alternative method of storing return addresses, which allows subroutines to be nested recursively, is the use of a **system stack**. This is a reserved area of memory into which data to be preserved is put. Addresses can be piled up on the stack as necessary; when a subroutine ends, the return instruction address is retrieved from the top of the stack. The location of the top of the stack is held in a special register called the **stack pointer**. The stack pointer is automatically adjusted on each subroutine entry and return. In actual implementation, the stack frequently starts from the highest address and grows towards lower addresses; for example, if the stack pointer is currently &78 and a two-byte address is pushed onto the stack, the stack pointer will be reset to &76. (In the BBC computer, page 1—the memory locations from &100 to &1FF—is reserved for use as the system stack. Consequently, the stack pointer holds a one-byte address, the offset from location &100. Its initial value is &FF.)

Execution of a subroutine may change the status flags in ways not expected by the calling program. It is necessary, therefore, for the subroutine to save the *status word* (the contents of the program status register) as well as the return address, and restore it, wholly or partially, before returning control.

Exercise 6.9

List the registers and memory locations used in transferring control to a subroutine, and describe the sequence of events. You may assume that the jump instruction takes an absolute address.

6.5 Address Modification

Instructions which use absolute addresses or immediate data enable a range of fairly simple programs to be written. It is frequently desirable to incorporate into an instruction an address which is not yet known at the time of writing the code. This happens typically when the address depends on the circumstances at the time when it is executed. Another situation in which the address field of an instruction cannot be fixed at the time of coding is where the same instruction is required to refer to a sequence of different addresses. This happens, for example, when processing an array of values.

These situations are handled by the provision of addressing modes in which the address field is *modified*. There are two methods of address modification—indexing and indirection.

Indirect addressing

An instruction which uses **indirect addressing** accesses its data by a two-stage process. The contents of the location addressed by the operand field is treated as a **vector**, which points to the location holding the data. Thus, if location &561C points to location &24A2, which in turn holds the byte 5F, then the indirect instruction

    LDA (&561C)

loads the value &5F into the accumulator. An indirect address is usually indicated by enclosing it in parentheses. (Alternatively, some assembly languages use the @ symbol for indirect addresses.)
This is illustrated by figure 6.5, where the two-byte address &24A2 is held in the

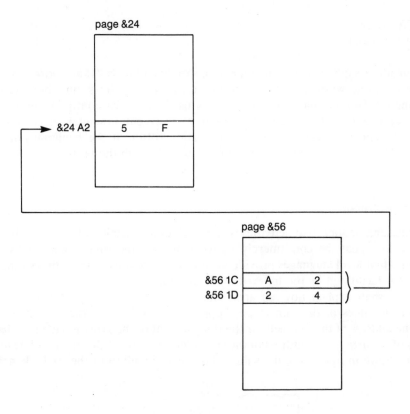

Figure 6.5 Indirect addressing

two adjacent locations &561C and &561D, low byte first. The corresponding direct instruction

    LDA &561C

would have the effect of loading &A2 into the accumulator.

An example of the use of indirect addressing would be for an operation on a parameter of a subroutine. The address of the parameter is passed to a specified location, say &561C. Indirection through this location now accesses the parameter, which is actually in location &24A2, say. The parameter can now be updated with the value held in the accumulator by the instruction

    STA (&561C)

Indirection is also of use in controlling the destination of a jump. If a jump has to be made to an address which varies according to circumstances prevailing during execution of the program, the jump is indirected through a vector. The vector has a fixed address, and its contents locate the destination. The instruction sequence

STA vector
JMP (vector)

stores an address in the vector and then jumps to that address. (If an address vector is more than one word long, the code for storing that address must be adjusted accordingly.) This mechanism is sometimes used to return control from a sub-routine, or an interrupt service routine, to the main execution sequence. The return address is held in a vector at a known location (often at the beginning of the routine). Control is returned by an indirect jump through the vector.

Indexed addressing

When the same sequence of activities is required for a collection of data, we should not have to repeat the code merely to accommodate the small change on each occasion. High-level languages provide arrays for this purpose. Array processing at low level is facilitated by the **indexed** mode of addressing.

First we shall explain how an array may be held in memory. An array is a sequence of values of the same type. Suppose each value occupies two memory cells. The address of the first cell for the first element of the array is called the **base address** of the array. The address of the sixth element, say, of the array will be *base* + 10, as shown in figure 6.6; the value 10 is called the **offset** of the sixth element.

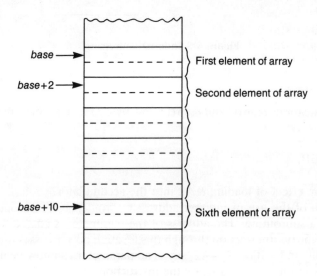

Figure 6.6 Array storage

(In BBC BASIC, all arrays have an index range starting from 0 upwards. The element $d(0)$ is stored at the base address; the offset for $d(i)$ is then i times the number of bytes required for each element.)

To address the elements of an array it is desirable to modify the base address by the offset. The base address is fixed for all operations on array elements; by adjusting the offset, the desired element is addressed.

In order to use indexed mode, one or more **index registers** are required. We shall assume that X and Y registers are available to be used for indexing. To address an array element, the offset is put into an index register. In indexed addressing mode, the address given in the instruction is modified by adding to it the contents of the index register. So if the X register holds the number 10, and *base* is the base address of the array then

        LDA base

loads into the accumulator the first word of the first array element, whereas

        LDA base, X

loads the first word of the sixth array element. The symbol following the comma indicates which register is to be used for indexing. For example, if we have

        LDX #&2A   \load the X register
        LDA &0E00, X

the first instruction loads the hex code 2A into the X register (immediate mode) and the second instruction loads the contents of cell &0E2A (that is, &0E00 modified by the offset &2A) into the accumulator. To illustrate indexed addressing, the following program sets up an array of twelve bytes, and stores in the array the numbers 101 to 112.

```
.array  EQUD 0
        EQUD 0
        EQUD 0          \reserve twelve bytes of memory
.start  LDX #0          \load 0 into X register
        LDY #100        \load 100 (decimal) into Y register
.loop   INY             \add 1 to contents of Y register
        TYA             \transfer contents of Y register to accumulator
        STA array, X    \store contents of accumulator in array (with
                        offset)
        INX             \add 1 to contents of X register
        CPX #12         \compare contents of X register with 12
        BNE loop        \if not equal, branch to loop
```

Exercise 6.10

Write an assembly code routine which prints the text string "Computing Science" using indexed addressing. Assume that a subroutine which prints the character in the accumulator is held at the location given by the label *write*. The effect of each instruction should be carefully explained.

Does your program work for all text strings?

It is sometimes necessary to combine both modification modes to indirect through an indexed address. One example of this could be the implementation of a string array in BASIC. In a string array, the amount of memory occupied by each element varies according to the length of each string, and it is not possible to use simple indexed addressing. Instead the array is accessed through a table of vectors. Since each address has a fixed length (say two bytes) the *address table* can be accessed as a simple array. Figure 6.7 illustrates the use of an address table. The instruction sequence

        LDX #4
        LDA base, X

stores in the accumulator the binary code 10110010 (= &B2); indirect addressing allows the contents of memory cell &13B2 to be stored in the accumulator. This is written as

        LDA (base, X)

and loads the accumulator with the first byte of the third string element.

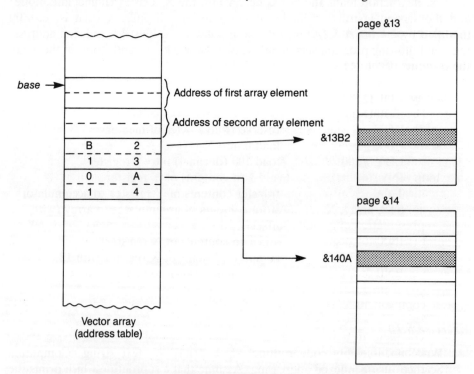

Figure 6.7 Indirection through an address table

Indirection may also be used in conjunction with indexing to provide a controlled jump. A *jump address table* is set up (as in figure 6.7) of addresses to which the jump may be required; the jump is programmed as

    LDX offset
    JMP (base, X)

Machine-code representation

With all these different addressing modes, how does the processor know how to interpret a given instruction? The answer is that the operation code for, say, LDA is not entirely fixed. It has a variable part as well as a fixed part. This is shown in figure 6.8, in which it is seen that bits 2, 3 and 4 of the operation code determine the addressing mode.

Instruction	Mode	Operation code
LDA #49	Immediate	10101001
LDA &F29	Absolute	10101101
LDA &F29, X	Indexed	10111101
LDA (&F29)	Indirect	10100001

Figure 6.8 6502 machine-code dependence on addressing mode

Summary of Chapter 6

The contents of the registers and memory locations are binary patterns which may be interpreted variously as instructions, characters or numeric data. The meaning attached to a bit pattern is determined by the field of the instruction in which it occurs. The distinction between different data interpretations is entirely in the hands of the program which accesses the data. For convenience, hexadecimal code may be used to represent binary codes.

Characters are represented internally using a standard collation sequence. Arithmetic is performed using the binary system. Pure binary is preferred for mathematical and scientific calculations, but binary coded decimal is available for commercial programs with a high proportion of input and output to arithmetic.

The representation of negative numbers requires the most significant bit to act as a sign bit (with 0 for positive). The following notations are in use:

- signed magnitude: the remaining bits represent the magnitude;
- twos' complement: the most significant bit has minus its usual value;
- ones' complement: each bit is inverted to obtain the negative from the positive.

In twos' complement notation, overflow is indicated when the carry into the most significant bit differs from the carry out of it.

Integer arithmetic can provide only a limited range of numbers, although it is accurate so long as the answer does not overflow. For a wider range of numbers, and to handle fractions, floating-point arithmetic is used. This is frequently implemented in hardware or firmware. The degree of accuracy depends on the number of bits available for the mantissa. Floating-point arithmetic within a fixed number of significant figures suffers from inherent inaccuracy.

Although programs derived from algorithms are written in high-level languages, the processor itself works in binary machine code.

Programs which manipulate the registers directly are written at low level. To ease the task of the low-level programmer, an assembly language is used. This provides mnemonics for the instructions and allows symbolic names for the memory locations. Modes of addressing by instructions can be immediate, absolute (direct), index modified, and indirect. Control in assembly code is provided by branch and jump instructions, which may be conditional. Program clarity and efficiency are aided by subroutines and macros.

The execution of an assembly-code program is a two-stage process. In the first stage, the assembly code is translated to machine code. This stage may involve several phases, including macro processing and two passes of the assembler. The resulting machine code is then a working program which can be executed under control of the software. The assembled machine-code version of a program can be saved for later execution.

Answers to Exercises

6.1
Binary	Octal	Hexadecimal
10011010	232	9A
001011	13	B
00010011	23	13

In converting between octal and hex, it is best to use the binary form as an intermediate stage.

6.2 $1001 \longrightarrow 1 \times 2^3 + 1 \times 2^0 = 8 + 1 = 9$
$100 \longrightarrow 1 \times 2^2 = 4$

(For each 1 in the binary representation, the number of digits after the 1 gives the corresponding power of 2.)

6.3 The method is to find the largest power of 2 which is less than the given number, and then consider the remainder.

2^6	2^5	2^4	2^3	2^2	2^1	2^0
64	32	16	8	4	2	1

$49 = 32 + 17$
$\quad = 32 + 16 + 1 \quad$ decimal
$\longrightarrow 110001 \quad$ binary

$21 = 16 + 4 + 1$ decimal

$\longrightarrow 10101$ binary

6.4 (a) 1988 DIV 256 = 7 remainder 196

    196 DIV 16 = 12 remainder 4

So $1988_{10} = 7B4_{16}$

111 DIV 16 = 6 remainder 15

So $111_{10} = 6F_{16}$

Similarly, $300_{10} = 12C_{16}$

(b) FF = $15 \times 16 + 15 \times 1 = 255$

BCD = $11 \times 256 + 12 \times 16 + 13 \times 1 = 3021$

$111_{16} = 273_{10}$

6.5 The largest negative number in twos' complement is 10 000; this corresponds to decimal $-2^5 = -32$

6.6   0 1 1 0

      1 0 1 1

      ———

      0 0 0 1

      1 1 1   carries

This sum corresponds to $6 + (-5) = 1$. Since the carries into and out of the most significant bit are equal, the correct result is obtained.

6.7   00111001 (57)   10111001 (−71)

(a) 00011100 (28)   11011100 (−36)

(b) 01110010 (114)   01110010 (114)

The decimal equivalents are given in parentheses.

(a) 57 DIV 2 = 28, −71 DIV 2 = −36 (rounded down).

(b) 57 ⋆ 2 = 114, −71 ⋆ 2 = 114 (true result out of range).

6.8 The accuracy depends on the length of the mantissa, that is, 36 bits. Of these, one is the sign bit; on the other hand, the leading 1 after the binary point is not stored as the mantissa is normalised. Since $2^{-36} \approx 3.6 \times 10^{-12}$, the corresponding decimal numbers are accurate to eleven significant figures.

6.9 This answer assumes that the data to be restored is saved in a stack.

Registers: program counter (PC), program status word (PSW) and stack pointer (SP)

Memory locations: area reserved for system stack

The operation JSR *address* is implemented by the following sequence of transfers:

Stack ← (contents of PC) + *n* (where *n* is the number of words occupied
by the JSR instruction)
SP ← SP − 1 (assuming a one-word address)
Stack ← PSW
SP ← SP − 1
PC ← address

6.10

	.text	EQUS "Computing Science"	\assembler directive
	.start	LDX #0	\initialise X register
		LDY t	\load address of text into Y register
	.loop	LDA text, X	\load a character of text string into accumulator
		JSR write	\write character using subroutine
		INX	\increment X register
		INY	\increment Y register
		CPY s	\compare address of next character with start address
		BNE loop	\branch to *loop* if *start* not yet reached
		RTS	\end of subroutine
	.t	EQUB text	\store *text* address
	.s	EQUB start	\store *start* address

This subroutine works by printing each character of the string until reaching *start*, which is the next address after the end of the string.

The subroutine will fail for an empty string. It will also not work if the string has more characters than the largest number which can be held in an index register. (For example, if the word length is 8 bits, the maximum string length is $2^8 = 256$ characters.)

Further Exercises

1. Write down the bit pattern for the storage of 27 in an eight-bit word. How would you represent -27 using the following conventions?

   (a) signed magnitude;
   (b) twos' complement;
   (c) ones' complement.

2. A particular machine supports manipulation of both fixed and floating point numbers utilising its 32 bit word length. For fixed point, all 32 bits are used to store integers in twos' complement form. Floating point uses the first 24 bits to store a fractional mantissa in sign and magnitude form and the remaining 8 bits

to hold the exponent in excess-128 form, these numbers being automatically normalised.

(a) Explain in detail these two different methods for storing numbers. The explanations should include
  (i) both the maximum positive value and also the negative value nearest to zero capable of being stored; bit settings are also required.
  (ii) the relative advantages of each form of representation.
(b) Some models within this particular range of machines do not support floating point arithmetic in hardware but use software instead. Explain why this is the case.
(c) Outline an algorithm for the addition of two floating point numbers.

(AEB—1986/1/15)

3. A 16-bit word computer has an instruction format with an 8-bit address field. This means that instructions can only have addresses in the range 0 to FF (hex). How can a word with a greater address be accessed?

4. (a) Express as a binary number
  (i) decimal 41 (ii) octal 3715 (iii) hexadecimal 3715.
(b) Give the 2's complement of the binary number 00101001.
(c) Compare the advantages and disadvantages of fixed point and floating point representation of numbers.
(d) A particular system uses floating point numbers in which the six-bit exponent is biassed so that zero exponent is represented by 100000, and the mantissa is a ten-bit 2's complement number. For a standardised (i.e. normalised) floating point number in this format, express in decimal:
  (i) the exponent 100101,
  (ii) the exponent 000101,
  (iii) the mantissa 0101000000,
  (iv) the mantissa 1010000000.

(JMB—80/1/13)

5. (a) A word in computer memory may contain
  (i) a floating point number,
  (ii) an instruction,
  (iii) a fixed point number.
  Suggest and explain a format for each of these forms of data assuming
      the fixed point numbers must cover a range of at least five
         decimal digits of both positive and negative numbers,
      there are at least four ways of addressing data,
      the main store may have a capacity of a least 64K bytes.
(b) State three of the methods of addressing data. Using a suitable example in each case, explain its usefulness.
(c) Compare fixed and floating point data formats for
  (i) range of representable numbers
  (ii) accuracy.

(JMB—85/1/15)

6. Write an assembly code program to perform the assignment

    n = n + size − 2

    using typical one-address instructions. Precise syntax is not important but you should state clearly the purpose of each instruction.

7. (a) Many computers use a status register to hold condition codes which communicate the outcome of previous actions to conditional jump instructions.
    (i) Describe three different condition codes.
    (ii) What types of instructions affect condition codes?
    (iii) Illustrate the action of a conditional jump in the execute phase of the fetch–execute cycle describing the function of any registers you mention.
   (b) It is required to write a section of program that transfers control to one of 18 different locations dependent upon an integer in the range 0 to 17. This integer is held in a location labelled SELECT.
       The machine upon which this is to be programmed supports one-address instructions with indexing (address modification) and indirect addressing available.
       Describe two different methods of implementing the required function. In each case your description should consist of a set of one-address instructions.

                                                                    (AEB—84/1/2)

8. Distinguish between an instruction and a directive in an assembly language program.

9. Using one-address instructions, write an assembly-language program to add the corresponding elements of two arrays, with base addresses *array1* and *array2*, leaving the results in the locations occupied by the first array. You may assume that each array element occupies one memory cell.

10. The assembly language of a particular computer uses two-address instructions. Thus

    ADD 100, 200

    causes the number in location 100 to be added to the number in location 200 and the result left in 200. Here 100 and 200 are *direct* addresses. If an address part is to be used *indirectly*, it is preceded by the symbol '@'. If the address part is to be used in *immediate mode*, it is preceded by the symbol '#'. All addresses and contents are written in octal.

Certain locations have contents as listed below.

location: 100 101 102 103 104
content: 107 104 103 134 555

For the following instructions, each executed from the *above initial state*, what is the effect of executing each instruction?

(a) ADD   101, @102
(b) ADD   101,   104
(c) ADD #100,   100

(ULSEB—84/1/5)

11. Assembly languages usually provide the *bitwise* logical operations NOT, AND and OR. A 1 corresponds to logic T, a 0 to logic F.

(a) Which operation effects ones' complementation?
(b) Show that 00000111 ANDed with a bit pattern acts as a mask to select the three least significant bits of that pattern.
(c) Describe a sequence of shifts which has the same effect as the mask in part (b).

12. (a) With the aid of an example, explain the term *single-address instruction format* as applied to binary machine code instructions.
(b) The assembly language instructions for addition, ADN 27, ADD 27 and ADI 27 will be executed in different ways because of their different modes of addressing (*immediate*, *direct* and *indirect*, respectively).
  (i) Distinguish between the three modes, showing the effect of the instruction in each case.
  (ii) Explain how the processor would distinguish between each mode of addressing when executing the machine code instructions. Relate the explanation to the individual instruction format and to the appropriate steps in the execution cycle.

(AEB—1983/1/2)

13. The following table shows the representations in a 12-bit word of the integer values **P** and **Q**, in twos' complement integer, sign and magnitude integer, signed binary coded decimal integer and floating point notations, not necessarily in that order. The floating point representation uses an 8-bit fraction and a 4-bit exponent, each in twos' complement form.

	A	B	C	D
P	0010 1001 1100	0000 0001 1101	0111 0100 0101	0000 0001 1101
Q	0001 0100 1101	1111 1111 0010	1001 0000 0100	1000 0000 1110

(a) What are the values **P** and **Q**?
(b) What notations do **A**, **B**, **C** and **D** stand for?

(c) What are the largest positive and negative values that can be stored in a 12-bit word in each of these notations? (Express your answers in powers of two if you wish.)

(d) Choose any three of these notations and, for each, describe in outline the steps necessary to add the two values **P** and **Q**. You may assume that there is a simple binary adder for two 12-bit operands, which also has the ability to act as a subtractor of twos' complement values by inverting one of the operands and adding an additional 1 bit.

(Camb.—1986)

13. Using an assembly language, rather than machine code, normally provides the programmer with the following extra facilities:
    (i) symbolic addresses,
    (ii) directives (or pseudo operations).

(a) Describe two ways in which symbolic addresses are used and explain how they are processed by a two-pass assembler.

(b) What is a directive? Give two distinct examples of typical directives and the tasks they perform.

(c) A piece of code comprising several instructions is to be used in a large assembly language program. Give *one* technique that the programmer could employ to minimise the writing of duplicate code.

Using a language with which you are familiar, or otherwise, explain carefully how this technique is implemented. What factors influence the efficiency of this technique in terms of storage and timing?

(ULSEB—1987)

7 All About Data

A computer is a device for processing data. We have expended many words on the processing, far fewer on the data. This deficiency will be remedied over the next three chapters, which cover the way data is organised and structured for the purposes of processing and storage.

Data is but an abstraction from information. Consider the timetable in figure 7.1. Taken as a whole, the timetable may be interpreted as a complete listing of the times at which buses on route 770 stop at selected points. This interpretation depends on understanding how bus timetables are constructed. Thus, it is necessary to know that opposite each place name (such as Hassocks) are given the times at which buses stop there, and these times are given in the format of the 24-hour clock. The place names are printed for convenience alongside each section of the timetable; of course, if you memorised the place names, they could be dispensed with and the timetable would still make sense. The entries in the timetable are just numeric codes—in this form they are raw *data*. When interpreted in the sense given above they provide *information*.

To process the information, it is sufficient to process the data in an appropriate context. We may assume that a processing algorithm has been designed which provides the right context. Consequently it is not necessary to input total information to the execution of an algorithm, merely the relevant data.

In this chapter we look at issues surrounding the collection of data for processing, and methods of ensuring the validity of the data in context. We have previously encountered the *array*, a collection of a number of data items of the same type. In this chapter we shall meet a new method of structuring data, the *record*, which can be used to describe a collection of associated data of different types.

7.1 Data Capture

In order that data may be processed by a computer, it must be collected and, if necessary, converted into a suitable form compatible with the hardware. The conversion process depends on the particular input device in use and an appropriate interface, as explained in chapter 5. Collection of data can take place in a number of ways. One of the factors influencing data collection is the nature of the source of information. Other important factors are cost, speed and accuracy. This last is vital, for there can be no purpose in carefully processing inaccurate data.

STAGECOACH 770 — LINDFIELD · HAYWARDS HEATH · BURGESS HILL · BRIGHTON — LIMITED STOP

Mondays to Saturdays

	★ NS	★ NS	NS	NS	NS	NS	NS	NS	NS	s	NS	s	762 NS
LINDFIELD, The Witch	0652	0742	0857	0957	1057	1157	1257	1357	1457	1557	1607	1702	● 1803
Lindfield, Post Office	0654	0744											
Haywards Heath, Muster Green													
HAYWARDS HEATH, Perrymount Road	0657	0747	0900	1000	1100	1200	1300	1400	1500	1600	1610Δ	1705	
HAYWARDS HEATH, South Road	0700	0750	0910	1010	1110	1210	1310	1410	1510	1610	1620Δ	1715	
Worlds End, Janes Lane/Valebridge Road	0710	0800	0913	1013	1113	1213	1313	1413	1513	1613	1623	1718	
Burgess Hill, Wendovers/Junction Road	0713	0803	0915	1015	1115	1215	1315	1415	1515	1615	1625	1720	
BURGESS HILL, Church Road Shops	0715	0805	0918	1018	1118	1218	1318	1418	1518	1618	1628	1723	
Burgess Hill, Royal George	0718	0808	0920	1020	1120	1220	1320	1420	1520	1620	1630	1725	1813
London Road, Chanctonbury Road	0720	0810	0923	1023	1123	1223	1323	1423	1523	1623	1633	1728	
Hassocks, Stone Pound	0723	0813	0926	1026	1126	1226	1326	1426	1526	1626	1638	1731	1818
Clayton, Jack & Jill	0726	0816	0932	1032	1132	1232	1332	1432	1532	1632	1642	1737	
Preston Park, Lovers Walk	0732	0822											
Edward Street, American Express	0739	0839											
BRIGHTON, Old Steine	0742	0842†	0942	1042	1142	1242	1342	1442	1542	1642	1652	1747	1837
BRIGHTON, Churchill Square	0745	0845	0945	1045	1145	1245	1345	1445	1545	1653	1652	1750	1840

STAGECOACH 770 — BRIGHTON · BURGESS HILL · HAYWARDS HEATH · LINDFIELD — LIMITED STOP

Mondays to Saturdays

	NS	NS	NS	NS	NS	NS	NS	NS		s	NS	s	NS
BRIGHTON, Churchill Square		0855	1000	1100	1200	1300	1400	1500	1605	1700	1700	1805	1805
BRIGHTON, Old Steine	0748	0858	1003	1103	1203	1303	1403	1503	1608	1703	1703	1808	1808
Edward Street, American Express	0755	0905	1010	1110	1210	1310	1410	1510	1615	1710	1706	1815	1811
Preston Park, Lovers Walk											1713		1818
Clayton, Jack & Jill	0804	0914	1019	1119	1219	1319	1419	1519	1624	1719	1722	1824	1827
Hassocks, Stone Pound	0807	0917	1022	1122	1222	1322	1422	1522	1627	1722	1725	1827	1830
London Road, Chanctonbury Road	0810	0920	1025	1125	1225	1325	1425	1525	1630	1725	1728	1830	1833
Burgess Hill, Royal George	0812	0922	1027	1127	1227	1327	1427	1527	1632	1727	1730	1832	1835
BURGESS HILL, Civic Way	0815	0925	1030	1130	1230	1330	1430	1530	1635	1730	1733	1835	1838
Burgess Hill, Wendovers/Junction Road	0817	0927	1032	1132	1232	1332	1432	1532	1637	1732	1735	1837	1840
Worlds End, Janes Lane/Valebridge Road	0820	0930	1035	1135	1235	1335Δ	1435	1535	1640	1735	1738	1840	1843
HAYWARDS HEATH, South Road	0830	0940	1045	1145	1245	1345Δ	1445	1545	1650	1745	1748	1850	1853
HAYWARDS HEATH, Perrymount Road	0833	0943	1048	1148	1248	1348	1448	1548	1653	1748	1751	1853	1856
Lindfield, The Witch											1754		1859
LINDFIELD, Post Office											1756		1901

CODE   S – Saturdays only.   NS – Not Saturdays.   Δ – Calls at St. Francis Hospital on Wednesdays.   ★ – Peak Fares apply to these journeys, see back page.

● – Passengers with 770 Day Return tickets may travel on this Service 762 journey between the points shown.

† – Time at Palace Pier.

Figure 7.1 A bus timetable *(courtesy of Southdown Bus Company)*

The whole activity of collecting data accurately and making it available to a process, such as a functioning computer program, is known as **data capture**.

Data collection

The collection of data may take place offline or online to the computer. Offline methods may be purely manual, so that a further activity is required to convert the data into machine-readable format, or maybe directly to machine-readable form.

Examples of purely manual methods include the assembly of data through interviews and other conventional techniques such as copying relevant items from source documents. The assembled data may be laid out on a sheet of plain paper prior to being keyed in. More often, however, special forms matching the input format for the program are printed in advance. These forms are filled in by data-entry clerks and are then conveyed to keyboard operators who can input the data by rote, quite oblivious of their information content. Such formats are used, for example, by meter readers to record the current readings on domestic gas and electricity meters. Application forms, similar to that shown in figure 7.2, have a fixed format into which the applicant inserts the particulars, a character at a time, for subsequent keyboard entry.

Sometimes information from initial documents is transferred to a single ledger document. Thus, deposits to accounts with the National Savings Bank can be made over the counter at Post Offices. Each deposit must be accompanied by a deposit slip, the details of which are transferred to a ledger sheet which lists all the day's deposits at that Post Office. The daily ledger sheet is sent to National Savings Bank headquarters for processing. Such copying operations are common in manual data collection. For reasons of convenience, data may be captured in one format (for example, the deposit slip) and accumulated in another format (for example, a ledger sheet). The copying operation is a particular source of error. Whenever data is copied there exists the danger that it will not be copied accurately. It should also be borne in mind that when data is collected manually and then subsequently input at a keyboard, this too is a form of copying liable to error.

We call errors arising out of copying operations **transcription errors**. These errors are mostly by way of copying a single character incorrectly, such as 511 for 611. Characters may also be transposed, such as 4798 for 4789. In order to minimise transcription errors, data is often collected using special documents capable of direct input via document readers. By removing a copying step, the scope for errors is reduced.

Closely related to these are errors of *duplication* and *omission* of characters or of data items. In order to ensure the **integrity** of data, that is, that the data processed is the true data, care must also be taken to avoid inputting the same data twice (for example by repeating a sheet of data) or failing to input a sheet of data (for example, because it has got lost). This is often achieved by numbering source documents in strict sequence.

Data may be input online at a terminal which is connected to the processor on which the data will be processed. An obvious form of online input is keyboard entry at a terminal, such as the terminals used by the tellers in building society offices to enter details of deposits, withdrawals and other transactions directly for immediate

Application for Credit

Please complete in BLOCK CAPITALS and tick where appropriate.

Mr   Mrs   Miss   Ms   Other title
☐   ☐   ☐   ☐   [   ]

First name(s)
[   ]

Surname
[   ]

Address
[   ]

[Postcode [   ]]

Date of birth [   ]   No. of dependants [   ]

Marital status: Married [   ]   Single [   ]   Widow(er) [   ]

Home telephone number (include STD code)
[   ]

Business telephone number (include STD code)
[   ]

Home details: '

Owner [   ]   Tenant [   ]   Furnished [   ]   Unfurnished [   ]

Time resident at present address   [   ]   years

If less than three years please give previous address.

[   ]

[Postcode [   ]]

Standard credit limit is £500
Should you require a higher limit please indicate by ticking the appropriate box.

£1,000 [   ]   £2,500 [   ]   up to max £5,000 [   ]

Figure 7.2 Fixed-format application form

processing. Other examples of online data capture include sensors for temperature, weight and other physical characteristics which are input directly to computers engaged in process control. The point-of-sale terminals now becoming increasingly popular in many supermarket checkouts incorporate devices for reading bar codes or magnetic stripe cards into computers which calculate and print out the price and also the current stock position.

Verification

When data is keyed in using key-to-tape and key-to-disc systems, an accuracy check, known as *verification*, is made. A second key operator, using the key station in verify mode, keys in all the data again. On this occasion, however, the characters keyed are not recorded (on tape or disc). Instead they are compared with the characters previously recorded. When a discrepancy occurs, the machine stops. The second key operator must then check whether the original character or the newly keyed character agrees with the source document. In the latter case, the recorded character(s) can be overwritten. After making the correction or accepting the original character, the operator continues verifying the rest of the document.

A similar verification procedure is employed when data is transferred between backing storage and main memory. The processor transfers the data twice and then compares the two versions of the transferred data. If they agree the transfer is deemed to be successful. Otherwise a further attempt is made to transfer the data or an error is reported.

7.2 Data Validation

The data which is processed by a program must be correct and valid. Correctness means that the data being processed is the data which is meant to be processed, without error. Validity means that the data input for processing can be satisfactorily processed by the program. It is clearly a prime function of every program to perform checks which *validate* data submitted to it. We shall discuss a number of methods of validating data.

Range checks

A *range check* may be applied to data to ensure that it is within its range of validity. The check must establish both that the data is of the right type and that the value lies within prescribed limits. Thus a program to handle positive numbers should explicity check for and reject negative numbers. The date of the month must be an integer in the range 1 to 31 and again this can be established by a range check. If an error in the input produces data which is outside the range of validity, this error will be trapped by the range check. However it is still possible for erroneous data to be within range, so that additional techniques are required to trap errors.

Encoding data

Further errors can arise in any encoding process, during which the format of data is changed. This may happen more than once between collection and processing. There will certainly be an encoding stage when data is converted to the internal format intelligible to the processor, but there may well be previous stages.

The stream of characters which typically comprise the input data must, at some stage, be converted to the internal binary form (ASCII or EBCDIC) of the processing computer. This conversion may be performed by an online input device, such as a terminal. When data is prepared offline on key-to-disc or key-to-tape equipment, it is converted to internal form ready for subsequent installation as part of the backing storage of the processing computer. Conversion to internal binary code is a form of *data encoding*.

The data may well be encoded at an earlier stage, prior to input. For example, bar codes represent numerical data as a set of black and white stripes of varying widths. They are widely used on packaged goods (and books) where they are pre-printed on the packaging or on a label. In the clothing industry it is more convenient to use mass-produced punched card tags (*Kimball tags*). The pattern of holes punched on the tag is a coded representation of the size, colour and style of the garment, and can be read by a machine. Mechanically produced codes such as these have a high degree of reliability, but in a small number of cases an erroneous code may occur.

Sometimes, codes may be encoded manually to present data in the format required by a program, such as the age conversion table in figure 7.3. The age conversion may well be performed by a clerk filling out a form.

If, for example, the age 27 is inadvertently coded E, this would be an encoding error. This error would not be discovered by a range check, which will accept any of the letters A to E as a valid age letter.

Age	Code
0–18	A
19–25	B
26–40	C
41–64	D
Over 65	E

Figure 7.3 Conversion table for age groups

Check digits

There is considerable experience of validation schemes for numeric data, which is more likely to be misread by a human reader than an alphabetic code to which a meaning can be attached. Several methods have been devised of building internal checking facilities into numeric data. One such facility is the use of a **check digit**. Here is an illustrative example.

A weekly magazine operates a subscription list, and each subscriber has a unique identification number. It is not expected that there will be more than half a million subscribers so a six-digit identification number is adequate. These numbers are modified by the addition of a check digit. So subscriber number 4719 is actually allocated the seven-digit identification number 0047191. How was the check digit 1 calculated? In this example all identification numbers are subject to a **modulo 7** check digit. The number now has the property that

$$(0 \times 7) + (0 \times 6) + (4 \times 5) + (7 \times 4) + (1 \times 3) + (9 \times 2) + (1 \times 1) = 70$$

which is divisible by 7. Each digit in the identification number is multiplied by its position, counting from the right. The check digit is arranged so that the sum of the digit-times-position for each digit in the numeric code comes to a number divisible by 7. The multiplier for each digit (the position in our example) is called a **weighting factor**. Other systems exist using different arrangements of weighting factors.

The calculation of the check digit is a laborious job for a person, but a trivial task for the computer. When identification numbers are initially allocated, the computer is instructed to print out a sheet of valid numbers, including the check digit; these can then be allocated manually. Alternatively, in an online system, the computer will itself allocate the next available valid identification number when a new subscription is entered into the data bank. Subsequently, whenever an identification number is input, the program calls a procedure to validate the number, using the modulo 7 check digit method.

This method allows seven possible check digits, from 0 to 6, since it depends on a computed number being divisible by 7. Consequently it can distinguish at most seven error conditions, and is thus suitable for numbers containing not more than seven digits. In principle, any modulus could be used, but only prime numbers are efficient at tracking down errors uniquely. The next prime number, 11, is used frequently as a modulus for check digits.

The Standard Book Number was introduced in the 1960s by book publishers in the United Kingdom as a means of identifying uniquely any book published in this country. Since then the scheme has expanded to provide each new book published in any country with an International Standard Book Number (ISBN). The ISBN is an 11-digit number divided into four fields, as shown in figure 7.4.

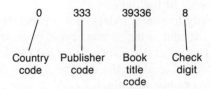

Figure 7.4 An ISBN

Exercise 7.1

    (a) Validate the ISBN shown in figure 7.4, assuming a modulo 11 check digit.

    (b) What is the next valid ISBN?

The use of a modulo 11 check digit allows numbers of up to ten digits (besides the check digit) to be handled reliably. There is one problem, however, with the use of modulo 11. Consider the book whose number should be 0 333 37097 * where the asterisk stands for the check digit. A calculation shows that the check digit should be 10! But 10 is not a digit. This problem has been overcome by using Roman numeral X for 10 when it is required as a check digit. Thus the book concerned actually has the ISBN 0 333 37097 X. This should clear up the mystery of why sometimes an ISBN, and indeed some other identification number used for all sorts of other purposes, ends with an X although it is meant to be a number.

This has an implication for the programmer. The input routine for an ISBN cannot just expect a number—if it did the range check would invalidate all ISBNs whose final character is X. Instead the input routine must specifically cater for the possibility of an X in the final position, whose interpretation as a check digit is 10.

Activity 7.1

Write a validation procedure (in any suitable programming language) for a numeric code with a modulo 11 check digit.

Control totals

Although a check digit can be used to maintain the integrity of an individual item of data, it cannot guard against the loss (or duplication) of whole data items. One of the checks against loss of items is the use of a **control total**. The simplest control total is just the number of documents or items in a given batch. Control totals may also be derived from specific data items. In an invoice each part has a price, and the total price is the sum of all the part prices. After the contents of the invoice have been transferred (whether manually or by machine) a consistency check can be made to ensure that the total price remains equal to the sum of the part prices. This use of the total price is another example of a control total. It is not strictly necessary to transfer the total at each stage, because it could always be recalculated (a trivial task for a computer). However, including it in the transfer proves a further check on the validity and accuracy of the data.

Control totals apply only to numeric data, but it is perfectly legitimate to use a control total even when the sum of the data is devoid of meaning. For example, if a statement is issued covering several invoices, the serial numbers of the invoices can be added to produce a control total for the statement, as in figure 7.5. This control total has no meaning—you cannot meaningfully add invoice numbers—but acts as a check on the invoices input. When addition (and multiplication) are used to compute codes from numeric data, this is called hashing; such a control total is consequently referred to as a *hash total*.

Exercise 7.2

Explain the difference between data verification and data validation.
Is it possible for verified data to be invalid?

```
Maverick Office Supplies

                    Statement
                                    £           £
To:  Invoice no.   01747        189.91
     Invoice no.   01792         27.03
     Invoice no.   01843        240.25
                                _____

     Sub-total                              457.19
     Less payment received                 216.94
                                            _____
                                To pay      240.25
                                            _____

Control code:   005382
```

Figure 7.5 Use of a hash total as a control code

7.3 Structured Data

We have discussed at some length (in chapters 2 and 3) how to organise programs so that they reflect the logic of the problem being solved. Various control mechanisms are available—repetitive constructs, branch constructs and procedures. Each mechanism has its uses. Data, too, can be structured in a variety of ways, each reflecting a different mode of use. The array is one form of data structure; we shall be considering a variety of other data structures in the coming chapters.

A library catalogue

Suppose you are a librarian. You want to keep track of the books in your library so that you can check whether the library has any copies of a particular book, whether a book is on the shelves or on loan, and so on. You will need to keep a record of each book. Since there are several items of information about each book which are worth having to hand, you may well decide to fill out a *record card* like the one shown in figure 7.6 for each book, and store these cards (in some suitable order) in a box.

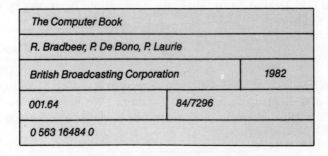

Figure 7.6 A library record card

On each card we would certainly want to record the title, name of the author, publisher and year of publication. We would probably also find it useful to note the library classification number, an acquisition number (especially where multiple copies of the same book are held) and the International Standard Book Number. Of course there are no rules as to how the information should appear on the record card, and if the library employs several librarians, each might use a different scheme for all this information. For most titles this would probably not create any ambiguity in the mind of a human user. But if 1984 appeared on a card, how could we be sure that it was the year of publication and not the title? And Macmillan could certainly give us cause for doubt—the publisher, the author, or even (in a biography) the title!

Matters would certainly be eased if each record card were clearly divided into specific labelled parts, as in figure 7.7.

Title	
Author	
Publisher	Year of publication
Library classification	Acquisition number
ISBN	

Figure 7.7 A labelled record card blank

Each labelled part or **field** of the record card holds an individual item of data. The whole is a structured data aggregate called a *structure* in some languages (such as ALGOL-68) and a *record* in others (such as COBOL, Pascal, Ada). BASIC, however, is deficient in data-structuring facilities and most versions of BASIC do not enable a general data structure to be defined as such.

Different types of data may be held in the different fields, but each field holds data of a specific type. In the case of the library record card, the fields *Title*, *Author* and *Publisher* may be of type *string* and *Year of publication* may be an integer in a suitable range (say 1800 to 2000). Similarly, appropriate types may be determined for the other fields.

Records

We have seen how a structured data type, a **record**, is a useful tool to describe an aggregate of data built up in a specified manner. We illustrate the handling of records with a further example, a *date* record. A date record might have three fields:

day	month	year

A particular instance of a date record might be

29	nov	1987

The *day* field is an integer in the range 1 to 31; the *month* field is an enumerated type (*jan*, . . . ,*dec*) and *year* is an integer in the range 1901 to 2000. In Pascal the *date* record type would be defined as follows:

```
type date =
    record
        day: 1 . . 31;
        month: (jan, feb, mar, apr, may, jun, jul, aug, sep, nov, dec);
        year: 1901 . . 2000
    end
```

Following this type definition it is permissible to declare variables of this type, for example

```
var today, tomorrow: date
```

To access the various fields of the record, Pascal uses a dot notation; the variable *today* may be given the value (29, nov, 1987) by the assignments:

```
today.day: = 29;
today.month: = nov;
today.year: = 1987;
```

Thus, for example, *today.year* names the *year* field of the record variable *today*.

You may have noticed that our definition of date does not prevent you having a 30th of February. This type of logical error cannot be handled by a record definition—it is the programmer's responsibility to take suitable action to protect a record from being assigned a phoney value.

Activity 7.2

Write a procedure
advance (**var** d: date)
to advance the date by one day. Be careful of the last day in each month.

It is interesting to compare the method of defining a record in Pascal with the way it is achieved in COBOL. It is not possible to predefine data types in COBOL, but a named record variable can be defined as follows.

```
01    DATE-OF-BIRTH
          05 DAY      PICTURE 99.
          05 MONTH  PICTURE XX.
          05 YEAR    PICTURE 9999.
```

Each field is a variable name (not a data type) and DATE-OF-BIRTH is the name of the whole record. The picture clause indicates the field size and type; for example, DAY is a two-digit number, MONTH is a string of three characters.

Exercise 7.3

It is desired to set up a telephone directory with each entry consisting of a name, address and number. (In Pascal or COBOL the entries could be records with three fields). Such a directory can be sorted by name (the usual form of indexing). Alternatively, a directory enquiries service might also require the same directory sorted by address. The telephone company might use the directory sorted by number, to identify the subscriber on any given number.

In BBC BASIC there is no facility for defining records. Simulate such a facility as follows. Each record is modelled as a string with two asterisks (*) in it. The characters until the first asterisk form the name field, the characters between the asterisks form the address field, and the characters following the second asterisk form the telephone number field. For example,

dir_entry = "Dan Archer * Glebe Cottage, Ambridge * (0991 47) 82"

(a) Give suitable function definitions for extracting the three fields from an instance of a directory record.
(b) How would you effect a change of address?
(c) Suggest an improvement in the design of the record to simplify your functions.

Record structures can be simulated in BBC BASIC, using strings as in exercise 7.2. However, this is not the same as the real thing. What are the disadvantages of not having proper record types? There are two significant drawbacks.

Firstly, our data is insecure. Any string might inadvertently be construed as a telephone directory entry. The only check available is that which the programmer might specifically write in. For example, it is possible to introduce checks to ensure that the spacer symbols appear precisely the right number of times, and that the telephone number field includes only digits and parentheses. In Pascal (or any other language which provides proper support for records) each record type is a distinct data type. It is a requirement of the language that variables of a given type be properly declared and appear only in legal contexts. These constraints are checked by the compiler, and if the programmer should use a record variable in the wrong context, an error message will be issued.

A second consideration concerns ease of use. In Pascal it is not necessary to rebuild the entry from scratch when we make a partial change. Suppose we have a record type

```
type dir_type =
    record
        name, address, tel_no: string
    end;
var old_man: dir_type
```

We can represent a change of address to 5 Hawthorn Villas, Ambridge (with no change in name or telephone number) by

old_man.address := '5 Hawthorn Villas, Ambridge'

Each field of a record variable (when accessed using dot notation) behaves like an independent variable.

Records and arrays

We have now met two methods of structuring data—the *array* and the *record*. Let us contrast record variables with array variables.

Each element of an array is a variable of the same type (such as all integers) and is accessed using an index (in one or more dimensions). An array is therefore suitable for a family of objects of the same type, which are to be indexed by some variable. For example, the names of the occupants of a hotel can be stored as a string array indexed by integers—the room numbers. The use of an index implies a specific ordering of the elements of the array.

In a record, on the other hand, each field may be a variable of a different type and is accessed using a field name. A record is therefore suitable for aggregating data which relates to a single object (such as the personal details of an individual). The fields are not logically constrained to any particular sequence.

Both arrays and records are examples of static data structures, that is to say, each requires a fixed allocation of memory space. For example, an array of integers indexed from 0 to 10 requires the allocation of 44 bytes of storage (in the BBC computer) which would (normally) be allocated in contiguous locations. In BASIC, the allocation is made when the statement

DIM occupant(10)

is encountered

The declaration of a record variable requires an allocation of storage for each of its fields. For example, given **type** *dir_type* above, each variable declared with this type requires space for three strings.

Tables of data

There is no particular restriction on the base type of an array. You are familiar with real arrays, integer arrays, string arrays and, maybe, character arrays and boolean arrays. A two-dimensional array is rather like an array of arrays (indeed in Pascal there is no distinction—a two-dimension array *is* an array of arrays). So why not an array of records?

If we wish to deal with a collection of records of the same type, the natural structure is an array of records. So a telephone directory is just an array of directory entries; for example, the Pascal declaration

var directory: **array** [1 . . 5000] **of** dir_type

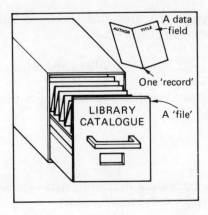

Figure 7.8 A library catalogue is an array of record cards

declares *directory* to be an array of 5000 entries (and reserves the necessary space). We can print all the names by looping through *directory[i].name* as *i* runs from 1 to 5000.

Arrays of records abound in all sorts of situations; they are often known as **tables** and are a popular format ıor presenting a spread of information.

The table shown in figure 7.9 is an array of six records, in which each record has three string fields—description, manufacturer and model—and one real field—price.

	Description	Manufacturer	Model	Price (£)
1	Radio-cassette	Pioneer	SK 353	99.90
2	Music centre	Philips	F 1231	179.95
3	Clock radio	Bush	6800	17.95
4	Disc camera	Kodak	8000	69.95
5	Kettle	Russell Hobbs	Highline	19.95
6	Typewriter	Brother	BP30	175.75

Figure 7.9 A table of product and price information

A payroll program for salaried employees could calculate each person's monthly pay cheque using a salary table, as shown in figure 7.10. Such a table is usually called a *look-up table*. This information could be coded as a seven-element array of records, where each record has two fields—*job_title* and *salary*.

A real-life payroll program has to be highly sophisticated. Besides having to calculate a monthly salary, it must also take into account such factors as pension payments, voluntary payments, National Insurance and expense allowances. To calculate a person's tax deduction, it is necessary to keep track of accumulated salary and tax payments for the current year, as well as tax allowances, which vary between individuals according to a tax code. In fact, it is necessary to supply several

1	Managing Director	45,000
2	Director	32,000
3	Store Manager	24,000
4	Department Head	17,000
5	Secretary	11,000
6	Salesman	16,000
7	Clerk	6,500

Figure 7.10 Salary table

pieces of information for each individual. Yes, you've guessed it, each individual will have a record associated with him or her. Even in a small firm with few employees, it rapidly becomes a laborious task to key in all this information each month. In a large firm with thousands of employees the task is more enormous. Enormous and unnecessary. Because a computer does not need to take its input from the keyboard. The records containing the data for program can be prepared once, offline, or even by another program, and saved on backing storage just like programs are saved. A collection of similar records is called a **file**.

The study of files is a large topic which will occupy us in the next chapter.

Summary of Chapter 7

Information which is to be processed is held in the form of data. Data is prepared for processing in three stages. The first stage is data capture. The data is collected from source by manual or automatic methods and is then encoded into a form suitable for processing. Offline data capture results in machine-readable data which forms part of the backing store. Online data capture feeds data from a primary or intermediate source directly to the computer which is running the processing program. The following types of error may arise in data:

- transcription errror;
- omission;
- duplication.

A common form of transcription error is the transposition of two adjacent characters.

The second stage is data validation, in which checks are carried out to ensure validity. To some extent this step can overlap data capture—data validation can be carried out by personnel engaged in data collection and entry. Data validation by computer includes range checks, which check that the type and the value of data supplied conform to the program specification. Check digits and control totals are used as additional checks on the integrity of data which is input.

The third stage relates to the organisation and structure of data within a program. A collection of data, all of the same type, may be structured as a one-dimensional or multi-dimensional array. Where a collection of associated data of differing types has a fixed format, the appropriate data structure is a record.

Answers to Exercises

7.1 (a) $(0 \times 10) + (3 \times 9) + (3 \times 8) + (3 \times 7)$
$+ (3 \times 6) + (9 \times 5) + (3 \times 4) + (3 \times 3) + (6 \times 2)$
$+ (8 \times 1)$
$= 176$

which is divisible by 11.

(b) The number, except for the check digit, is increased by one, and a new check digit is calculated. The next ISBN is therefore 0 333 39337 6.

7.2 Data verification is the activity which checks that the data has not been corrupted during transcription. It is frequently achieved by reinputting the data and comparing the two versions. Data validation is the activity of checking that the data presented for processing meets certain constraints.

It is quite feasible for corrupt data to be valid, by meeting the constraints. Conversely, verified data may be invalid, because it is not within the scope for which the processing program was intended.

7.3 (a) DEF FNname(entry$) = LEFT$(entry$,INSTR(entry$,"*") − 1)

```
DEF FNaddress(entry$)
LOCAL temp$
temp$ = MID$(entry$,INSTR(entry$,"*") + 1)
= LEFT$(temp$,INSTR(temp$,"*") − 1)

DEF FNtel_no(entry$)
LOCAL temp$
temp$ = MID$(entry$,INSTR(entry$,"*") +1)
= MID$(temp$,INSTR(temp$,"*") + 1)
```

(b) Assume that the change of address is local, and that the telephone number is unaltered. We need two parameters—the old directory entry and the new address.

```
DEF FNnew(entry$,new_add$)
= FNname(entry$) + "*" + new_add$ + "*" + FNtel_no(entry$)
```

(c) The functions to access the fields were complicated by the fact that both 'spacers' are asterisks. We can use two different symbols (for example * and %) as spacers to simplify the function definitions. An entry would then look like

"Sid Perks*The Bull, Ambridge%(0991 47) 69"

Note that it is crucial that the spacer symbols cannot appear in any of the fields. In our case no names, addresses or telephone numbers contain a * or % symbol.

Further Exercises

1. Write a program which reads in names of employees and their job titles and calculates their monthly pay by using a look-up table. Deduct tax on the following basis: the first £2000 of annual income is tax free, the next £20,000 is taxed at 25%, and any excess is taxed at 50%.

    Do not forget that your program needs to print out its results.

2. A certain clothing retailer with over 300 retail outlets uses a computer system to record garment sales on a weekly basis. Every garment offered for sale has a garment ticket attached to it which uniquely identifies that garment. The tickets are produced by the computer at head office. When a sale is made the salesman uses a "point-of-sale" (POS) terminal to enter the garment number, price and salesman number. The salesman number is required for bonus payments calculations. The data is validated by the "POS" terminal and, if correct, is written onto a magnetic tape cassette which is sent to head office at the end of the week.

    One of the data items input is checked by the "POS" terminal using a *modulo 11 check digit* system, one has a *range check* applied to it, and the other is checked by reference to a small table held in the limited memory of the "POS" terminal.

    (a) Describe the two validation techniques in italics.
    (b) Associate the above three validation procedures with the data items input.
    (c) The entry of information from the garment ticket by the salesman may introduce errors into the system. Briefly describe a modification to the printing of tickets which, together with suitable modification to the "POS" terminal, would eliminate these human-induced errors.
    (d) At the end of the week the "POS" terminal writes a batch control total on to the cassette tape. What is a batch control total and for what is it used?

    (AEB—83/2/7—part)

3. A program requires data in the form of positive integers. The integer may contain a decimal point and trailing zeros, but no leading zeros. The end of a data item is signalled by a space or a carriage return. Examples of valid input are 76, 430.0 and 215. ; 8.9, 0067 and 52B are all invalid.

    Design a procedure to validate the input.

4. A medium sized company with several sites distributed throughout a large town uses a microcomputer based system, with a hard disc backup, to store and process its payroll and personnel files. The data relevant to the calculation of the pay of employees is collated on a regular basis in preparation for a weekly payroll run. The main processor is housed in one of the sites. Each site has a device for encoding data on a portable medium. The encoded data is transported to the main site each week in order to prepare the transaction file.

(a) Outline the practical steps that can be taken when collecting the raw data to minimise the number of errors.

(b) Describe the functional characteristics of a data encoding device appropriate to this application. Explain the role of this device in the process of data capture.

(c) The transaction file for the weekly run contains records which include, amongst others, the fields employee number, department, hours worked and date.

Describe validation checks that could take place on these four fields including at least one example of

   (i) a range check,
   (ii) a type check,
   (iii) the use of a check digit.

(d) Suggest a method for streamlining the current system.

(ULSEB—1987)

8 Files

Go in to the general office of any commercial enterprise or administrative unit, and you will surely see a filing cabinet. This item of furniture houses the information store of the enterprise. The information may include correspondence and other previous records, and also administrative procedures for the activities conducted by the organisation. A large volume of information must be arranged in a satisfactory fashion if any part of it is to be readily available. Filing cabinets are arranged in drawers, each holding twenty or more files. Each file is a collection of information grouped under a specific heading. Correspondence files may be grouped under the names of individual correspondents. Employee details are held in a personnel filing system grouped according to employers' work numbers. Records of invoices may be held in an accounts file, stock details in an inventory file.

Backing storage for a computer installation is usually organised as a filing system, by analogy with the manual systems which preceded the advent of computers. The files are held nowadays on magnetic media—mainly discs and tapes. A considerable amount of computer time in commercial data processing departments is occupied with the processing of data files. Much of this processing involves extracting data items, sorting records and producing new or updated files. Some arithmetic computation also takes place, but it often occupies but a small fraction of the total processing time. Round 1960 the COBOL programming language was developed for use in such business applications; an updated COBOL standard was introduced in 1975. Although Pascal has made some inroads on business applications, it is somewhat defective in the area of file handling and COBOL remains the most widely used programming language.

Data files which are accessed from magnetic tape must be sequential, but the use of direct-access devices, such as discs, allows data to be organised in indexed and random files. We shall consider how data files are handled within programs, using appropriate techniques. Data which is required to be accessed by a number of different programs may be held in a more highly organised form, the database.

File organisation is not restricted to data handling. Textual documents, source programs and machine code can all be held in files. We shall look briefly at a uniform filing system which caters for all these uses.

8.1 Serial Processing

A **file** is a collection of data which exists independently of any program. A file may consist of purely binary data, such as a machine-code program, in which case it is called a *binary file*. Alternatively, the data in the file may consist of characters (suitably encoded) which can be typed out at a terminal—this is a *text file*. A special class of text files are those which contain the code for a program in a programming language—these are often referred to as *program files*. However, when we discuss *data files* in general, we usually mean a collection of records which may be accessed and processed by suitable programs.

Let us consider a personnel file. Each record in the file contains personal details about a member of staff. For convenience they may be arranged in some order, or sequence. This could be alphabetical by surname, but that would still leave open the problem of identifying one of the 29 Smiths working for the firm. In practice, large employers allocate to each employee a *staff number*. This number becomes part of each individual's record and can be used to sequence the records. A field of a record, like staff number, which serves to identify that record uniquely, is called a **primary key**.

A further illustration is provided by an estate agent who maintains a file of house-for-sale records. Each record has fields for address, asking price, number of bedrooms, rateable value and type (detached, semi or terraced). The address field is used as a primary key.

Magnetic tape

Large data files are kept in backing storage. The payroll program needs to produce a pay cheque for each employee, so it processes the personnel file *sequentially*. A suitable medium for maintaining sequential files is magnetic tape. Magnetic tape comes in reels of up to 2400 feet in length and half an inch wide. Data encoded onto the tape can be accessed as the tape is wound from one end to another. A *magnetic-tape unit*, which accesses data from its medium (tape) in strict sequence, is a **serial-access device**. We shall digress a little to study how information is held on tape.

Magnetic tape has a plastic base coated with ferric oxide, a magnetisable substance. On 9-track tape (the commonest type) each byte is coded in a frame as nine bits, one extra bit serving as a *parity check bit*, as shown in figure 8.1.

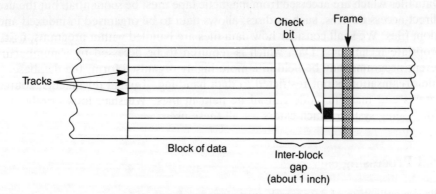

Figure 8.1 Nine-track magnetic tape

Character codes are usually recorded with even parity; all codes with an odd number of 1s have 1 in the check bit track, so that *every* code has an even number of 1s. When the tape is read, the data is checked to ensure that each code is even. If it turns out to be odd, this indicates an error, which will be reported to the user program.

When data is recorded onto tape, we say it is being *written*, when it is retrieved it is being *read*. To avoid accidental erasure, data cannot be written to a tape unless a special **write-permit ring** is affixed to the reel. There are nine read and write heads, one for each track on the tape.

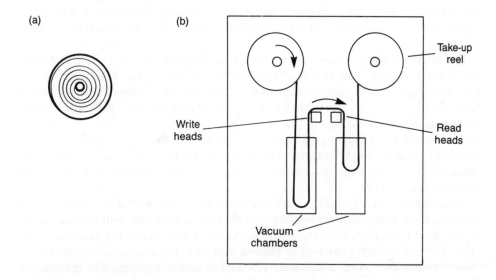

Figure 8.2 (a) Tape reel. (b) Tape drive unit

The principle of recording (and retrieving) data from a magnetic tape is much the same as that used on the domestic audio cassette and video cassette player. A capstan drives the tape against a pinch roller and a tape guide aligns it onto the reel; as the tape is unwound from one reel it is wound onto a fixed reel. However, the data held on a computer tape is stored using a fixed magnetic density in digital form, whereas audio tape is recorded with a range of magnetic densities to capture analogue information. A tape drive is very fast—between 80 and 120 inches per second (compared with $1\frac{7}{8}$ inches per second for audio cassettes). At this speed it would take about 4 minutes to read a whole tape from end to end.

The time to locate a block of data *and* transfer it into main store is called the **access time**. To accommodate the high speeds, the tape is held slack in vacuum chambers between the reels and the read heads, so that the inertia of the reels cannot affect the reading speed. This is illustrated in figure 8.2, in which the arrows show the direction of tape travel.

The drive must run at a precise constant speed to avoid errors. Acceleration to (and deceleration from) normal running speed is very fast (a few thousandths of a second), but during this time the tape moves by a quarter of an inch or so. Data is therefore read/written in blocks of records and a gap (about half an inch long) is left between blocks. When a block of data is written to the tape, it is immediately read back to verify its accuracy. In case of error, the same block is written again before writing the next block.

Data on magnetic tapes is commonly packed at 800 or 1600 characters per inch so that typical data speeds are 100 000 or 200 000 characters per second—many times faster than a card reader. A magnetic tape can hold something like 20 million characters at 800 characters per inch—equivalent to the whole of the London telephone directory. Very high density tape drives can handle data packed at 6250 characters per inch. On such drives much faster access times can be achieved; in addition, these drives allow up to 180 million characters to be stored on a single tape.

The effective transfer rate, that is, the actual number of characters transferred per second, is less than the true rate because of the space taken up by the inter-block gaps and the deceleration of the drive over these gaps. These gaps are a fixed size, so the effective transfer rate is increased by having longer blocks. However, to set against this, it must be borne in mind that a buffer area of main memory must be set aside to hold a block of data, since the whole block is read (or written) as a single unit of transfer. Moreover, the time taken by the gap is used to check for errors and take appropriate recovery action; longer blocks must therefore reduce this capability.

As the ends of the tape are threaded onto the reels, the drive needs some way of knowing from where to start reading. A reflective aluminium strip is fixed to the tape some 15 feet from each end—this marks the logical beginning and end of the tape. The unit does not attempt to read or write any data beyond the confines of these tape markers. After a tape has been read or written to, it must be rewound to the beginning. During data transfer the tape can travel in the forward direction only.

Frequently a file may not fill a whole tape, and it may be desirable to store several files on one physical tape. A physical unit of tape is often called a **volume** (just like a volume of a book, which might hold one long work or several short stories). A really long file might span two or more volumes. To avoid identification problems, many systems require that each tape file be preceded by a special character sequence, called a **label**. Before processing the file, the program can check the label.

Tape volumes are held offline, in a library. When a program requests a tape, a message is sent to the computer operator. It is one of the functions of the operator to mount tapes into tape drive units as requested by the system.

Exercise 8.1

A magnetic tape 1800 feet long has data recorded on it at a density of 1600 bytes/inch with an inter-block gap of 1 inch. If the block size is 2000 characters, how many megabytes can be stored on the tape?

Ignoring start-up and slow-down, how long will it take to read the entire tape, at 125 inches per second, and what average transfer rate does this represent in bytes/second?

Microcomputer tapes

Tape-drive units are neither cheap nor small—indeed they are both larger and more expensive than most microcomputers. But the backing storage function served by tape has a valid place in microcomputer applications. Manufacturers of computers have solved this problem by making use of the domestic cassette player/recorder. The cassette read/write head can transfer bit codes between a cassette tape and an external device. Since there is just a single head, character codes are stored along the tape, rather than across it. This makes data transfer to a cassette tape a very slow operation. A typical speed is 1200 baud, equivalent to 120 characters per second.

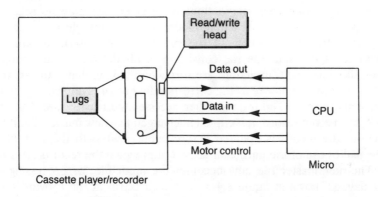

Figure 8.3 Cassette tape storage for microcomputers

Standard connections (such as the 5-pin DIN socket on most domestic machines) are utilised to wire up the cassette player as a tape unit. A minimum of four wires is required—two for the 'writing' circuit and two for the 'reading' circuit—and a fifth wire is usually kept at 0 volts (ground level). Where a cassette player has motor control, an additional circuit can allow the computer to start and stop the cassette as required, under program control. (Cassettes cannot, however, be rewound under program control.) Unlike the large reel systems, cassettes can be used on both 'sides' with conventional equipment. In fact, there are two tracks, which are accessed in opposite directions of tape travel. Although cassette tape of any length can be used, the tape driving speeds are such that for most applications five or ten minutes per side is a convenient size. It should be borne in mind that domestic cassette players are not precision devices and there may be some sensitivity to tape head alignment. In particular, tapes written by one player cannot always be read by another.

Write protection of a cassette is achieved by removing a plastic lug; there is one for each side of the tape. Write permission is regained by sealing the lug-hole with a patch of sticky tape.

Batch processing

In our payroll example, each record on the file was accessed and processed. This is not always the case. Consider the Billingsgate Building Society, which has computerised its accounts. An accounts file has been set up, containing a record for each account holder. Twice a year interest is added to each account-holder's balance. This requires a simple sequential updating process—each record is updated and the new versions are saved in a new file. Between interest dates, account holders may make deposits or withdrawals. Each such transaction requires the corresponding account-holder record to be updated.

It is not particularly economical to search the whole file from the beginning to access the record, and then produce a new file with just the one change. Nor is it usually necessary. Numerous transactions on a given day may be relayed to a central computer site. Each transaction is identified by a suitable key—the account number. After five-thirty, when all the branches are closed, an applications program takes as its input the file consisting of all the day's transactions—the **transaction file**. First the transactions are *sorted* on the key, that is to say, they are arranged in the same sequence as the corresponding records appear on the **master file** of accounts records. The program then accesses the master file; if there is no transaction for a given record, it is copied unchanged to a new master file; if there is a transaction, the record is updated before being written to the new file. This procedure makes use of the particular sequence in which the records are stored in the file. The new master file now becomes the input file for processing on the following day, as shown in figure 8.4.

This method of collecting all the day's transactions into a single batch is known as **batch mode** processing. After the processing is complete on Monday night, the no. 2 master tape contains all the data about the current status of the accounts. All previous information could now be destroyed. However, for security reasons—in case of loss or damage to the master tape, or in case a program error has occurred in writing the new tape—the previous (no. 1) master tape and the day's transaction tape are kept. After Tuesday evening's run, the no. 2 tape is kept as well as the new no. 3 tape, and the no. 1 *grandfather* tape is transferred to a fireproof store. Only after Wednesday's run is the no. 1 tape (plus Monday's transaction tape) disposed of. The no. 2 tape then becomes the new grandfather tape as shown in figure 8.5.

At each stage, the three latest versions of the master file are retained, as a security precaution. The older versions are no longer required, and the tapes can then be reused. Magnetic tape can be recorded over, just like new audio material can be recorded onto used cassettes. The reusability of magnetic tape is a factor which contributes to keeping down costs in a magnetic tape library.

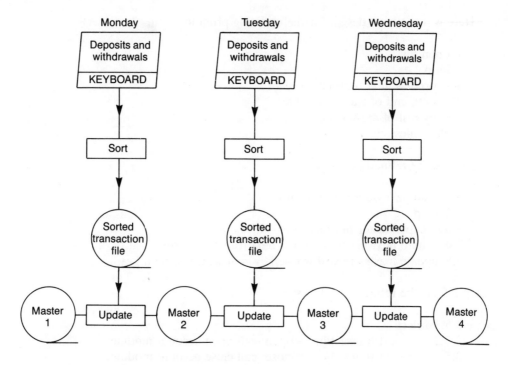

Figure 8.4 Daily update cycle

	Grandfather	*Father*	*Son*
Monday night	—	1	2
Tuesday night	1	2	3
Wednesday night	2	3	4

Figure 8.5 Grandfather–father–son routine

A sequential file update

In batch mode processing, a master file is updated on each run using a transaction file. The master file may be empty initially, and the first transaction file could consist of suitable insertion transactions to generate the first version of the master file. Subsequently, each run will generate a new version of the master file.

As an example, we shall consider how the master file of the Billingsgate Building Society is updated daily. Transactions take place in branches, where they are entered into a local, on-site computer. At the end of each working day, the transactions are sorted and transmitted to the Society's central computer. Transactions include opening and closing accounts, deposits and withdrawals. At the central computer, the incoming branch files are merged into a single, sorted transaction file. This file is then used to update the master file.

Here is a top-level design for the updating program.

```
1 open files
2 loop
3   process next transaction record
4   until end of transaction file
5 copy rest of master file
6 close files
```

Step 3 can be refined as follows:

```
3.1 read next transaction record
3.2 loop
3.3   copy master file records
3.4   until next master key >= next transaction key
3.5 update master record whose key = next transaction key
```

Step 3.5 can be refined as follows:

```
3.5.1 select
3.5.2   if next transaction = open: call open account module
3.5.3   if next transaction = close: call close account module
3.5.4   if next transaction = deposit: call deposite module
3.5.5   if next transaction = withdrawal: call withdrawal module
```

The transaction modules can then be developed separately. Here are top-level designs for the *close account* and *deposit* modules.

close account

transaction key, master key
check that keys are equal order closing statement write master record to closed accounts file

deposit

transaction key, master key, amount
check that keys are equal new balance = amount + old balance write record with new balance to new master file

The update program as now structured consists of a main program with four transaction modules. Further development may indicate the need for additional modules. For example, at present transaction records are checked simply for agreement with master file records. However, it may be desirable to perform more elaborate validation on the transaction key (the account number). In this case, a validation module would be appropriate.

In this way you can begin to see how a fairly complex update program can be developed. An important part of the software design is the selection of suitable data structures for the transaction and master file records.

8.2 Direct-access Devices

Since a tape unit is a serial device, it can only handle sequential files. The use of sequential files has its limitations. Suppose you are responsible for mailing a magazine each month to subscribers. The address file is held on tape and is used to print address labels for each issue of the magazine. If there are many thousands of subscribers, you may expect to receive notification each month of two or three address changes. This involves updating the file. Because the file is sequential, it is necessary to scan it from the beginning, record by record, to access the records which need to be updated. For a large file this can be excessively wasteful of time. How could access be improved?

Here is an idea. If you want to look up a telephone number in a directory, you could scan all the names in the directory starting from Aalborg (or whatever the first entry is). To find the name McCallum would probably take you longer than walking from London to Inverness. However books are no longer written in scrolls, but are bound in pages. Using the index names at the top of each page, you can probably open up the correct page of the directory within five seconds. You can likewise home in on the subscriber name you require without reading each name from the top of the page. So although the entries in the directory are arranged sequentially, you can home in fairly directly to any entry you may choose, because a book is a **direct-access device**. (Direct access is sometimes called *parallel access* or *random access*.) The telephone directory is an **indexed** sequential file—each page can be accessed directly using the index.

Hi-fi discs provide further examples of direct-access devices in common use. The conventional black disc may have several pieces recorded on each side. You can listen to the third song on the first side without hearing the first two, by locating the pick-up arm on the third track. It is not necessary to search through the first two songs first. On a compact disc you can select an item using an index number—thus going straight to the piece you want to hear.

Magnetic-disc storage

Direct-access backing store is provided using similar principles to hi-fi discs. The most widespread medium is the hard disc. A metal disc has its flat surfaces coated with a thin layer of magnetic material. Unlike the long-playing audio disc, which has but one spiral groove on each surface, a magnetic disc is divided into concentric circles known as **tracks**. There may be 200 or 400 tracks on one surface. To locate data on the disc, a read/write head moves in a straight line towards (or away from) the spindle into position above the desired track—this is linear tracking. The disc rotates continuously in a **disc drive** at high speed, say 60 revolutions per second. The **latency**—the average delay in waiting for a particular part of a track to reach the read/write head—is therefore $\frac{1}{2} \times \frac{1}{60}$ second, or about 8 milliseconds.

Usually several discs (between ten and twenty) are stacked together on a single spindle in a **disc pack**. The two outer surfaces are not used, but a comb of read/write arms can access the inner surfaces, with a separate head for each surface. These arms all move together, so that when one head is accessing track 83 on its disc, all the others are accessing track 83 on their discs. The set of all tracks which can be accessed from a given head position is called a **cylinder** (for example cylinder 83). The amount of storage on a given cylinder is critical, because it can all be accessed without moving the arm (the slowest part of the operation). Moving from cylinder to cylinder can be achieved only by physical movement of the arm. It is therefore desirable to organise related data (that is, individual files) on one cylinder. If a file is too large to fit on one cylinder, it should be stored on adjacent cylinders, to minimise head movement.

The read/write head records (writes) and retrieves (reads) data magnetically (like a tape head). The tracks are not physical grooves in which a stylus vibrates. Instead, the head hovers on an air cushion close to the track it accesses, moving in a horizontal direction only. Disc drives are manufactured to a high degree of precision; the distance between the head and the disc surface is between 20 and 50 microinches (a microinch is one millionth of an inch). At this distance, a signal can be picked up without physical contact. Any foreign particle which finds its way into the air cushion is liable to cause read/write errors, at least. In more serious cases, a **disc crash** may occur (physical contact between a head and a disc). This could be caused by a smoke particle, whose typical size is 250 microinches. Positive air pressure is therefore maintained in disc drives to repel foreign particles.

A serious disc crash may result in a ring being burnt through the magnetic coating, revealing the bare metal beneath. A damaged disc is likely to spoil a good head; a damaged head may ruin a good disc. Not only is the hardware expensive, but a damaged disc may result in the loss of data. Following a disc crash, the disc pack must be replaced; the data must also be restored to the new disc pack in as recent a form as possible. To help avoid disc crashes, disc packs must never be dropped and should be handled with care.

As shown in figure 8.6, each track is divided into, say, 16 **sectors**, with each sector holding a fixed numbers of words of data—maybe 64 or 128. The capacity of a disc pack is typically 100 or 200 Megabytes of storage—much more than a magnetic tape—and in larger installations drives with a storage capacity of more than one Gigabyte are in use. The time taken to transfer a sector of data is about one millisecond, yielding an actual data transfer rate of up to 1 Megabyte per second, ten times as fast as magnetic tape.

Only whole sectors of data can be addressed; the contents of a sector of a track is called a **block**. The disc operating software may specify the unit of transfer as two, three or more whole blocks. The actual unit of data transfer is called a **bucket**.

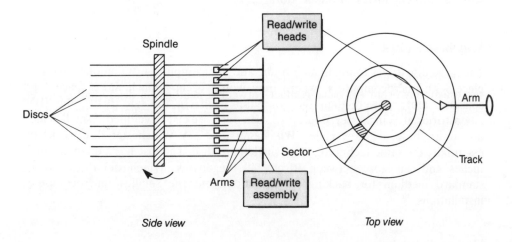

Spindle

Read/write heads

Discs

Arm

Arms

Read/write assembly

Sector

Track

Side view

Top view

Figure 8.6 Disc pack (showing operative parts)

1 Megabyte $= 2^{20}$ bytes
≈ 1 million bytes
≈ 1000 K
1 Gigabyte $= 2^{30}$ bytes
≈ 1 billion bytes
$\approx 1\,000\,000$ K

Figure 8.7 Large units of storage

The access time to locate and transfer a bucket or from an online disc is governed by whether a head movement is required. Repositioning the read/write head involves a physical movement of the arm, which can take 20 or 30 milliseconds. This is called the **seek** time. We have

access time = seek time + latency + transfer time

If all the data is transferred to or from the currently accessed cylinder, the average access time depends only on the latency and the number of sectors transferred. Each individual sector is addressed by a cylinder number, sector number and head number. Usually, one of the reading surfaces of a disc pack is not used for data—instead it contains location information such as the disc addresses at which files are located and the current cylinder and sector numbers.

Magnetic disc packs as described here are usually exchangeable. It is possible to retract the arms completely to enable the disc pack to be removed and replaced by another. In practice, larger installations do not often change disc packs, in view of the time loss incurred. Such installations usually have a number of disc packs permanently online (and spinning continuously), with a control unit selecting which drive is in communication with the computer at any one time. These drives are often organised in clusters of two, four or eight disc packs, acting as a single device with several Gigabytes of online storage.

Winchester discs

The large disc drives found in mainframe and minicomputer installations are out of place with microcomputers, where they would occupy much more space (and consume more power) than the computer itself. In the late 1970s, the IBM laboratories at Winchester Boulevard, San Jose, Texas, developed a small sealed disc unit; these are now called *Winchester discs*. A Winchester disc works on essentially the same technology as a single hard disc. The disc has a diameter of $5\frac{1}{4}$ inches and can store between 10 and 40 Megabytes. Winchester discs are the standard medium for backing storage in all but the smallest microcomputer installations.

Floppy-disc drives

In small installations, it is not necessary to have the same amount of data online at any one time, nor do they require such high access speeds. In such cases a floppy-disc drive is used. These disc drives use **floppy-discs** (sometimes called **diskettes**), which are made of a flexible material and are kept in a square cardboard sleeve with a small aperture for the read/write head to access the disc. They may have one or two recording surfaces and 40 or 80 tracks. Unlike hard-disc systems, the read/write head not only has to be positioned but must also be lowered onto the recording surfaces and makes physical contact. An indicator light on the drive housing shows when the arm is active, to avoid damaging the disc by switching off or removing the disc whilst it is in motion.

(a)

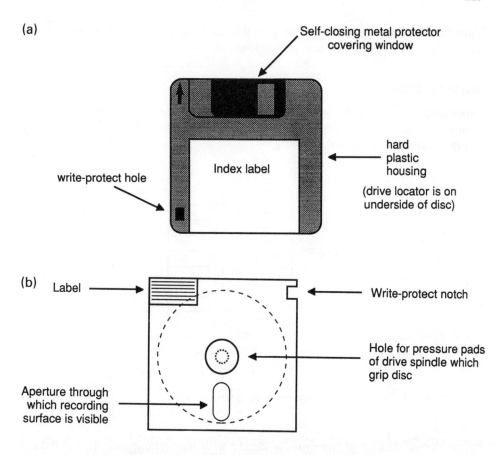

Self-closing metal protector
covering window

Index label

write-protect hole

hard
plastic
housing

(drive locator is on
underside of disc)

(b)

Label

Write-protect notch

Hole for pressure pads
of drive spindle which
grip disc

Aperture through
which recording
surface is visible

Figure 8.8 (a) Micro-floppy disc. (b) Floppy disc

Floppy discs come in standard sizes of $5\frac{1}{4}$ inch and 8 inch diameter. Their capacity may be 200K for a single-sided disc, or up to 1 Mbyte for a double-sided, double-density disc.

A new $3\frac{1}{2}$ inch floppy disc in a plastic housing is becoming popular. Of course, the name floppy disc is a bit of a misnomer for a rigid package. Despite their size, they have the same capacity as larger discs, because capacity depends on the number of tracks rather than physical size.

We have discussed at length two forms of backing store. Magnetic tape is less convenient than discs, but not so expensive. In practice, there is a trade-off between speed and efficiency on the one hand and cost on the other. In large installations, data files which are frequently accessed will be on disc, and tapes are used for long-term storage. Another advantage of tapes is portability—it is easier to transport a reel of tape from place to place than a disc pack. Also, tape is cheap enough to allow a supply of spare capacity to be held. On cheap microcomputers of the home computer variety, at the other end of the scale, economic considerations may loom large. A disc drive can be more expensive than the microcomputer to which it is attached, whereas cassette recorders sell for less than £50. On the other hand floppy discs are every bit as portable as tape cassettes, and much more convenient since cassette drives are so slow.

Magnetic drums

Tapes and discs are not the only forms of backing storage available. Magnetic drums used to be very popular, and were in fact the first direct-access backing storage devices to be manufactured.

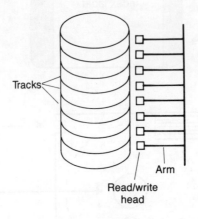

Tracks

Arm

Read/write
head

Figure 8.9 A magnetic drum

The *curved* surface of the drum is coated with magnetic material, and data is stored in circular tracks on this surface. There is one read/write head per track, and as the drum rotates at high speed, each point on the drum passes a head. The appropriate track is selected electronically, so that the only delay is until the drum rotates to the point where the data sought is at the head position. Since no physical movement of the head occurs, data is accessed rapidly. An access time of 10 milliseconds is typical, several times the speed of a disc access.

Magnetic drums are, however, no longer popular. Because only the curved surface is used, the amount of data that can be stored on a drum is small compared with the capacity of a disc. The difference could be a factor of 20 or more. This lack of capacity resulted in greater cost, and an increase in space occupied at a time when the accent is on reduced size has effectively edged drums out of the picture.

Security of data

When files are held on tape, each time the file is processed it must be rewritten. Typically both the old and the new tapes are online simultaneously and so the old tape remains available. This allows the grandfather–father–son security routine to be employed. The older tapes may be retrieved either in the case of physical damage to the new tape or corruption of the new file during processing.

With direct-access devices, files are updated in situ. This can generate a great saving in processing time, as it may no longer be necessary to rewrite the file completely when it is updated. On the other hand, a grave security risk now exists, as only one copy of each file is held. One way to deal with this problem is to maintain one (or more) old versions of a file on disc as **back-up** in case of corruption of the current version of a file. Another security measure is for the files to be copied to tape at regular intervals (daily or weekly). This copy is known as a **dump**, and allows the files to be recovered in case of corruption or physical damage to the files on disc. A further refinement is to maintain a complete record of all file transactions between dumps on a **journal** file. Provided the journal remains intact, the current files can be **recovered** from the last dump, by using the journal file to update the dump.

On micro and minicomputer systems which use floppy discs, an alternative is to maintain back-up copies of whole discs in place of a tape dump. Unlike a tape dump which must first be copied onto disc before use, a back-up disc can be used itself for recovery

Activity 8.1

Find out the backing storage capacities of the computers at your school or college. If you have access to a minicomputer or mainframe, find out the capacities of its disc drives and tape drives.

Exercise 8.2

Why is it generally desirable for a computer system to use magnetic tape as backing storage as well as magnetic discs?

Exercise 8.3

Explain the relationship between integrity and security of data.

8.3 File Handling

We have discussed the role of files in data processing and the physical hardware on which they are stored. We now turn our attention to the way in which files are accessed within programs. The programmer must be concerned with two things: handling the logical file operations, and linking these to the physical file on a storage device.

The linkage between the representation of the file in the program and the name by which the file is known to the operating system may be made either within or outside the program. COBOL adopts the former convention, with the file names being linked to logical file identifiers inside the program. Standard Pascal does not allow references to external file names within programs; the logical file identifiers are linked to actual file names outside the program. There is no standard for file handling in BASIC. Some versions require filing commands to appear outside programs, whereas BBC BASIC allows the filing commands to appear within programs.

File operations

A program is attached to a physical file in BBC BASIC using one of the commands OPENIN, OPENOUT or OPENUP. In UCSD Pascal the procedures *rewrite* (for opening new file) and *reset* (for opening existing files) are available for attaching file variables to physical files.

OPENIN	Read only
OPENOUT	Write only
OPENUP	Read or write

Figure 8.10 File commands in BBC BASIC

OPENOUT and OPENUP can only be effective on devices with write permission. OPENUP—like *rewrite* and *reset* in UCSD Pascal—enable two-way communication between a program and a file.

The program statement

A = OPENOUT "Library"

assigns a **channel** A to a file which will ultimately be stored with the name "Library". A file buffer, consisting of a page of memory, is reserved for channel A, and the title "Library" with other general header information is written to the device.

If more than one device is accessible, it may be necessary to select the appropriate device. This selection must usually be made before program execution begins.

*TAPE	Cassette
*DRIVE 0	Disc drive 0
*DRIVE 1	Disc drive 1
*DRIVE 2	Disc drive 2
*DRIVE 3	Disc drive 3

Figure 8.11 Device selection commands in BBC BASIC

A record of data is written to the file buffer using the following variant of the PRINT keyboard.

PRINT #A,number   writes a numeric record (the value of the variable number) to channel *A*.

PRINT #A,title$ writes a string record (the value of the variable title$) to channel *A*.

In Pascal, a character or string may be written to a text file as follows:

  write(library, title)

where *library* is a variable of a suitable file type and *title* is a variable of type *char* or *string*.

In BBC BASIC the first byte of each record in a file is a code byte which identifies the record as integer, real or string. This enables the record to be read back when the file is subsequently used for data input to a program.

Code	Record type
&40	Integer
&FF	Real
&00	String
(&FE	End of file)

Figure 8.12 Table of code bytes for BBC files

A single byte may be written to the file buffer using the BPUT keyword, for example

  BPUT #A, &25

The byte to be transferred, which may be in decimal or hex format, must be an integer in the range 0–255 (0–&FF) or a variable whose value is in this range.

Data is transferred to the backing storage device when the file buffer is full, that is, in units of one page. Thus the block size is one page (= &100 bytes). The inter-block gap on tape is normally set to 0.6 second (about 1 inch), but this may be changed using the operating-sytem *OPT command; for example

  *OPT 3,11

changes the inter-block gap to 1.1 seconds.

The final block is not transferred until a CLOSE statement is encountered, for example

  CLOSE #A

This statement also puts an end-of-file marker onto the file and releases the file buffer page in memory. If the CLOSE command is not given, the final block of data will not be written. Moreover, the file on backing storage will be unreadable. The *close* procedure performs a similar function in UCSD Pascal.

If a channel is opened for reading, as in one of

```
namefile = OPENUP "Directory"
book = OPENIN "Library"
```

the channel may be used to read a record or byte. The OPENUP or OPENIN statement transfers the first block of data to the file buffer reserved for access by the channel. Subsequent blocks are transferred when the previous block has been read through. A record is read from the file using a variant of the INPUT statement, for example

```
INPUT   #namefile, subscriber$
INPUT   #book, title$
INPUT   #data, value1
```

Unlike keyboard input (which can coerce a number into a string variable), the record type must match the variable on file input, because the code byte (which was placed at the beginning of the record when it was written) will be read by the INPUT statement.

The facility for reading a single byte is the function BGET, which behaves like GET for reading a single byte from the keyboard, for example

```
byte% = BGET #channel
char   = BGET #document
```

How a channel works

A channel assignment statement makes a file available to the program. In the case of OPENIN and OPENUP, the file must exist on backing store prior to the call. In the case of OPENOUT, an empty file is made available, to which the program can write. The file buffer is a window (of size one page) onto the file and the channel points to a single record within the window. All references to a given file area are through the channel variable, which is henceforth always identified by the hash sign #. This is illustrated in figures 8.13 and 8.14.

When a writing channel is opened, it points to the first location in the file buffer. After several records have been output to the file, the channel points to the first empty location in the file buffer, as shown in figure 8.15. When a block has been transferred from/to the file buffer, the channel is repositioned at the beginning of the buffer.

An attempt to output on a read-only channel, or input from a write-only channel, will upset the BASIC system, which will respond with a channel error message when the program is run.

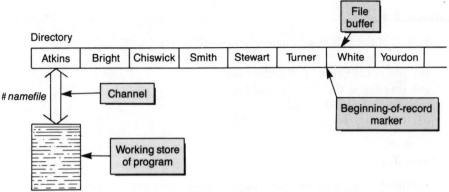

Figure 8.13 namefile = OPENUP "Directory"

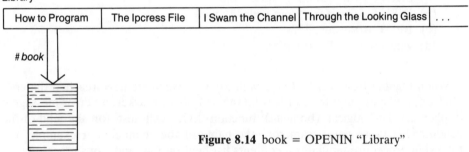

Figure 8.14 book = OPENIN "Library"

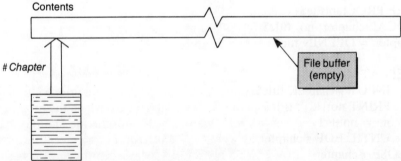

PRINT #Chapter, "Information Processing", "Keep Under Control", "Watch Your Language", "All About Data"

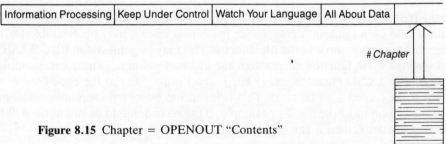

Figure 8.15 Chapter = OPENOUT "Contents"

Exercise 8.4

Which of the following channel assignments are valid?

(a) file = OPENOUT "Wednesday"
(b) transfer = OPENIN stockfile$
(c) #A = OPENUP "file"
(d) Channel$ = OPENIN "Dayfile".

Exercise 8.5

Assuming that channels have been opened as in (a) and (b) of the previous exercise, which of the following are valid statements?

(a) PRINT #file, "John", "Jack", 8.5
(b) INPUT #transfer, "item code", code$
(c) BPUT #transfer, 27
(d) value = BGET #transfer.

When reading from a file, it is as well to know when we have reached the end. (Indeed, if you attempt to read *beyond* the end-of-file marker, an error message is displayed.) The logical (boolean) function EOF will test for the end-of-file condition. It takes one parameter—the name of the channel. For example, the following procedure tabulates a contents list held on file, and stops gracefully.

```
DEF PROCtab(file$)
LOCAL chapter, no, title$
chapter = OPENIN file$
no = 1
REPEAT
    INPUT #chapter, title$
    PRINT no; ". "; title$
    no = no + 1
    UNTIL EOF #chapter
CLOSE #chapter
ENDPROC
```

Random-access files

All the file operations discussed so far are suitable for sequential processing. Where a file is held on a random-access device (such as a disc) it may be desirable for a program to access records in the file directly. This may be achieved in BBC BASIC by using the PTR function to reassign the channel pointer. (The corresponding procedure in UCSD Pascal is *seek*.) The pointer must point to the code byte of a record if the record is to be read. This is identified by its byte sequence number from the beginning of the file. For example, if the record sought begins at the 420th byte on channel Z then it can be read as follows:

```
PTR #Z = 420
INPUT #Z, record
```

On its own, the pointer variable is a rather blunt instrument, since the file must be scanned first to identify pointer values of interest. In the next section we shall look in detail at the way files can be organised to maximise the advantage of random access.

Structured files

Files on the BBC system are unstructured, that is, records of different types can be mixed *ad lib*. Pascal and COBOL require the programmer to define structured files: a suitable record type is first defined, and a file consists of records of that type only. In Pascal you could have the following:

type
    book = **record**
               title, author: string;
               catalogue_no: real;
               publication date: 1800 . . 2000
        end;
    library = **file of** *book*;
var
    volume: book;
    lib: library;   *lib* serves as a channel name
    .
    .
    .
    lib ↑ := *volume;*   These statements append
    put(lib);   the record *volume* to the file
                addressed by channel *lib*

Note how a single *put* statement writes a whole record (however complex) to the file. A similar facility (*get*) exists for reading whole records from structured files.

Activity 8.2

Devise procedures in BBC BASIC which will notionally read and write book records to a 'structured' file.

Activity 8.3

Transaction processing is usually concerned with sequential files. Suppose you have a master file of all book titles currently on loan from a library. At the end of each day two transaction files are constructed—one of book titles borrowed that day, the other of titles returned that day.

Construct a program to update the master file using the two transaction files. You may assume that each file is held in some definite order (such as alphabetical) which you should specify.

Does your program work if someone attempts to return a book which has not been borrowed?

Investigate the suitability of your program for use in your school or college library.

8.4 File Organisation

The file manipulation facilities of the previous section are geared towards sequential files. Although these facilities are available equally for use with serial-access (tape) and direct-access (disc) devices, they assume a sequential mode of file organisation in which each record is accessed following its predecessor. An exception to this is the PTR function which allows a file to be addressed at random.

On a direct-access device, the unit of data transferred between a file and main memory is the bucket. The logical unit of data is the record, and a bucket may hold one or several records. The method of file organisation determines the address of the bucket in which a given record is to be found. The bucket is then read into main memory where it is scanned to locate the given record.

Consider a file of employee records, in which the primary key (identifying field) is the employee's works number. Suppose that initially there are 7000 employees, with works numbers from 00001 to 07000. If each bucket holds five employee records, the following simple arrangement suffices. Bucket 1 can hold records whose keys are 00001 to 00005, bucket 2 holds records 00006 to 00010, and so on until all the records are allocated. Additional (empty) buckets are reserved to cater for new appointments to the workforce. With this simple arrangement the bucket number can be calculated directly from the key. (The actual addresses of the allocated buckets depend on the availability of space on the device—we shall just number buckets from 1 upwards.)

Over the years, employees may leave the firm, creating more and more gaps in the early part of the file. This can cause a problem of some magnitude, especially when a firm has been in existence for many years before its payroll is computerised. Moreover, different departments may use different bands of works numbers, all processed by the same payroll program. If the firm has about 7000 employees whose works numbers range from 00001 to 99999, it would be terribly wasteful to have a file with space for 100 000 records when just 7000 are stored, a utilisation rate of 7 per cent. A better method of file organisation is called for. The choice of file organisation for a particular application is made by a *systems analyst*, who must be familiar with the likely modes of processing and the available methods of file organisation.

In this section we consider three types of file organisation available for files held on a direct-access device—random, indexed and indexed sequential.

Random files

In a random file, the sequence in which records are stored bears no simple direct relationship to the order of their keys. Looked at in this light, a random file appears to be unsorted. However, there must be some algorithm by which the bucket number is determined from the record key.

In our payroll example suppose that the works number is in the range 00001 to 99999, and that five records can be held in each bucket. Then 2000 buckets can hold up to 10 000 records. If we take a works number, ignore the first digit, and then divide by five, the result is a number in the range 0 to 1999 (ignoring remainders). This provides a good scheme for allocating bucket numbers. A rule like this, for calculating a number in a fixed range from a larger key in somewhat arbitrary fashion, is called a **hash function**.

A problem arises when too many records hash to the same bucket. In the example above 03041, 23042, 33044, 43040, 53042 and 73041 all hash to the bucket number 608, which cannot hold six records. If six employees actually have these works numbers, we shall be in trouble. When two records keys hash to the same bucket we say that a **collision** has occurred. Once a bucket is full, no further collisions can be stored.

A hash function should be chosen so as to minimise the number of collisions. You should note that, since it is permissible for several records to hash to the same bucket number, it is not necessary to hash the primary key. An alternative key, such as the employee's postcode, may provide a more even distribution of records across the buckets. Of course, if we try to fill up all the buckets to avoid wastage of space, then, however good the hash function, as we try to accommodate the last few records, there will be more likelihood of a collision. It is usually considered good practice to aim for about two-thirds occupancy in a random file. (In our example, we could reasonably expect to accommodate about 7000 records.)

Even with the best hash functions, and generous provision of storage space, some excess collisions may occur, causing **overflow**. One method of handling overflow is as follows. If the appropriate bucket for a record is already full, the record is put into the next bucket. If that too, is full the record is put into the next bucket that has space. If the last bucket is full, the search for a space continues with the first bucket. Naturally, if some records are likely to be accessed more frequently than others, the more used records should be placed in the file first. Records which overflow take longer to access, as they are not held in their correct buckets.

Indexed files

If you want to look up a certain topic in this or any other book, the chances are that you will first flick through the index. For while the topics in the book are arranged in an order which is opaque to the outsider, the index is arranged in alphabetical order. So a quick search of the index should yield the number of the page on which the chosen topic is covered.

This approach can work well with files. To return to our employee files, suppose we were to set up the file with all the employee records in works number order. Fine. Now, when an employee leaves, the corresponding record is removed from the file. This creates a space which can be used for a new employee. The new employee's works number may be out of sequence, though, To cope with this problem we create an index file. The index file does not contain as much information as the main file. In fact, each record in the index file has just two fields—the works number and the bucket number of the corresponding record in the main file. However, unlike the main file, which can be in random order, the index file is sorted on the record key, that is, it is stored so that the works numbers are in sequence. Records can be added to or deleted from the main file at will, but on each occasion the index file will need to be re-sorted. The main file, to which an index now exists, is called an **indexed file**. There is no overflow problem with indexed files. However, the price to pay is that the index must be sorted after every insertion or deletion.

If the index is held in backing storage, accessing a record in the main file will be slow by comparison with the hashing method, because two disc accesses are necessary to retrieve a record from the file. If the index is held in main memory, though, it can be accessed faster than evaluating a hash function. Thus indexed files are feasible when the file is not too large for its index to be held in main memory. To keep the size of the index small enough so that it can be held in main memory, only the cylinder number is stored for each record. When the cylinder holding the record is found, the *cylinder index* (usually held on disc surface #1) is accessed to locate the exact bucket (addressed by disc surface and sector) which holds the corresponding record. The fastest record access achievable occurs when the appropriate cylinder index and the bucket containing the record are already in main memory, as a result of a previous access. (A running note is maintained by the operating system so that the pages of secondary storage currently held in the IAS can always be identified.) In the worst possible case the cylinder on which the record is held is far from the current cylinder, causing a large seek time, and neither the cylinder index nor the required bucket are available in the IAS, so that two disc transfers are needed (delay = 2 × latency).

Exercise 8.6

The Old Bangers Company maintains a file of vehicles for sale. The following is an extract from the file.

Bucket	reg-no	colour	type	make	model
1747	XYA 123R	green	saloon	Morris	Marina
1748	ABC 456S	blue	saloon	Ford	Cortina
1749	PPQ 789T	red	estate	Austin	Allegro
1752	NML 129R	grey	saloon	Vauxhall	Chevette
1753	RST 228P	white	saloon	Rover	3500
1754	TXY 97S	black	hatchback	Fiat	127

Construct the corresponding part of the index file.

Indexed sequential files

The indexed file, as described above, suffers from a severe drawback—the index must be updated at every insertion or deletion. This drawback can be overcome by maintaining a sequential file with an index. The sequential order of the file allows serial processing, and the index enables records to be accessed directly. To avoid having to sort the file following each insertion, the buckets are not filled completely when the file is created. Instead, each bucket is left about 40 per cent full, leaving adequate space for future insertions.

Not every record is indexed; the index file contains the primary key for just the first record in each bucket of the main file. This method reduces the size of the index file. Instead of needing one record in the index for each record in the main file, we have one index record for each bucket of the main file. In the index, each record gives the bucket number of the indexed data record. Since the file is sequential this allows any record to be located.

Figure 8.16 shows an indexed sequential file in which, for simplicity, only the key field of each record is shown in the main file. To access the Burton Group record, a search of the index file reveals that it must be in bucket 432, since Burton Group follows Bremner but precedes Cantor. Bucket 432 is then searched to retrieve the record. If it is desired to insert a Courtaulds record, the correct bucket is number 751, Courtaulds being between Cantor and Dunhill. The new record may then be placed in its correct position in bucket 751, rearranging existing records as necessary. Note that the buckets used need not be consecutive, but will be allocated by the disc operating system according to availability. In the even of a large file, it may be necessary to occupy space on several cylinders. In this case, each cylinder has its own index; in addition, there is top-level index which identifies the cylinder containing a given record. The main file should be organised so that it is partitioned sequentially between cylinders. This allows the top-level index to reference only the first data record (or home record) on each cylinder. An index which has more than one level (such as file index and cylinder index) is a **multi-level index**.

Progressive insertions will eventually fill some buckets, so that they can accommodate no further records. An attempt to insert a record into a full bucket causes overflow. The simplest method of handling overflow in indexed sequential files is to have some spare **overflow** buckets. When a record needs to be inserted into a full bucket, a pointer is set up from the full bucket to an overflow bucket (on the same cylinder) and the record is placed in the overflow bucket. Likewise, when a record is being retrieved, if it is not found in its home bucket, the overflow pointer must be examined. If the overflow pointer has been set, the corresponding overflow bucket is searched. After many insertions an overflow bucket can become full; in this case the overflow pointer of the overflow bucket can be set to point to a further overflow bucket. Eventually, all the overflow buckets on a given cylinder may become full. To deal with this situation, a cylinder may be set aside to act as a **second level overflow**. The last record in the last overflow bucket on a given cylinder is set to point to the second level overflow.

This indexed sequential access method (**ISAM**) can be used to handle overflow without any need to update the index. The index established when the file was built remains valid after subsequent insertions. It may possibly need updating in the

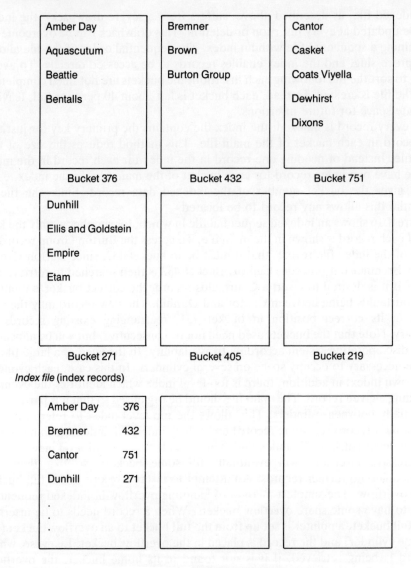

Figure 8.16 An indexed sequential file

event of the removal of an indexed record (the first record of a bucket) from the file, though this is not strictly necessary.

After a while, when there are a large number of overflow bucket, the retrieval of some records becomes inefficient. When the average time taken to access a record *degrades* to an unacceptable level, it is desirable to rebuild the file, sequentially, and create a new index.

The details of setting up the index file are usually left to be handled by the *system software*. The programmer of an individual application can then specify that a particular file is required to be an ISAM file, without worrying about the implementation details.

8.5 Information Retrieval

The computer comes into its own as a repository of data. A large file can be searched rapidly to retrieve a particular record whose primary key is given. However, this is frequently not the best method of accessing data. We shall consider two design methods which are in use for accessing a large collection of data.

Inverted files

It should not be assumed that it is always appropriate to access a record on its primary key. Often it is desirable to retrieve a set of records with particular attributes. Consider a flight information file, whose records have the following fields.

FLIGHT

Flight code		Departure		Arrival		Aircraft	Seating capacity	Days of week
Airline	Flight #	Airport	Time	Airport	Time			

The following is an example occurrence of a flight record.

BA	001	LHR	1115	JFK	1055	Concorde	190	M–F

The primary key is the flight code—a unique flight record can be retrieved by the flight code. But a travel agent may be more interested in finding which flights (irrespective of airline) depart from London (Heathrow) for New York (Kennedy) between 0930 and 1200 on a Tuesday. One way to obtain this information is to search the complete flight information file and extract each record which satisfies the condition. In a large file, the time taken for a complete search could be prohibitive. Instead, since this type of information is frequently required, subsidiary files are held which index the main file on suitable fields called **secondary keys**. These files are called **inverted files**.

Our travel agent could use two inverted files—one for departure airport and one for arrival airport. In each inverted file the airport codes are used as keys. The only other information held in each inverted file comprises lists of flight codes (the primary keys) for each airport of origin or destination airport, as the case may be. Corresponding to each choice of the secondary key there may be many records in the main file.

From these inverted files, two lists are rapidly extracted—a list of all flights out of London (Heathrow) and a list of all flights to New York (Kennedy). Those flights common to both lists are then extracted from the main file and scanned for time

Departures

LHR	AF 317
	AI 001
	BA 001
	BA 010
	BA 927
	PA 001
	PA 101
	TW 311

Arrivals

JFK	AA 991
	AI 001
	BA 001
	EA 761
	PA 001
	PA 101
	TW 244
LHR	BA 002
	BA 274
	LY 315

Figure 8.17 Inverted files ordered on airport code

information. In this way the travel agent can be provided with the flight information that he requires. This is much more efficient than scanning the whole master file. Of course, the travel agent may input his request without being aware that an inverted file has been used in the search process. The actual method of execution is transparent, but the time taken to access the information will be much less when an efficient method is used, and that is what the travel agent notices.

Inverted files, or other similar methods, provide a convenient method for accessing records via fields other than the primary key and can, at small cost, yield a great reduction in time spent on searches.

Of course, the program which produces the inverted file will need to scan the main file record by record, but this does not need to be run while a user is waiting. The inversion program can be run (possibly overnight) on such occasions as required. This may mean that the inverted files are not always up to date. Alternatively, the inverted file can be created once, and then updated each time the main file is updated.

Databases

In a large corporation, the quantity of information held may be enormous. It will not necessarily be held all in one file—different users may have different files each containing selected data. We shall illustrate some of the issues with reference to data held in connection with running a school.

A school needs to maintain information about its teaching structure, accommodation and pupils. Each class register contains names, dates of birth, addresses and attendance records of pupils in that class. The school secretary's file may include the name and address of every pupil in the school and a record of lunch payments. The teacher in charge of external examinations may maintain a file of names and dates of birth of pupils in the fifth and sixth forms and their examination statuses.

Travel passes are issued by local authorities. To facilitate communication, the school secretary may consider it desirable to maintain an index of pupils listed by local authority of residence.

From time to time pupils move and change their address. This information might be communicated to the school office, and the secretary's file will be suitably amended. Unless the form teacher is also informed to make a similar change in the class register, the address information will be *inconsistent*. This is a problem which arises in file information systems because of *duplication of data*. The very fact that data is duplicated is itself wasteful of space, and is more wasteful the more data is duplicated. Making the same change several times in different files is wasteful of processing time.

A further problem relates to the programs which access and manipulate the files. If any change is made to the structure of a file, then all programs using that file must be amended, even if they do not access the changed field of the records. For example, the class files of pupil records might be amended to include a new field indicating a report grade. If the school examinations are handled by a program which accesses this file, that program will have to change (to reflect the new record structure), even though it makes no use of the report grade field.

One answer to these problems is the centralisation of data storage. But putting all the information into a single file is not necessarily the answer. We have already emphasised how it is necessary for the structure of data to reflect the structure of the problem. This is true not only for the internal structure of data (arrays, records) but also for the *organisation* of data. Moreover, a single large file may take an enormous amount of time to access, and even more to update.

The organisation of a mass of data of varying types and with different processing requirements calls for a **database**. A database is a highly organised collection of data accessible to all the application programs within a system. Within a database, duplication of data is carefully controlled, and each program is afforded a selective view of the data, which is appropriate to that application. A database allows for the storage of different types of records, with appropriate interconnections using pointers. Since data is not usually duplicated in a database, the problem of consistency, which results from failing to update duplicate copies of the same data, is effectively solved.

In order to operate a database, special software is required; this is called a **database management system** (DBMS). The DBMS enables collections of records to be set up, with suitable interconnections as described by the **database administrator**. The global data design is called a **schema**. The schema makes provision for all the data items which are required by any program. Individual programmers no longer access files; they access the whole database, but their view is constrained. The database administrator arranges for each program to have only a partial view of the database, or **subschema**, seeing only those data items which are relevant to that program. In this way sensitive data, such as medical history, can be kept in the database and yet be invisible to users who have no right to know the information.

Because each user has only a restricted view, the problem of amending the database is solved. If a new data field is added to the database, no existing program is aware of the change, since the local view of the database by the program remains unchanged. If a data field is removed from the database, only those programs which formerly accessed this field need to be rewritten; all other programs remain unaffected.

The existence of the database makes it easier to develop new programs. If all the data fields for the new program are already available in the database, the new program is allocated its subschema. The data structure on which the new program operates is now determined, and does not have to be defined from scratch. If the new program will need data fields not yet in the database, then the database administrator must enhance the database to provide for the new program.

A database is a highly complex integrated data structure. It contains not only all the data for some real-world system, but also reflects suitable interrelationships between various data fields. This is illustrated in figure 8.18, which shows the partial view of a school database schema which is accessed by a program used to maintain a record of performance in examinations. The Pupil record may contain additional information, such as name and occupation of parents, which is invisible to the examination program. The Pupil record has one pointer to a Class record, and several pointers to different Subject records. The examinations taken by each pupil are recorded in a set of Exam records. The Pupil record has a pointer to the first Exam record, which itself has a pointer to the second Exam record, and so on. Using this chain of pointers, all the Exam records for a given pupil may be accessed.

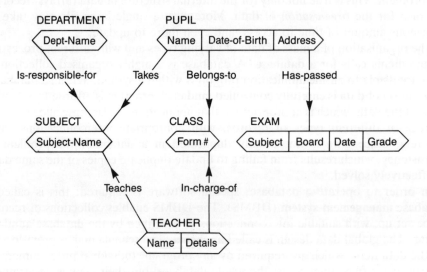

Figure 8.18 Partial view of a school database

The use of a database entails a quite powerful management program—the database management system. For large applications this means an initial expense which may be rapidly recouped through time saved in obtaining rapid access to a reliable store of data—the database. Many proprietary database management systems exist now. They range from large mainframe systems, and even a dedicated computer (the Britton–Lee database processor), to the dBase III system which runs on a microcomputer.

8.6 The Filing System

The organisation of data into directly accessible files or a database, as described in previous sections, is appropriate to a data processing environment where users access a store of data via transaction-processing software. An alternative method of organisation is more relevant where a single user, or each user in a multi-user environment, requires a filing system to manage a set of named files. With this method, access to data within files is under the control of the user.

The logical unit of storage is the file, whereas the physical unit of storage is the block. A file may occupy one or more blocks. The user is largely uninterested in the number of blocks occupied by a file (except insofar as there is, in practice, an upper limit on the number of blocks available to a given user). The objectives of a filing system include the following:

- creation and deletion of files;
- facilities to enable files to be written to and read from;
- control of access to files by users (in a multi-user system);
- ability to name files logically (avoiding reference to physical file addresses);
- management of file allocation to backing storage.

Directories

The method of organisation is to establish a **user directory**. This is a special file, maintained by the filing system, which contains details about the user's files. In particular, the directory will contain the following data for each named file: the address of the first block of the file, control information regarding access rights to the file, the length of the file in blocks, and the date and time when the file was created or last updated. In a multi-user system there must also be a **master file directory** which acts as an index to all the user directories, according to each user's **user-id**. It is permissible for different users to give identical names to their files; no confusion will arise because the full name by which each file is known to the filing system includes the directory name. Thus, in figure 8.19, the system distinguishes the files [JSMITH]PROG and [FCOTTON]PROG.

Some filing systems, such as UNIX and VMS, provide facilities for a multi-level directory. This may be used in two ways. One way is to enable the directory structure to reflect the departmental hierarchy of the user base. Thus, in a company with many users of a single computer system, the master directory might index departmental directories, such as Marketing, Stores, Research, Sales and Manufacture. Each department itself has many users, each with their own user directory. So, if C. Lawson of Sales has a file called JAN1989, the full file name would be [SALES.CLAWSON]JAN1989. The CLAWSON directory is called a **subdirectory** of SALES. To save users having to type in long file names frequently, a process which is both tedious and liable to error, the system keeps a record of the **default**

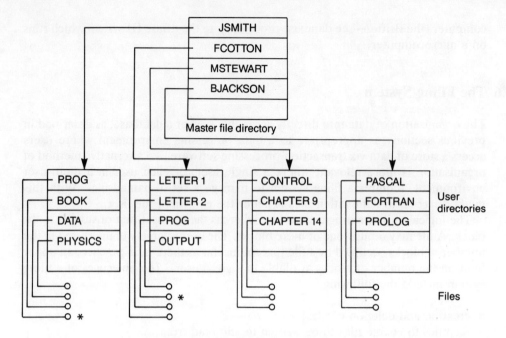

Figure 8.19 Directory structure

directory. When C. Lawson logs in to his user directory, the default directory is set up by the filing system to be [SALES.CLAWSON]. All files in this directory can be referred to without giving the directory name as prefix. (The names of other files have to be typed out in full.) When appropriate, the default directory can be changed by the user, using a *file utility* program.

The concept of a multi-level directory has a further use. Each user is able to divide his files into groups, by creating subdirectories. Thus, a user who is writing a book, engages in research and maintains correspondence, might group his files into three subdirectories. The files are then created within an appropriate subdirectory, such as [TPRITCHARD.BOOK]CHAPTER9. On login, the default directory is set to [TPRITCHARD]. If the user wishes to work on his book during a session, he will reset the default directory to [TPRITCHARD.BOOK], so that files in this subdirectory can be referred to without a prefix.

File sharing

Each file has, associated with it, access permissions. Typically, the filing system may recognise three categories of users—the owner, a group of users to which the owner belongs, and the world (all users). For each category, the owner of a file may specify the level of access; for example—no access, read-only access, execute access, full access (including the right to delete the file). When this book was in draft form, each chapter was held as a file in the author's user directory on a mainframe computer. Only the author had full access to the files. However, read access was granted to other users, so that the author's secretary could print out the draft chapters. (For this, the secretary requires permission to read the file.)

When a file has been fully developed, the owner might withdraw full access from himself, in order to avoid accidental deletion. Of course, the owner always retains the right to change the protections on each file.

Summary of Chapter 8

We have discussed a variety of methods of data organisation, and the ways in which they are influenced by hardware considerations.

At the basic data-item level, a record may be used to describe a data type consisting of several fields, not necessarily identical. When data is required to be saved between program runs, it is held as a file. A structured file of records (all of the same type) is a familiar feature in a commercial data processing environment. Backing storage for files is usually in the form of magnetic tapes and magnetic discs. For microcomputers the usual media are tape cassettes and floppy discs. Tape is cheaper than disc, but is slower (being a serial medium). Typical transfer rates for magnetic tape are 100 Kb/second for a tape drive and 120 b/second for a cassette unit. Where a program has to access a high proportion of the records on a file, sequential processing is an appropriate method. Typically, such processing will take place in batch mode on an overnight run.

Programs can read from or write to files using channels. Although the program communicates with the file as a whole, at any instant only a part of the file need be in a buffer in main memory.

Files must be organised in a manner which reflects the likely mode of processing. Random files, whose records are accessed using a hash function, are relatively easy to update. Indexed files, with an index held in main memory, can handle frequent accesses rapidly. An indexed sequential file requires only a small index, and is also capable of sequential processing. In practice, a multi-level index is usually required. Excess insertions of records are handled using overflow buckets, chained by pointers from the home bucket.

Complex data requirements are generated by the need for information retrieval. In smaller environments, the use of secondary indexes may be sufficient for all purposes. In a large organisation with multiple uses of the same data held in different files, a more centralised approach is desirable. A database holds all the data for a system, including interconnections between related data, while the database management system restricts each user program to a limited view of the database.

Where users maintain their own files, a filing system provides the file utilities. Each user has a directory within which files are created. Some systems allow a hierarchy of subdirectories.

Answers to Exercises

8.1 Each block occupies 2000/1600 = 1.25 inches, plus 1 inch for the gap. The total length of the tape is $1800 \times 12 = 21\,600$ inches. Since $21\,600/2.25 = 9600$ blocks (ignoring those unavailable at the beginning and end of the tape), the tape can store 9600×2000 bytes = 19.2 Mb.

21600/125 = 172.8 seconds (about three minutes); this gives an average transfer rate of

$$19200000/172.8 \approx 111111 \text{ bytes/second}$$

8.2 Magnetic tape is useful to archive files which are accessed only infrequently. It is also convenient for holding back-up copies of files. Tape is portable, and so can be used to transport files physically between computers which are not linked electronically, or for very large files which would take a long time to transmit between computers by wire.

In each case the main benefit is cost (tape is cheaper than discs) or space (tapes are more compact than discs).

8.3 Integrity refers to the correctness of data, either after a copying process or after being updated. Security relates to the mechanisms employed to ensure the integrity of data from corruption, and also to protect devices which hold data from damage or loss.

8.4 (a) and (b) are valid, but (b) will succeed only if the values of *stockfile$* is the name of a file accessible on the current device (tape or disc). (c) and (d) are invalid because the left-hand side of a channel assignment must be a numeric identifier.

8.5 (a) and (d) are valid. (b) is invalid because a string constant may not appear in a channel INPUT statement. (c) is invalid because you may not write on a read-only channel.

8.6 The registration number of a vehicle uniquely identifies it, so this is used as the primary key. Index records consist of the primary key and the bucket number (in the main file), and the index file is sorted on the primary key. The given data has the following index file.

reg-no	bucket-no
ABC 456S	1748
NML 129R	1752
PPQ 789T	1749
RST 228P	1753
TXY 97S	1754
XYA 123R	1747

Further Exercises

1. What are the main differences between hard discs and floppy discs?

2. What is a block of data on tape and on disc? Name one major difference between them.

3. Why is a tape considered to be a serial-access device, whereas a disc is a direct-access device?

4. A public library is an information store in which the 'items' are books. Is it a serial-access or random-access store?

5. (a) Explain the purpose of a parity bit when storing data on magnetic tape.
   (b) (i) A magnetic tape, which is 2400 feet long, can store data at a density of 1600 characters per inch. If 2000 characters are stored in each block, and the inter-block gap length is $\frac{3}{4}$ inch, how many blocks of data can be stored on the tape? (Note: twelve inches = one foot.)
   (ii) Assuming that there are approximately 480 000 characters in an average length novel, how many novels can be stored in this format on one magnetic tape?
   (c) A file stored on magnetic tape usually begins with a header record. What purpose does this record serve, and what information may it contain?

   (Camb.—1987/1/1)

6. A disc pack has some 20 recording *surfaces*, 400 *tracks* and 12 *sectors* per track. In operation, the pack spins at constant speed. Data is accessed by moving the read/write assembly (comprising 20 read/write heads) to the required *cylinder*, then reading the sector concerned into main store.

   (a) With the aid of diagrams, explain the terms in *italics*.
   (b) When reading data, a read/write head must be positioned over the desired track and must be able to identify the required sector as it spins under the head. To provide positioning information, one surface is formatted so that its read head can pass data on radial and angular position to the control unit. Since all the read/write heads are synchronised, the positioning data is common to all surfaces. Suggest what information might be recorded on this surface:
   (i) to indicate the track number currently under each read/write head,
   (ii) to indicate the sector number which is currently under each read/write head.

   (AEB—1983/1/3)

7. A supermarket uses a computer to keep a daily check on its stock levels. Information regarding the sale and delivery of goods is recorded, resulting in a transaction file containing records which consist of the following three fields.:

   Item number; Quantity; Marker.

For goods sold the marker is S, for goods received it is R. At the end of each day this file is used to update the master file, the records of which consist of the following fields:

   Item number; Description; Quantity-in-stock; Re-order-Level.

Both of the above files are sorted into ascending item number sequence.

Construct a flowchart or an appropriate pseudo-code description for a program to update the master file with the stock movements from the transaction file and to produce a report of all those items where the update quantity in stock is less than the re-order level on one printer and an error report on another.

You may assume that each file is terminated by a dummy record containing a 'high value' item number.

(AEB—1983/2/6)

8. A disc pack has 18 surfaces with 400 tracks of data on each. The average time taken to position the heads is 30 milliseconds, and the discs rotate at a speed of 50 revolutions/second. If the actual data transfer rate is 500 000 bytes/second, what is the average access time for a block of 2000 bytes with random processing?

9. A master file is held on magnetic tape with the records sequenced on a numeric key. A transaction file on magnetic tape, and sequenced on the same key, contains records which are to be deleted from the master file.

   (a) Why is it desirable for both files to be sequenced on the same key?
   (b) Suggest how the data could be stored on the transaction file to make processing more efficient.
   (c) Using a top-down design or a structure diagram, present an algorithm for deletion of the records from the master file.
   (d) Discuss the advantages/disadvantages of writing the output file to
       (i) the master tape
       (ii) the transaction tape
       (iii) blank tape.

10. (a) Explain the following terms:
        (i) file creation,
        (ii) file reorganisation,
        (iii) master file.
    (b) A magnetic disc cartridge has 10 usable disc surfaces. Each surface has 200 tracks, with 10 blocks per track. The timing for the disc is as follows.
        Time for one revolution   25 mseconds
        One track seek   10 mseconds
        Average time for a random block   40 mseconds
        (i) For this disc calculate the file size for 20 000 records packed at 10 records/block.
        (ii) The above file is to be updated with 200 records. Calculate the time for this update for both a sequential and a random update, stating any assumptions you make. Comment on your answers.

(JMB—1983/2/2)

11. (a) Describe, without giving details at machine code level, how, giving a key, a record could be found
　(i) in a simple sequentially organised file, that is, one that has no index,
　(ii) in a randomly organised file.
　(b) Under what circumstances is it better to use:
　(i) a simple sequentially organised file instead of a randomly organised file?
　(ii) a randomly organised file instead of a simple sequentially organised file?
　(c)　(i) What is meant by index-sequential file organisation?
　(ii) Suggest, giving reasons, where the indexes of an index-sequential file should be placed.
　(iii) Suggest a method for inserting into an index-sequential file a record that causes overflow.
　(iv) Give an example of a situation where index-sequential would be preferable to both random and simple sequential file organisation.

(JMB—1979/1/17)

9 Dynamic Data Structures

A file is collection of records; a structured file is a collection of records each having the same structure. A file may thus be thought of as a type of data structure. Unlike an array or record, a file does not have a fixed size; it can even be empty. Writing to a file alters its size. A data structure whose size can be altered by inserting and deleting elements is called a *dynamic data structure*.

Another example of data structure which you have met, albeit in disguise, is a string. We have probably given you the impression, so far, that a string is a primitive data type. This impression might be reinforced by an awareness that in some programming languages, string variables can be defined much like real or integer variables. In BBC BASIC, it is merely necessary to suffix a variable name with $—no other declaration is required. In some versions of Pascal, too, it is permissible to use string as a data type without specific definition. However, in standard Pascal it is necessary to define something like

    type string = **array** [1..15] **of** char

before string variables can be declared. This gives us a clue to the nature of a string. In standard Pascal, a string is a static structure of a fixed number of characters, in other words it is a *character array*. This automatically imposes a maximum size for a string identifier, once it has been defined.

In BBC BASIC, there is no language limitation on the size of a string (although the implementation does not allow strings of more than 256 characters). When a string is initialised, the appropriate amount of space is allocated, for example

    school$ = "Kent County"

reserves eleven bytes of memory for *school$*. If, subsequently, the assignment

    school$ = "Queen Elizabeth"

is encountered, additional memory is allocated to accommodate the longer string.

In fact, a new copy of the string *school$* is defined with its own allocation of memory (and the old copy is now dead space). This is a crude method of providing, to the programmer, a structure which can grow in size as the need arises. Again, unlike arrays and the record types which we have considered so far, a string is being expected to behave as a dynamic data structure.

In this chapter we introduce a number of data structures which can grow dynamically during program execution. A fundamental type of dynamic data structure is the sequence or list. Two special types of list, with restrictions on the way items may be inserted and deleted, are the stack and the queue. Another important data structure is the tree. We shall meet a use of trees for sorting ordered data.

9.1 Lists

To all intents and purposes, a string is a sequence of characters of unspecified length. Such a sequence is called a **list**. In a shopping list, there is no predefined limit as to the number of items, it is just as long as necessary. If a string has no predefined length, we need some way of determining its current length. BASIC has thoughtfully provided the function LEN, which returns the length of a given string. But we can reconstruct this function ourselves if we are given some basic building blocks. Clearly, we must be able to start with the empty string " ". The primitive notion is a (single) character, so we shall build our strings using characters and the concatenation operator +. So

$$\begin{aligned}
\text{"program"} &= \text{"p"} + \text{"rogram"} \\
&= \text{"p"} + \text{"r"} + \text{"ogram"} \\
&\quad \vdots \\
&= \text{"p"} + \text{"r"} + \text{"o"} + \text{"g"} + \text{"r"} + \text{"a"} + \text{"m"}
\end{aligned}$$

In general, lists can be built provided we have an operation which constructs a new list from a single item and an existing list.

In addition to building strings, we need a means of decomposing strings. We assume the existence of a function *FNtail* which decapitates a string and returns the remainder, for example

FNtail("Fred")	returns the value	"red"
FNtail("list")	→	"ist"
FNtail("a")	→	" "

Notice how we can now recognise a single character—it is a string whose tail is empty; that is, the condition

FNtail(string$) = " "

is true provided *string$* has a single character. Likewise, if a string has length n its tail has length $n - 1$. It is easy to see now that the diagram in figure 9.1 defines an elegant recursive algorithm.

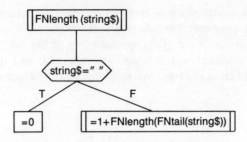

Figure 9.1 The function FNlength

Exercise 9.1

(a) Write a function (in any suitable language which supports strings of indefinite length) for finding the length of a string according to the structure diagram in figure 9.1.

(b) Use locally available predefined functions to define the tail function.

The operations of building a string, decapitating a string and finding the length of a string apply equally to lists of any type. For example, we can build a shopping list by appending items to the list; we can remove the top item from a list; and we can use the same formal procedure as for a string to determine the number of items in a shopping list.

Abstract Lists

The abstract data structure which comprises a list is characterised by having a **pointer** field, which points to the next element in the list. Figure 9.2 illustrates a list of names.

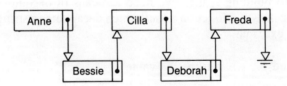

Figure 9.2 A list of names

The pointer of the last element of the list points to no other element; it is called a **nil** pointer and is usually drawn with a special symbol, as in the diagram.

To insert an element into the list, it is necessary to *redirect* or *reassign* pointers. For example, the element with the name Judith can be inserted at the head of the list by making its pointer point to the current head of the list (that is, Anne). Likewise, the element with the name Esther could be inserted between Deborah

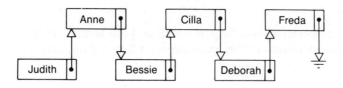

Figure 9.3 Insertion into a list

and Freda by entering the list at its head and moving down the list until Deborah is reached, directing Esther's pointer to Freda and redirecting Deborah's pointer to Esther.

Thus a (linked) list provides a flexible data structure in which items can be inserted (and deleted) at will. Unlike an array, there is no need to reserve all the space in advance. Another advantage of the insertion facility is to enable lists to be maintained in correct sequence at all time. If the names had been held in an array instead of a list, inserting a name in the middle would have entailed moving all the subsequent names to new array locations, in addition to the problem of identifying where the names end. On the other hand, the array structure offers the advantage that all its elements are directly accessible, whereas the elements of a list can be accessed only through the head of the list.

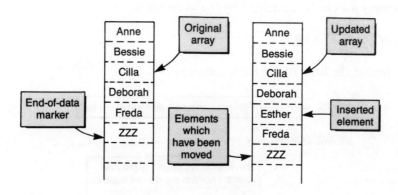

Figure 9.4 Insertion into an array

We have assumed, for simplicity, that the only data field in each element of the list is a name. But there is no reason why each element should not be a record with several fields, such as address, telephone number, status. An alphabetical membership list which is frequently updated might well be maintained in this form.

Exercise 9.2

    (a) What operations can be performed on both arrays and lists?

    (b) What operations can be performed on lists but not on arrays?

Exercise 9.3

What is the length of a newly created list?

Pointers and cursors

Setting up a linked list within a program is a task normally left to the programmer. The pointer representation can be implemented in Pascal using *pointer types*. A list is named using a pointer to the head element. The following definitions can therefore be used. (A pointer is indicated in Pascal using an up-arrow.)

```
type
        list = ↑ element;
        element = record
                    name: string
                    next: list
                  end;
var
        ListOfNames := nil
```

An empty list can be initialised by the assignment

    ListOfNames := **nil**

Insertion at the head of the list is achieved as follows:

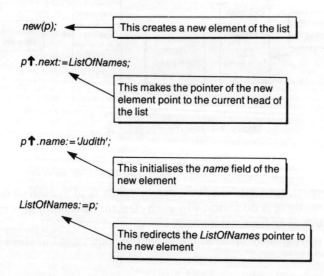

Insertion in the middle of the list may be achieved in much the same way.

The use of pointers means that the elements of the list need not be held in adjacent memory locations. Instead, whenever a new element is created, space is reserved at a convenient point in memory. The pointer is actually the address of the first memory cell reserved but, of course, the high-level programmer is not concerned with this detail.

Alternatively, it is possible for a table to be used to implement a linked list. The secret here is to have a **cursor** field, which holds the pointer to the next array element. The nil pointer can be implemented using a non-existent value for the cursor field (such as zero). Figure 9.5 illustrates a tabular representation of the list depicted in figure 9.3. Note that when using a tabular representation, the whole of the space required must be reserved in advance. (In BASIC, a parallel pair of arrays can be used as a table.)

Head — 7

Names

1	Deborah	5
2	Anne	3
3	Bessie	8
4		
5	Freda	0
6		
7	Judith	2
8	Cilla	1
9		
10		

Figure 9.5 Tabular representation of a list

Activity 9.1

Write algorithms for (a) insertion of an element into a linked list, (b) deletion of an element from a linked list.

Consider carefully where your algorithm needs to define actions which are specific to the choice of representation (table or pointer) for your list.

9.2 Stacks

Where it is necessary to have full freedom of access to insert and delete elements, the list is the appropriate data structure. But not all applications require this freedom.

Guiseppe works in a restaurant washing dishes. When he comes in at six each evening he is faced with an empty counter. As patrons finish courses their empty plates are brought in one by one. The first waiter puts an empty plate on the counter; subsequently the plates are stacked up on top of the existing pile. Guiseppe takes the top plate from the pile and washes it up, placing the clean plate on a rack; he repeats this operation as many times as necessary. As the evening wears on the pile seems to grow inexorably, despite Guiseppe's manful attempts to keep up. Gradually as the evening draws to a close, fewer plates are piled on and the stack decreases in size.

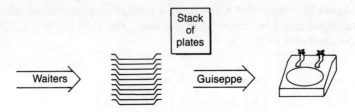

Figure 9.6 Guiseppe's input—a stack

The mode of operation here is known as last-in, first-out (**LIFO**). Plates are added to, and taken from, the top only. A data structure which works on this principle is called a **stack**. New items may be *pushed* onto the stack. Only one item is accessible—the *top* of the stack. The top item can be removed or *popped* to leave a stack whose new top item is now accessible. We have already encountered a hardware stack in chapter 5, and a subroutine stack in chapter 6; we shall see a further use of stacks in chapter 10 when we study the evaluation of arithmetic expressions.

In BASIC and Pascal there is no stack type. We can, however, simulate a stack using an array as a model for a stack. We shall assume a dimension statement for _stack$() sufficiently large for our purposes. Two operations are required: *push* and *pop*. We also need an operation to determine whether the stack is empty; to achieve this we shall use the global variable _top%, whose value equals the number of items currently on the stack.

```
DEF FNempty = (_top% = 0)
```

The push operation pushes an *item* onto the stack, above the current top item. We therefore model it using a procedure with one parameter.

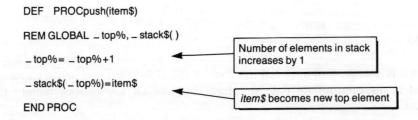

Strictly speaking, we should guard against an attempt to push an item onto a full stack. In principle there is no such thing as a full stack, but a real computer has a limited memory size and so a maximum stack size must be imposed. We may describe an attempt to overfill a stack as *stack overflow*.

The popping operation requires no parameter but must return a value—the former top element. An attempt to pop an empty stack is an *underflow error*.

```
DEF FNpop

REM GLOBAL _ top%, _ stack$( )

IF FNempty THEN PRINT "Stack underflow error" : STOP ◄──── [ Trap illegal use of FNpop ]

        ELSE _ top%= _ top%−1

= _ stack$( _ top%+1)
```

Note how in this implementation *FNpop* does not actually destroy the old top value—it merely hides it from the user who can communicate with the stack only through *FNempty, PROCpush* and *FNpop*. The variables *_top%* and *_stack$()* are assumed to be hidden from use. This can be achieved vividly by replacing the stack procedures with calls to assembly code. (Of course, the array model is not the only one possible. You could write a set of procedures/functions for a stack using Pascal records and pointers.)

It is usually desirable to have another function *FNtop* to inspect the top of the stack. *FNtop* returns the same value as *FNpop*, but does not move the *_top%* pointer.

The user of a stack should not be permitted to manipulate the elements of the array directly. The array is merely used to model the stack. User access is restricted to take place by means of the visible operations — *PROCpush, FNpop, FNtop* and *FNempty*.

Exercise 9.4

An empty stack is set up to hold items of type string. Show the contents of the stack and the value of *data$* after execution of lines 20, 50 and 80 of the following program.

```
10 PROCpush("Manchester")
20 PROCpush("London"
30 data$ = FNpop
40 PROCpush("Basingstoke")
50 PROCpush("Edinburgh")
60 PROCpush("Reading")
70 data$ = FNpop
80 data$ = FNpop
```

Exercise 9.5

A sequence of integers is held in a numeric stack. Use the basic stack operations to obtain the average of these values.

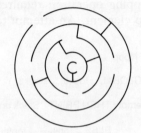

An amazing problem

A problem that lends itself to solution on a computer is that of tracing a path through a maze. The computer can be programmed to make an exhaustive search, printing out each position visited until the 'home' is reached. For simplicity, let us assume that the maze is on a rectangular grid, as shown in figure 9.7.

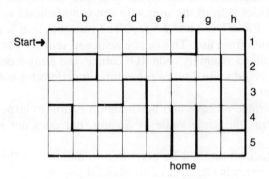

Figure 9.7 A maze problem

The labels *a–g* and *1–5* enable each square to be uniquely identified. Thus the start square is *a1* and the 'home' is reached at *f5*. Tracing the maze by 'hugging' the right-hand wall yields the following path:

$$a1 \quad b1 \quad c1 \quad c2 \quad c3 \quad b3 \quad a3 \quad a2 \quad b2 \quad a2$$

$$a3 \quad b3 \quad b4 \quad c4 \quad d4 \quad d5 \quad c5 \quad b5 \quad a5 \quad a4$$

$$a5 \quad b5 \quad c5 \quad d5 \quad e5 \quad e4 \quad e3 \quad f3 \quad f4 \quad f5$$

This is evidently a valid path through the maze which could be used by a newcomer who does not know his way round. But it is utterly inefficient, leading our visitor up blind alleys only to lead him back out again.

However, if we record the squares visited on a stack, pushing each new square onto the stack, but popping the stack whenever leaving the way we came, the blind alleys are automatically removed. In our case we are left with the direct route.

a1	b1	c1	c2	c3	b3	b4	c4	d4	d5
e5	e4	e3	f3	f4	f5				

The details of the algorithm are slightly tricky, so we leave it as an activity for anyone sufficiently interested.

Activity 9.2

Devise a procedure *PROCmaze* which takes an input stream (of strings) representing squares visited and pushes them onto a stack, popping any which are up blind alleys. The availability of *PROCpush(square$)*, *FNtop* and *FNpop* may be assumed.

Exercise 9.6

Given a stack, devise a procedure to print out the items on the stack from the bottom to the top. State clearly any assumption you make.

9.3 Queues

It is not always appropriate to use the last-in, first-out structure provided by a stack. Many situations require items to be deal with in a first-come, first-served fashion. We usually call such arrangements (for example, people waiting for a bus or a teller in a bank) *queues*.

Guiseppe (remember him?) arranges his washed plates on the rack in a queue. Those washed first will dry first, and so they are reused in strict rotation. Guiseppe accesses only the *back* of the queue (to deposit his washed plates); the waiters collect plates from the *front* of the queue only.

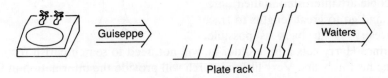

Figure 9.8 Guiseppe's output—a queue

Modelling a queue

A list in which insertions are made at one end, and deletions from the other is called a **queue**. In computing terminology, a queue is a *first-in, first-out* (**FIFO**) structure.

Queues are appropriate when several users are sharing a printer. In this case, several files may be sent to a printer which can handle one at a time. As files arrive they are appended to a queue, held in a buffer memory linked to the printer. When a printing job is completed, the file at the head of the queue is sent to the printer to be printed, and so on.

It is possible to model a queue using an array (much as we did for a stack). You might appreciate the difficulties entailed in this model by considering what Guiseppe does with the next plate when the rack becomes full (as it will!). He pushes the rack down the counter and puts an empty rack behind it, so extending the space available for his queue. And so on. By the time he runs out of empty racks, some of the front racks will have been emptied and he can salvage these for further use.

In the array model we need two variables—for the *front* and the *back* of the queue. New items can be added to the back of the queue; items may be removed from the front of the queue. If the back of the queue reaches the end of the array, and there is space (from removals) near the beginning of the array, this space can be used for the continuation of the queue. An array used in this way is a circular representation of a queue. The size of the array imposes an upper bound on the length of the queue.

Alternatively queues may be implemented using lists with pointers. (No insertions or deletions are allowed in the middle of the queue.) Eventually the queue may grow so large that no space remains in memory for further insertions. So we must reclaim the empty locations. But wait—there is no such thing as an empty location in memory. In fact, what happens is that those locations removed from the front of the queue are no longer accessible to the program. They have become useless garbage. When more space is required this garbage is collected (by the management software—see chapter 10) and made available for reuse.

9.4 Trees

Genealogy has become very popular. Many people are interested in their antecedents, and go to great lengths to trace their ancestry as far back as possible. When Prince Harry gets a little older he will not need to search parish records to determine his forebears. Very little research will provide the information in figure 9.9.

You may wish to continue the diagram to include further information but it is sufficient for our purposes. The diagram contains a collection of data items called **nodes**. In our diagram the nodes contain strings, but they could hold integers or even records. What interests us is the relationship between the nodes. At first sight it looks like a family tree, until you realise it is upside down. Computer scientists habitually draw trees upside down. (The reason for this is that the entry point of the tree is the root, and as the tree 'grows' more information must be added. Since we write downwards, it is easier to 'grow' trees downwards.) A tree is a type of

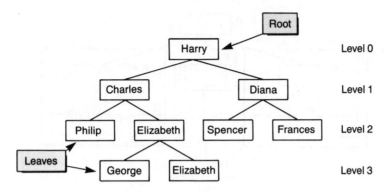

Figure 9.9 Prince Harry's lineage

dynamic structure with a 'special' node called the **root**. The number of nodes encountered on the journey indicates the **level** of the destination node. If it is not possible to go from a node further away from the root, the node is called a **leaf**. The tree in the diagram has the additional property that each node has no more than two nodes attached to it at the next level. Such trees are called *binary trees* and have a particular role in computing. Unlike the data structures considered until now, a tree is not *linear*.

An assembly may be described in terms of subassemblies using a tree (not necessarily binary), as in figure 9.10.

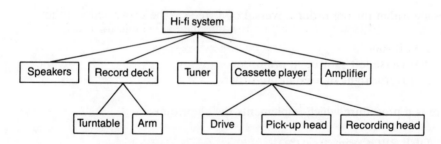

Figure 9.10 Subassemblies

A structure tree for an algorithm conveys not only the structure of the algorithm but also the sequence in which the nodes should be visited to write a corresponding linear program.

An enumeration of the nodes of a tree is called a *tree traversal*. The order of traversal appropriate to the structure diagram in figure 9.11 is

A B C D E F G H I

This order is known as **pre-order** traversal, because the root is visited before the subtrees are traversed. Each subtree in turn is traversed in pre-order. (A **subtree** is

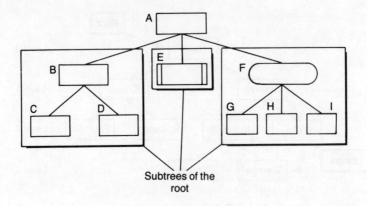

Subtrees of the
root

Figure 9.11 Traversing a structure tree

what you are left with if you delete the branch leading into a node and all the nodes attached to the top of the branch. The node now becomes the root of a new tree coming from the node.) In the case of a binary tree, each node has precisely two subtrees (which may be empty)—a left subtree and a right subtree.

Exercise 9.7

Characterise a leaf node in terms of its subtrees.

The algorithm for pre-order traversal of a tree can be expressed as follows:

1 visit root
2 traverse left subtree in pre-order
3 traverse right subtree in pre-order.

Here is a procedure which implements the algorithm.

```
DEF PROCprint_tree(t%)
REM pre-order traversal of tree with root at t%
If t% <> NIL
    THEN PRINT FNvalue(t%): print_tree(t%!_left):
                            print_tree(t%!_right)
ENDPROC
```

The procedure *PROCprint_tree* for executing this algorithm assumes the existence of a package of 'binary tree' functions. *FNvalue* extracts the value of the root node, and *t%!_left*, *t%!_right* respectively point to the left and right subtrees of the node whose pointer is *t%*. An empty tree is indicated by the pointer *NIL*. Figure 9.12 shows a binary tree package, where each node is a string. The maximum string length is determined by the initialisation procedure *PROCinit*.

```
DEF PROCinit(size)

REM Tree initialisation allowing nodes of up to 'size' bytes

REM GLOBAL _ S%, _ left, _ right, NIL

NIL=0

_ S%=size+7 : _ left=0 : _ right=4

ENDPROC


DEF FNvalue(t%)=$(t%+8)


DEF FNroot(node$)

REM Insert value node$ as the root of a new tree

IF LEN node$ > _ S%-7 THEN PRINT "Tree Error" : STOP

DIM new% _ S%

!new%=NIL : new%!4=NIL

$(new%+8)=node$

=new%


DEF PROCleaf(node$,n%,branch)

IF branch= _ left OR branch= _ right

    THEN n%!branch=FNroot(node$)

ENDPROC
```

Figure 9.12 Binary tree package

Exercise 9.8

Modify the procedure in PROCprint_tree to indent each node value by a number of spaces equal to the level of the node in the tree. (This prints out a 'graphic' representation of the tree.)
Hint: Introduce another parameter.

Sort trees

Data may frequently be amenable to sequential organisation. We have seen how a structure tree represents a sequential program. A stream of names is made accessible if the names are in alphabetical order. If a set of names is held in an array it will be necessary to sort the array using a method like those discussed in chapter

3. A tree, being a dynamic structure, can be built up as required. We shall discuss here how to generate a binary tree so that its structure reflects the sequential organisation of the data. We call this structure a **sort tree**.

Suppose we wish to store the following names in a sort tree:

Shakespeare, Shelley, Keats, Byron, Wordsworth, Gray, Browning

We wish the tree to reflect alphabetical order. The rule we adopt is that a left branch is used for a *preceding* name, and a right branch for a *following* name. To begin, Shakespeare is inserted as the root. Shelley *follows* Shakespeare so it is inserted on the right branch. Likewise Keats, *preceding* Shakespeare, is inserted on the left branch. Following the insertion of Byron we have the tree shown in figure 9.13.

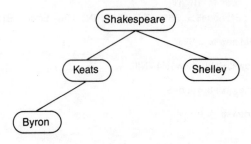

Figure 9.13 Poets' tree (partial)

Wordsworth *follows* both Shakespeare and Shelley; Gray *precedes* Shakespeare and Keats but *follows* Byron. Finally Browning *precedes* all others, yielding the tree in figure 9.14.

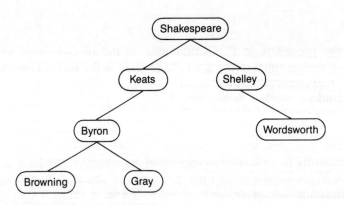

Figure 9.14 Poets' tree (complete)

Thus the program design is:

```
visit the root node
loop
    select
        if next data item precedes this node
        then
            branch left
        else
            branch right
        endif
until node is empty
insert data item
```

Note how the new node is always a leaf of the new tree

Activity 9.3

Using the tree package (figure 9.12) write a program which generates a sort tree.

The next task is to produce a sorted list from the sort tree. It is clear that pre-order traversal will not deliver the goods. The correct algorithm is

```
traverse left subtree
visit root
traverse right subtree
```

since all names in the left subtree *precede* the root, and all in the right subtree *follow* the root. This must always be true, because that is how we constructed the tree. We call this route through the tree an **in-order** traversal.

Exercise 9.9

It is now desired to expand the poets' tree by the addition of Tennyson. Where will the new node be inserted?

Activity 9.4

Modify PROCprint_tree (exercise 9.8) to execute in-order traversal.

Activity 9.5

Note carefully how the tree grows in a rather straggly fashion. The precise shape of the tree is dependent on the order in which the data is presented to the program. Using your procedures you should experiment with presenting the same data in differing sequences, and compare the resulting trees.

Searching a sort tree

One use of trees is to maintain a collection of records. Each record has a key identifier, and the keys may be integers or strings, which can be sequenced numerically or alphabetically. By keeping a collection of records in a sort tree, we can economise on the time taken to access a record. By searching the tree for the required key, we can access the desired record; the maximum number of nodes visited will be the highest number of levels in the tree. The longest search time is therefore proportional to the length of the longest branch.

A tree is more efficient if it is *balanced*. In a balanced tree no leaves are introduced at a new level until the preceding level is full. In such a tree the maximum search time is proportional to $1 + \log l$, where l is the length of the longest branch. This increase in efficiency must be paid for—the overhead is the effort required to maintain the tree in balance, which may necessitate moving nodes afer they have been inserted.

Summary of Chapter 9

Where it may be necessary to vary the number of records, it is appropriate to use a dynamic data structure.

An important example of a dynamic data structure is a list, whose elements are linked by pointers. Stacks and queues are dynamic data structures with specific insertion and deletion rules. It is possible to model these structures using arrays or pointers to records.

A more complex dynamic data structure is the tree. Examples of trees abound; a structure diagram is one example of a tree. Trees can represent sequential data by a suitable traversal of the nodes. A sort tree is built by inserting leaves to maintain sequencing under in-order traversal.

Answers to Exercises

9.1 (a) DEF FNlength(string$)
       IF string$="" THEN = 0 ELSE = 1 + FNlength(FNtail(string$))
   (b) DEF FNtail(string$) = MID$(string$,2)
       [Note: This function definition is not wholly satisfactory because it fails to trap an illegal attempt to find the tail of an empty string. Can you fix this defect?]

9.2 (a) Arrays and lists can both be created, elements can be updated (by assignment), and the value of an element can be retrieved.
   (b) Insertion and deletion.

9.3 A newly created list has no elements, so its length is 0.

9.4

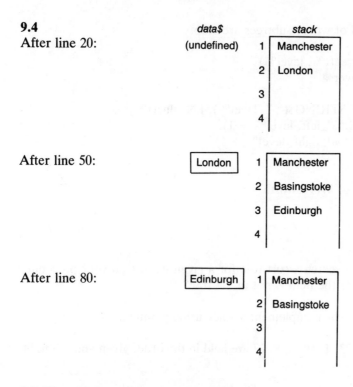

After line 20:   data$ (undefined)   stack
1 Manchester
2 London
3
4

After line 50:   London   stack
1 Manchester
2 Basingstoke
3 Edinburgh
4

After line 80:   Edinburgh   stack
1 Manchester
2 Basingstoke
3
4

9.5 The simplest method is an UNTIL loop.

```
sum = 0: count = 0
REPEAT
    sum = sum + FNpop
    count = count + 1
UNTIL FNempty
average = sum/count
```

9.6 Assume that the size of the stack is less than *max%* (where *max%* has been previously assigned), and that the stack is not empty.

```
DIM temp$(max%)
DEF PROCprint_stack
LOCAL i,j
i = 0
REPEAT
    i = i + 1
    temp$(i) = FNpop
UNTIL FNempty
FOR j = i TO 1 STEP −1
    PRINT temp$(j)
NEXT j
ENDPROC
```

9.7 A leaf is a node all of whose subtrees are empty.

9.8 DEF PROCprint_tree(t%, level%)
   REM pre-order traversal
   IF t% <> NIL
      THEN PRINT STRING$(" ", level%), FNvalue(t%):
         print_tree(t%!_left, level% + 1):
         print_tree(t%!_right, level% + 1)
   ENDPROC

9.9 As the left subtree of Wordsworth.

Further Exercises

1. Write a procedure to search a sort tree for a given item. Can your procedure handle the case where the item is not in the tree?

2. Develop procedures which implement a stack using pointers.

3. The numeric values 23, 1, 19, 3, 8, 27 are held in the order given and are to be organised as
   (i) a linked list,
   (ii) a binary tree.
   (a) Describe, with the aid of diagrams, each of these two data structures.
   (b) The above values are held in a one-dimensional array A. By using an additional array NEXT and a variable FIRST show how these values may be represented in ascending numeric order using a linked list. Show clearly the value of FIRST and the elements of NEXT.
   (c) Construct a flowchart or a pseudo-code algorithm to show how an additional value may be inserted into a linked list of this form. Assume that a variable FREE gives the subscript of the first free location in A.
   (d) Construct a diagram showing how the above values would be held in a binary tree which facilitates sorting, assuming the value 23 to be the root.
   (e) Comment upon the number of comparisons required to locate a particular value in a binary tree as compared with a linked list.

   (AEB—1984/2/2)

4. A certain computer system has approximately 2000 users each of whom is allocated a unique user-id (user identifier) consisting of two alphabetic characters followed by two denary digits. In order to gain access to the computer system a user enters his or her own personal user-id and the computer system then determines whether this has been allocated or not. Access is denied if the user-id has not been allocated.
   For reasons of efficiency it is considered necessary that the allocated user-ids are held in main store and the following two methods have been suggested:

(i) the user-ids be held in a table and accessed by use of a hashing algorithm,

(ii) the user-ids be held in binary tree form.

(a) Describe these two methods of holding the data. In each case show how a particular user-id would be accessed and comment upon the efficiency of access.

(b) Discuss the relative merits of these two methods with respect to the addition and deletion of user-ids.

(AEB—1982/2/1)

5. A publisher maintains a list of his books currently in print. Each book is represented in the list by its standard book number. The list is maintained in ascending numerical order of code numbers, and is updated by inserting and deleting entries for books as they are published or become out of print.

Discuss the suitability of sequential storage in a one-dimensional array structure (or vector) for computer storage and processing of this information.

Describe by means of diagrams and written explanation, an alternative storage structure using links (pointers).

For the alternative storage organisation you have described, give detailed instructions for effecting each of the following operations:

(a) deleting a book-number as the book becomes out of print, and freeing the space which becomes available,

(b) adding the book-number of a newly published book.

Take care to allow for the case of a book-number which precedes all those currently on the list. Take all possible steps to ensure that the attempted addition of a new book-number does not fail while unused storage exists.

(ULSEB—Specimen/2/8)

6. A binary tree is to be used to hold data about a collection of items. The items in the collection are changing frequently. The data held for each type of item consists of a part number (integer), and the tree is to be maintained in ascending order of part number.

The structure is illustrated by the following diagram (figure 9.15) which contains some example data.

The quantity of any particular item may be changed; this includes a decrease to a zero quantity, in which case that type of item is to be removed from the tree, or an increase from a zero quantity, in which case the new type of item is to be added to the tree. It is known that there will never be more than 500 types of items in the tree at any one time.

(a) Show, by means of diagrams and the example given, how this binary tree may be represented in a computer by using arrays. Include provision for the organisation of the free space.

(b) Using your suggested representation, describe algorithms for the following operations:

(i) given a part number, find the quantity (or indicate that the part number is absent);

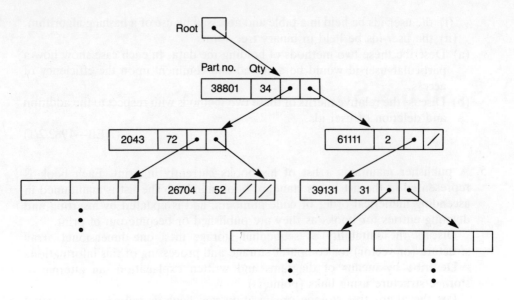

Figure 9.15 Stock control tree

(ii) given a part number and a positive quantity, update the data in the tree; your algorithm should include provision for the case where the part number is not present in the tree and needs to be added.

(Camb.—1983/2/4)

7. (a) By means of diagrams explain how data is added to and removed from the following data structures:
   (i) a queue,
   (ii) a push-down stack.
   (b) What is a linked list? Describe in detail how you would implement such a list when it is to be stored
   (i) in immediate access storage,
   (ii) as a file on disc.
   (c) A linked list is held in immediate access storage and each element of the list contains five fields. The first field is the key field. By means of a flowchart or other technique, describe a procedure to find an element in the list. The first parameter of the procedure is the value of the key field which is to be found. The second parameter returns either the value zero if the element is not found, or the value of the pointer to the element if it is found.

(JMB—1983)

10 Systems Software

Computer hardware responds to a repertoire of elementary instructions, its machine code. We have seen the nature of low-level programming in chapter 6—it is cumbersome, highly prone to undetected errors and unfriendly in appearance. High-level programming, on the other hand, provides the user with a somewhat more friendly mode of communication.

Human beings communicate with each other by way of a spoken dialogue, and using ordinary handwritten or printed manuscript. We might like to communicate with computers in a similar fashion. To some extent this is already achievable, as we shall see in chapter 11, but it requires that the computer be first primed to understand this 'foreign' mode of communication. More realistically, we are willing to meet the computer half way. We accept that we should be expected to codify our problems and specify programs in a computer-oriented language. But we hope equally that the language that we have to use may be readily intelligible to human beings, too, and that the formal reduction to machine code be performed by the computer itself. Indeed, so long as the conversion between program and machine code can be achieved according to a set of definite rules, this is a task to which the computer is admirably suited.

So we expect computers not only to 'solve our problems', but also to provide a more friendly environment. This environment is called a *virtual machine*, and is provided by what we shall call generically *systems software*. Broadly speaking, we may think of systems software as being a suite of programs 'in the background' which allows us to communicate with the computer in a less unfriendly fashion. It is the purpose of this chapter to examine the function of the major items of computer software.

The software which concerns our programs directly consists of *compilers*, *interpreters* and *assemblers* for the programming languages in which our programs are written. In addition, we may require *editors* with which to update our program files and other documents. More generally, the tasks of file management, of allocating resources to different users in a multi-user environment or on a network, of scheduling batch runs and of management of the memory are functions of the *operating system*.

10.1 Software and Firmware

The basic collection of programs which a computer user requires in order to make use of the hardware is frequently supplied by the vendor of the hardware, or by a specialist firm of software writers who produce software to the computer manufacturer's specification. Software may also be produced 'in-house' by a systems support group, and at a large installation there will certainly be such a group who will provide modifications to the systems software to meet local needs.

In the case of a mainframe or minicomputer, the software will most likely be supplied initially on magnetic tapes. This is not, however, a convenient medium for regular use as, by its very definition, systems software is required frequently and fast. (Indeed, in the case of an operating system, or supervisory software, it will be running continuously.) The software will therefore be held on disc backing storage for rapid transfer to main memory, as indeed will all user programs which are frequently accessed. On a microcomputer, software may be supplied on a floppy disk. However, faster access is available if the software is supplied as a read-only memory (ROM). This is a practical consideration as software is likely to be produced in large quantities, and so the cost of making the prototype is spread, and the price is effectively limited to the unit cost of producing the ROM.

The term software has come to be associated with complete flexibility, in contrast with hardware. Where the software resides on a disc, or another magnetic medium, it can be easily relocated to suit changing requirements. The program in a ROM has been 'burnt in' and is immutable (except in the case of an EPROM, which can be reprogrammed at some expense). This difference has led to the introduction of the term *firmware* to describe 'software' which is not quite soft.

Typical modern microcomputers, such as the Acorn BBC series of computers, Archimedes and the Research Machines RM Nimbus PC, have been designed to allow ROMs to be plugged in directly. This feature enables not only systems software but also widely marketable applications programs—such as word-processing and educational 'software'—to be made available on ROMs.

Applications software

The end user of a machine is not interested in the 'nuts and bolts' which, in the long run, make things work. His aim is to switch on (or log on to) the computer and be faced immediately with an environment in which to perform the relevant processing. The teacher using an educational program to teach French wants to be able to switch on and find a suitable teaching environment which requires the pupils to type in appropriate words or sentences that increase their knowledge of French. The businessman wants to be able to key in specific financial data and then view a spreadsheet of consequent information. The programs which provide these environments are called **applications programs**. Some applications programs are highly sophisticated packages, like travel booking programs, Lotus 1-2-3 for financial analysis and the statistical package for social scientists, SPSS. Spreadsheets are very popular with businessmen for performing calculations with numerical data in an easily understood layout. Packages for payrolls and stock control are available in numerous formats and are used in businesses of all sizes. Packages of this sort are used by huge corporations running mainframes, by large businesses on minicomputers and by small firms with microcomputers.

The applications programs may be held in a *library* which is accessed by users. In large installations there may be several libraries, each available to specific classes of authorised users.

10.2 High-level Language Support

Programs may be written in a variety of programming languages, depending on the availability of language support on the computer which has to run the program, and the suitability of the language for the task in hand. A program written in a high-level language may be executed in one of two fashions. The program can be *compiled* into machine code; in this case the original version of the program is called **source code**, and the corresponding machine code version is called **object code**. The object code is held in a file, and is available to be run directly (using appropriate utilities). Alternatively the program may be *interpreted*, that is, each statement is analysed and executed as and when it is encountered.

In this section we shall explain the translation process which enables high-level code to be used to control the execution of a computer. We shall examine some of the detailed aspects in the following two sections.

The translation process

The systems program which compiles or interprets a source code program is called a **compiler** or an **interpreter**, as the case may be. Compilers, interpreters and assemblers (which you encountered in chapter 6) are all programs which take source code as their input and then perform a translation process. We may identify three conceptually distinct functions within the translation process:

- *lexical analysis* in which the program text is broken down into a uniform stream of *tokens*;
- *syntactic analysis* where the grammar of the program is checked, and the structure of the program is organised for further processing;
- *code generation* in which executable code is prepared which reflects the meaning of the high-level program.

In practice, the three functions of a compiler will not necessarily be carried out by distinct routines.

The successful compilation of a program presupposes that the source code is syntactically correct and obeys the grammar rules of the programming language. A compiler must, however, also be capable of handling source programs which are incorrectly formulated. To this end the code analysis phases are designed to pass on, to an *error analysis* phase, any source code which cannot be successfully analysed. If any errors are discovered, appropriate error messages will be output and no object code is generated. If no errors are found, then the *report generator* will report that object code has been successfully produced, and a message may be included indicating the amount of space occupied by the object code program. Some compilers report errors merely by a number, which must then be looked up in a table. This is unfortunate because a computer is very adept at looking up tables and the compiler should at least print an intelligible description of the error. Good compilers also indicate clearly (on a program listing) exactly where the error has been noticed.

Many compilers allow user programs to incorporate routines from a program library held on disc. To enable this process a **linkage editor** is invoked. This inserts

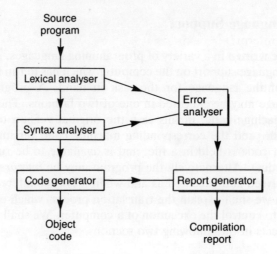

Figure 10.1 Schematic layout of compiler

the necessary references in the object code to the library routines, which are stored as precompiled code. Some compilers also allow the user to prepare routines or segments (as source code) which are compiled separately and are subsequently linked into the main program. It may also be possible to incorporate segments whose source code is written in another language.

The difference between an interpreter and a compiler becomes significant at this stage. When a *compiler* is used, the binary code of the object program is saved as a **relocatable** binary file; that is, the machine code is ready to run, but the addresses are stored *relative* to the beginning of the program. Actually to run the program, it is necessary to *load* the object code (including any linked routines) into the computer's memory. An *interpreter* acts in a different fashion. As each machine-code instruction is generated, it is immediately executed by the processor. These instructions are not consolidated into a file, but are discarded on execution. A syntax error need not be reported until it is about to be executed, and it is possible for an erroneous program to run satisfactorily if it contains an error in a 'dead' code statement which is never executed. This could not happen with a compiler, which has to produce an object code program for the whole of the source code.

What are the implications of the difference between compilation and interpretation, and which is preferable? If there were a clear cut answer it is unlikely that both methods would remain available. The truth is a matter of 'horses for courses'—each has advantages in appropriate situations.

An interpreter saves time because it does not produce an object code file which must then be loaded. It therefore provides a rapid method of running programs one-off and testing them to ensure that they are error free. This is of particular value when developing programs in an interactive environment where response time is an important factor. An interpreter is often simpler (and less expensive to produce) than a compiler, and can offer much better debugging facilities. Since the program is run while it is being analysed, if anything should go wrong the program variables are immediately available for inspection.

Where space is at a premium, it may not be possible to store in memory the program and an interpreter at the same time. A compiler, on the other hand can accept the source program in segments and produce the object program in corresponding segments. The linked object program, a machine-code file, can then be executed without the compiler being in memory. A second advantage of compilation relates to frequently used programs. Compilation may be a slow process, but executing the resulting object code is much faster than running source code under an interpreter. Besides the obvious overhead of generating the machine instructions from the source code during execution, there is the hidden overhead of each statement being translated separately on each execution. So a statement in an inner loop may need to be processed numerous times during interpretation. A compiler, on the other hand, translates the text of the source as it is scanned from beginning to end, so each statement is compiled only once, no matter how many times it will be executed. When a program has been developed and is going to be run many times, the saved (relocatable) object code which is produced by a compiler is a machine-code program which can be executed directly.

The most popular interpreted languages are APL, BASIC, LISP and Prolog. These have been designed as *interactive* languages, to be input and run from a terminal (or on a microcomputer). They are, therefore, natural candidates for interpretive execution. In each case, the interpreter has been designed as part of a command *environment* for the language. The user can develop and run programs in these environments insulated, largely or entirely, from the general operating system. On some microcomputers, such as the Acorn BBC series, the machine automatically enters the BASIC environment when it is switched on. Other languages—including Algol, Pascal, FORTRAN, COBOL and Ada—are most frequently run in compiled form. Historically, compilation was appropriate for batch programs, where the response time depends on factors outside the program. Nowadays all languages are available in interactive environments, and some systems offer both an interpreter (for development) and a compiler (for production runs) for the same language.

An important use of interpreters is in the command environment of an interactive system. The user types in commands which are translated and executed by the *command language interpreter*.

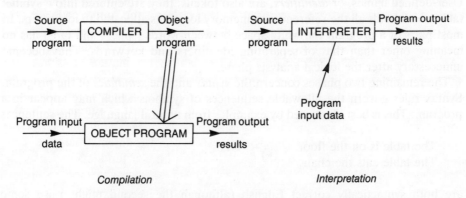

Figure 10.2 Two ways of executing a program

To sum up, compilers and interpreters are systems programs (or library programs) which take source code as their input (from either the keyboard or a file). A compiler generates a machine-code file (which may be run at will) as its output, whereas an interpreter executes the source program.

Although the computer on which the compiler runs is usually the same as the computer which executes the object code, this is by no means an absolute requirement. A **cross-compiler** may be used to produce object code for execution on a different computer. A typical case where a cross-compiler might be used is where the machine which has to run the object code has a small memory. For example, a cross-compiler running on the IBM 3090 mainframe might be used to produce object code for a 6502 microprocessor.

Exercise 10.1

Why are compilers and interpreters both desirable as methods of translating computer languages?

10.3 Syntax of Programming Languages

We have already mentioned that programming languages exist to provide a relatively friendly medium in which the human programmer can convey an algorithm to the computer, which then converts it to an internal form according to a predetermined set of rules, using a special program—an interpreter or a compiler. We identified three phases in this process.

The first phase, *lexical analysis*, is concerned with the stripping out some of the 'wrapping' which makes a program more appealing to the programmer, but has no significance for the computer. Thus *comments* are removed, and character sequences are grouped into tokens. A **token** is an indivisible unit of the programming language. Thus, examples of tokens are *keywords* (whose literal meaning is relevant only to the English-speaking humans) and symbols with fixed meanings (like $\star$ and $+$), as well as *numeric constants* (which are converted to a suitable binary format) and character constants (which are converted to ASCII code, say). User-defined names, or *identifiers*, are also tokens; they are entered into a **symbol table** which holds all the references to memory locations allocated to identifiers. In most parts of a program the white space between words (spaces and tabs) has no meaning other than that of separating identifiers and keywords. They become unnecessary after the lexical analysis phase.

The remaining two phases concern the *syntax* and the *semantics* of the program. Syntax rules govern the allowable sequences of symbols which may appear in a program. This is best illustrated by examples from natural language. The sentences

> The table is on the floor. $(\star)$
> The table eats the chair.

are both syntactically correct English (although the second might raise some eyebrows). On the other hand

The chair green floors with

is syntactically unacceptable. Likewise the BASIC statement

name$ = title$ + initial$ + FNsurname("fred", "joan")

is syntactically correct, whereas

PRINT FOR I TO NEXT Mary = 19

fails to conform with the rules.

Once an English sentence, or a BASIC statement, is written in correct syntax, it is necessary to determine its **semantics** or meaning. For example, of the two correct sentences written above (⋆), the first is clear and unambiguous, whereas the second is devoid of meaning.

The *syntax analysis* phase establishes that a program is *syntactically correct* and puts it into a form suitable for *code generation* according to the *semantics* of the programming language. In order that these phases be achieved by an automatic computer, they must be properly defined. Language *syntax* is frequently defined by precise formulas or diagrams. Programming language *semantics* have been studied mathematically, but are usually described in natural language.

Defining syntax rules

Early attempts at devising high-level programming languages were very much *ad hoc* efforts. In the late 1950s a committee was formed to define a new, advanced algorithmic language (that is, a language in which computer algorithms could be readily expressed). Two members of that committee, John Backus and Peter Naur, devised the formalism in which the syntax of their new language, ALGOL-60, is expressed. The formalism is straightforward to master and is known as **Backus-Naur form** (BNF). BNF is often called a *metalanguage*, because it is used to describe another language (such as ALGOL-60, BASIC, Pascal).

An illustration of the use of BNF to describe a simple language is shown in figure 10.3. Here the object described is a post-1983 British car registration mark. There are four rules or **productions**. In each the left-hand side is a grammatical construct enclosed in angle brackets (called a **non-terminal**) and is followed by the composite symbol ::= which means 'is defined by'. The right-hand side consists of a sequence of terminal or non-terminal symbols. A **terminal** symbol belongs to the basic

<registration mark> ::= <letter> <numeral> <letter> <letter> <letter>

<letter> ::= A | B | C | D | E | F | G | H | J | K | L | M | N | P | R | S | T | V | W | X | Y

<numeral> ::= <digit> | <digit> <digit> | <digit> <digit> <digit>

<digit> ::= 0 | 1 | 2 | 3 | 4 | 5 | 6 | 7 | 8 | 9

Figure 10.3 BNF description of car numbers issued in Great Britain since August 1983

'alphabet' of the language, that is, it is an allowable symbol. For car numbers these terminal symbols are digits and capital letters (other than I, O, Q and Z). In a programming language, any symbol which can actually appear in program code is a terminal symbol. A vertical bar indicates alternatives, so the third rule can be paraphrased as

"A numeral consists of a sequence of one, two or three digits."

There is precisely one non-terminal which does not appear in any right-hand side, namely <registration mark>. This is known as the *root*. Loosely speaking, the grammar defines the root in terms of the terminal symbols, by way of intermediate grammatical constructs. The intermediate constructs are the non-terminals which appear on the left-hand side in their defining productions, and are used elsewhere on the right-hand side of one or more productions. The root of the grammar for a programming language will typically be called <program>. In general, the root of a grammar is often called a <sentence>.

The BNF description above gives a precise set of rules for (a) generating all possible registration marks which conform to the specification, and (b) checking that any given registration mark is legal. This scheme is frequently used to define the syntax of a programming language. In the syntax analysis phase, the language processor can check the program code against the definition of the language. This is called **parsing** the code. If no possible match can be made to fit the program into the rules, a *syntax error* is flagged.

In order to define the constructs required in a program, it may be necessary to indicate that something may be repeated an arbitrary number of times. For example, an integer is defined as an arbitrary sequence of digits. This is achieved as follows:

<integer> ::= <digit>|<digit><integer>

Thus an integer is either a single digit, or a digit followed by an integer. Thus any sequence of digits found in a program, appearing where an integer is expected, will be correctly identified as an integer. A production rule of this sort, which is defined (partly) in terms of itself, is *recursive*.

In practice, there will be a restriction on the size of an allowable integer. However, this is not a syntactical restriction; it is an implementation restriction due to the manner in which integers are stored. It is likely, though, that such a restriction will be checked by the lexical analyser, when it encounters the integer and attempts to represent it as a token.

Example

The following grammar rules give the syntax for a procedure definition in a dialect of BASIC.

<procedure definition> ::= <procedure head><separator>
<procedure body><separator><endproc statement>

<procedure head> ::= <line number> DEF <procedure call>
<procedure call> ::= <procedure identifier>|<procedure identifier>
(<identifier list>)
<procedure identifier> ::= PROC<identifier>
<procedure body> ::= <body statement>|<body statement><separator>
<procedure body>
<body statement> ::= <local statement>|<statement>
<local statement> ::= LOCAL <identifier list>
<identifier list> ::= <identifier>|<identifier>, <identifier list>
<endproc statement> ::= ENDPROC
<separator> ::= <carriage return><line number>|:

Of course these rules presume that <line number>, <identifier> and <statement> have been defined.

Exercise 10.2

Write a production rule for <identifier>.

Expression analysis

An important element of syntax analysis is that of analysing expressions so that they may be evaluated. High-level languages have facilities for writing arithmetic expressions, such as

30 * month + day

and boolean expressions, such as

(pay < 120) AND ((age > 65) OR female)

These expressions are conventionally written with the *operators* (such as *, +, AND) between their respective **operands** (for example, 30 and month for the operator * in the first expression above). Operators used in this form are called **infix** operators. Our normal rules for evaluating infix expressions include:

(a) work from left to right;
(b) * and / take priority over + and −;
(c) parentheses may be used to give overriding priority.

These rules encapsulate a hierarchical view of an expression, which may be realised diagrammatically as a binary tree (as discussed in chapter 9):

Constants and variable are the operands, and appear as *leaves* of the tree; the other nodes are the operators. Suppose *month* = 4 and *day* = 17; evaluation of the tree proceeds as follows. We start with the tree

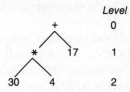

Evaluation commences from the deepest level, in this case level 2. Evaluation of the subtree

is equivalent to 30 ⋆ 4 = 120; this subtree is therefore replaced by its value. We now have the tree

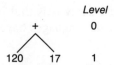

which evaluates to 120 + 17 = 137. This leaves a tree with a node and no branches, and this is the value of the tree. This simple example illustrates how a simple expression tree can be evaluated.

Given an expression tree, the infix form of the expression corresponds to in-order traversal of the tree, as follows:

    put the left subtree in infix form
    insert the root
    put the right subtree in infix form

In practice, parentheses must be inserted round each subexpression deduced from a subtree unless the current root is + or −.

Exercise 10.3

Refine the above form of traversal of an expression tree into a program design for a function to produce an infix expression from a given tree.

Reverse Polish notation

The *evaluation* of an expression, though, corresponds to a somewhat different traversal of the tree. In order to evaluate the expression, both the left and right subtrees must be evaluated first. Thus we are led to a **post-order** traversal of the tree:

> evaluate the left subtree
> evaluate the right subtree
> apply the root operator.

If the expression were *generated* from the tree using this order of traversal, each operator would appear following both of its operands. Thus

3 + X	becomes	3 X +
2 ⋆ Y + 7	becomes	2 Y ⋆ 7 +
(11 − A)/B	becomes	11 A − B /

It is interesting to note that, in this *postfix* form, there is no need for brackets; evaluation proceeds in regular fashion from left to right, and there is never any ambiguity. Postfix notation for expressions was used in work by the Polish logician Jan Lukacziewicz; it is usually known as **reverse Polish notation**.

You might care to note that in a valid reverse Polish expression the following are true:

- the total number of operands is one more than the number of operators (of course, this is equally true for an infix expression);
- if you start from the left of the expression and proceed to any symbol (before the last), the number of operands is at least two more than the number of operators so far.

Exercise 10.4

Convert the following infix expressions to reverse Polish notation.
(a) u − 2 / y
(b) p⋆p − 4⋆q⋆r

(It may help to draw the expression tree first.)

Exercise 10.5

Compute the following expressions in reverse Polish notation. (The up-arrow ↑ means 'raise to the power of'.)

(a) 4 7 ⋆ 10 4 + /
(b) 5 18 16 − ↑ 5 +
(c) 1 2 3 4 5 + + + +

Activity 10.1

Modify your algorithm from exercise 10.3 to produce an expression in reverse Polish notation from a given expression tree. Test your function (or procedure) on the following tree.

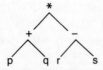

The evaluation stack

We have spent some considerable effort studying expressions but it is not yet clear how this study is useful to a language translator. To reap the benefit of our newly acquired wisdom, we shall use another data structure studied in chapter 9, the

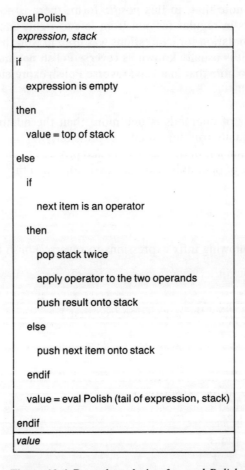

Figure 10.4 Procedure design for *eval Polish*

stack. Remember that a stack grows by pushing data items on it, and we can retrieve the top item of a stack by popping.

Now, a reverse Polish expression is evaluated by simply marching along from left to right, retaining all operands so far, and operating on the two most recent when encountering an operator. This process can be formalised as an algorithm using a stack as shown in figure 10.4. The function *eval Polish* must be presented with a reverse Polish expression and an empty stack as input data. This function will work satisfactorily if the expression is properly formed; otherwise an error situation will arise. If there are too many operators, at some stage an attempt will be made to pop an empty stack; if there are two few operators in the expression, more than one operand will be left on the stack at the end.

Activity 10.2

See if you can improve the algorithm to cater for incorrect expressions, as described in the text.

Exercise 10.6

Using the stack routines (chapter 9), write a function definition which will evaluate an algebraic expression given in reverse Polish notation. You may assume that the expression is held in a string, with items separated by spaces.

Test your function on the expressions in exercise 10.5.

Exercise 10.7

The user of a Hewlett–Packard calculator is required to enter expressions to be evaluated in reverse Polish notation; the calculator holds the number in a hardware stack. What advantages and disadvantages does such a calculator have over one which accepts expressions in infix order?

Activity 10.3

Modify the function of exercise 10.6 to handle boolean expressions.

You might like to compare the operation of the evaluation stack with the stack processor described in chapter 5.

Unary operators

We have made the tacit assumption that each operator has two operands (such as 7 ∗ 5). These are called **binary operators** (nothing to do with binary numbers or binary arithmetic). In fact we also need to use **unary operators**, which have only one operand; for example, a negative number is written

−12

and a boolean variable can be negatived by writing

NOT p

The analysis of unary operators is as follows. In an expression tree a unary operator has a right branch but no left branch. The rules for reverse Polish expressions (given just before exercise 10.4) apply to the count of binary operators only—unary operators are not included in the count. Of course, in the postfix form, the distinction between binary minus and unary minus must be carefully preserved.

In evaluating a reverse Polish expression by the stack method, the processing of each new item now requires a three-way selection. This is illustrated below.

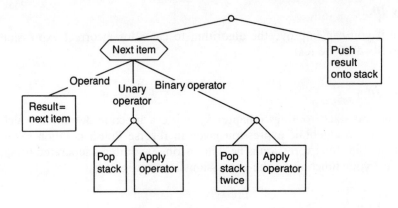

Evaluation of postfix expression

10.4 Code Generation

A compiler produces a code version of the source program as its output—this is called the object code. (An interpreter produces no object code but executes the source program directly.) In principle, it would seem appropriate for the object code to be in the machine code of the computer hardware on which it is to run. But this can be a very expensive proposition. For each high-level language you may wish to use, a compiler must be provided for each and every machine! To make things worse, most compilers are extremely long and complicated programs, as you might expect from the discussion of the previous section.

For this reason, a different approach is sometimes adopted. The compiler for a given language compiles the source program into **intermediate code**. This code looks much like assembly code, but in fact is not the assembly code of any real computer. However, because the intermediate code is rather like assembly code, the task of translating it for any particular machine is a relatively easy task. The main burden of compilation is borne by a portable compiler which produces intermediate code.

For example, many Pascal compilers work by compiling into *p-code*. In order to use such a Pascal compiler on a new type of machine, it is merely necessary to write a p-code translator for that machine.

One question remains—in what language is the compiler written? If it has to be written in a language understood by the machine, the compiler will still have to be rewritten for every new machine! There are two approaches to this problem. One method is to use a standard systems language. BCPL was designed as a language for writing compilers, so that once it is available on a computer, it could be used for building all other compilers written in BCPL; this is popular in some quarters. Nowadays a wide range of computers (including most minicomputers) have available the C programming language (which was influenced in turn by the older BCPL). Once a compiler for a language is available in C, it can be used to produce intermediate code for any machine which understands C; in particular, it can be used on any computer which runs under the UNIX operating system.

There is another answer to the compiler problem. Many Pascal compilers are themselves written in Pascal. So, they can be used, provided they have themselves been compiled—by a Pascal compiler! This is a classic chicken-and-egg situation. To resolve it and produce a compiler for computer A, you must have a machine (say a PDP-11) which already runs Pascal programs.

We require a translator from p-code to machine code which will itself be in the machine code of computer A. The p-code translator for computer A is first written in Pascal. As shown in figure 10.5, this translator can be compiled (on the PDP-11) so that the PDP-11 is now equipped to translate p-code into machine code for computer A. Together with the compiler from Pascal to p-code (which the PDP-11 already has), the PDP-11 is now able to produce machine code for computer A from any Pascal source program. This process is an example of cross-compilation. If computer A is a small machine (an Acorn BBC, perhaps) which cannot support its own compiler, all Pascal programs for computer A are first cross-compiled on the PDP-11; the resulting object code can be executed directly on computer A.

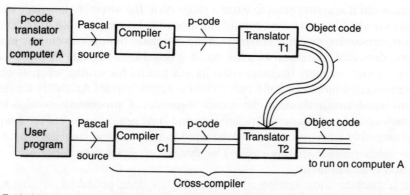

Each thick box represents the PDP-11 computer running the software described in the box

Figure 10.5 Cross-compilation

If computer A is large enough to hold its own compiler, the cross-compiler on the PDP-11 can be *bootstrapped* onto computer A as shown in figure 10.6. First the p-code translator to machine code of computer A is itself translated on the PDP-11; the resulting machine-code program is a p-code translator which runs on computer A. The main Pascal compiler is now itself compiled into p-code on the PDP-11; the resulting p-code version can be translated on computer A. Now any Pascal program can be compiled and executed on computer A.

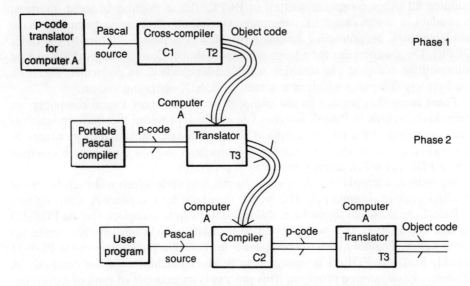

Figure 10.6 Generating a compiling system for another computer

Assemblers

Although programs are normally written in high-level languages, there are some occasions when it is appropriate to write a program in the assembly language of the computer on which it is to be executed. The assembly language, as we have seen in chapter 6, mirrors the machine language of the computer but uses mnemonic names for instructions and addresses. In addition, it is possible to allocate memory using directives. Some assembly languages also have a facility for writing macros, which are parameterised blocks of code called by a symbolic name. Assembly-language programs need to go through the same sequence of processing as high-level programs—lexical analysis, syntactic analysis and code generation—but the simpler form of assembly language and its relationship to the machine language make the process much simpler in this case. The system program which performs this translation is an assembler.

Once a machine-code version of a program has been produced, it no longer matters (to the computer) whether the source program was written in a high-level language or in assembly code. The machine-code program can be executed directly by the processor.

10.5 Utility Programs

Compilers, interpreters and assemblers are general-purpose programs which are available to users. In particular, they are employed by users for processing applications programs. Such general-purpose programs are known as *utilities*; we shall describe a number of other utilities in this section.

A **load-and-go** compiler produces object code ready for execution. If this program is, however, saved on backing store it must be loaded back into main memory, by a **loader**, for execution. If the addresses in the object code are absolute then the program must be loaded into the specific locations where it will run correctly. Object code can also be **relocatable**, in which case internal address references are given relative to a starting location. In this case it may be necessary for the loader to make certain adjustments to address fields as well as loading the program.

Programs which are composed of several modules use symbolic names within segments to reference symbols defined in other, separately compiled modules. A **linker** or **linkage editor** resolves these references so that the various modules can be loaded together as a single machine-code program. Library modules are frequently written in assembly code and linked into programs by the linker. Programs which manipulate external files (on backing storage) require the linker to match up the internal and external file names.

The routines which perform input and output are used much like library routines. Unlike library routines, which are held on backing storage as relocatable modules, the input and output routines are usually held in ROM nowadays. Since they are therefore part of the system, they are also considered to be utilities. Commonly used functions like SIN, COS, SQRT and LN are also implemented in ROM and handled as utilities. However, unlike the language and control utilities, which are used to process programs, these utilities are used within programs to perform specific functions.

File utilities

We have discussed data files, which are manipulated by programs, in chapter 8. Filing systems are not restricted to data files, though. Instead of storing records on files it is possible to store text. Thus, it is possible to store a source program or indeed any document as a file. Text files may be held in ASCII or EBCDIC format. Of course, the files are actually held as the corresponding binary patterns. Indeed machine-code programs can be saved directly as binary files; binary files are also used for other purposes such as the intermediate data of some applications programs, and BASIC interpreters actually produce a tokenised binary file from a source program written in BASIC.

A number of utility programs are available for manipulating files. A *copy* utility is generally available for copying files (such as backup). Other utilities enable files to be *renamed* or *deleted*, and two or more files can be *merged* into a single file. A *sort* utility may be available to sort the contents of a data file.

Editors

A most important utility is one which enables users to create and update text files. Such a utility program is called a **text editor**. Editors allow text to be inserted into or deleted from a file at a specific place. More sophisticated editors also allow

- global searching of a file for a particular string;
- systematic replacement of a given string by some other given string;
- copying a portion of text to another part of the file or to another file;
- moving a portion of text within a file.

As a protection against unintentional deletion of file contents and systems failures, files are not edited *in situ*. Instead a *workfile* copy is edited; at the end of the session the user can save the workfile in place of the original version.

There are two general types of editors. **Line editors** address a file line by line (by attaching a line number to each line). At any time, there is a *current* line which can be edited. Line editors are particularly suitable for use on hard-copy terminals, where a line of text must be addressed for use. **Screen editors** display a portion of a file, known as a *window*. The cursor is moved to the desired position on the screen, at which point editing may take place. In a screen editor there is no need for line number addressing. Screen editors can be used at terminals with VDU screens and on a single-user system which uses a screen output (that is essentially all microcomputer systems).

Some screen editors are equipped with facilities for margin justification, control of the general layout of text by single-key commands, insertion of text parameters into files or documents and for printing copies of documents. Other facilities may include spelling checks, alternative typefaces and foreign modes of script. Such all-embracing editors are called **word processors**. They may be available as software (for example, WordMarc, Microsoft Word, View on the Acorn BBC series, TXED on the Research Machines 380Z and a host of packages with names like WordWise, WordStar, WordCraft) or firmware in the form of a plug-in ROM for a microcomputer. Word processing is widely used in the office environment and many computer systems are available with an inbuilt word-processing capability, and not able to do much or anything else. These machines are *dedicated word processors*.

A few interactive language environments (such as APL, BASIC, micro-Prolog) have an editing facility built into the operating environment, which itself takes care of the form in which program files are organised in backing store. This approach keeps the user interface simple.

Most environments, however, provide the editor as a separate program (as indeed the filing commands are handled by separate programs). For example, UCSD Pascal provides an Editor, Filer, Compiler and other features as distinct subenvironments.

Exercise 10.8

What type of editor does BASIC have?
Can you think of any historical reason why this type of editor was chosen?
Does *your* computer possess any other editing facility?

10.6 Operating Systems

In any computer system there is a need for housekeeping. The various programs which are available and active must perform under the control of an *operating system*. The operating system consists of a suite of supervisory programs, which provides the environment in which all activities take place, and a **nucleus**, through which these programs actually communicate with the hardware. Users of BASIC not only have a programming language in which to write high-level programs, but also have complete access to facilities for running, saving and loading programs. BASIC is, in fact, a complete environment superimposed upon an operating system.

A popular general-purpose operating system for computers based on the Z80 microprocessor was CP/M (*Control program for microcomputers*), developed by Digital Equipment Corporation and based on the operating system of the PDP-11 minicomputer. CP/M is a disc-based operating system; that is to say, one or more tracks on each disc are reserved for the operating system, which must be loaded each time the system is switched on. CP/M is used, for example, on the Research Machines 380Z. CP/M provides the usual range of general utilities, but no language capability. Typically, on CP/M systems the BASIC interpreter runs under the control of CP/M; however, the user does not (for the most part) need to be aware of this—he can safely assume that BASIC is the whole operating system.

The programming language Pascal is usually supplied as a compiler to work under some resident operating system. But an extremely popular microcomputer version of Pascal is UCSD Pascal (developed at the University of California, San Diego) which provides a complete environment, including full editing and filing support. So popular has UCSD Pascal proved that it is now available on numerous mainframes.

These simple operating systems allow a single program to run at any one time. There is also a concurrent CP/M which allows a user to run several processes concurrently.

A single-user operating system which is very popular on 16-bit microcomputers such as the PC machines, is MSDOS. By way of contrast, the popular multi-user operating system UNIX was developed at Bell Laboratories to run on PDP minicomputers, and is now available on machines of all sizes. Operating systems are an important part of a computer system, and are often produced by the companies who market the hardware. IBM have a number of operating systems for their mainframes, such as OS/VMT and MVS; ICL has an operating system called VME; and the DEC corporation have standardised on VAX VMS as their operating system.

The use of a standard operating system across a range of hardware means that the user, who interfaces with the operating system, can use different machines within the same range without having to learn a new structure. This is important when a user of a computing system requires a larger one, because the volume of work has grown, or because it is desired to computerise more processes. With a standard operating system, the user can **upgrade** his system, obtaining a larger, or faster, machine which will continue to run the old programs.

Nucleus

The central core of an operating system, through which it obtains access to the basic hardware, is the **nucleus**. The main components of the nucleus are the dispatcher and the interrupt handler. The nucleus provides the environment in which programs can run. The **dispatcher** selects which job should next have control of the processor. In a simple system where only one user job can be submitted for running at any one time, the function of the dispatcher is to select the user job or one of the supervisory programs for running as appropriate. The supervisory programs in this case will be utilities for handling peripherals. In *multiprogramming* environments where many jobs may be handled simultaneously—we shall discuss this arrangement shortly—the dispatcher maintains one or more queues of user jobs. When a user job can have control of the processor, the dispatcher selects one according to some definite criterion. Typically, the rule may be to select the job at the front of the queue of runnable jobs.

Interrupt handling

The **interrupt handler** is the part of the nucleus which deals with interrupts. Hardware interrupts are generated by peripherals which need to be served; they indicate an input device waiting to send, or an output device which has finished receiving data. Software interrupts are generated by programs which require a transfer of control to an operating system process, to initiate a peripheral transfer, for example, or to deal with an error situation.

As an example of a hardware interrupt, the internal timer or **real-time clock** is usually used to keep track of elapsed time. Each 'tick' of the clock needs to be counted. To achieve this, the clock sends an interrupt to the CPU at each pulse. The CPU services the interrupt (by updating a memory location, perhaps) and returns to its normal business until the next pulse. And so on.

Another source of interrupts is the keyboard. Each time a key is depressed, an interrupt occurs; this interrupt must be serviced (or handled) before the next key is depressed or a character will be lost. (It is not necessary that the incoming character be processed immediately; typically it will be sent to a *keyboard buffer* from which the program can collect characters at its leisure. It is the presence of a keyboard buffer which allows *type-ahead*.)

Interrupts are used in this way by slow input devices. Autonomous output devices (such as disc drives) also use interrupts—after a block of data has been transferred to the device buffer, the program in memory can continue until the output device is ready to receive more data. An output device therefore issues an interrupt when it is ready to receive. Buffered devices, such as tape and disc drive units, use interrupts in a similar way. A tape drive, fast though it is, does not match the speed of a CPU transfer. When data is requested from a drive, the required data is first put into the drive buffer, which is under the autonomous control of the drive unit. An interrupt is then sent to the processor and the CPU can service the incoming data.

It is seen that interrupts play a great part in enabling the efficient use of hardware. Peripheral units can operate concurrently with the main processor, with communication taking place using interrupts. The main processor and the peripheral devices have a master/slave relationship. Input and output are initiated by the main processor, which does its own thing during the autonomous transfer of data.

The existence of an interrupt is detected by a flag in the program status register. After each fetch–execute cycle, before the next fetch, the interrupt flag is inspected. If it is set, program control is transferred by the interrupt handler to an *interrupt service routine*. The service routine requires, for its own purposes, that the program status register be initialised in a particular way. Since different sources of interrupts require servicing in different ways, the interrupt handler must first determine the source of the interrupt. One method is the use of a *skip chain*. Each device has an associated flag which is inspected by the interrupt handler. This is called **polling** the devices. The device whose flag is set is serviced by the appropriate service routine. For each device an interrupt vector is held in a fixed memory location, as shown in figure 10.7. This vector contains the information for the appropriate interrupt service routine to be executed. Thus a service routine is entered by loading its vector into the program counter and program status register.

IPC   Address of interrupt routine

IPS   Program status word for interrupt routine

Figure 10.7 An interrupt vector

The interrupt vectors are initialised by the supervisor program, but they can be modified by a user who wishes to provide his own interrupt routine. On completion of the interrupt routine, control will have to be returned to the interrupted program. This is allowed for by saving the program counter (PC) and program status word (PS) on the hardware stack on entering the interrupt sequence. Transfer of control to and from an interrupt service routine operates in a similar fashion to transfer of control between a program and a subroutine.

An alternative method used to identify interrupts is the inclusion of special hardware which automatically transfers control to the interrupt vector. On some computers a compromise method is used. Devices are grouped onto *interrupt lines*, which are identified by hardware. Each interrupt line has associated with it a skip chain, through which the interrupt handler selects the appropriate interrupt vector.

Exercise 10.9

Which registers and memory locations must be updated on conclusion of an interrupt service routine, and how?

It is possible for a second interrupt to occur during the servicing of the first one. If, for example, the clock service routine is itself interrupted, there is a danger of another clock interrupt occurring before the first has been serviced. This would result in the computer losing track of the time. The problem of some interrupts being more important than others is dealt with in two ways. Firstly, it is possible for specific interrupts to be disabled; servicing of a disabled interrupt is deferred until it is enabled again. In this way it is possible to 'switch off' the keyboard, say, while other interrupts are being serviced. More sophisticated control is provided by a system of priorities. The supervisor assigns priorities by setting appropriate flags in the program status word associated with the interrupt. The CPU can be interrupted only if the device has a higher priority than the current processor priority.

The number of priority levels available varies between processors. The PDP-11 caters for eight levels of priority (numbered 0 to 7); the clock, for example, has priority level 6 and its service routine can be interrupted by a device with priority 7. When the processor is running at priority 7, it cannot be interrupted at all. Small microcomputers have only two priority levels; all devices must therefore have priority 1 and their service routines cannot be interrupted.

When two devices with the same priority are awaiting service, they are handled in a sequence determined by the supervisor. Interrupt handling on the Acorn BBC works in this manner. When an interrupt is detected, a general service routine is entered; this routine polls the interrupt flags of all the devices in a definite sequence. When a flag which has been set is found, the device service routine is entered as described previously.

Exercise 10.10

How does a skip chain implement a system of priorities for interrupts?

Multiprogramming

We have discussed how the supervisor enables several hardware devices to function simultaneously. Our next topic is the scheduling of several programs to run concurrently.

In the early days of computing, when a computer that filled a large room provided less processing power than today's desktop micro, a computer could be used by only one user at a time. With faster and more expensive processors, it became wasteful of resources to restrict access to a single user at one time. When a processor can run a sizeable program in a few seconds, one running program cannot keep the processor fully occupied. **Multiprogramming** is the name given to the operating system facility which allows several programs, or **tasks**, to be active simultaneously. Of course, the processor cannot do two things at the same time; however, the operating system can take advantage of the time during which a task is waiting for a data transfer (to or from a peripheral device) to run a different task.

Nowadays, a multiprogrammed single-user system is usually only found on a microcomputer operating system which supports multiprogramming. On larger computers, provision is made for **multi-user** access. One form of multi-user access is the **time-sharing** system, in which each user has his own terminal and seems to be the sole user of the system. For other purposes, there is the **transaction-processing** system (such as an airline booking system, or a building society accounts system), in which users at remote terminals initiate transactions made available by the

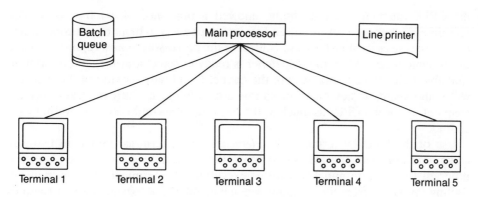

Figure 10.8 Share access

transaction-processing software. These transactions provide the users with shared access to a common store of data.

Consider the user at terminal 1, in figure 10.8. At times the processor may be waiting for input from the terminal. Even the fastest typist in the world cannot send more than 10 characters per second, a minute fraction of the rate at which the procesor is capable of receiving them. So, each second the processor is waiting for 99 per cent of the time. Or suppose that the program from terminal 1 requires a disc access; this is much faster than keying in at the terminal but will still take at least 10 microseconds, a long time compared with the processor's instruction speed. Instead of dealing solely with input from terminal 1, the operating system transfers attention to input from terminal 2 as soon as a wait happens on terminal 1. When terminal 2 is in wait mode, control is transferred to terminal 3 and so on.

Eventually control returns to terminal 1. Terminal input which has taken place during the intervening period is queued in a buffer which is now inspected. This may all happen within a second or less, so that the user at terminal 1 does not notice that the processor has not been 'listening'. In fact, each user experiences 'sole use' of the computer. Only when the CPU is very busy, with a large number of simultaneous users running long programs, does any individual user begin to notice degradation of the **response time**, that is, the time taken by the processor to respond to input from a terminal.

This all works very well as long as each program needs to communicate with terminals and peripheral devices. Such tasks are **input/output bound**. Suppose a terminal user is running a **compute-bound** program, which requires little or no input/output, that is, the program is engaged in a long computation. In a multiprogramming environment, all the programs are available in memory, but the CPU can execute only one at a time. Now, in the absence of any input/output demand or backing store transfers, one task could hog the CPU for seconds or minutes or . . . No other program would even get a look in.

It is necessary for the operating system to exercise some control over this situation. It achieves this by a **scheduling** mechanism. One method is *time-slicing*. Each running program is allowed a maximum time for consecutive occupation of the CPU. Each program might be allowed a time-slice of 1/100 second. The real-time clock can be set up to send an interrupt every 1/100th of a second. Since this causes the current task to lose control of the processor, it must rejoin the queue of runnable tasks. When the dispatcher is ready to select a task again, a different runnable task will be at the head of the queue. Eventually the turn of the first task will come again. If not many programs are running, a given program may get frequent use of the CPU, as much as 0.5 or even 0.8 second CPU time within each second.

Use of the CPU by terminals is *interactive*. Each terminal user is in two-way communication with the system. If more than a minute or so elapses before a program from the terminal completes execution, the terminal remains 'tied up' waiting for output from the program, when it could be put to use. Longer programs are often submitted in *batch* mode. The program is sent, complete with any necessary input, as a whole job to be executed. Batch jobs may be run overnight (when there are no interactive users on the system) or they may be run simultaneously with interactive jobs in a multiprogramming environment. The operating system can allocate priorities to programs so that programs with a higher priority are always given precedence over those with a lower priority. Batch programs are assigned the lowest priority and run in *background* mode, utilising gaps in CPU usage. Compute-bound interactive programs are allocated the next priority above batch programs. Input/output-bound programs are always allocated a higher priority, in the knowledge that they will soon give up control of the CPU when they demand a peripheral transfer. Important users can be given higher priority than less important users, according to a priority scheme built into the operating system. The highest priority is attached to the supervisor programs.

Exercise 10.11

A holiday company accepts bookings from the public through travel agents' terminals and by postal application from the public. Payment for bookings made through agents is sent to the company by post when the agent receives an invoice from the company.

(a) What type of computer system is appropriate to this form of operation?
(b) Which activities require interactive operation, and which ones are suitable for batch operation?

Real-time processing

We have discussed the use of a computer in batch mode and in interactive mode. The computer runs a program and produces a response to the programmer—in seconds or minutes for an interactive program, or in hours (or days) for a batch program. The adequacy (or otherwise) of the response time is measured in terms of the programmer's priorities, but not in relation to the program content. A program to *model* traffic-light switching at a junction will produce a series of results, but the elapsed time would not need to relate to the actual times within which the traffic signals change.

Suppose, however, that a computer program were being used actually to control traffic-light signals. The response must not only be appropriate, but must occur at precisely the right instant. Similarly, if a fire alarm system is controlled by a microprocessor, the alarm must be set off within a specified number of seconds following activation of one of the sensors. Minicomputers are often used in process control, where the response must be fast enough to maintain the required standards of safety and product quality. Likewise, an automatic aeroplace landing system must compute the flight path and adjust the controls fast enough to be effective.

Figure 10.9 An air-traffic control room (*courtesy of the Civil Aviation Authority*)

All these examples are illustrations of situations where processing must occur within a timescale imposed from the outside. This is called **real-time** processing. Different areas of information processing have developed differing styles of high-level languages, and real-time processing is no exception. Two examples of real-time languages popular in this country are RTL/2 and CORAL-66. The latter was developed by the Ministry of Defence. The Ada language, sponsored by the United States Department of Defense, was specifically commissioned in order to make available the advances of high-level languages to real-time applications, especially embedded systems.

There are also some circumstances which, in principle, demand real-time response, but in response can be operated in batch or interactive modes. Consider a payroll program. The cheques have to be available on time each Friday for weekly-paid employees, and the magnetic tape files for bank transfers to monthly-paid staff must be available by the 25th of each month. In practice, the programs can be run overnight (every Thursday night and every 24th of the month) and the results will be available in time. (For added safety, in case of a computer failure, they could even be run a day early.) The important factor here is that the programmers submit the program in time—the actual run-time response is not constrained by the real-time requirements. Such programs are sometimes called pseudo real-time systems. However, if the volume of processing becomes too large, this sort of task could become a genuine real-time system. In 1987, the Bank of America undertook to provide trust facilities for clients. This required the production of certain financial reports. The number of clients grew to such an extent that it took more than 25 hours to process each day's input. Consequently a backlog of work built up and it became impossible to provide clients with information on time. By the end of the year the backlog became so large that the bank had to hand over a large number of clients to another bank with better processing facilities.

10.7 Memory Management

The available main memory may not always be sufficient to run a particular program or suite of programs. The user has various methods at his disposal for controlling the use of memory. If several separate activities are being processed, each can be run as a separate program. The programs are saved on backing storage, and one program at a time is brought into memory and executed. Where one program is itself too long to fit into memory it may be segmented, with later segments overlaying earlier segments. Compilers are sometimes overlaid in this way to fit on hardware with insufficient memory.

With a multiprogrammed computer, the fact that several programs are live simultaneously creates a distinct risk of interference. It is one of the functions of the operating system to control such situations. Suppose two programs, P1 and P2, are currently being executed. Perhaps P1 requires data input—what is there to stop it reading a record into an area of memory which is used by program P2? It is an important function of the operating system to assign space to the programs, and to protect each area of space from use by other programs. This is called **memory protection**. These memory assignments may require more space than is available. It may be necessary to transfer some areas of memory onto backing storage while they are not in use, and to call them back into memory as they are required. This is *memory management*.

One simple method of memory management is to partition the main store into fixed areas. Each area holds just one program. The IBM operating systems DOS and OS/MFT work in this way. This method can be very inefficient. The partitions must be large enough to hold a large program, but when a small program is run it too will be given exclusive use of a partition. This could be very wasteful of space.

Dynamic memory management overcomes this problem by tailoring the sizes of a partition to the size of the program which occupies it. Naturally this is a more complex operation than fixed memory management, as the partition boundaries will be constantly changing as user programs are moved in and out.

However, dynamic memory management has its own problems. When a program occupying 50K (say) is completed, its partition becomes available for a new program. The new program might occupy only 40K, wasting 10K of space. This waste may be repeated several times throughout memory.

Exercise 10.12

What data structure would be suitable for use by the operating system to keep track of the free space in main memory?

A more flexible approach to memory management is to divide programs into small chunks, or **pages**, occupying 4K maybe. Backing storage is organised in pages and addressed as though it were main memory. The whole main memory is organised into **page frames**, each of size 4K, into which pages may be copied from backing storage. Each program being executed is allocated a limited number of page frames. When a location in backing storage is addressed, the page containing it is copied into one of the allocated frames in main memory.

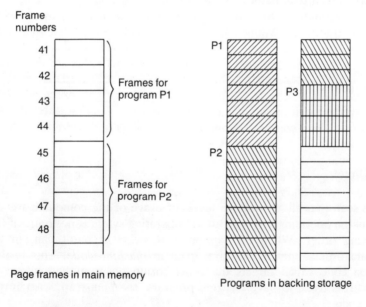

Figure 10.10 A snapshot of main memory occupancy

As far as users are concerned, the whole of the backing storage behaves as though it were main memory. Programs are divided into fixed-length chunks which bear no relation to the logic of the program. The paging is transparent to the user, being controlled by the operating system. At any one time the whole of a program need not be in main memory. As a new portion of memory is required the operating system reads in new pages, swapping them out again to reclaim space as required. The operating system uses an **address map** to locate the page frame, if any, in the IAS that is currently occupied by a given page. This is achieved using a **page table**, which lists the page frame occupied by each page. For a page not currently in main memory, the entry in the page table is empty. An attempt to address a location in such a page generates an interrupt. The program is suspended, joining the queue of suspended tasks, while the required page is transferred from backing store into main memory, with a corresponding update in the page table.

It follows that a page table must be maintained for each program, with as many entries as determined by the size of the program in pages. Typically this will result in numerous page tables most of whose entries are empty, corresponding to pages not currently in main memory. Furthermore, the time required for each memory access is doubled as it must be preceded by consulting the page table. A method used to alleviate these problems is to use a portion of the high-speed *associative memory* (contents addressable filestore) as page address registers. These registers are labelled by the page frames in main memory; the contents of each register are the page number of the page currently occupying the given frame. For each memory access the page address registers are searched associatively; for example, if page 17 is required, a search of the page address registers will return the corresponding frame number, provided the page is resident in main memory. If the page is not currently in main memory, the search will fail.

Memory organised in this way using pages is called **virtual memory**; as far as the user is concerned, the whole backing storage behaves as though it were main memory.

Acitivity 10.4

Discover what form of memory management is operated by the computer centre to which you have terminal access. What is the size of each page?

10.8 Black Boxes

We have seen that all the various levels of usage of the computer are subject to control by the operating system. But the operating sytem is not quite at the top of the pecking order. When the computer is switched on it can, in principle, understand orders only if they are given in *machine code*. This is the binary instruction code which directs the processor to position the switches or logic elements. It is usual to have just one program, the **bootstrap**, written directly in machine code.

Given a bare machine, it could be programmed in machine code, paying attention to details of input/output handling. With the operating system running, most of the details of input/output are taken care of. With an assembler, programs do not need to be written in machine code at all. So, with each layer of software, the machine takes on a different appearance.

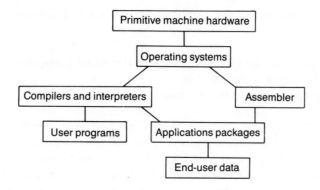

Figure 10.11 The 'computeraucracy'

Figure 10.11 shows the hierarchy of control. Each user has a view of a **virtual machine**. Thus the end user only 'sees' the application package and views the responses to his submission of data as a functional black box—the computer. As far as he is concerned, the environment he sees *is* the computer. Indeed, that whole environment could be manufactured in hardware, without affecting the user's perception of the computer. Likewise, the applications programmer sees the compiler interface for his high-level language as 'the computer'. From the user's point of view the hierarchy is rather like figure 10.12, with most 'users' seeing only the layer immediately below. The operating system makes itself felt at all levels, but its existence is transparent to the end user.

Thus, layer upon layer of black boxes are constructed so that a primitive but powerful kernel appears as a sophisticated machine. Each layer depends on its

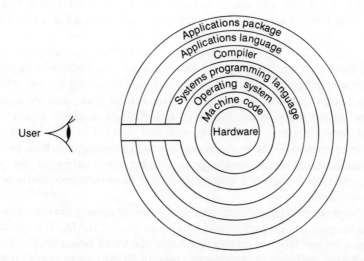

Figure 10.12 Layered user view of a computer

predecessor. But ultimately how is the bootstrap loaded? The bootstrap itself must be

- loaded manually (using switches) to set up the initial configuration;
- permanently stored in memory; or
- directly incorporated into the internal logic of the processor.

The PDP-11, for example, uses the second method, with the bootstrap held in read-only memory at a specific address. This address is loaded into the program counter in a special option at switch-on. Many microcomputers are constructed using the third method. The Research Machines 380Z bootstraps the cassette operating system, which accepts single key commands; the command b then invokes a further bootstrap to load the operating system from tracks 0–2 of disc drive A.

Typically, the bootstrap resides in ROM, at an address which is automatically loaded into the program counter when the computer is powered up. When the bootstrap is run, it invokes a special system routine which in turn loads the operating system. There is usually a special switch, or BREAK key, which can be used to reinvoke the bootstrap; this is called *rebooting* the system.

The Acorn BBC

As an example of the configuration of a microcomputer, we present here a brief overview of the immediate access store of the Acorn BBC computer. The BBC series of microcomputers has its own operating system, which resides in a ROM. (This is the usual arrangement for microcomputers; on larger machines the operating system, like most systems programs, is held on backing storage.)

The IAS of the BBC B consists of 64K bytes, 32K of which (with addresses from 0 to &7FFF) are RAM and the remaining 32K (from &8000 to &FFFF) are reserved for read-only memory. Most of the top 16K (from &C000 to &FFFF) is occupied by the so-called machine operating system, except for three pages which are used as registers for controlling input and output. This is actually an extension of the bare hardware operating system but, because it is enshrined in read-only memory, the user perceives it as part of the machine operating system. However, each byte is addressable so that individual bytes can be read, if necessary.

The other 16K of ROM (from &8000 to &BFFF) are available to four plug-in ROMs, only one of which is active at any one time. The BASIC interpreter occupies one of these ROMs, but equally any system program which provides a complete environment could reside here. Under the control of the BASIC interpreter, the user perceives a computer whose hardware apparently acts as a BASIC environment.

To function properly, the resident operating system requires the use of an area in which housekeeping can be performed, that is, an area of RAM. The allocation of RAM for use by the BBC operating system is shown in figure 10.13. The main private work area available to the selected plug-in ROM (for example, BASIC) is 1K from &400 to &799. The 1K of RAM from 0 to &399 is largely used as workspace by the machine operating system but some is also available to the

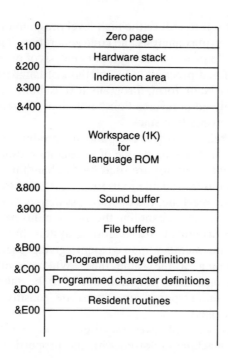

Figure 10.13 Usage of RAM by BBC operating system

BASIC interpreter and user-provided low-level programs. The RAM between &800 and &D99 is normally reserved as buffer space for various system activities.

When additional features are installed, such as a disc filing system or a networking system, additional workspace may be required. Additional commands are available to the user and their definitions need to be stored so that the appropriate communication takes place between the operating system and the disc-drive controller. Likewise, there are housekeeping activities in maintaining the interface between the local processor and a network. The disc filing system includes an auto-boot facility for loading programs from disc. With this facility, the end user can switch on the computer which then appears as a black box version of an applications package.

Summary of Chapter 10

We have discussed the role of systems software as the intermediary between a user and the bare machine. At the highest level, an unsophisticated user of an applications program perceives his interaction with the program as a direct interaction with the computer. More sophisticated users may have access to a menu of library programs. Programmers in high-level languages require the service of a translator—either a compiler or an interpreter.

The job of a translator is to reduce the high-level program to executable form, by way of lexical analysis, syntax analysis and code generation. This may involve error trapping at each stage. In order to allow proper analysis of programs, programming languages must be defined precisely. One method of language definition is using productions in Backus–Naur form. Program text is built up using expressions, which may best be analysed in reverse Polish notation. These expressions can then be evaluated using an evaluation stack.

Sophisticated users require software support for producing files, in the form of text editors. In particular, the source code of a program is usually produced using a text editor. Other utility programs are used for file handling.

In order to make facilities available to users, access is controlled by an operating system. On a single-user machine, the operating system provides the editing, filing and language facilities as well as handling the autonomous peripheral devices. In a multi-programming environment, the operating system has also to take care of program scheduling and memory management, giving users the impression of several programs running at the same time. Where a processor is accessed interactively, the response time required needs to be taken into account. In real-time processing, the response time must be sensitive to the process or application being controlled.

The virtual machine concept gives the user (or each user in a time-sharing system) the use of a machine endowed with the properties of a given software environment.

Answers to Exercises

10.1   Advantages of compilation:

- compiler does not need to be resident in memory during program execution;
- object code runs faster than interpreted code;
- object code file is available for further runs.

Advantages of interpretation:

- for a single run, interpretation is faster than compilation followed by execution of object code;
- programs can be debugged interactively.

10.2   <identifier> ::= <letter>|<letter><identifier>
<letter> ::= a|b|c|d|e|f|g|h|i|j|k|l|m|n|o|p|q|r|s|t|u|v|w|x|y|z|£|_

10.3   Each node of the tree is represented as a record with three fields: *value*, *left* subtree and *right* subtree. The tree is represented by a pointer to the root node.

In the following design, *expression*, *operator*, *l* and *r* are variables of type *string*.

infix

```
  tree
  if
      tree=NIL
  then
      expression=""
  else
      operator=tree↑.value
      l=infix(tree↑.left)
      r=infix(tree↑.right)
      if
          operator <> "+"
      then
          put parentheses round r
          if
              operator <> "-"
          then
              put parentheses round l
          endif
      endif
      expression=l+operator+r
  endif
  expression
```

You might like to code this function and try it out on trees constructed using a tree construction package (like the one presented in figure 9.12).

10.4 (a) u 2 y / −
         (b) p p ⋆ 4 q ⋆ r ⋆ −

10.5 (a) = 28 10 4 + /
              = 28 14 /
              = 2
         (b) = 5 2 ↑ 5 +
              = 25 5 +
              = 30

(c) $= 1\ 2\ 3\ 9 + + +$
      $= 1\ 2\ 12 + +$
      $= 1\ 14 +$
      $= 15$

10.6 1000
1010 DEF FNevalPolish(expr$)
1020 LOCAL space%, head$, tail$
1030 IF expr$ = " " THEN =FNpop
        ELSE space% = INSTR(expr$, " "): head$=LEFT$(expr$, space%−1):
               tail$ = MID$(expr$, space%+1): PROCeval(head$):
               = FNevalPolish(tail$)
1100
1110 DEF PROCeval(item$)
1120 LOCAL op1$, op2$
1130 IF INSTR ("+−*/↑", item$)
        THEN op2$ = FNpop : op1$ = FNpop:
               item$ = STR$(EVAL(op1$ + item$ + op2$))
1140 PROC push(item$)
1150 ENDPROC

10.7 The advantage is a complete avoidance of brackets. The disadvantage is the need to become familiar with reverse Polish notation, which is not usually well known.

10.8 BASIC has a line editor in which any program text preceded by a line number is automatically placed in correct sequence. The BASIC editor has a renumbering facility, and usually an AUTO command for repeated insertions into a program file.

  BASIC was originally developed as a teaching language on a multi-user system with teletype terminals for which screen editors are inappropriate.

  The BBC computer has a rudimentary screen editing facility for copying text already on the screen to a new location using the cursor arrows and the COPY key.

10.9 PC, PS, SP(stack pointer) and Stack
        PC ← pop Stack
        SP ← SP + 1
        PS ← pop Stack
        SP ← SP + 1

This is achieved by a single machine instruction—return from interrupt (RTI). It cannot be achieved in two stages because that would leave an incompatible PC and PS at 'half-time'.

10.10 The skip chain polls the devices in a definite order. Thus the devices higher up the chain are always serviced before devices lower down the chain, if both are awaiting service simultaneously. The order in which the devices are polled acts as a prioritisation system.

10.11 (a) The holiday company should run a transaction-processing system. The following transactions are required: booking a holiday, recording payments, producing invoices.

(b) Bookings by travel agents from terminals must be run interactively. The other transactions can be run in batch mode; say, payments on a daily basis, when the post arrives, and invoicing once a week.

10.12 Since the number of distinct regions of free memory is not fixed, a suitable data structure is a linked list. In this context the list is often called the *free list*.

Further Exercises

1. What is meant by *batch processing*? Under what circumstances might it be advisable to submit a batch job from an online terminal?

2. Why is magnetic tape unsatisfactory as a backing store device for real-time processing? To what extent does your answer also apply to an interactive system?

3. What does *system software* mean?

4. Is time-slicing more important:
   (a) for a batch service
   (b) in a multiprogramming environment
   (c) on a stand-alone machine?

5. Which of the following methods of memory management requires the most complex operating system:

   (a) fixed partition method
   (b) variable partition method
   (c) virtual memory?

   Discuss your answer.

6. What do a compiler and an assembler have in common? Do they serve a similar purpose?

7. Describe one feature of an available operating system which is particularly helpful to an unsophisticated user. Describe a feature which you find less than helpful and suggest an improvement.

8. Many microcomputers are used nowadays in stand-alone mode, like the very earliest computers. What considerations prompted the introduction of multi-programming?

9. (a) What are the advantages of an interpreter compared with a compiler for a *programmer* of a microcomputer, who is developing in a high-level language a program which is to be used *infrequently*?
   (b) What are the advantages of a compiler compared with an interpreter for a *programmer* of a main frame computer, who is developing in a high-level language a program which is to be used *frequently*?
   (c) What differences would there be for a *user* of a program on a compiler-based system compared with an interpreter-based one?
   (d) When the command for running a program is given, some interpreters allow for a preliminary scan of the program before the execution proper is begun. What advantages and disadvantages might this provide during development of a program compared with an interpreter which does not give a preliminary scan of the program before execution?

                                            (ULSEB—1984/1/9)

10. (a) Explain the techniques of compilation and interpretation, distinguishing between them.
    (b) Under which circumstances would each technique be most appropriate?
    (c) For each technique, give **two** advantages for the user of a high-level language.

                                            (JMB—1982/1/20)

11. An operating system carries out several functions which ensure the efficient operation of a computer system. Three such functions are

    (i) optimising use of the CPU,
    (ii) memory management and
    (iii) management of files and peripherals.

Describe techniques which can be used to implement these functions.

                                            (JMB—1983/1/16)

12. What are the objectives of an operating system?
    In a multi-access time-sharing system used to provide a commercial bureau service, the operating system maintains a job-queue; the initial placing of a job in this job-queue depends on the priority requested by the user when the job enters the system.
    Describe a data structure suitable for maintaining this job-queue, which will allow jobs to be placed at any position in the job-queue. Indicate what data will be held in this data structure, and where the program code will be stored.
    The job at the head of the job-queue will be considered for execution. Describe circumstances under which this job would not be able to be executed and would need to be suspended.

If the job at the head of the job-queue is capable of execution, it is given the use of the central processor. What conditions may cause this use to cease?

A more sophisticated time-sharing system maintains two job-queues; one of jobs capable of execution, and another of suspended jobs. Describe what the operating system must do from the time one job issues an input–output request until another job is given the use of the central processor.

(ULSEB—1983/1/8)

13. (a) Briefly describe **four** functions of an operating system that encourage efficient utilisation of the hardware.
    (b) On one particular multi-access computer, two versions of the operating system are available:

    Version A allocates a fixed time period, 50 milliseconds, to each user terminal regardless of tasks in hand. At the end of the period, control is passed to the next terminal in sequence. Version B allows a particular terminal's program to run until delayed waiting for an input or output transfer. When a delay occurs, control is passed to the next terminal in sequence.

    (i) Compare the effectiveness of versions A and B of the operating system when each manages the following combination of jobs:
    Job 1.   A slow teletypewriter interactively running a game of noughts and crosses.
    Job 2.   A visual display unit where a long mathematical calculation has been initiated and no further input–output activity is expected until the end of the computation.
    Job 3.   A teletypewriter printing a long list of names and addresses.
    (ii) Suggest two methods of improving one of the above versions of the operating system.

(AEB—1983/19)

14. Interrupts are a mechanism that permit various hardware components of a computer configuration to function concurrently.

    (i) Explain what is meant by this statement.
    (ii) Show, with the aid of a flowchart or otherwise, at what stage an interrupt may be detected in the fetch–execute cycle and what happens when one is detected.
    (iii) With the aid of an example, explain why it can be advantageous to have priorities associated with interrupts.

    Multiprogramming operating systems permit tasks to run concurrently.

    (i) Explain what is meant by this statement.
    (ii) Describe three different functions performed by an operating system.

(iii) With the aid of an example, explain why it may be advantageous to have priorities associated with tasks in order to improve utilisation of hardware.

(AEB—1984/1/9)

15. A firm has two computers, a Prime running under UNIX and a VAX running under VMS. A Pascal compiler is available on each system. The firm now wishes to replace both computers with a new, more powerful VAX running under UNIX. You are offered a £5000 contract to port a Pascal compiler to the new system.

    (i) Which existing Pascal compiler would you choose to work from?
    (ii) Will any changes have to be made to application programs written in Pascal in order that they should execute satisfactorily with the new compiler?

11 How to Communicate

Communication is about bridging gaps, where the gap may be conceptual or spatial. A conceptual gap exists between the computer and human users. Modes of conversation between people assume certain conventions such as visual clues, tone of voice and a dialogue between the participants. To use computers, people have had to adapt by becoming computer literate. In the first section of this chapter we look at some ways in which computer programs can be written so as to meet the user half way and enable the computer to become person literate.

A spatial gap exists where there is a need to use a computer situated at a remote site. The site may be a different town, a different building or just a room across the corridor. This situation arises with shared access to minicomputers and mainframes using terminals. We look at remote access in section 11.2. Another circumstance in which a spatial gap exists is when several independent processors are linked. The purpose of the link may be either for users to send messages to each other or to access resources (software or hardware) available elsewhere. In the final section, we shall take a glimpse at the growing field of computer networks through which communication between processors may take place.

11.1 Human–computer Dialogue

We have remarked previously that the various components of a computer system must be properly interfaced if there is to be any internal communication whatsoever. At the human–computer interface, however, there was a tendency to assume that the person would make almost all the accommodation necessary for communication to succeed. As long as the computer provided an input/output interface in terms of conventional alphabets and symbols, the rest was left to the user. Inevitably this meant that using a computer was itself an acquired skill, best left to computer operators and programmers and few others. Since the mid-1970s this approach has become less and less tenable. Three important developments have taken computer use out of the domain of the professionals into the sphere of every man. The first was the development of shared access to mainframes by several simultaneous users, as opposed to the previous system of collecting all jobs into batches for input. This resulted in the availability of interactive terminals to senior management in the commercial world and to users in academic environments to whom the computer was a tool in their research. The second development was the development of large-scale networks through which members of the public,

313

such as clients of banks and building societies, and subscribers to the Prestel viewdata service, were given direct access to computer terminals. The third development was the explosive growth of cheap computing power, first in the personal computers for businessmen and then in home computers. Making microcomputers available so widely has generated a demand for easy accessibility to computers; this means that the mode of input is straightforward and that the computer's responses can be readily understood.

Prompting for input

A bare program design which solves a problem provides for input and output of data, but makes no concession to the need for dialogue. If a value needs to be input at an interactive session, a signal or **prompt** will be sent (displayed); but this prompt may give no indication of the nature of the value required to be input. Thus the prompt may be a special symbol, such as $ or >, or an alphabetic character identifying a disc drive (or a computer within a network), or it may be the name of the currently active program. The prompt indicates the need for input at this point, but gives little or no clue as to what sort of input is required. On some systems, online help is available in response to typing H or ?, but its value depends both on knowing what to type to get help and, more importantly, on the foresight of the programmer in providing a useful help feature.

However, an immediate improvement is to provide a meaningful prompt. Thus, if the input to be required is a number in the range 1 to 7 representing a day of the week, a meaningful prompt might be:

> Input day of week
> (type 1 for Sunday, 2 for Monday, etc.)

In this example, the user response is a single keystroke; the admissible values for the response are integers in the range 1 to 7. In some cases a longer response is required—this may be a number or a string of characters may be input. This is appropriate for programs which process numbers or strings directly, such as sorting programs. Where single-key input is used, the key may produce either a printable character or a control code—the computer cannot tell the difference anyway, as they are all transmitted as bit patterns.

If the input by the user is unacceptable, there are several possible forms of response from the computer. There may be no response (not very helpful). The response might be "Illegal Input" (not much better). The response might be "Error no. 27" (helpful only if you have the user manual). Or the response might actually diagnose the error and indicate a suitable correction: "Your input must be a number in the range 1 to 7". The program designer should bear in mind whether the system will be used mainly by inexperienced and irregular users, in which case more verbose error messages are called for, or experts who prefer short error messages. A system which tends to be used by a wide variety of users may well offer the user a choice of interface—novice or expert.

The following two programs perform essentially the same task, but Version B has a much friendlier interface.

Version A

```
 10 INPUT N%
 20 DIM sequence (N%)
 30 FOR i% = 1 TO N% : INPUT sequence(i%) : NEXT i%
 40 position% = 1 : max = sequence(1)
 50 FOR i% = 2 TO N%
 60     this = sequence(i%)
 70       IF this > max THEN max = this = position% = i%
 80 NEXT i%
 90 PRINT "LARGEST NUMBER IS", max, "IN POSITION", position%
100 END
```

Version B

```
 10 REM *********************************
 20 REM * Program to read in a sequence of  *
 30 REM * numbers and identify the largest   *
 40 REM *                                                    *
 50 REM *                   by O. Gram                  *
 60 REM *                                                    *
 70 REM *                   July 1984               *
 80 REM *********************************
100
110 INPUT "How many numbers are there" N%
120 PRINT "Enter" N% "numbers followed by RETURN"
130 DIM sequence(N%)
140 FOR i% = 1 TO N%
150     INPUT sequence(i%)
160 NEXT i%
200
210 REM position% gives position in sequence of max, the maximum so far
220 position% = 1: max = sequence(position%)
230 FOR i%=2 TO N%
240     this = sequence(i%)
250     IF this > max THEN max = this : position% = i%
260 NEXT i%
300
310 PRINT ' ' "The largest number is "; max ", which is the ";
        position% "th in the input sequence."
400 END
```

These programs take as input an integer which specifies the length of a list, followed by a list of numbers. The program then finds the largest number in the list and its position. The first program just issues the standard basic input prompt (?). The user who is unfamiliar with the program has no hope of providing appropriate input, unless documentation for the program is at hand which explains what to do. The second version, on the other hand, issues a clear prompt for the length of the list ("How many numbers are there?") followed by a clear instruction to enter the numbers in the list. While this is a relatively trivial example, it illustrates the need for a program designer to worry not only about the data and the way in which it is to be processed, but also to consider carefully the interface between the program and the user.

The extent to which a program attempts to communicate sensibly with the user determines the range of people who will be able and willing to use the program. Careful attention to this feature of programs is a subject, worthy of study in its own right, called **dialogue engineering**.

Menus

Consider a personnel database. The insertion of a new entry requires the input of a name, address, telephone number and other details as yet unknown to the system. The insertion program might prompt for each of these as follows. (On each line, the program prompt finishes with a colon, and is followed by suitable user input.)

Name:	Jack Jones
Address:	19 River Drive, Sheffield
Postcode:	SD1 3XY
Telephone:	0742 12345
Staff Number:	907339

On attempting to retrieve this record, the staff number can be used, if known. Most people, however, find it more difficult to memorise numbers than names. It may turn out, though, that there are several employees called Jones. The system may have a search facility which lists names and addresses of all employees with a given name, alongside their staff numbers, as shown in figure 11.1. In this way, the correct one can be chosen. The staff number, once known, can be used as input for the retrieval of the full staff record. This method uses the index in the same way as a manual index.

A more powerful use of the computer, which both saves the user the chore of retyping something already on the terminal screen and protects the user from making an error, is to treat the list now on the screen as a **menu**. A menu is a list of items, provided by the computer, from which the user makes a choice. Two methods are available for the user to express his choice. In figure 11.1 the names in

Name index: Jones

(1)	Jones AC	17a Terrace Green, Doncaster	451237
(2)	Jones B	24 West Street, Cardiff	219078
(3)	Jones H	81 Upper Road, Swansea	209426
(4)	Jones J	19 River Drive, Sheffield	907339
(5)	Jones P	431 Hampstead Road, Bayswater	114032

Figure 11.1 Index of staff named Jones

the menu are identified by line numbers (1 to 5). Typing in the appropriate line number is sufficient response by the user to identify the staff number whose record is to be retrieved.

An alternative form of menu selection makes use of the cursor (the symbol, usually flashing, whose normal function is to indicate where on the screen the next character will be echoed). In this form the program responds to a special key or keys (such as the spacebar) to move the cursor alongside each menu item in turn. When the cursor is alongside the desired item, the selection is confirmed by pressing a special key, such as RETURN or ENTER. This use of the screen display creates a simplified user-friendly interface.

On some microcomputers, selection from a menu is aided by the use of a pointing device called a **mouse** (see figure 11.2). The mouse has two inputs: an analogue input and a button. The mouse, about 4 by 2 inches in size, sits on a table top and is controlled by the palm of the hand. A ball in the base controls the analogue input; as the mouse is rolled over the table top, a special cursor or pointer on the screen moves in the corresponding direction. When the pointer is steered to a suitable menu item, the item can be selected by pressing the mouse button.

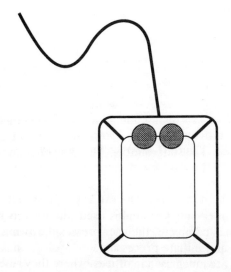

Figure 11.2 Mouse

Selection from a menu is equally applicable when making a choice from a suite of programs. A typical package of business software may provide access to word processing, payroll, invoicing and stock control programs. The choice of program could be indicated either by typing in the name (in full or in shortened format) or making a menu selection. Likewise, each program can be driven either by typing appropriate keywords or by selecting from a menu.

One factor which may influence the choice between offering a menu selection and requiring a keyword to be typed is the time taken to print the menu on the screen. If the menu is long and the user knows which selection he wishes to make, typing the keyword might be the preferred method.

It is possible to use a menu approach even where the number of possible responses is large. The Prestel database, for example, allows access to information on enormous number of topics using a multi-level index. At each level, the index is presented as a menu. For the user who knows exactly which page of information he wants to access, it is possible to bypass the menus by keying in the page number directly.

Form filling

Another method of requesting user input is by provision of a form. This method is ideally suited to transaction processing systems. The system offers a choice of forms, which can be called up on the screen by the user. A typical form is shown in figure 11.3.

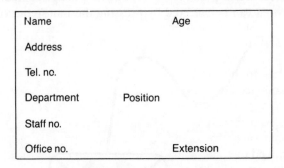

Figure 11.3 Screen form display

The user fills in each field of the form. The TAB key is pressed to advance to the next field. If a transaction processing terminal is used, the form is filled in under local control; when the form is complete, the user presses the TRANSMIT key to send the input to the processor and initiate processing.

Form-filling systems are much used in offices, where they resemble manual office techniques. Often, when a manual system is computerised, the format of the forms used will be maintained in the computer system so that the system remains familiar to the users.

Free-format dialogue

Because a computer is a pre-programmed device, dialogue with a program tends to be formal. The greatest degree of formality is found where the human response is constrained to a fixed set of responses. So, where a command is to be entered, the response must belong to the set of commands which is understood by the system. Such responses are amenable to menu formats. When the human response required is the input of a data string, greater flexibility is possible. The format may still be limited somewhat by the needs of the processing program, but the actual content of the data is relatively unconstrained.

The use of a fairly formal dialogue has some definite advantages. Communicating through a formal dialogue fixes in the user's mind the nature of the computer as a machine with no innate intelligence. It has, however, been the aim of many research workers to provide a more human interface to the computer, enabling dialogues to take place in more natural language.

There are two aspects to the use of natural language in computer dialogues. The easier one to tackle is the use of natural language by the computer for its output. This can be achieved by storing a collection of natural language sentences for use in response to specific inputs. This provides a system which appears more friendly to the user. However, since the user can input from only a fixed repertoire, the computer continues to appear mechanical.

The second aspect is the ability of computer programs to respond sensibly to natural language input by the user. This is a much more difficult problem to tackle, because of the immense complexity of the structure of natural language. A typical approach to handling natural language input is to look for specific keywords in the input, treating the rest as a form of noise. Depending on the programmer's skill, such programs can display a degree of apparent intelligence. The design of this sort of program is just one area of study in the field of artificial intelligence. The user input typically has to be verbose to eliminate ambiguities, and sometimes a dialogue may take place between the computer and the user to establish the user's meaning.

Because a program which accepts natural language appears to display intelligence, it may bamboozle the user into thinking that it is possessed of greater wisdom than is indeed the case. This was demonstrated dramatically by Professor J. Weizenbaum, who developed the ELIZA program at the Massachusetts Institute of Technology. By responding in certain set ways, ELIZA appears to conduct a meaningful conversation. So much so, that many of its users refused to believe that it was a mere computer program, thereby creating unfounded expectations in its users.

Graphics

We return to methods which improve the conveyance of actual, rather than apparent, information. The simplest forms of output are modelled on writing, or printing, using limited character sets. Characters are output onto a sheet of paper which is wound, as on a typewriter. A device accepting such output is called a teletypewriter, or teletype. The simplest screen output devices work in the same way, serving as glass teletypes. Cathode ray technology can, however, offer more dramatic effects. These may be achieved in several ways.

One method of improving the output display is by cursor movement. This movement may be relative to the current cursor position—back, up and down as well as forward—or it may be by addressing a chosen position on the screen. Any attempt to overwrite an existing character on the screen results in the loss of the original character. This is used to good effect to delete characters from the screen by overwriting them with spaces. Screen editors, for example, take advantage of screen addressing to provide a snapshot of a section of a file on the screen. As the file is edited, the snapshot is updated to show the current version of the edited file.

Another technique which can be used with character displays is the partitioning of the screen display into **windows** (see figure 11.4). Within each window, text continues from the end of one line to the beginning of the next, and the whole text in the window can be scrolled up to insert an additional line. This technique allows several different displays to be presented on the same screen, and may be used to display different aspects of the same process. For example, a word-processing program may display a large window on the current text and smaller windows on the status of the current command and the type of formatting being used. Some software allows several processes to be active simultaneously. Windows on each process may be displayed on a single screen, possibly in an overlapping fashion. Interaction between the user and the currently selected process takes place in the appropriate window.

So far we have indicated how a character display may be manipulated. Human dialogue, primarily a verbal interchange between people, also makes use of timing, intonation and stress as well as visual clues such as facial expression and gestures. Computer dialogue can likewise be enhanced by the use of non-text features. This can be the use of different sizes and colours to provide a range of emphasis to various components of a display. Graphical features, as in figure 11.5, are a well-established element in the presentation of the printed word. The ability of a screen to display graphics depends on two technological enhancements. A character display is produced by selecting one out of a hundred or so available characters to occupy each position on the screen. The number of positions is typically 80 per row with 25 rows. One possible enhancement is to increase the range of display characters. By simply providing for a number of block shape characters, low-resolution graphical displays can be built up. A standard set of low-resolution graphics symbols, known as the teletext standard, is used in viewdata systems. Alternatively, individual graphical symbols, called **icons**, may be made available by the software for use in a given context. An office utility program may have icons to represent files, a clock and a wastepaper basket.

A greater enhancement is achieved by abandoning the restriction that the screen be addressed as 25×80 matrix, and allowing each individual pixel, or picture element of the screen, to be individually addressed. By this method, elaborate graphical designs can be shown on the screen. The quality of the display depends on the number of pixels in the screen. Good-quality high-resolution graphics may address a matrix of 1000×1000 pixels, requiring special high-technology graphics terminals. Traditionally, such graphics have found uses in the field of computer-aided design. With the introduction of low-cost microcomputers in the early 1980s, graphics capability has become more widespread. Nowadays, it is the rule rather than the exception to use graphical output. Numerical data, for example, is frequently displayed as a histogram (bar chart) or as a pie chart.

A further use of a graphics capability is to provide a choice of character sizes and fonts (typefaces) for text. This has a particular value in conjunction with a printer with graphics capability. Documents can then be produced with a full range of styles approaching printing quality.

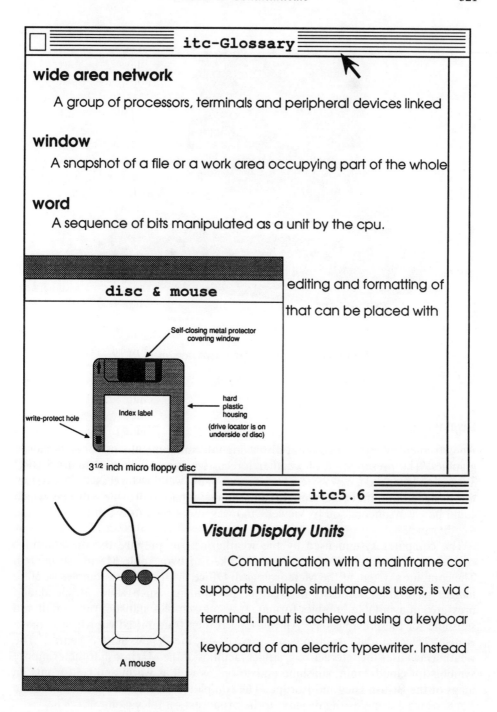

itc-Glossary

wide area network

A group of processors, terminals and peripheral devices linked

window

A snapshot of a file or a work area occupying part of the whole

word

A sequence of bits manipulated as a unit by the cpu.

disc & mouse

Self-closing metal protector
covering window

write-protect hole

Index label

hard
plastic
housing

(drive locator is on
underside of disc)

3¹/₂ inch micro floppy disc

A mouse

editing and formatting of

that can be placed with

itc5.6

Visual Display Units

Communication with a mainframe cor

supports multiple simultaneous users, is via c

terminal. Input is achieved using a keyboar

keyboard of an electric typewriter. Instead

Figure 11.4 Window

Figure 11.5 Graphics output (*courtesy of ICL*)

Displaying information

An extremely effective method of displaying information is the use of well-chosen graphics. The presentation of weather forecasts is a case in point. In 1985 BBC Television launched a new system for presenting the weather forecasts. This system was designed to fulfil two essential requirements: it had to provide a display which could be easily understood by viewers and was also straightforward to use for the weatherman.

The computer system used by the weatherman to prepare the presentations consists of a VAX 11/750 minicomputer linked to two Apple Macintosh micros. The computer system at the Meteorological Office in Bracknell assembles satellite images as well as forecasts of weather phenomena, such as wind speed and pressure, in a suitable graphics format. It also assembles statistics on rainfall and sunshine for the previous day. All this data is then transmitted via Kilostream—a British Telecom data transmission service—to the VAX at TV centre. The weatherman uses the interactive graphics facilities of the Macintosh to superimpose symbols for clouds, rain, sunshine and so on, as well as warm and cold fronts on maps of the British Isles and Europe. The completed displays are sent back to the VAX which assembles the displays to be broadcast on television.

Before the advent of this system, weather displays were prepared on board maps using magnetic strips and symbols. Use of a computer system with an advanced human–computer interface has provided a highly flexible medium.

11.2 Remote Access

Nowadays, the ubiquitous microcomputer provides most people with their first introduction to a computer. Its compact design includes a keyboard, screen and processor in close proximity—often encased in one box. In the case of mainframes and most minicomputers, this arrangement is out of the question. For a start, the processor with its associated peripheral equipment may fill a room; moreover, these larger computers may be accessed simultaneously by several users who have no need or desire to be near the computer suite or each other. The important peripheral device to which regular and immediate access is required is a terminal, which allows both input and output, and thus serves as the interface for human–computer dialogue.

Terminals are connected to the main processor using wires which carry the input and output signals. The simplest device of this sort, the **dumb terminal**, does no more than send signals from the keyboard and display received signals on the screen. It has the limited capability of intercepting the binary codes it receives and acting accordingly. Thus it may display on the screen the appropriate character, or perform the appropriate control function such as new line or clear screen.

The more sophisticated screen capabilities required by the need to be able to handle the character- and graphics-display modes outlined in the previous section are provided by increasing somewhat the technological capability of the terminal. Such terminals are said to be endowed with a degree of intelligence.

Special-purpose terminals

Terminals may be designed for very specific purposes. This category includes **automated teller machines** and **point-of-sale terminals**. These terminals allow digits to be input and also have one or two special-purpose keys related directly to the program under which they operate.

The automated teller machine provides access to the accounts of a bank or building society. The user has to key in a personal identification number (PIN) to gain access to his or her own account information. Access to accounts is not available without using the PIN, so preserving the privacy of this information. Processing of the accounts may take place at one or two central locations, but the terminals are available at a large number of places throughout the country. The special keyboard includes a *numeric keypad* (which is used to key in the PIN and for selecting a sum of money) and special keys which are aligned with a screen and are used to make a menu selection. These machines have a second input medium which reads an account number from a magnetic stripe on a plastic account card. This is a security feature, as the user must produce the card in order to interrogate the account. The output may be a message on the screen, a printed ticket or a bag containing currency notes. In each case, the input and output media are designed to fit the particular needs of the users.

Point-of-sale terminals are used in supermarkets and stores to serve several functions of the retail trade. The code number of a product may be input from a bar code or magnetic stripe on a label attached to the product. The price of the product

Figure 11.6 An automated teller machine: Halifax Building Society Cardcash machine
(*courtesy of Halifax Building Society*)

is determined by the computer from a *look-up table*. Recording the sale may also trigger the stock control program to update the stock levels. A customer who has an account with the store can have his or her account debited and the invoice printed as part of the same operation. The interactive link between the terminal and the processor allows continual updating of the central information store.

Off-line point-of-sale devices are also in use. These contain a very limited processing capability. The information which needs to be transmitted for central processing is recorded on a tape cassette. Each evening, the tape cassettes are then sent to the data processing department to be run as batch updating jobs.

Modems

The simple model of a link between a terminal and the main processor makes sense when both are in the same building or on the same site. If the processor is at a remote location, it is unlikely to be feasible to run special cable links between the terminals and the processor. The most popular solution to this problem makes use of an existing nationwide communications network—the telephone system. By making a telephone connection between a terminal and a processor, the two can communicate. This has an obvious beneficial by-product. The same terminal can be

Figure 11.7 Point-of-sale terminal (*courtesy of ICL*)

used, on different occasions, to link with any computer to which the user is allowed access.

The telephone network serves the transmission of voice information in electrical analogue form. The variations of amplitude (loudness) and frequency (pitch) are converted by the mouthpiece into corresponding variations of electrical current (with a certain range of frequencies) and then converted back by the earpiece at the receiving end. Sending digital signals requires a different technology; a digital signal sent across the telephone network is likely to be corrupted *en route*. To overcome this problem, the digital signal is converted into an analogue signal by a process called *mo*dulation. At the other end the signal is *dem*odulated into a digital signal. The device which performs these functions is called a **modem**.

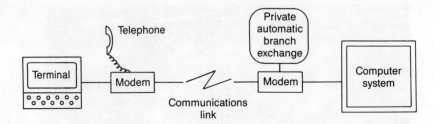

Figure 11.8 A telephone link using modems

One method of converting digital signals is *amplitude modulation*. In this method, the modem transmits a signal at a fixed frequency. This signal is called the carrier wave. The amplitude of the wave is modulated between two levels—high and low—in response to the bits 1 and 0. The speed with which the amplitude can be changed is called the baud rate; in this method, the number of bits transmitted per second is almost equal to the baud rate. (There is some slight loss of speed because certain extra bits have to be transmitted in conjunction with the actual message.)

An alternative method of sending digital signals through a telephone line is to use an acoustic coupler. This device has a pair of rubber cups which grip the handset of the telephone receiver. This acoustic coupler converts the binary signal from the terminal into an audio signal (of fixed pitch) which can then be transmitted through the mouthpiece of the receiver. The reverse conversion is performed on the incoming audio signal from the earpiece. Acoustic couplers used to be popular for two reasons. Firstly, they were a lot cheaper than modems. Secondly, acoustic couplers are portable since they use the handset of the telephone for transmission, whereas a modem must be wired into the telephone line. Against these two advantages, the acoustic coupler is less reliable than a modem because an additional layer of conversion—the audio signal—is inserted into the sequence.

Both advantages of acoustic couplers have now disappeared. Solid-state technology enables modems to be purchased for under £100. In the United Kingdom the price has also come down as a result of the removal of controls over telecommunications equipment; previously modems had to be hired from the GPO, who used to control the telephone network. Portability is also no longer a problem because telephone lines are now accessed by a standard plug-and-socket arrangement, enabling modems to be plugged in as and when necessary. Finally, telephone receivers no longer conform to the standard shape which fits an acoustic coupler.

11.3 Intercomputer Communication

Our conception of a computer has been, so far, one of a single processor in communication with a number of peripherals. There is no reason, though, why computing power should not be spread over several locations linked in a single system. The low cost of microprocessors has given a considerable boost to this notion of distributed processing. One development has been the intelligent terminal, which is capable of doing some processing. Stand-alone microcomputers can run terminal programs so that they behave just like terminals to a central computer. By switching between terminal and stand-alone modes, the user can process data locally or on the central processor. Microcomputers used in this way, as local computers which are also part of a computer network, are often called *workstations*.

Automated teller machines are frequently linked to a local minicomputer in the same building. The full details of all the accounts, however, are held in the central building society computer at a remote location. When access is required to data held on the main computer, use is made of an inter-computer link or network.

Networking

Direct communication between computers may be desirable in order to share an expensive facility between users. While each office in a firm may have its own workstation, it is likely that only one lineprinter or graph plotter is required for the entire firm. Attaching this peripheral to a stand-alone computer means that users have to process jobs requiring lineprinter or graphical output at that computer. Linking the workstations in a network enables jobs processed at any workstation to send the output to the lineprinter or graph plotter. Such shared use of resources is likely to be an important factor in setting up a local area network to serve an office complex, university campus, school or town hall.

Commercial organisations whose offices and warehouses are spread across several towns may find that they are using a minicomputer at each site. In the interests of sharing data between warehouses and head office, a *wide area network* might be established to link the computers, using a line leased from a public communications company. Networks provide a convenient system for users to send messages to each other; this use of a network is known as **electronic mail**.

There are two popular designs for a local area network—the Cambridge ring and Ethernet. In the **Cambridge ring** system, the devices are attached to a circuit made of two pairs of twisted-pair cable, as shown in figure 11.9. Data is sent round the ring in one direction only; since all devices are attached to the ring, the data will eventually reach its destination. Data can be transmitted round the ring at 10 Megabits per second, and there is no limit to the length of the ring provided repeaters (to amplify the signal) are included every 100 metres. Data is carried round the ring in packets. When a station wishes to transmit, it must capture an empty packet. The address of the receiving station is placed at the head of the packet. Each station checks the packets circulating the ring and collects any which are addressed to it.

The **Ethernet** is based (in its simplest form) on a bus, as shown in figure 11.10. To reach all devices on the network, the signal must travel along the bus in both directions. This means that packets of signals travelling in opposite directions could collide with each other. Ethernet provides a special mechanism to handle collisions. Ethernet networks are built using coaxial cable. A device is attached or *tapped* to the cable by making an electrical connection which does not break the cable, as a

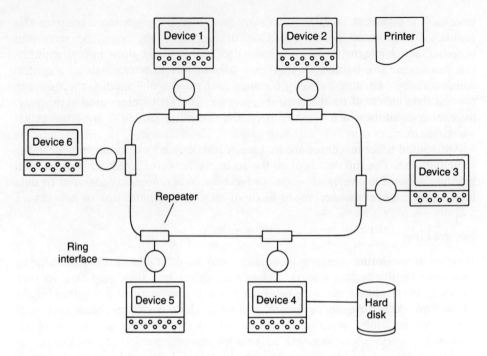

Figure 11.9 Cambridge ring network

break would change the operating characteristics of the cable. A **terminator** must be attached at each end of the bus to prevent old signals from being reflected and interfering with new signals. The maximum distance between any pair of stations on the network is 2.5 km, and data is transmitted at 10 Megabits per second.

Local area networks frequently use digital signals, as this avoids the need for modems. This is called **baseband** signalling. Provided there is no noise on the line,

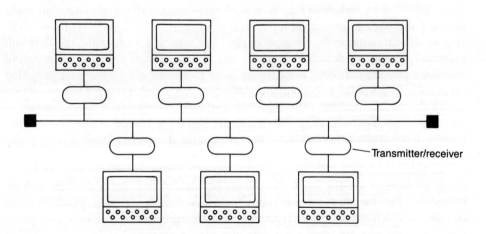

Figure 11.10 Ethernet bus network

and the distances are not too great, this works well. An alternative is to use a network in the same way as a telephone line, using modems to modulate the signals. Since analogue signals can be transmitted at a wide range of frequencies, the same cable can be used to carry numerous distinct messages simultaneously. This is achieved by assigning a different frequency to each device, using *frequency modulation*. This method of data transmission is called **broadband** signalling, and is desirable where there are heavy flows of data traffic.

Acorn Computers market the Econet system for linking their computers in a bus network like Ethernet. Using a cheaper technology, Econet operates with two twisted-pair cables and the data speed can be set between 70 and 307 kilobits per second, with the higher data rates available on shorter networks. The maximum length of the cable between two stations is 1 kilometre. Each station has a unique address which is a numeric code.

A small local-area network may link devices in a single office. A larger network may connect devices at various locations within the same building. A single organisation covering a large site, such as a university campus, may also share a local-area network. In practice, however, each unit is likely to have its own network. These networks are then linked together via *gateways*. Gateways may also be used to access public networks from any point on a local-area network.

Wide-area networks

Linking computers across large distances can be achieved using the public telephone system. Dialled lines tend to suffer from errors introduced into transmissions; this limits the transmission speed. Where flexibility is not a criterion, fixed telephone lines can be leased (by the year); these lines can carry transmissions at up to 2400 baud. Another disadvantage of telephone lines is the high cost. Where several terminals in one location are linked to a computer at another location, the signals from the terminals can be transmitted through a multiplexer which shares the usage of the telephone line among the terminals. A simple method of multiplexing is to divide the usage of the line into fixed-period time slots.

The telephone system, which sends data through switches at telephone exchanges, can be a source of errors in data transmission. A more reliable method for networking computers is **packet switching**. In a packet-switched network, messages are split up into packets of a fixed length; each packet carries the destination address. The network consists of direct links between computers, which can hold packets if the route is busy. If there is more than one route between the source and the destination, different packets may conceivably travel by different routes and arrive in a different sequence from the one in which they were transmitted. At the receiving end, the packets must be reassembled to form the original message.

Unlike the telephone system, which gives exclusive use of a line to form a circuit which remains in use for a period of time, packet-switching networks act like the postal service. The packets are taken from the sender and transmitted, at the convenience of the network, to the destination. Use of packet-switched networks is therefore both cheaper and more reliable than the telephone service for inter-computer communication.

British Telecom operate a public packet-switching network for data transmission, called PSS. Three computers are used as message-switching exchanges, situated at London, Manchester and Glasgow. Access to the network is available at these points as well as at multiplexers located in a number of major cities. There is also an international system, IPSS, through which messages can be transmitted worldwide.

Wide-area networks can be of use to a group of organisations who wish to communicate with each other. Large businesses tend to produce their order lists by computer. These orders are submitted (by post) to the suppliers, who resubmit the order into their own computer. The supplier's computer is used to prepare paper invoices, which are entered into the retailer's computer. The repeated conversion between paper documents and machine-readable data is wasteful as well as a potential source of error. To cater for the communications need exemplified by this problem, private networks are being set up (using lines leased from telephone companies) through which the computers of participating companies can communicate with each other directly. One such network to which retailers and their suppliers can subscribe is Tradanet. British Airways operate a network called Travicom, through which some 6000 travel agents in the United Kingdom can book and print airline tickets. It has joined in a consortium with other European airlines to develop a new networked booking system called Galileo. It has been estimated that the cost of developing Galileo is in the region of £100 million.

In the academic world a large number of universities, polytechnics and research institutions in the United Kingdom, who are major research users of computers, are linked together by Janet, the Joint Academic Network. By means of a gateway at the Rutherford Laboratory, Janet is connected to EARN (the European Academic and Research Network) and thereby to several other international networks. EARN links more than 400 host computers in Western Europe, Turkey and Israel. In this way, it is possible for academics worldwide to communicate with each other using electronic mail. The mail is sent across the network using a *store and forward* system, that is, it is sent to the next computer down the line, which then forwards it further, until it reaches its destination. Electronic mail networks usually incorporate automatic requeueing, so that if a connection fails, the same message is automatically transmitted again.

Summary of Chapter 11

In this chapter we have been concerned with some general issues surrounding communication with computers. Dialogue between people and machines can be improved by a greater awareness by programmers of the need for user-friendliness. A computer-initiated dialogue may operate on the basis of an intelligible prompt, or question, to which the user types an answer. A user-initiated dialogue is established by the user typing a command or, where the choice of commands is small, the user may select a command from a menu.

Technological improvements allow the screen to be developed into a fully addressed output device, possibly with graphics capabilities.

Terminals may be used for input and output at remote locations. Where the public telephone system is used for the communications link, modems are needed at each end to convert the signal between digital and analogue form. Remote access to computers has enabled the development of automated teller machines and point-of-sale terminals.

Communication between computers is achieved by linking the processors and peripheral devices in a network. Local-area networks allow the sharing of costly software and hardware and the use of an internal electronic mail service. The most popular layouts for these networks are Ethernet (in which data is broadcast along a bus) and Cambridge ring (in which data circulates). Wide-area networks exist between computers in locations remote from each other. The difficulties arising with using the telephone system for computer communications are largely avoided with packet-switching networks.

Further Exercises

1. Give an example of a menu-driven program (or suite of programs) with which you are familiar. What advantages are there for the user in this system? How would the user input his choices in the absence of a menu?

2. What features are used in commercial application packages to make them more attractive to business executives? Distinguish between features requiring different types of terminals.

3. Computers have been used by banks for more than twenty years. Why are automated teller machines such a recent development?

4. What function is served by a modem in a computer system? Give an example of a computer system in which modems are not required.

5. What are the essential differences between computer networks which use the telephone system and packet-switched networks?

6. (a) Describe the advantages of having computers and peripherals linked together in a computer network.
   (b) Draw a diagram showing the structure of a computer network which is such that a user at a terminal can access any of the computers and peripherals in the network.
   (c) Indicate what problems would arise if large amounts of data need to be transferred from one computer to another.

(ULSEB—1986)

7. A company with its head office in town A and branches in towns B, C and D has a computer system in each office. It now wishes to link the four computer systems together. Two ways of doing this are being considered.

Method 1 involves connecting the head office to each of the three branch offices as shown in figure 11.11(a).

Method 2 involves connecting each office to two other offices to form a ring as shown in figure 11.11(b).

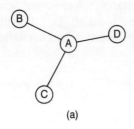

(a)

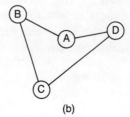

(b)

Figure 11.11

(a) Why is method 2 more satisfactory than method 1 if
  (i) a communications line breaks down between two computers?
  (ii) one of the computers in the system breaks down?
  What advantages has method 1 over method 2?
(b) When transferring a file of data from one computer to another it is important that the computer receiving the data should be able to check that the data it receives is the data that the transmitting computer actually sent.
  (i) Describe the checks you would expect to be performed during the data transfer, and explain what sort of error each check is designed to detect.
  (ii) If during the transfer of a file no errors are detected can one be sure that the file has been transferred correctly? Give reasons to support your answer.
  (iii) What part do modems play in the transmission of data between two computers that are long distances apart?

(Camb.—1985)

Further Reading

B. R. Gaines and M. L. G. Shaw, *The Art of Computer Conversation*, Prentice-Hall International, London, 1984.
This book is wholly concerned with human–computer communication. Chapters 5 and 6 are particularly relevant.

12 Computing Today

The computer is an inescapable component of our society and culture, along with electricity, the telephone and piped water. Computers have invaded and revolutionised every conceivable sphere of human activity. Offices and publishing houses, manufacturing industry and the world of finance—all have entered a new computer era. These innovations have set in train new currents in society. Jobs done under computer control when they previously gave work to people constitute a destabilising effect on employment patterns. We examine some of the social consequences in section 12.2. The existence of large data banks holding information on individuals is seen as a threat to privacy. We shall look at the new procedures which are needed to protect the rights of people in respect of computer-held data which concerns them. Finally, we take a brief glance at some of the newer avenues of endeavour which are being opened up by the use of computers.

12.1 The Growth of Computing

The development of computers has spawned machines in several shapes and sizes—supercomputers, mainframes, minicomputers and microcomputers. When these terms were first introduced, they described classes of machines quite different in size, performance, hardware and functionality of use. Most of the dividing lines have now been blurred. There is a complete spectrum of size and performance available among the computers now on the market. Differences in hardware have become less marked as new technologies pervade the manufacture of components. Even functionality is no longer a discriminator—the corner shop may run a stock control program on a micro, the local store may run its stock control on a minicomputer, and Marks and Spencer may use a mainframe to perform the same function. The most significant division of computers into classes is between single-user systems and multi-user systems. This division is software based, as the same hardware could run either sort of operating system. That is as it should be, for many different computers are configured from essentially the same set of hardware components. Indeed, a typical computer system will grow as the demands on it increase.

In this section we survey some of the current areas of activity in which computers play a major role.

The electronic office

Round about 1980 it was being confidently predicted that the conventional office, with its dependence on paper as the primary medium of storing and sending information, would be rapidly transformed into a paperless office as a result of the introduction of computer technology. Let us examine how far this prophecy has been fulfilled at the time of writing this book, some nine years later.

We may identify a number of major commercial functions:

* manipulating and storing information;
* preparing statistical reports;
* typing documents;
* communication (within the office and outside it); and
* performing arithmetic calculations.

The last function, which used to be carried out using books called ready reckoners, was 'computerised' by the advent of the cheap calculator in the 1970s. At about the same time, dedicated word processors began to come on the scene. These were able to relieve the drudgery of retyping whole documents to correct minor mistakes and of typing virtually identical letters to different addresses. In organisations where larger computers were in use, terminals were provided to give managers direct access to information held on the computer. Through the use of personal computers, computing power is now available to a large proportion of staff in large offices to handle a large range of office functions.

Correspondence may be typed using a word-processing package, reviewed by its author, and amended by the typist—all before a single word is committed to print. If the typist makes a typing error, she can correct it online before anything is printed. No hard copy need be made until the letter is satisfactory and ready for signature. Even the file copy can be retained on disc, rather than keeping a typed copy in the filing cabinet.

Software packages for office use typically include appointments diary systems which automatically indicate clashing appointments and buzz the user when the appointment is due. They also provide indexes for addresses and telephone numbers of colleagues and clients. These serve not only as repositories of information; they can also be used to control the addressing of envelopes and to dial up telephone calls automatically.

Individual computers are usually linked in a local-area network to enable shared use of printers and disc storage and internal electronic mail. Gateways to external networks are enabling telex communications to be incorporated into the electronic office; current developments are now extending this facility with the provision of networks which can handle both voice and data transmission. Gateways can also be used to good effect for organisations which have offices on several sites. Each office has its own local-area network, which can access a public wide-area network via a gateway. In this way, communication is possible between all the sites of the organisation as though it were linked in a single network.

These uses of the computer in the office should have caused a vast reduction in the volume of paper. So far this has not happened. Here are some reasons why.

Firstly, sensitive documents often must be produced on paper as legal proof of their existence. Furthermore, most organisations communicate with clients who can, at the present time, receive information on paper only. It would require every household to be equipped with computers before electronic mail begins to be an alternative, rather than an additional medium of communication. Anyway, many executives, let alone the large proportion of the population who have never seen the inside of an electronic office, are diffident about relying on the computer; the tangible piece of paper has more appeal.

In fact, far from reducing the volume of paper documentation, the net effect so far of computerisation has been a vast increase in the paper mountain. After all, the computer can process and supply information so much faster than previous manual methods, so that much more information is readily available. And high-speed computer-controlled printers can produce more printed documents than a typist ever could.

The writing of this book is a case in point. The drafts were typed using a word-processing package on a DEC System-20 mainframe. After the first draft was typed, subsequent drafts took much less time because those parts of the text which were unchanged did not need to be retyped, since they were already stored in the computer. This was a great improvement in efficiency and, one hopes, a less boring task for the typist. But did it generate less paper? Not a bit of it. Each draft was printed out in full. For although the author has direct terminal access to the computer, the terminal is tied to a socket in the office. It is not readily available outside office hours, although some terminal access is possible outside the office. So a hard copy was still necessary. Moreover, this author (in common with the majority of the population) lacks the necessary keyboard skills to type rapidly and prefers to scribble away on a pad of paper. A portable computer which could also be used as a terminal would certainly make a difference, but these machines are expensive at present and not necessarily compatible with any given mainframe. And the word processor cannot handle the drawings anyway.

When the drafts of the book were ready for sending to the publisher, no network was readily available for electronic transmission. So the good old-fashioned postal service was used. And, of course, you readers are studying this text on paper and not perusing a copy stored on a disc file.

No, the paperless office is still a long way off, if indeed it will ever come. Computers are certainly revolutionising office methods and procedures, but for the time being their impact is one of piecemeal evolution. Computers are associated with speed, and information stored therein is perceived to be short-lived. People still prefer to have access to a more permanent medium.

Exercise 12.1

Specify four applications of office computers which reduce dependence on paper.

Electronic publishing

There is, however, one area where the electronic office has really taken off, and that is where paper itself is used as only a transient medium. Newspapers, especially daily newspapers, are by their very nature short-lived. There is, after all, nothing so out-of-date as yesterday's newspaper. At the point of sale, the customer still expects to read a news*paper*. But at the point of production, there is a great deal of mileage in the paperless office. In newspaper production, speed is of the essence. Sending a report from a distant capital by post is out of the question in any event. There is a great role for the high-speed computer here. In the conventional newspaper office, a reporter writes an article; no sooner is it ready than a subeditor gets his pencil ready to alter it; then the editor gets his hands on it. After each stage it is retyped—on paper. The final version is sent to the compositors who set the type for final printing—and their machinery uses a keyboard.

In the electronic newspaper office, the reporter types his report straight into the computer. All the editing functions are performed—on the computer. When the article is ready for printing, the compositors need do no more than enter an instruction sequence; the text for composition is already on the computer which can compose the film from which the actual paper will be printed.

Such newspapers are becoming commonplace now. The *Washington Post* has been produced this way for many years, and almost all newspapers in the USA have followed suit. When the first draft of this book was being written, electronic publication of the daily newspapers in the United Kingdom was being spoken of in futuristic terms. Since then, great changes have swept the British newspaper industry, and many titles are now published using the latest computer techniques.

Exercise 12.2

What advantages does electronic publishing offer

(a) journalists,
(b) newspaper editors,
(c) publishers?

Exercise 12.3

Why did printers and the print unions oppose the introduction of electronic publishing?

Information retrieval

Although the prime motive for the use of computers has been information processing, the greatest actual use is the retrieval of stored data. The most straightforward examples are the use of computers by businesses to ascertain current stock levels, amounts owed by customers or to suppliers, and prices of goods. On a larger scale, there is the data held by Government agencies and quasi-governmental organisations. The registration details of vehicles are held on computer. So is information about the licensing of drivers. Hospitals maintain information about patients on computers, and now general practitioners are also turning to computers to maintain patient records.

Police forces have traditionally been great hoarders of information, and they have not been slow in putting computerised data banks to use. Even fingerprint information has been coded for computer storage. At the time of writing, Scotland Yard was in the process of developing and installing its Crime Report Information System. This is a computer system which assembles reports from 2000 terminals all over London and is able to highlight specific information as well as produce reports on crime trends.

In addition to information which is stored for subsequent use within the organisation which collected and stored it, there is information which is collected for use by a wider community. Library catalogues are held for perusal by potential users of the library. The British National Library maintains on computer not only a catalogue of publications in its holdings (all big libraries do this) but also a collection of abstracts of learned papers, known as BLAISE. These abstracts can be consulted online. If a copy of the abstract is all that is required this can now be achieved within minutes, obviating the delays occasioned by manual searching of catalogues and the use of the postal service. Searching of several abstracts in succession can lead to the selection of one or more documents (which may have to be sent by post!).

Another example of a data bank held for use by a wider community is the list of prices at which shares are traded on a stock exchange. This information is needed in up-to-the-minute form by stockbrokers and others engaged in share dealings. Before computers were used for this purpose, the only way to obtain this information (other than by direct approach to a dealer in shares to propose a deal) was through information relayed from an agency. This could not be kept so up-to-date, nor was it as convenient, as perusing a screen which could access a computerised database. With prices changing by the minute, share price information was an obvious candidate for this treatment. An immediate outcome of this development was the promulgation of a new market index. Stock market indices are used as a guide to performance of the market as a whole. The *Financial Times* 30 share index has been in use for many years as such an indicator. However, because of the time taken to compute the value of the index, it was updated only once an hour. In late 1984, a new FT-100 index of 100 company shares was introduced; this index is maintained by a computer program with access to a current share information database. As a result, the new index is kept up-to-date at all times. An even more significant introduction of computer technology, known popularly as the Big Bang, was ushered in during 1986 to replace the whole share-dealing system on the London Stock Exchange by one in which the official share dealing firms—called *market makers*—promulgate their dealing prices via a City network. One consequence of this has been that the floor of the Stock Exchange is now virtually deserted since all dealing takes place by telephone.

Computerisation of the City is by no means complete. The new electronic dealing systems have generated a vast increase in turnover. Every share deal which takes place needs to be followed up by work in the back office. This work includes financial settlement of the deal, registration of the new ownership of the shares, and transmission of documents between brokers and the parties to the deal. To help cope with this increase in paperwork—caused by the introduction of computer technology on a vast scale—a further massive software initiative is under way. The Stock Exchange automatic execution facility became fully operational in early 1989. Even before it was introduced, voices were being heard that this additional helping hand from the computer would be insufficient to stem the growing tide of paperwork. How much more investment in new technology is required to achieve a genuine reduction in routine documentation?

Teletext and viewdata

Accessibility to information banks by 'public' users has improved with the development of public data networks, especially packet-switched networks designed for use with digital computers. These public services have enabled network facilities to be provided for wide access to information banks. The travel industry has made wide use of specialised networks on which information is provided by airlines giving details of flights and package holidays. These enable the travel agent to provide clients with information (which can be kept up-to-date) without thumbing through innumerable brochures to access the desired product. Several organisations may feed information into the same network to be accessed by travel agents who are more interested in the destination, say, than the actual airline providing the flight.

The provision of information across a network in an easily assimilated form has been enhanced by the development of **teletext**. Teletext technology has been developed to harness the general availability of television screens as receivers for information transmitted from a computer. An adaptor receives and decodes the transmission for display of the information. In a teletext system, information in screen-sized chunks is held in a database. An index is provided so that the users can home in on the screen or screens in which they are interested. The medium of transmission can be open-circuit broadcasting—this method is a passive system giving the user control over the selection of information but no opportunity to respond. Telephone transmission allows greater flexibility, in terms of selection of information and a response capability.

Broadcast teletext—such as the Ceefax and Oracle systems in the United Kingdom—make use of the fact that television broadcasts actually transmit 50 frames per second, with a short interval between each frame to allow the screen scanning beam to return from the bottom right-hand corner of the screen to the top left-hand corner. During this interval, one or two screenfuls of digital data can be broadcast. This data is stored in the teletext receiver and can be called up onto the screen. One or more screenfuls of data contain indexes to enable information screens to be selected. The data can remain static over a period of time. However, each screenful of data is refreshed by a repeat broadcast every three seconds or so, allowing rapid updating of material such as news and Stock Exchange prices.

Teletext systems using telephone links now exist in several countries, providing a general **viewdata** service. The organisation which runs the service invites information providers to supply frames of information to be held on one or more computers within the network. The information can be updated by the providers as and when necessary. The network is usually organised so that the bulk of the population can reach a node of the network via a local telephone call (this keeps down telephone charges). Information providers can make a charge for the information provided—this charge is debited automatically to the account of the telephone lines from which the call originated. The frames (or pages) of information are organised as a tree; the user enters at the root and can descend either branch by branch or directly to a numbered frame. The Prestel public viewdata service began operation in Britain during the 1970s, and the Teletel service in France started not long after. By 1985 some thirty countries were operating viewdata services. The telephone allows the user to input data to a viewdata system (using a numeric keypad) as well as receive frames of information. This facility is being used in the next phase of development to provide *teleshopping* services. The subscriber can key in order details which are received by the information provider, who can fulfil the order, simultaneously debiting the user's credit card account.

In an analogous development, the TSB Bank operates a Speedlink service, which allows customers online access to their account files using an ordinary telephone receiver. Customers may order statements, issue cheque payments, and transfer funds between accounts. Synthesised voice output is used by the computer to echo input and communicate with the customer.

Process control

The simplest example of process control is probably a fire-control system, which detects smoke and fire, using sensors, and switches on sprinkler valves in the appropriate zones under computer control. The function of the computer in this application is to monitor continuously the input from the sensors and use the information to switch on (and off) the appropriate sprinklers, and initiate an alarm call to the local fire station. There is no reason why a computer must be dedicated to this task. A computer which spends almost all its time on commercial data processing, say, could also incorporate the program to implement a fire control system.

Computers are used, however, as dedicated controllers for industrial processes, such as manufacturing. Temperatures and pressures can be sensed, leading to valves being opened and closed. Computer control is commonplace in the oil refining and petrochemicals industries. The computer is used to monitor the volume and density of liquids being manufactured. In a steel mill the thickness of the steel produced can be monitored, and suitable adjustments can be made to the process as necessary. The amount of fuel and feedstock in input hoppers can also be monitored, and refill requests can be made to a screen to warn the process operator.

Many industrial chemical works use products with lethal capabilities; a proper control system is capable of detecting dangerous and abnormal concentrations of toxic or flammable substances. In these circumstances the whole, or part of, the industrial complex must be shut down. It may be necessary for the shut-down to proceed in an orderly fashion to avoid dangerous substances accumulating further, or to prevent damage to equipment. These factors will be built into the control program. Maintenance of such systems must be at a high level, to ensure that no malfunction occurs, and it may be that the computer is used in the routine maintenance procedures. The software must be of the highest standards of correctness, as there is rarely any margin for error in the control and monitoring of industrial processes.

Other processes subject to computer control include the distribution of electricity, gas and water through national grids, and the handling of waste water, sewage and industrial effluents. Air traffic control, blind landing systems for aeroplanes and the supervision of space flights have some similarities with industrial process control, though typically these systems may require more sophisticated mathematical calculations as well as straightforward control functions. At the other end of the spectrum, domestic processes are increasingly coming within the province of microprocessor control. Washing machines nowadays have electronic control mechanisms instead of the mechanical controllers which have been in use until now. A small processor chip controls the hot and cold water valves, the timer, water level and spin speeds. Similarly, microprocessors are being built into cars to monitor performance of the engine and the braking system, and even to determine the odometer display.

Exercise 12.4

What are the two essential features of process control? Why are computers useful in performing these functions?

Scientific calculations

The greatest initial impetus for the development of Computing Science came from areas of scientific endeavour which required complex mathematical calculations. These include missile guidance systems for military use, weather forecasting and fundamental research in theoretical physics at the subatomic level.

The really complex nature of these mathematical calculations may be gauged by the way in which they devour processing power. Weather forecasting is very much a case in point, for it is no use having a computer to forecast tomorrow's weather—a convenience for city dwellers, but vital for farmers, fishermen and transport operators by sea and air—if the program takes 48 hours to run. The United Kingdom Meteorological Office uses a Cyber 205—an extremely powerful computer—to gather weather information and produce weather forecasts.

The development of supercomputers many times more powerful than commercially used mainframes, and array and vector processors which can perform an arithmetical operation simultaneously 64 or 256 times, have been almost entirely in response to the need to support such calculations. Special programming languages, such as DAP FORTRAN, are used to exploit the particular processing capabilities of these machines. Computations which currently engage supercomputers are high on the list of applications for the new fifth-generation computer architectures.

Computer-aided design

In the field of manufacture—be it aeroplanes and cars or furniture and washing machines—objects must be designed before they are fabricated. The first design drawings are unlikely to be definitive. Improvements and modifications to the original design are frequently required; very often several alterations will be needed before the final design is achieved. Redrafting all the working drawings can be an arduous task, especially when only small changes are being incorporated into the design. The computer can ease this task by the use of special software for editing graphics displays.

Computer-aided design (CAD) techniques provide facilities for the input of design drawings, for displaying screen images represented by these drawings, and for making specified modifications to the designs. Specialised graphics software is required as well as a graphics terminal with suitably high resolution. Graphics **workstations** based on microcomputers can handle reasonably sophisticated software for colour displays with fairly high resolution (512 × 342). For more powerful software and displays of higher resolution, a powerful minicomputer or mainframe may be needed. One facility often available in this context is the ability to *zoom*. The design or artwork is actually stored at very high resolution—maybe 100 000 × 100 000. The whole design is displayed on the screen at reduced resolution. A particular feature of the design can be selected to zoom in on. A small area of the whole design is then expanded to fill the screen at greater resolution.

The simplest method of obtaining graphical input is by using a graphics tablet on which grid lines, corresponding to pixels on the screen, have been ruled. *Synthetic-camera* techniques work from a set of primitive objects provided by the CAD package which can be programmed into a particular configuration. The primitives may be circles, squares, lines, spheres and other geometric shapes, and may include shapes programmable using mathematical functions. The configuration is viewed from an assumed camera point, which defines a boundary beyond which the configuration is *clipped*. The clipping window is a rectangle for two-dimensional configuration and a pyramid for a three-dimensional configuration. Standard graphics packages available are Graphical Kernel System (GKS) for 2-D and Core Graphics System for 3-D.

A graphical design which is in store can be modified using the editing features of the CAD package. Typically, the portion of the design is selected from the screen using a light detector pen. This portion can then be redrawn, rescaled to a different size, rotated or translated to another part of the design. Two designs can also be merged.

The production of a high-quality design drawing of a three-dimensional object is achieved by the CAD software in a sequence of stages. The design usually begins with an outline or *wire-frame* drawing, consisting of a multitude of polygons. This drawing will include edges which cannot be seen from the viewpoint. Such hidden edges and faces are removed from the drawing.

There will remain some parts of faces which are obscured from the viewpoint by intervening objects. There are two techniques for dealing with this. In the **painter's algorithm**, the objects are placed in the design in order of distance from the viewpoint, furthest first. This then ensures that nearer objects, as they appear on

Introduction to Computing

Figure 12.1 Three-dimensional solid modelling on a Sun-4/260C Workstation (*courtesy of Sun Microsystems UK Ltd*)

the screen, automatically overwrite further objects. The **z-buffer algorithm** works by associating with each pixel, in addition to its x- and y-coordinates on the screen, a z-coordinate corresponding to depth of the line or surface. Where two or more images map to the same pixel, only the one with the lowest z-coordinate is retained.

At this stage, the drawing consists of the visible polygons only. Each polygon is now coloured in the appropriate colour, as specified by the designer. To obtain a more natural appearance, the colouring over the polygons is smoothed out using *shading algorithms*. These can take into account ambient illumination as well as individual light sources whose positions must be specified. Finally, the jagged edges which appear on slanting boundaries—a feature of the pixels in raster graphics—are smoothed out. This is achieved either by increasing the resolution of the display along the boundary or by adjusting the intensity of the pixels along the boundary to blur the edge.

Closely allied with CAD is the field or *computer-aided manufacture*. This harnesses the power of the computer to automate manufacturing processes. Specialist programming languages are used to specify actions by industrial robots and numerically controlled cutting machines. The design and manufacture of machine tools is often combined using CAD software to produce the data which drives the manufacturing software.

Exercise 12.5

Why are text-editing techniques inappropriate for graphic designs?

Exercise 12.6

Enumerate the stages in producing a high-quality image from a wire-frame drawing.

Education

The world of education, from school to university, has always been seen as a prime user of computing resources. Of course, an educational institution has the same reason to computerise its administrative procedures as any other organisation. Moreover there will be departments engaged in teaching computing science, where the direct experience is vital, and areas of teaching which could use the obvious attributes of a computer such as its number-crunching power and the ability to manipulate text for those engaged in the critical study of the composition of texts.

But over and above these uses, it has been long felt that computers have a role as a vehicle of instruction. This has led to the development of *computer-aided instruction* and *computer-aided learning*. The former is concerned with the computer as an adjunct to the conventional human teacher, capable of presenting subject matter in a readily assimilable form. In its early years, computer-aided instruction has not been the unmitigated success claimed for it by its early protagonists. For a computer program to gain acceptance, it must be written by an expert programmer who is also well-versed in the subject matter to which the program relates. Such people are often difficult to find. In the field of computer-aided instruction (CAI) there is an added dimension of difficulty. A computer program cannot replace the human teacher—it can only assist in a classroom activity. So there has to be some definite advantage in using it before teachers on the ground see any point in learning a new skill merely to incorporate into their lesson structure something that they were already doing. So the hopes for CAI are in breaking new ground—tapping areas which are difficult to teach by conventional methods or presenting new angles in a particular subject. Since by its very nature CAI must break new ground, it needs to be of a proven high standard before gaining acceptance. And much of what has been produced has failed to satisfy this criterion.

To take just one example, considerable attempts have been made to show that the computer is a useful tool in all areas of the curriculum. Spurred on by programmers whose use of the machine has developed round its arithmetical capabilities, simulation programs have been devised in geography, history, biology and other subjects. These have been hailed as a great advance, because before the days of the computer the simulations were not feasible in a classroom situation. Unfortunately this approach belies the reality of the educational issues. Teachers in many subjects do not reduce their subject to mathematics precisely because there is no adequate mathematical model; and an attempt to present one using the mighty computer does not necessarily make it educationally sound.

Computer-aided learning is a more sensitive issue, as it is an attempt to replace the human teacher, or to provide a teacher where face-to-face tuition is not available. Educational programs of this type seek to build up an interaction, on an individual basis, with the learner. Thus the learner is continually tested on his or her knowledge, and the path taken through the teaching material is adjusted (by the program) to take account of the learner's responses. Weak answers require reinforcing material, or more drill exercises, whereas good answers allow the next topic to be embarked upon.

12.2 The Age of Information Processing

We shall now try to survey briefly the way in which the use of computers actually shapes the development of our society. Machines have been with us since the Industrial Revolution and the computer is, at first sight, just a machine. The introduction of machines into the economy wrought wholesale changes in the lifestyle of society; and the large-scale use of computers is likewise exerting a revolutionary influence over the manner in which we live our lives.

Social effect of computers

The manner in which our lifestyle is adjusting to the computer society can be compared with certain other modern inventions, such as the telephone and automobile transport, whose impact on society has been out of all proportion to their direct purpose. The motor car enables journeys to be completed rapidly, allowing the user a substantial saving of time. In practice, the widespread availability of mechanical transport has had a profound effect not only on mobility but also on work patterns and on the way in which urban centres have developed. The motor car telescoped the time to move from A to B. Likewise, the invention of the telephone telescoped the time to send a message from A to B. Its widespread availability changed completely the nature of communication, again setting in train the development of different lifestyles. The computer has telescoped the time taken to process information. This alone has many implications for society.

One result has been the use of computers in industry to perform tasks which have previously been labour intensive. In this respect the information age is giving a repeat performance of the Industrial Revolution, when mechanical devices replaced labour-intensive manufacturing processes. In both cases, there are improvements in speed and quality of the final product.

In our description of the computerisation of newspaper production, we have indicated how the vast majority of the jobs in producing a newspaper simply disappear. The immediate net effect is therefore to throw thousands of employees out of work. Unless handled sensibly, this can be catastrophic. If computers are introduced to save money, some financial compensation should be given to those made redundant. This has happened in many US newspapers, where former employees whose jobs have disappeared are still paid to do nothing, this being cheaper in the long run than maintaining the pre-computer methods of production.

On the other hand, a person doing nothing at all day is no asset to society. He or she is unproductive, and the boredom can induce physical and mental ailments as well. A computerisation programme must be sufficiently far-sighted to tackle these projected issues and plan for their solution. In some set-ups the redundancy problem is not so severe. Where the job losses can be contained within reasonable proportions and phased over a period of time, they can be handled within natural wastage. In most firms, some people leave employment each year for a variety of reasons. If the job losses are contained by not replacing these natural losses, then no individual suffers from redundancy, although there may be an overall effect in terms of the level of employment within the local community.

On the other hand, computers do not only destroy jobs—they also create them. Apart from the obvious fact that computer hardware has to be manufactured, in a factory which employs people, there is the even larger software industry. Indeed, much more money nowadays goes into the purchase of software than into the purchase of hardware. Paradoxically, this is because software production is so labour intensive! In addition, the industry has spawned new applications—and consequently new demand for computers—in areas which take no jobs away. For example, personal computers used by executives and computer-controlled telephone exchanges largely serve to handle an explosion of information processing which would otherwise not be performed at all.

Computer Crime

The spectre of unemployment is just one danger which the computer revolution could bring. Computer crime is another danger. The new science has brought with it its own opportunities for criminal activity. The management and disposition of funds is a large application of computers. It is, therefore, possible for a criminal to tinker with the legitimate processing in such a way as to siphon off funds. With computer giving direct access to bank accounts, the whole crime can be contained within the computer. For many purposes nowadays, money is an entry in a computer file. Financial bonds and securities are also transferred to new owners using computers and telecommunications links. Thus anyone who is able to obtain physical access to a computer which handles financial transactions, and is able to bypass the security mechanisms on the computer, is able to indulge in fraud on a large scale. Likewise, computer systems which handle inventories and distribution of goods can have their data doctored so that goods can be pilfered without trace.

Physical access to the computer is frequently no problem. With many computers being linked in networks which can be accessed from the public telephone system, a terminal and a modem in a private house are all that is needed to make contact with the computer. The only protection here is the telephone number of the computer, which should not be known more widely than necessary. Security mechanisms, such as passwords, are the next line of defence. Those with the greatest scope for crime here are those in the greatest position of trust—the staff of the financial institutions. They may well have legitimate rights of access to certain data and software on the computer, and this may make it feasible to breach internal security. This is particularly true in some firms where security and the need to prevent unauthorised access is not treated seriously enough. It is even alleged that in some firms it is possible to obtain passwords to login directories and restricted software merely by telephoning the relevant department posing as a legitimate user. It is a fact that crime perpetrated by computer professionals, even if detected, may never be brought to the attention of the public. A bank, for example, might hesitate to prosecute a programmer who successfully committed a computer fraud; publicity could lead to a loss of confidence in the bank.

One method of detecting computer crime is the use of an *audit trail*. Computers are good at remembering things. So it is possible to build into a computer system a means of recording all transactions (or all transactions of a certain type) and the identity of the initiator of each transaction. Suspicious events can then be automatically monitored. Alternatively, a human monitor could check through a sequence of transactions to establish their legitimacy. After all, the ability to put through fraudulent transactions depends on the lack of monitoring; in a system where every cheque has to be signed personally by the managing director he, at least, should know what is going on.

The development of public access to computer networks has increased the danger of infiltration from the outside. Persons who have no right to access may nevertheless work their way in along the communications links to the secrets of computer-held data and may corrupt that data to their advantage. Protection against corruption, from within or without, is the function of a security system. We discussed physical security in chapter 8—the need to hold back-up copies of data as a protection against the destruction of the medium on which the data is held. This needs to be extended to cover electronic security, to provide protection against corruption or invasion of the data held within a computer system. We shall take a look at security of data in section 12.3.

The Computer Straitjacket

Human interaction is characterised by an ability to accommodate, to adapt to changing circumstances. So trains can be controlled readily by computer; they are already constrained to travel on tracks, so their motion is controlled by speed and knowing when to stop. Buses, another form of public transport, are not so simple to control. The first driverless train is here, but the first driverless bus is a long way off. The need to respond to such a variety of circumstances, such as the pedestrian who darts across the road, a bus stop which need to be moved temporarily, or a diversion because of road works, is a skill not yet within the domain of the computer.

A lack of adaptability is typical of machines. In the case of computers it may be tempered by a level of flexibility built by the programmers into the software. The difficulty, though, is that the software is written in advance. The problems have to be foreseen, and the foresight is not always there. The person who can do the right thing at the right time cannot always foresee all possible situations which will need handling.

This general limitation on the capabilities of a computer-controlled activity has a pervasive influence as society becomes more and more dominated by computers. Of course, it is possible to use both hardware and software that is increasingly reliable and tailored to do the task required of it. But there is always the tendency to cut corners and allow human beings to adapt to the computer, and not vice versa.

If a customer receives a bill for £0.00, then is it the computer's fault and nothing can be done about it. *You* know better—it is the programmer's fault, and something could be done about it. But the computer is sometimes used as a weapon, or as a shield, rather than as a tool, in order to condition human responses.

When computer threaten unemployment or undesirable changes in work conditions, trade unions take an interest to protect their members. When computers threaten to invade the privacy of the individual citizen (an issue we shall address in the next section), this is such a major issue in a democracy that governments are expected to legislate. But the insidious takeover of lifestyle by the computer, like the similar takeover by earlier generations of technology, is perceived as progress without anyone giving it much thought.

Most people are filled with awe in the presence of a mysterious power. The computer and its manipulation of information represent power. And since a high proportion of the population does not grasp its mode of operation, that power is a mystery. The result is that people are prepared to invest the computer with an intelligence that it does not have. People therefore react to computers with varying degrees of credulity. We are quite prepared to let machines (meters) monitor our consumption of gas, electricity and telephone usage. Only a few people question the accuracy of meters; in the same way, not many people question the accuracy of computers.

If you go to an insurance broker for a quote on motor insurance you will probably expect him to give the cheapest quote, or a reasoned explanation why another quote would serve you better. However, if the broker uses a computer terminal to provide the quote, there is a tendency to believe the computer without question. If you go to a travel agent and he suggests that you go to a different holiday resort from the one you have chosen, you might well suspect that he gets a larger commission on the alternative package holiday. But if he produces the evidence on the screen of a terminal, few people will query it.

That indeed is the paradox of computers. The intelligence of computers is severely limited, yet people are prepared to ascribe human powers of reasoning to the computer, which do not exist. The processing power of computers grows easily and can be tailored to meet many of the needs of society. Yet expense, or inertia, frequently leads to an installation of inadequate systems, and the public is induced to accept that these limitations are inherent and part of the price of computerisation.

12.3 Privacy of Information

We have alluded to the fact that information is power. This is most dramatically seen by the way in which people hide personal information from those they do not wish to be exposed to. Privacy of the individual incorporates his wish to control information about himself. People will trade privacy for the benefits it bestows. Thus they may keep funds in a bank for the advantages conferred by a bank account, although this means that bank staff have access to details about their financial status. However, a person expects that the bank will not divulge such information to outsiders. The exception to this is where the Government legislates the right of its agencies, such as the Inland Revenue, to be given this information.

In what ways do computers pose a threat to this privacy? We can identify two distinct areas of concern. Firstly, the sheer speed and volume of computerised data allow the accumulation of evidence by organisations which can be accessed only too readily. The second area of concern is the relative ease with which an unauthorised person might gain access to information legitimately stored. The solutions to these two problems lie in different hands. The unauthorised accumulation of data is a matter for legal controls. Unauthorised access to data properly held is a design issue in the construction of computer systems.

Laws of privacy

The first country to enact a law to impose controls on the use of data about individuals held on computers was Sweden in 1973, followed by the United States in 1974. Other countries have followed since. The United Kingdom Government had previously appointed a committee, the Younger Commission, to report on the issue of privacy. This committee reported in 1972, pronouncing the following principles:

- personal information should be held for specific lawful purposes only;
- it should not be excessive for those purposes;
- it should be accurate and up to date;
- it should not be retained longer than it is needed;
- the individual should be entitled to inspect it.

No legislation ensued, but subsequently the Data Protection Committee was set up under Sir Norman Lindop. The Lindop Committee produced a thorough report on the issue in 1978. It recommended the establishment of a Data Protection Authority with whom all users of computer held information would have to register. It also proposed that data users would have to apply for permission to use data for any purpose other than that for which it was originally gathered, and to exchange data between computers. The unauthorised possession of information on a computer was to be a criminal offence. A particular recommendation was that data held on computers by the police should be subject to supervision.

The Lindop report was not accepted by the Government. However, legislation was brought in incorporating most of the proposals of the Younger Commission, including the right of the individual to know what information was held on him. This passed into law as the Data Protection Act in 1984. Exempted from its provisions are personal data held for the prevention or detection of crime, for the apprehension of offenders and for the assessment of taxes.

The safeguards built into the Act provide a measure of protection for individuals from firms who accumulate information on them. The law requires that anyone who holds personal data about identifiable individuals must register with the National Data Register. Privacy of data is protected by a legal requirement on *data administrators* to refuse access to personal data to anyone who does not have a justifiable need to know.

A related issue is that of **data integrity**—that the data held is actually correct. Data held on computer can become corrupted by hardware failure, software faults or human error. The law gives individuals the right to check that information held on them is correct and to challenge the need to hold the information. Examples of data that an individual might choose to challenge are creditworthiness ratings listed by credit agencies and information held by employers which could affect promotion or pension rights.

A major threat arises, however, from the possible use by Government of information legitimately held on computers for a variety of purposes. Government departments hold records of driving licences, vehicle licensing, health records, National Insurance records, tax information and police records. In addition to this, various firms and public utilities also hold data concerning bank accounts, business accounts and usage of gas, telephone and electricity. Correlated rapid access to all this data could give someone considerable information about any chosen individual. Many people consider the sum total of information accessible in this way to provide for an unwarranted degree of governmental control. It becomes imperative, therefore, that restrictions should exist over the allowable degree of correlation of this information as well as strict supervision over who may access which data. One safeguard is the lack of a single identity number. Health records are accessed via a National Health Number, tax records via a tax file number and so on. However, it is not too difficult for a computer to do a complete search using the person's name as a key; and modern advances in hardware are bringing down the time taken to perform such searches.

Security of data

Even correct data which is held legitimately must be protected. Steps need to be taken to ensure that no-one has access to data to which he or she has no right. Access controls can be introduced at several levels. The systems administrator needs certain privileges to obtain access to programs which generate new directories (for new users) and to impose memory usage restrictions on such directories. Individual users can access their own directories freely but should not be able to access other users' directories without permission. Users may create files to which they wish to allow wider access—either to an identifiable group of users or to individual users. This access could be at several levels—for example, read-only access, execution access (for programs), write access (allowing modification of the file contents) and deletion rights.

One method of enforcing control is the use of passwords to gain access to directories and files. These passwords should be changed frequently to prevent them becoming known to outsiders. Credit cards and cash cards which can be used at automatic tills use password protection to prevent unauthorised use. The password is usually a four-figure number called a **personal identification number** (PIN). It is not known to the bank or data processing staff as it is generated at random by the computer system and posted to the authorised user in a sealed envelope.

In a typical computer system, however, there is a hierarchical access structure. The data administrator has access to all files. Users at other levels have access to any directories at lower levels beneath them, for example, users within their departments. There is no good reason, though, why a data administrator should have free access to everyone's files. A better system would allow all users, at any level, to protect totally from access any files with sensitive data.

Another method of controlling access is the **encryption** of data. Data can be encoded according to a secret formula so that only legitimate users can decode it. One particular method of encryption of data uses a pair of very large prime numbers. In this method, the product of the two numbers is used to encode the data but the numbers themselves are needed to decode the data. The elegance of this system lies in the fact that, because of the size of the numbers concerned, it would take an enormous amount of time (even using a computer) to work out the decoding numbers, even knowing the encoding number. This is called a **public key** system, because data can be safely encoded by other people, with only the recipient being able to decode it.

Exercise 12.7

Passwords on computer systems are usually composed from alphanumerics, possibly with one or two other characters being allowed. Why are personal identification numbers for plastic cards strictly numeric?

12.4 Developing Applications

Research continues apace in extending the frontiers of computer applications. In 1981 an international conference was held in Japan on the fifth-generation programme. The aim of this programme is to design and build computers which operate in modes of logical inference more akin to human thought than the present-day computers whose instruction modes are a development of the original computational requirements of the early computer builders. Such computers, it is said, will speak and understand speech, and will be able to read handwriting and printed books. They will learn from their experience to improve their mode of operation. In short, they would display artificial intelligence. The fifth-generation strategy implies a major change of direction for both software and hardware. One direction in which much research is being conducted is *functional programming* and the associated data-flow computer architectures. Another popular direction is based on the logical programming language Prolog.

In the field of hardware, the research emphasis is on parallel processing architectures. One product already on the market is the **transputer**, a complete computer on a chip. Several transputers can be linked up, in a variety of ways, to provide a genuine parallel processing capability. It is claimed that a suitable array of transputers can provide the processing power and flexibility of a supercomputer at a fraction of the price.

Another field of active research is into *superconductors*. A major problem in hardware construction is the disposal of heat generated by the electrical currents in computer circuitry. In the old days of valve technology this was a massive problem, and even now mainframes require an air-conditioned environment. However, the use of transistors has mitigated the problem to a considerable extent, and most smaller computers can function adequately with natural ventilation. Nevertheless, if the amount of heat generated could be reduced further, more components could be packed closer together, thus multiplying the power of the processor. Superconductors hold the key, because they generate no heat at all. At present their use is impracticable, as no superconductor is known which can function without being cooled by liquid nitrogen. Even this is a considerable advance over recent years, when the only superconductors known required a temperature of only three degrees above absolute zero. It is the aim of current research to develop a superconductor which can function at room temperature.

Expert systems

One field in which it is hoped to use these fifth-generation computers is in the area of expert systems. Such systems are programmed to mimic the deductive processes of the greatest expert in a given field. Thus a medical expert system is programmed with expert medical information, so that any doctor can reach the sort of conclusions currently reached by only the most experienced specialists. Or so the theory goes.

Expert systems are planned for all areas where there is a large body of facts to be learned and then juxtaposed using inference based on experience. Such sytems could eventually replace lawyers in litigation, and advisers in all fields.

Robotics

One of the fields in which it is hoped to make great strides is in the use of robots. Computer-controlled robots are currently in use in manufacturing industry where they can take over boring assembly-line jobs from human workers. In the field of quality control they can be used to apply standards consistently to components manufactured for motor cars or aeroplanes.

A long-term vision is that of the robot available to act in a service capacity to save individuals effort. Such robots would require a high degree of sophistication. It is considered by the proponents of the fifth-generation project that such robots could more easily be built using this more advanced technology.

Is it worthwhile?

At the end of the day, will all these advanced techniques actually yield an improvement in our way of life? We may marvel at the way in which drudgery is banished from our lives, but are we sure that we know how to replace it with something better?‹

Will the net result of greater and more widespread use of computers lead to more centralised power and a destruction of individual initiative? Or, on the contrary, will greater access to personal computing power result in the greater independence of individuals from large-scale forces in society which tend to dominate one's life?

Man is gregarious. Society depends on human interactions. Will more computerisation bring greater opportunities for social contact, or are more and more individuals going to get out and seek to communicate with machines rather than other people?

As the computer takes over an ever larger share of our environment, these are some questions which should be pondered.

Summary of Chapter 12

Computers have, in the space of a few decades, wrought tremendous changes in the way people live. The office and the shop floor, where many people spend a large part of their waking day, are changing beyond recognition. The home itself is invaded by computers and by systems which depend on computer control. The telephone itself provides access to computers the world over.

Employment patterns have changed as the computer destroys the need for existing work-forces. The computer industry has generated new jobs and new computer-based activities generate their own employment, but there is no guarantee that this will balance the job loss in the long term.

The present-day computer is insidiously making its mark on human activity. The speed and volume of processing capable with a computer lead to new problems in terms of the confidentiality of personal information. New legal frameworks are being introduced to handle the new situation. The computer itself has been harnessed to provide security against unauthorised access to data. Access control methods include passwords and encryption of data.

New applications using fifth-generation computers displaying artificial intelligence are intended to include expert systems and robots.

Answers to Exercises

12.1 Electronic mail—replaces paper memoranda.
Documents which need to be read by several members of a department can be held in a central filestore and accessed from terminals.
Appointments diaries and telephone numbers can be held on computer.
Executives can review drafts of outgoing correspondence and make amendments and comment online.

12.2 (a) Journalists can experiment with different versions of the same story without rewriting parts common to the different versions. The computer can do a word count and new material can be added or excessive words removed with relative ease. The text as typed can be incorporated into the newspaper without the danger of new errors creeping in at the composition stage.
(b) Amendments can be made directly to journalists' copy without the need for complete retyping. The page make-up can be inspected before the type is composed and different layouts can be experimented with. Late news stories can be inserted right up to the minute the presses begin to roll.
(c) The publisher benefits from more streamlined procedures which save on labour costs.

12.3 The printers engaged in the composition process had the most to lose since it is largely their jobs which have been superseded by computers.

12.4 Measurements must be taken to determine the current state of the process, and modifications must be made to the process if necessary. The first of these is the input to a process control system, the second is the output. A computer is capable of making numerous simultaneous measurements and analysing them rapidly so that modifications can be computed and implemented in real time.

12.5 Text editors are designed to handle text files, which are essentially a stream of characters displayed sequentially on the screen. The units of text as perceived by the human user are characters, words and sentences; that is, contiguous groups of characters. The units of a graphic design are, from the user point of view, objects which are part of a two-dimensional screen display. This does not tie in directly with the sequence of pixels which make up the internal representation of the picture. The techniques required here are, therefore, quite different from the character manipulation routines of a text editor.

Another difference is that graphical objects may need to be rotated or rescaled, operations which are not relevant to text. A graphics manipulation routine is, therefore, a much more complex piece of software than even a sophisticated screen-based text editor.

12.6 The steps are: hidden-edge removal, invisible face removal, colouring of faces, shading of colour and jagged-edge smoothing.

12.7 Automatic teller machines and other card-accepting machines do not have full alphanumeric keyboards. They usually have a numeric keypad augmented by a small number of menu-selection keys.

Further Exercises

1. A centralised computer system is to be replaced by a network of microcomputers held in separate departments of an organisation. Comment on the likely effects on the security of information.

2. Discuss three ways in which computers have affected your life indirectly. Do you consider these aspects to be beneficial to you?

3. (a) Explain the difference between the terms 'privacy of information' and 'security of information'.
   (b) Briefly describe two developments in computing which might increase public concern about privacy of information.
   (c) Briefly discuss and justify **two** steps which might be taken by government to alleviate such public concern.

(JMB—1982/1/19)

4. It is proposed to create a national database which would contain much of the information about individuals currently on government files. This would link the records of such organisations as the Passport Office, the Inland Revenue, the Registrar of Births and Deaths, the Department of Health and Social Security, the Driver Vehicle Licensing Centre.

   It is anticipated that many government departments will need to continue independent processing after this database has been established but that each will have on-line access to the database.

   (a) What sort of information would be held on this database and how might access by different departments be controlled?
   (b) How might such a database be established and maintained?
   (c) What advantages might there be in such a database?
   (d) What are the social implications of this proposal?

   (JMB—1984/2/6)

5. A credit-card company issues its card holders with a numbered card which may be used in the purchase of goods or services from any merchant who has agreed to accept cards from this company. At the time of receiving the goods, the card holder presents his card so that the number may be recorded on the sales receipt. The merchant forwards his copy of the receipt to the credit-card company and the purchase price is refunded to the merchant. Each month, the credit-card company sends a bill to each card holder listing all purchases made during the previous month. Each card holder has an upper limit to the credit he is allowed; this 'credit limit' is determined by the credit-card company after requesting a reference from the card holder's bank.

   The data concerning card holders and their purchases is held on an interactive computer system.

   In an essay, discuss the security implications of this sytem with reference to the following:

   (a) the preservation of reasonable privacy of the data held,
   (b) card holders who are themselves employees of the credit-card company,
   (c) whether the monthly statement should contain details of individual purchases, or simply an overall total,
   (d) the loss of a card.

   (ULSEB—1983/1/13)

6. Many organisations now collect personal information about you and others and store it in computer-based files.

   Suggest, with reasons, the types of information likely to be held by:

   (i) the Police,
   (ii) your school or college.

State what inherent threats to personal privacy you consider are implied by the storage of personal information on a widespread basis.

Discuss safeguards that may be implemented.

(ULSEB—1984/2/9)

7. If you were planning a database system for confidential data what action would you take to cope with the following requirements?

(a) To minimise unauthorised access.
(b) To detect unauthorised access.
(c) To recover the database after a system failure or a catastrophe (such as a fire in the computer room).
(d) To obtain information about the use of the data in order to make improvements in the right way.

Give examples to illustrate your answers, and explain why some people require more privileged access than others.

(Camb.—1983/2/7)

8. Discuss **two** of the following computer applications:

(a) computer-aided design,
(b) computerised stock control and financial accounting,
(c) word processing and electronic mail.

Your answer should include:

(i) why a computerised system is used in the particular application.
(ii) the hardware which is a specific feature of the application,
(iii) the software used in the application,
(iv) the effects of using computers on the people who work in the application described, and on society in general.

(AEB—1986/2/15)

9. Describe two processes which each use different computer techniques for parts of the process. For each of your chosen examples, explain briefly the advantages of computerising the process, and illustrate how the output from the first part of the process is interfaced with the second part.

10. Systems involving computers and communications are now very widely used in many areas of business and government. Much of the data in these systems needs to be kept secure because it is personally or commercially sensitive. One example application of such systems is Electronic Funds Transfer which, in the City of London alone, accounts for many billion pounds worth of transactions every working day. A high proportion of computer crime involves the improper access to, use of or interference with data such as this.

Discuss the nature of computer crime and the type of personnel most likely to be involved. Describe the steps that can be taken to attempt to prevent computer crime or to detect it, and explain why such steps are not always successful.

(Camb.—1987)

Further Reading

Alfred Z. Spector, 'Computer software for graphics', in *Computer Software*, W. H. Freeman, New York, 1984.
This 12-page article gives a more detailed account of interactive graphics software.

I. O. Angell and G. H. Griffith, *High-resolution Computer Graphics Using Pascal*, Macmillan, London, 1988.
This book discusses the implementation of the methods for producing screen graphics.

Appendix A: ASCII Codes

Hex code	Character	Hex code	Character	Hex code	Character	Hex code	Character
0	NUL	20	(space)	40	@	60	
1	SOH	21	!	41	A	61	a
2	STX	22	"	42	B	62	b
3	ETX	23	#	43	C	63	c
4	EOT	24	$	44	D	64	d
5	ENQ	25	%	45	E	65	e
6	ACK	26	&	46	F	66	f
7	BEL	27	'	47	G	67	g
8	BS	28	(	48	H	68	h
9	HT	29	)	49	I	69	i
A	LF	2A	*	4A	J	6A	j
B	VT	2B	+	4B	K	6B	k
C	FF	2C	,	4C	L	6C	l
D	CR	2D	–	4D	M	6D	m
E	SO	2E	.	4E	N	6E	n
F	SI	2F	/	4F	O	6F	o
10	DLE	30	0	50	P	70	p
11	DC1	31	1	51	Q	71	q
12	DC2	32	2	52	R	72	r
13	DC3	33	3	53	S	73	s
14	DC4	34	4	54	T	74	t
15	NAK	35	5	55	U	75	u
16	SYN	36	6	56	V	76	v
17	ETB	37	7	57	W	77	w
18	CAN	38	8	58	X	78	x
19	EM	39	9	59	Y	79	y
1A	SUB	3A	:	5A	Z	7A	z
1B	ESC	3B	;	5B	[	7B	{
1C	FS	3C	<	5C	\	7C	|
1D	GS	3D	=	5D	]	7D	}
1E	RS	3E	>	5E	↑	7E	~
1F	US	3F	?	5F	_	7F	(delete)

The characters in the first column are *control characters*; they may be produced from the keyboard by depressing the CTRL key and the corresponding key from the third column simultaneously. For example, ASCII code &1B can be produced by the combination CTRL-[. Several control characters can be produced by special keys, as follows:

BS	backspace
HT	tab
LF	linefeed
CR	return
ESC	escape

DC1 to DC4 are *device control codes*; DC1 and DC3 are frequently used to control scrolling of the screen. CTRL-G (bell) sounds an audible tone. CTRL-L (form feed) is used to start a new page on a printing device. The other control codes are mainly used in connection with data transmission.

Appendix B: Other BASICS

The version of BASIC used in this book is BBC BASIC. Initially introduced on the Acorn BBC computer in 1981, it has become the standard BASIC, available not only on Acorn computers, but indeed on all computers intended for the educational user. However, for the benefit of readers who prefer to use RM BASIC (the version supplied with the RM range of computers) or BBC BASIC V (installed in the Acorn Archimedes), this appendix highlights some of the important differences.

RM BASIC

RM BASIC includes a number of improved program structures, as well as one or two important notational differences from BBC BASIC.

Assignment symbol

The preferred assignment symbol is := but = is also accepted.

Loops

The repetitive constructs are FOR/NEXT and REPEAT/UNTIL as in BBC BASIC.

Branches

The alternative construct IF . . . THEN . . . ELSE (on a single line) is available as in BBC BASIC.

Subprograms

The major differences between RM BASIC and BBC BASIC are in the definition and use of subprograms. In RM BASIC any legitimate identifier may be used to name a subprogram—it does not have to begin with FN or PROC.

Procedures

A procedure definition begins with the reserved word PROCEDURE, and the parameters are not enclosed in brackets. In addition, it is possible to call parameters by reference, and arrays may be passed as parameters. By way of example, here is how the *output_bill* procedure (section 3.4) would be coded in RM BASIC.

```
500
510 PROCEDURE Output_bill name$, address$, tel_no$, rental_charge,
                                                         call_charge
520
530 vat := 0.15 : REM constant value
540 PRINT name$ ! address$ ! tel_no$
550 REM ***output charges***
560 PRINT "apparatus:", rental_charge
570 PRINT "calls:", call_charge
580 vat_charge := vat*(rental_charge + call_charge)
590 PRINT "vat:", vat_charge
600 PRINT "total:", rental_charge + call_charge + vat_charge
610 ENDPROC
```

There is no LOCAL declaration in line 520 as all identifiers are automatically local in RM BASIC unless specified to be global. On those occasions where a global variable is required, this is achieved by a GLOBAL declaration which must appear as the first line in the main program (or the subprogram which calls the procedure) *and* as the first line in the body of the procedure definition.

The main program of the Telecom billing system which calls this procedure looks like this in RM BASIC:

```
REM***Telecom billing***
INPUT telephone_no$, name$, address$
INPUT number_of_telephones, initial, final
used := final − initial
Compute_charges number_of_telephones, used  RECEIVE  rental_charge,
                                                         call_charge
Output_bill name$, address$, telephone_no$, rental_charge, call_charge
END
```

This program illustrates the use of *output parameters*, which must follow all the input parameters and be prefixed by the reserved word RECEIVE. A procedure definition with formal output parameters is coded as follows:

```
PROCEDURE Compute_charges no_of_telephones, used
                              RETURN rental_charge, call_charge
REM CONSTANTS
line_charge := 13.60
receiver_rental := 2.45
unit := 4.4 : REM pence
REM BEGIN
```

```
rental_charge := line_charge + (no_of_telephones*receiver_rental)
call_charge := used*unit/100
ENDPROC
```

Note how the reserved word RETURN takes the place of **var** in Pascal. However, in RM BASIC, if a variable is used as both an input and output parameter, it must appear in both lists—before and after RETURN.

RM BASIC makes some provision for exception handling within procedures (section 4.3). The LEAVE command may be used to cause a premature exit from a procedure to the calling statement.

Functions

Function definitions begin with the reserved word FUNCTION and finish with ENDFUN. A value is returned to the calling statement using the reserved word RESULT. Here is the wage function (section 3.4).

```
1200
1210 FUNCTION Wage(rate, hours)
1220
1230 IF hours <= 38 THEN wage0 := hours*rate
                         ELSE wage0 := (38 + (hours − 38)*1.5)*rate
1240 RESULT wage0
1250 ENDFUN
1300
1310 FUNCTION Tax(gross)
1320 RESULT 0.25*gross
1330 ENDFUN
```

An array parameter is passed by reference, just like a **var** parameter in Pascal. No specification is required. The following is the RM BASIC version of the linear search function in exercise 11 of chapter 3.

```
FUNCTION Search1(data$(), size, item$)
index := size + 1
REPEAT
    index := index − 1
UNTIL data$(index) = item$ OR index = 0
RESULT index
ENDFUN
```

Since *data$()* is passed as a parameter rather than a global variable, the actual array could be called something else other than *data$*. In fact, in RM BASIC it is not even necessary to pass *size* as a parameter, because there is a built-in function *BOUNDS* which can determine the size of an array.

This covers very briefly the major structural differences between BBC BASIC and RM BASIC.

BBC BASIC V

The extended version of BBC BASIC supplied with the Acorn Archimedes range of microcomputers is also available on some other computers. The following significant extensions implement some of the structures discussed in this book.

Loops

In addition to fixed loops and until loops, BBC BASIC V implements while loops. The syntax is

```
WHILE <condition> DO
    <statements>
ENDWHILE
```

Branches

Most versions of BASIC to data have provided the single-line IF . . . THEN . . . ELSE as the only alternative construct. As a result the only practical way of implementing a branch is often by the introduction of procedures for the consequent statements. In BASIC V, there is a proper IF statement which can be used to code a two-way branch:

```
IF <condition> THEN
    <statements>
ELSE
    <other statements>
ENDIF
```

There is also a CASE statement to code a multi-way branch.

Array operations

A useful feature in BASIC V is that the array is a fully supported data structure, with operations on whole arrays. Thus a single statement can be used for an operation on a whole array. The following illustrates the use of array operations on compatible arrays.

```
DIM a(200), b(200), m(100, 200)
a() = 6*b()
b() = a() + b()
a() = m()*b()
```

Appendix C: Coursework and Projects

The Common Core in Computing at Advanced Level, as published by the GCE Examining Boards [*Common Cores at Advanced Level—First Supplement* (GCE Boards of England, Wales and Northern Ireland, 1987)], contains the following statement:

Project work should
(a) encourage the sensible use of computers to solve problems which are within the experience or understanding of the candidate;
(b) emphasise the analysis and design skills involved in problem solving using the computer and so involve the development of a piece of work over an extended period of time;
(c) involve the development, documenting, implementing and testing of a software based package which might or might not include the use of pre-written software;
(d) involve the organisation and presentation of a report on the work that has been carried out, including an evaluation of this work.

Typically the project will count for about 25 per cent of the marks, and so will need to be a substantial piece of work. Candidates following the usual two-year course should select a project topic at the end of the first term. This will leave a clear period of fourteen months over which to develop the project in time for completion during the fifth term.

Any application area is acceptable, but in practice a candidate must choose an application which is not too difficult to analyse and also not too time-consuming to be completed in good time. Stock control, a spelling checker, crossword-solving aid and invoicing are just a few areas which could form the basis for a suitable problem. Other project ideas may be found in the contexts of the following exercises set in this book: exercise 2.3 (bank transactions), further exercise 2.3 (timetable), further exercise 7.1 (payroll).

It is not always necessary to code everything from scratch; it is perfectly permissible to use a pre-written module (such as a sort module) or to program a suitable application in a database language such as dBase III. Any use of such material in a project must of course be acknowledged in the documentation. Candidates would do well to choose a project topic which allows them to display an understanding of the use of topics specified in the syllabus they are following.

The development of the program will include the various phases described in chapters 1 to 4. This includes:

analysis of the problem,
consideration of possible solutions,
reasons for selecting a particular approach,
design of the program structure and data structures,
consideration of error conditions and data validation, and
refinement of the design,

as well as actual coding. Any acceptable project will be sufficiently complex to require conscious design. It should also pay attention to the feasibility of processing realistic volumes of data. This may have implications for the file structures used in the program.

The project report must describe the problem, document the whole development process and include concise user documentation. Due regard should be had to any limit imposed by the Examination Board on the length of a project—typically about 25 A4 sides in addition to an annotated program listing and the output from an adequate selection of test runs. (Only the final working program listing should be submitted.) It will be found helpful to isolate weaknesses in intermediate versions of the program by getting fellow students to try it out.

It is advisable for the project report to be preceded by a short abstract—about half a page.

Appendix D: Hints for the Solution of Selected Further Exercises

Chapter 1

1. Speed; updating.
   Cost, but consider Minitel (distributed in France).

3. withdrawal:
   1 input details
   2 reduce balance by amount
   3 record entry in passbook

   refinement:
   2.1 obtain old balance
   2.2 subtract amount to give new balance
   2.3 save data for statement

   1 input details
   2 select
   2.1 if transaction is deposit: handle deposit
   2.2 if transaction is withdrawal: handle withdrawal
   2.3 endselect

Chapter 2

1. loop for each account holder
       loop
             review borrowing limit
             loop until Monday morning
                   input withdrawal request
                   dispense amount if within limit or output message
                   reduce limit by amount
             endloop
       endloop
   endloop

Chapter 3

1. *Until* loop exits when condition is true; *while* loop exits when false. Also, *until* loop must be executed at least once.

   > loop
   >   action
   >   until condition

   may be replaced by

   > action
   > loop while not condition
   >   action
   >   endloop

   A language designer may choose not to provide an *until* loop construct on the grounds that a *while* loop construct can cover for both.

3. In a subprogram. Local variables are visible within the subprogram only, so that the behaviour of the subprogram is not influenced by unspecified outside factors.

5. Meaningful identifiers, comments, data structures, algebraic and logical expressions, program structures (loops, branches).

8. (a) Avoids need to specify a bogus value—in some cases may be difficult to ensure that bogus value does not arise in practice.
   (b) Allows input stream to be processed without having to decide in advance number of items in stream; also avoids possibility of specifying the wrong number of items by mistake.

   (a) requires fixed loop (number of items = number of iterations).
   (b) requires *until* loop (repeat until input = bogus value).

9. address
   _____

   instring
   _____

   > if instring is not empty:
   >   nextchar := first character of instring
   >   remove first character from instring
   >   line := empty string
   >   loop while nextchar <> comma instring is not empty
   >   append nextchar to line
   >   nextchar := first character of instring
   >   remove first character from instring
   >   endloop

```
    output line
    output newline character
    call address(instring)
    endif
```

Note that this procedure assumes that the input string does not begin with a comma.

Now code in a suitable high-level language.

Chapter 4

2. Pascal. (a) Control structures, expressions, recursive procedures. (b) Meaningful identifiers, comments.

3. Readability, maintainability.

Chapter 5

2. (a) Can be kept up-to-date; but users may require extensive training.
   (b) People feel more at home with hard copy; but may be bulky.
   (c) Fairly easy to peruse; if a reader/printer is available can print off pages required.

3. XOR.

4. $\overline{a.(b+c)} = \overline{a} + \overline{(b+c)}$

   $\qquad = \overline{a} + (\overline{b}.\overline{c})$

5. $2^4 = 16$.

13. large $= l$, small $= \overline{l}$; round $= r$, square $= \overline{r}$; wood $= w$, glass $= \overline{w}$.

   $(r.\overline{w}) + (\overline{r}.w) + (l.\overline{w}) + (\overline{l}.\overline{r}) + (\overline{l}.w)$

   $= (r + l).\overline{w} + (\overline{r} + \overline{l}).\,w + (\overline{l}.\overline{r})$

   Now, $(\overline{l}.\overline{r}) = \overline{l}.\overline{r}.(w + \overline{w}) = \overline{l}.\overline{r}.w + \overline{l}.\overline{r}.\overline{w}$, so the expression becomes

   $(r + l + \overline{l}.\overline{r}).w + (\overline{r} + \overline{l} + \overline{l}.\overline{r}).\,w$

   $= (r + l + \overline{r + l}).\overline{w} + (\overline{r} + \overline{l}).\,w$

   $= \overline{w} + (\overline{r} + \overline{l}).\,w$

Thus George will take either a glass top table, or a square or small wood top table.

Chapter 6

1. 00011011. (a) 10011011, (b) 11100101 (c) 11100100.

3. Indirection through a predetermined page.

11. (a) Bitwise NOT.
    (b) 0 AND x = 0; 1 AND x = x.
    (c) logical left shift (5 bits) followed by logical right shift (5 bits)

Chapter 7

1. initialise lookup table
   initialise tax bands
   initialise tax rates
   loop
       input name, job title
       gross := lookup (job title)
       select
           if gross < band(0) : tax := 0
           if band(0) <= gross < band(1) : calculate tax at standard rate
           if band(1) <= gross : calculate tax at higher rate
       end select
       print gross, tax, net = gross − tax
       until end of payroll file

3. posint

---
instring

---
call first(instring, string1, valid)
call.decimal (string1,endstring, valid)
call end(endstring, valid)

---
valid

---

first

---
instring

---
ch := first char of instring
select
       if ch <> 0 : remove leading digits to produce string1,
                                       valid:=true
       otherwise : report error, valid := false

---
string1,valid

---

decimal
string1, valid

if valid = true and string1 is not empty:
    ch := first char of string1, rest is endstring
        if ch <> decimal point : report error, valid := false

endstring, valid

end
endstring, valid
remove leading digits from endstring if next char is not space or carriage return: report error,   valid := false
valid

Chapter 8

1. Speed, storage capacity, durability, portability.

2. Size of tape block can be varied by writing software; size of disc block determined by disc operating software. Tape drives slow down between blocks.

8. Average seek time = 30 ms.
   Latency = $\frac{1}{2} \times \frac{1}{50}$ = 10 ms.
   Transfer time = 2000/500 000 s = 4 ms.
   Average access time = 44 ms.

9. (a) Process serially in a single pass.
   (b) Store keys only.
   (d) (i) Lack of security; if processing is unsuccessful or new master tape is lost, no old master tape available to rebuild file.
    (ii) Similar to (i).
    (iii) Securest method, provided tape is available. If anything goes wrong, original master and transaction tapes can be used to rebuild output file.

Chapter 9

2. Since we need pointers, we shall use Pascal. We use a linked list representation for the stack; each item in the list is a record as in section 9.1. We need a single variable to point to the current top of the stack; this can be either a global variable or it can be passed as a parameter to each of the stack procedures. Adopt the latter approach, and call the pointer variable *stack*.

```
type stacktype = ↑ element;
     element = record
                      data: itemtype
                  link: stacktype
              end;
var stack : stacktype;
function empty(stack: stacktype): boolean;
begin
    empty:= (stack ↑ = nil)
end;
procedure push(item: itemtype; var stack: stacktype);
var el: ↑ element;
begin
    new(el);
    el ↑ .link:= stack;
    el ↑ .data:= item;
    stack:= el
end;
```

A function *pop* may be defined similarly.

Chapter 10

1. Batching up programs to be run without user intervention.
   A job which can be pre-planned to be run at a specific time (for example, overnight run of monthly statements); a job which is known to take a long time.

2. Access to tape slows down response.

3. Operating system, utility programs.

4. Time slicing is a tool in a multiprogramming operating system. It may be relevant to batch programs running in the background on such a system. A stand-alone machine may be used by a single user for many programs simultaneously under a multiprogramming system.

5. See section 10.7

8. Economic use of a scare resource.

Chapter 11

2. Menus, icons, spreadsheets, charts, graphic displays.

3. Consider: plastic card technology, user resistance, installation cost, security; also cost of capital vs staff, cost of transmission.

4. Local area network; digital transmission line.

5. Message-switched communication requires a fixed connection for the duration of the call.

Chapter 12

1. Access to each microcomputer can be restricted to departmental users, with only limited access to network users. On the other hand, each department has a responsibility for local security, and this dispersed responsibility may be difficult to monitor and control.

9. Desktop publishing: A microcomputer sends a bit map or a program in a special language to a laser printer, which is in fact a dedicated microcomputer with a printing function.
Address lists: Sorting and printing.
Navigation: Calculation of desired route and feedback control to engines.

Glossary

References to other items within this glossary are given in *italics*.

Absolute addressing   Assembly-language addressing mode in which the *operand* is actual data for the operation.

Access control   Limitation on access to software by group of users or password.

Access time   Time taken to retrieve a data item.

Accumulator   A special *register* used to hold the most recent value output by the ALU.

Actual parameter   A value or expression used within a *subprogram* call.

Ada   High-level language with facilities for real-time tasking.

Address   A number which identifies a *register* or a location in memory.

Address space   The size of memory capable of being addressed by a given number of bits.

Algorithm   A set of rules for solving a problem or performing a specific task in a finite number of steps.

Allophone   A component of speech, used in a digital voice synthesiser.

Alphanumeric   A character which is either alphabetic or numeric.

Alternative control structure   A control structure for the execution of alternative actions depending on certain conditions.

ALU   *Arithmetic-logic unit*.

Applications package   Specially written programs with associated documentation for carrying out a particular function (such as payroll or navigation).

Arithmetic shift   An operation in which the contents of a location are shifted right or left by a number of bits and the sign bit is preserved.

Arithmetic-logic unit   The part of the CPU where the arithmetic and logical operations are performed.

Array   A composite data object consisting of a number of data items of the same type.

Array element   A single addressable data item belonging to an array.

Array index   A set of one or more values used to access a single element of an array.

Assembler   A *utility program* which assembles a program coded in *assembly language* into machine instructions.

Assembly language   A low-level language whose instructions are generally in one-to-one correspondence with machine instructions.

Assignment statement   A statement which assigns the result of an operation or computation to a variable.

Associative memory   Storage which can be identified by its content rather than by its address.

ATM   *Automated Teller Machine*.

Audit trail   A set of records of the file updating which takes place during transactions, enabling items to be traced.

Automated Teller Machine   A special-purpose terminal giving access to the computer system of a bank or building society.

Automatic sequence control   The fundamental control feature of the von Neumann architecture by which the *program counter* is automatically incremented during each fetch–execute cycle.

Backing storage   Storage of large quantities of data outside the *immediate access store*.

Backup   A copy of a file which may be used in the event of corruption of the original.

Backus–Naur form   A formal notation used in defining the *syntax* of programming languages.

Bar code   A pattern of thick and thin lines and spaces, representing a numerical code, which can be read by an optical scanner.

Base address   The lowest address in an area of storage, which is added to an *offset* (relative address) to obtain a storage location.

Batch processing   A procedure in which a collection of programs and their data are grouped together and then processed in sequence.

BCD   Binary-coded decimal.

Binary search   A method of searching an ordered list by splitting it successively into two halves and disregarding the half which cannot contain the desired record.

Binary tree   A *tree* structure in which each node has at most two branches.

Bit   A binary digit (0 or 1).

Block   A collection of records or bits, stored, transferred or transmitted as a unit.

Block structure   The organisation of a program in terms of subprograms

Boolean   A data type with two values, 'true' and 'false'.

Boolean algebra   A mathematical system for manipulating logical expressions.

Bootstrap   A short program (held in ROM) which is used to bring a larger program (such as an *operating system*) into memory.

Branch construct   A programming construct which allows a choice between two or more conditions to determine the subsequent action.

Bucket   A logical unit of storage consisting of a whole number of blocks.

Buffer   An area of memory which holds data temporarily during transfer (between IAS and a peripheral device).

Bus   A shared pathway for the transmission of address, data or control signals within a computer.

Byte   A string of eight *bit*s, which may correspond to one character or two digits.

Cache memory   A small, high-speed store between the CPU and a large main memory.

CAD *Computer-aided design.*

Call-by-reference A parameter mechanism which allows a subprogram to reference a variable in the calling program using a local name. It is used to return values to parameters.

Call-by-value A parameter mechanism which initialises a local variable of a subprogram with a value.

Case statement A programming construct which implements a *multi-way branch.*

Central processing unit The collection of components, including the arithmetic-logic unit and the control unit, which performs the processing of data.

Check digit An extra character attached to a number prior to data transmission to allow the *integrity* of the data to be checked on arrival.

Check sum A *control total.*

Clock pulse A signal, arriving at a fixed regular interval, which synchronises the activities of the CPU.

Code generation The final phase of compilation, in which the *object program* is produced.

Collision Occurrence of two data items hashing to the same key.

Comment Text appearing in a source program which is intended for human readers only and is ignored by the *compiler.*

Compiler Utility program which produces an intermediate-code or machine-code version of source programs in a given high-level language.

Computer A collection of resources which, under the control of a stored program, automatically accepts, processes, stores, retrieves and outputs data.

Computer-aided design The use of a *computer* in engineering and other design problems.

Concatenate To join two strings together.

Condition code A bit (or group of bits) whose value establishes the status of the most recently executed instruction.

Constant A data item whose value cannot change within a program.

Control store A ROM which holds *microcode.*

Control total An extra data item appended to a group of data items prior to transmission or transcription to allow the *integrity* of the group of data items to be checked on arrival.

Control unit The part of the CPU which controls the fetch–execute cycle.

Control variable The variable whose value controls the number of executions of a for loop.

CPU *Central Processing Unit.*

Crisis time The time within which a peripheral device must be serviced before data is lost.

Cursor A symbol which appears on a screen display to identify the insertion point for characters typed at the keyboard.

Cylinder The set of tracks in a disc pack which can be accessed by the read/write heads in a given position.

Daisy wheel A rotatable circle of spokes embossed with a set of characters, used in a particular type of impact printer.

Data A value or values which may be processed.

Data bus   A pathway for the transmission of data within a computer.

Data capture   Manual or automatic data collection for input to a process.

Data dictionary   A dictionary of *identifiers* and data formats used in a database or other software project.

Data error   An error in input data.

Data table   A list of identifiers used in a program or subprogram, with their types and meanings.

Data type   A class of data, characterised by its allowable values and a set of allowable operations.

Database   A collection of shared data with controlled redundancy.

Debugging   The detection, location and elimination of errors (bugs) in software.

Declaration   Program code to specify the *data type* of a given *identifier*.

Dialogue engineering   A systematic method of developing a human–computer interface.

Direct address   An address field which contains the data for an operation.

Direct memory access   Method of transferring data between a peripheral and the IAS without using CPU registers.

Directive   An *assembly language* instruction which does not correspond to a machine instruction.

Disc   A circular magnetic storage device which allows direct access to data.

Disc crash   Contact between a disc and its read/write head, causing physical damage and corruption of data.

Disc drive   Mechanism for rotating discs and accessing data on disc.

Distributed processing   Execution of a program on a network of computers and terminals.

Document reader   Input device which reads source documents.

Documentation   A written record of information about a piece of software, including its history, how it works and how it should be used.

Domain   The set of allowable values of a *data type*.

Dot matrix   A rectangular grid of dots within which characters are formed for a screen display and in printers using multiple styluses.

Duplex   A transmission system which allows transfer of data in both directions simultaneously.

Dynamic stucture   The hierarchy of subprogram calls at run time.

Editor   A *utility program* which allows a text file to be edited.

Electronic funds transfer   The use of a *wide-area network* to perform banking transactions.

Electronic mail   The transfer of messages between users via a computer network.

Encryption   A *security* device whereby the contents of a file are encoded in a special manner.

End-of-file   A symbol written to a file on backing storage after the last record.

Enumerated type   A *data type* whose values are enumerated explicitly.

EPROM   Erasable programmable *ROM*.

Error   A mistake in the logic, syntax or semantics of a program as a result of which the program fails to deliver the desired, or any, results. (See also *Data error*.)

Exception   An abnormal condition which occurs during processing.

Expert system   A database or other software, containing organised knowledge of a particular technical specialisation, which can perform some of the functions of a human expert.

Exponent   The index or power of the base in *floating-point* notation.

Fail safe   A system which is resistant to failure.

Fail soft   A system which mitigates the worst effects of exceptions.

Fault tolerance   The ability of a program to react properly to exceptions.

Feasibility study   A preliminary study of a data processing application, to determine whether and how to implement or upgrade a computer system.

Fetch–execute cycle   The fundamental instruction cycle of a computer.

Field   A specific part of a *record* or low-level instruction.

FIFO   First in, first out; describes the behaviour of a *queue*.

File   An organised collection of records.

Firmware   A sequence of instructions stored in *read-only memory*.

Fixed loop   A loop construct in which the number of repetitions is fixed at the outset.

Flag   A bit in a *program status word*.

Flip-flop   A storage element with two states.

Floating-point   A representation of a number as a mantissa (between 0.5 and 1) times a power of the base (2, in digital computers).

Floppy disc   A small disc, manufactured using a flexible plastic with a magnetic coating.

Function   A subprogram whose execution returns a value to its calling statement.

Global   A variable visible throughout a program.

Grandfather-father-son routine   A backup scheme whereby two previous versions of each file are always held.

Graphical Kernel System   A standard package for handling 3D graphics.

Graphics tablet   An input device which converts the movement of a pen over a sensitive pad into digital signals.

Graphics terminal   A VDU terminal on which graphics can be displayed.

Hard Copy   Printed computer output, as opposed to screen output, which is soft copy.

Hardware   Physical equipment used in data processing.

Hash function   A formula for computing a number (a hash total or hash key) from the value of a data item.

Hex digit   A digit or letter used in base 16.

High-level language   A programming language which enables program statements to reflect the vocabulary and structure of problems.

Highway   A *bus*.

IAS   *Immediate access store.*

Icon   A pictorial symbol representing a file on a screen display.

Identifier   A name which stands for a data item in a *program* or *program design*.

Immediate access store   Main memory, which can be accessed directly by the CPU.

Index The position of an element in array; also, the table of addresses for a file on disc; also, the power to which a number is raised.

Indexed address An address which is computed by adding the value of an index register to the address field.

Indexed sequential access A method of accessing a sequential file using a partial index.

Indirect address An address field which contains the address of the location holding the operand.

Infix An operator written between its *operand*s.

Input The supply of data to a program or main memory.

Instruction set The set of instructions available in the *machine code* of a processor.

Integration testing Testing to confirm the validity of a software system composed of modules which have each been validated separately.

Integrity A term which describes measures taken to preserve the accuracy of data and to prevent its corruption.

Intelligent terminal A terminal which has some local processing capability.

Interactive A conversational mode of program execution in which a user inputs data or commands in response to prompts.

Interblock gap The space between two physical blocks on magnetic *backing storage*.

Interface The hardware and software required to link two devices; also, the values shared by two modules.

Intermediate code An instruction set, independent of any particular processor, into which a given programming language may be compiled.

Interpreter A utility program which enables the execution of a computer to be controlled by a program which is not in machine code.

Interrupt A signal which causes a break in the execution sequence, which can subsequently be resumed.

Interrupt service routine An instruction sequence which is entered on receipt of an *interrupt*.

Inverted file A file indexed by a *secondary key*.

ISAM *Indexed sequential access method*.

Journal A file which maintains a log of every transaction taking place within some system.

Key A value which identifies a record.

LAN *Local area network*.

Laser printer A high-*resolution* dot image printer which forms characters on the printing drum using a laser beam.

Lexical analysis The first phase in language translation, in which individual characters are grouped into the symbols of the programming language.

LIFO Last in, first out; describes the behaviour of a *stack*.

Light pen A hand-held device which reads bar codes by emitting a light beam and sensing the reflected light.

Lineprinter   A high-speed printer which prints all the characters in a line in a single operation, rather than as a sequence of characters.

Linkage editor   *Utility program* that locates and links separately compiled routines to form a single module for loading.

List   A data structure in which each item contains a link to its successor.

Loader   *Utility program* which copies an object code module into the position in store it will occupy during execution.

Local   An identifier whose scope is restricted to a subprogram.

Local-area network   A group of computers and peripheral devices on a single site interconnected by direct cable links.

Logic gate   An electronic device with a single output whose value is a function of its inputs.

Loop   A program control structure which repeats a section of code.

LSI   Large scale integration; an integrated circuit with thousands of components.

Machine code   A sequence of machine instructions.

Machine instruction   A binary code which specifies a machine operation which is performed in a single *fetch–execute cycle*. This is the native binary format which is recognised by a CPU.

Machine-readable   Data recorded in a form whereby it may be read by an input device.

Macro   A command which generates several instructions.

Magnetic ink character recognition   Machine recognition of a standard set of characters printed in magnetic ink.

Magnetic tape unit   A peripheral device that reads and writes data on magnetic tape backing storage.

Main memory   The *immediate access store*.

Main processor   The CPU and *immediate access store* considered as a unit.

Mainframe   A large computer with several free-standing peripherals and accessed by numerous terminals, which requires an air-conditioned environment and reinforced floor support.

Maintenance   The ongoing process of changing software to accommodate changes which occur as well as errors which come to light.

Mantissa   The fractional part of a number in *floating-point* notation.

Master file   The main data file for an application, which may be updated using amendments from a *transaction file*.

Memory cycle   The sequence of events in transferring a byte or word between main memory and the CPU.

Memory protection   An operating system function which checks that programs do not access memory locations outside their allocated area.

Memory-mapped I/O   The arrangement whereby input and output ports are addressed as memory locations.

Menu   A list of choices displayed by an *interactive* program.

Merge   To combine two or more ordered sequences of data into a single ordered sequence.

Metal oxide semiconductor   A technology for making low-powered transistors.

Metalanguage   A language, such as BNF, used to define a language.

MICR *Magnetic ink character recognition.*

Microcode A sequence of *microinstructions.*

Microfiche A small sheet of film containing an array of microfilm frames which may be read or printed using a special viewer.

Microinstruction A binary code which specifies a sequence of register transfers at a lower level than a *machine instruction.*

Modem A device used to interface a digital device with an analogue telephone line.

Modular design A technique for developing a system or program as a set of separate *modules.*

Modular testing The validation of individual program modules or subprograms before incorporation into the whole system. Contrast *integration testing.*

Module A defined component of a system.

Mouse A hand-held input device which is rolled on a surface to move a screen *cursor* and has one or more buttons to select an item displayed on the screen.

Multiplexer A device which enables several signal streams to share a single communications channel.

Multiprogramming An operating system which allows the interleaved processing of several programs.

Multi-way branch A construct which allows a choice of several actions depending on the value of some expression.

Nested structure A program control structure contained wholly within another such structure, such as a nested *loop* or a nested *subprogram.*

Node An item in a tree, network or other linked structure.

Normalisation Adjusting a *floating-point* number to the standard form for a given system.

Nucleus Part of a virtual memory operating system which must be in main store when any program is running.

Object program A fully compiled version of a program.

OCR *Optical Character Recognition.*

Octal Base eight.

Offset The difference between the value of an actual address and the *base address.*

OMR *Optical Mark Reading.*

Operand Value on which an operation is performed.

Operating system A suite of programs which manage the resources of a computer, and control the operation of all other programs.

Operation code The part of a machine-code instruction which specifies the type of operation to be executed.

Optical Character Recognition Automatic recognition of characters by light sensing.

Optical Mark Reading Automatic input of marks made in pre-determined positions on standard documents.

Output The supply of data by a program to its environment or from main memory to a *peripheral* device.

Overflow   A numerical result which is too large to fit in the number of bits assigned; also, a record which cannot be placed in the area of storage where it belongs.

Packet switching   A data transmission method in which messages are divided into packets which are routed by the system to the destination.

Page   A fixed-size block of memory.

Parallel transmission   The simultaneous transfer of all the bits of a character over parallel lines.

Parameter   A value passed between a subprogram and its calling statement.

Parity   Whether the number of ones in a binary string is odd or even.

Parity check   A test on transmitted binary data to confirm that the parity is correct, as determined by the *interface*.

Password   A group of characters which must be input to allow access to a resource.

PC   *Program counter*.

Peripheral   A unit of a computer system which makes or receives data transfers, such as a *disc drive* or a printer.

Personal identification number   A numerical *password* used to access a network via an *Automated Teller Machine*.

Pixel   An addressable element in a graphics display.

Point-of-sale terminal   An input/output device used at a sales checkout for billing and stock control.

Pointer   A link from one data item to another.

Pop   Remove the item at the top of a *stack*.

Postfix   An operator which is written after its *operand*s.

Primary key   A *key* which identifies a record uniquely.

Privacy   The recognition that access to some data must be restricted.

Procedure   A named set of program statements which performs a specific task.

Process control   The use of a computer to monitor and regulate a manufacturing process.

Processor-controlled I/O   Data transfer in which each byte is transferred under control of the CPU.

Program   A complete statement of a solution to a problem capable of being executed on a computer.

Program counter   The *register* which holds the address of the next instruction.

Program design   A statement of an algorithm in sufficient detail that program code may be derived from it.

Program status register   A register in the CPU which holds the *program status word* of the program which is currently running.

Program status word   A *word* used by the operating system containing data about a program in the course of being executed.

Program verification   A procedure for checking that software meets its specification.

PROM   Programmable *read-only memory*.

Protocol   A set of rules governing a data transfer.

Pseudocode   A notation for *program design*s using keywords from a programming language interspersed with natural language.

Push   Add an item at the top of a *stack*.

Queue A *fifo* list, where items are inserted at one end and removed from the other.

RAM *Random-access memory*.

Random-access memory The part of main memory which may be written to or read by a program.

Read-only memory The part of main memory which may be read by programs but not written to.

Real-time Describes a system or program which is synchronised by some external process.

Record A collection of data treated as a unit.

Recovery Restoring a previous version of a file when the current version is corrupted.

Recursion The definition of a concept in terms of itself.

Register A storage location which holds a binary *word*; sometimes restricted to locations in the CPU.

Relocatable code An *object program* which will run wherever it is placed in memory.

Repetitive control structure A *loop*.

Reserved word A character *string* with a fixed meaning in a programming language, which is therefore not available for definition by the user.

Resolution The fineness of detail in a graphic.

Reverse Polish *Postfix* notation.

Robustness See *fault tolerance*.

ROM *Read-only memory*.

Root The *node* through which a *tree* is accessed.

Run-time stack A stack used to implement nested subprograms.

Scheduler (high-level) The module of a *multiprogramming* operating system which allocates priorities to programs waiting to run.

Schema A complete description of a *database*.

Screen editor An *editor* which allows the section of text to be edited to be selected and displayed on the screen.

Secondary key A *key* which identifies a group of records.

Sector The smallest addressable unit on magnetic *disc*.

Security Measures taken to secure the *integrity* and *privacy* of data.

Select . . . end select A pair of keywords which may be used in *structured English* to enclose a choice control structure.

Semantics The meaning attached to a sequence of symbols.

Serial access The method of accessing a data item in storage by first locating all its predecessors.

Serial transmission The transfer of a binary word bit by bit along a single line.

Software Programs and program modules which comprise a computer system.

Software engineering A collection of techniques for software development based on methods of engineering design.

Software life-cycle The complete period from the conception of a piece of software, including operation and maintenance, until it is no longer in use.

Source data Values, representing information, which are fed into a program.

Source program   A program, written in a programming language, as presented to a computer.

Specification   A precise statement of what a piece of software will achieve.

Spreadsheet   A program for manipulating rows and columns of numbers.

Stack   A *lifo* list, where items are inserted at, and removed from, the top.

Stack pointer   A *register* which holds the address of a dedicated *stack*.

Stepwise refinement   A *top-down* method of developing a *program design* in which each step is successively refined until all the steps are sufficiently detailed.

String   A sequence of characters.

Structured English   A notation for *program design*s using English text punctuated by formal keywords.

Structured programming   Any method of developing a program by systematic consideration of its control structures.

Subprogram   A named program unit which can be called from a program statement, such as a *function* or *procedure*.

Subscript   An ordinal value which forms the whole or part of an array *index*.

Subtree   A tree structure obtained by selecting a *node* of a *tree* and its subsidiary nodes at all levels.

Syntactic analysis   The second phase in language translation, in which sequences of symbols are matched to the syntax for the language.

Syntax   The rules for writing sequences of symbols in a language.

Systems analysis   The process whereby the requirements of a job, including the feasibility of computer involvement, are identified and specified.

Table   A one-dimensional array of data *records*.

Teletext   A text retrieval system distributed by television broadcasting.

Terminal   An input/output unit.

Terminal emulator   A program (usually in ROM) which enables a microcomputer to behave as a terminal to a multi-user system.

Test data   A set of special data (and the expected output) used to test a program.

Text file   A file of printable data, in which each byte stands for a character in a standard set.

Time-slicing   The allocation of a fixed time interval to each user of a shared resource, as in *multiprogramming* and multiplexing.

Top-down design   A method of program design in which a problem is expressed in terms of components which have not yet been designed themselves.

Track   A subdivision of magnetic storage which is one bit wide.

Transaction file   A set of records containing updating data for a *master file*.

Transcription error   An error in copying data.

Transfer rate   The average quantity of data transmitted per unit time.

Transputer   A complete main processor on a chip with in-built connections so that several transputers may be linked to provide a multiprocessor system.

Traversal   A systematic method of enumerating the nodes of a *tree*.

Tree   A hierarchical data structure with one data item at each node, consisting of a *root* node linked to zero, one or more subsidiary nodes, each in turn the root of a *subtree*.

Truth table   A table of values used to compute a boolean function (logic operation).

Turnaround documents   Computer-generated output to which data may be added for input to a *document reader*.

Two-dimensional array   An *array* in which each element is indexed by two subscripts.

Twos' complement   A system for representing negative binary numbers in a fixed-length store by subtracting the corresponding positive number from zero.

Underflow   The result of an arithmetical operation which is too close to zero to store; also, an attempt to access an item from an empty stack.

Utility program   A general-purpose program, such as an *editor* or a *compiler*, which aids in the development of user programs or is called by the operating system.

Validation   Checking that data conforms to certain conditions; also, checking that a program meets the user requirements.

Variable   A data name or *identifier* whose value may change during the course of program execution.

VDU   *Visual display unit*.

Verification   Checking that an input file has been keyed correctly (by repeat keying and comparing the two copies); also, checking that a *program* meets its *specification*.

Viewdata   An interactive data retrieval system accessed by telephone.

Virtual machine   The interface presented to a user by an *operating system* or a *utility program*, whereby a layer of software may be used as though it were part of the hardware.

Virtual memory   A method of addressing backing storage as though it were part of main memory.

Visual display unit   A computer *terminal* with a keyboard for input and a screen for output.

VLSI   Very large-scale integration; an integrated circuit with tens of thousands of transistors.

Volatile   A semiconductor memory which loses its contents when power is switched off.

Wide-area network   A group of processors, terminals and peripheral devices linked using public telephone lines.

Window   A snapshot of a file or a work area occupying part or the whole of a screen.

Word   A sequence of bits manipulated as a unit by the CPU.

Word processor   A computer system for production, editing and formatting of documents.

Workstation   An *intelligent terminal* or a microcomputer used in a network.

Bibliography

Most of these titles have been referred to at the end of the relevant chapter, together with a comment on the suitability of the book.

British Computer Society (ed), *A Glossary of Computing Terms*, Cambridge University Press, 1989.

Computer Software, W. H. Freeman, New York, 1984.

I. O. Angell and G. H. Griffith, *High-resolution Computer Graphics Using Pascal*, Macmillan, London, 1988.

L. Antill and A. T. Wood-Harper, *Systems Analysis*, Heinemann, London, 1985.

D. Barron, *Computer Operating Systems*, 2nd edn, Chapman and Hall, London & New York, 1984.

T. J. Bentley, *Making Computers Work*, Macmillan, London, 1984.

A. Berry, *The Super-Intelligent Machine*, Cape, London, 1983.

I. Birnbaum, *Assembly Language Programming for the BBC Microcomputer*, Macmillan, London, 1984.

P. Brophy, *Computers Can Read*, Technical Press, Gower, Aldershot, 1986.

B. R. Gaines and M. L. G. Shaw, *The Art of Computer Conversation*, Prentice-Hall International, London, 1984.

M. G. Hartley, M. Healey and P. G. Depledge, *Mini and Microcomputer Systems*, Macmillan, London, 1988.

P. Large, *The Micro Revolution Revisited*, Frances Pinter, London, 1984.

N. Willis and J. Kerridge, *Introduction to Computer Architecture*, Pitman, London, 1983.

The following title will be of interest to instructors and teachers who wish to go deeper into program design:

R. Bornat, *Programming from First Principles*, Prentice-Hall International, London, 1987.

Index

If you are looking for a short definition, consult the Glossary first

If you are looking for a short definition, consult the Glossary first

If you are looking for a short definition, consult the Glossary first

If you are looking for a short definition, consult the Glossary first

If you are looking for a short definition, consult the Glossary first

If you are looking for a short definition, consult the Glossary first